ACT Orange

A special thank you to C2 Education's Curriculum team for reviewing and supporting the creation of this book. Please contact Edward Kim at Edward.kim@c2educate.com to report any errors or issues with the content.

To C2 Teachers and Students:

This book was designed to provide a quicker comprehensive review of major concepts on the ACT exam to help fill the knowledge gap between ACT Green and ACT Purple. Students who have completed ACT Green should use this book to practice and review concepts in order to prepare for ACT Purple.

ACT Orange is not meant to be used in a belt-type system, so teachers and students should use this book as needed. If students are struggling with a number of concepts in ACT Green or Purple, this workbook has additional problems and simplified concept explanations to support student learning.

Please contact Edward Kim at Edward.kim@c2educate.com if you come across any content errors or issues.

Thank you!
- C2 Curriculum Team

Table of Contents

ACT English

Introduction 1

Subjects and Verbs 3

Basic Sentence Structure 6

Punctuation 13

Pronoun Errors 18

Verb Errors 23

Adjectives and Adverbs 28

Commonly Confused Words 32

Idioms 36

Parallelism and Modifiers 41

Transitions and Organization 47

Author's Intent 53

Relevance 59

Conciseness 63

Style and Tone 67

Practice Exercises 71

Practice Exercises Answer Key 106

ACT Math

Pre-Algebra Review 113

Number Properties 121

Ratios, Rates, and Percent 126

Algebraic Operations 133

Solving and Modeling Linear Equations 138

Functions 145

Solving and Modeling Linear Inequalities and Absolute Value Equations 150

Solving and Modeling Systems of Equations 155

Coordinate Plane Geometry 161

Quadratics and Polynomials 169

Radical Expressions and Complex Numbers 178

Rational Expressions 184

Exponential and Logarithmic Expressions 190

Lines, Angles, and Polygons 198

Circles 208

Conic Sections 215

Sequences and Patterns 219

Matrices 226

Statistics and Probability 233

Trigonometry 243

Practice Exercises Answer Key 253

ACT Reading

Introduction 257

Explicit Information 259

Implicit Information 265

Words in Context 270

Literary Narrative 274

Social Studies 279

Humanities 284

Natural Science 289

Paired Passages 294

Overview 298

Practice Exercises 300

Practice Exercises Answer Key 328

ACT Science

Introduction 330

Understanding Charts and Graphs 339

Understanding Questions 353

Analysis Questions 366

Generalization Questions 380

Data Representation Passages 393

Research Summaries Passages 404

Conflicting Viewpoints Passages 419

Practice Exercises Answer Key 434

ACT Essay

Introduction to the ACT Writing Test 437

Prewriting 441

Introduction and Thesis 445

Analysis and Examples 448

Conclusions 451

Organization 454

Style 458

ACT English: Introduction

The ACT English Test is intended to assess your mastery of English grammar and writing. Like other sections of the ACT, the English Test has its own unique benefits and challenges. This lesson will provide an overview of what you can expect from the ACT English Test.

Format of the ACT English Test

The English Test includes five passages accompanied by 75 questions; you will have just 45 minutes to complete this section. That means that you have just 36 seconds to answer each question.

The passages on the English Test include a variety of errors that you will be expected to identify and correct. These errors will be marked by numbered underlined sections or boxes; each of these numbered sections will correspond with a question provided next to the passage.

Content of the ACT English Test

Although the English Test requires speed, more than any other section of the ACT, the English Test assesses what you already know rather than what you can figure out from given information. This makes preparation for the ACT English Test somewhat more straightforward than for other sections.

The ACT English Test will focus on two broad content areas: Usage/Mechanics and Rhetorical Skills. Usage/Mechanics includes general grammar questions while Rhetorical Skills includes questions that focus on the less tangible elements of good writing, such as style.

USAGE/MECHANICS

Punctuation (10-15%): Questions in this category focus on both internal and end-of-sentence punctuation. There is an emphasis on punctuation errors that affect meaning, such as those that help to avoid ambiguity.

Grammar and Usage (15-20%): Questions in this category include errors such as subject-verb agreement, pronoun errors, verb errors, and idiomatic usage errors.

Sentence Structure (20-25%): Questions in this category focus on your understanding of the relationships between and among clauses, placement of modifiers, and shifts in construction.

RHETORICAL SKILLS

Strategy (15-20%): Questions in this category focus on your ability to develop ideas by choosing expressions that are most appropriate to a passage's intended audience and purpose; judging the effect of adding, deleting, or revising material; and judging the relevance of statements in the context of the passage as a whole.

Organization (10-15%): Questions in this category require that you organize ideas logically and coherently by choosing effective opening, transitional, and closing sentences and phrases or by reorganizing sentences or paragraphs within the passage.

Style (15-20%): Questions in this category focus on your ability to choose precise, appropriate words and images in order to maintain the style and tone of a given passage while avoiding wordiness and redundancy.

General Strategies for the ACT English Test

Quickly read the entire passage: Although the format of the English Test lends itself to focusing only on those parts of the passage that are referenced by the questions, you should take a moment to quickly read through the entire passage. This is necessary in order to effectively answer questions involving style, audience, and purpose, and such questions can make up 30-40% of the overall English Test.

Answer the questions in order: Since the questions are in the order in which they appear in the passage, it is logical to answer the questions in order. This will eliminate the need to go through parts of the passage multiple times. If, however, you find yourself struggling to answer a certain question, don't hesitate to skip it and come back to it later.

Use the process of elimination: Whenever the correct answer is not immediately clear to you, rely on the process of elimination to arrive at the correct answer. Even if you are unable to eliminate all of the incorrect answers, you will at least improve your odds of guessing correctly.

When in doubt, always guess: Don't leave questions blank. The ACT will not penalize you for incorrect answers, so there is no benefit to skipping questions entirely.

Don't be afraid to choose NO CHANGE or OMIT: Students often ignore these answer choices, believing them to be likely incorrect; however, these answer choices have just as much of a chance of being correct as any other answer choice. NO CHANGE will be right about 25% of the time, so don't be afraid to select NO CHANGE if you cannot find an error.

ACT English: Subjects and Verbs

One common error on the ACT English Test involves subject-verb agreement. All complete sentences must have both a subject and a verb; the subject is the noun or pronoun performing the action, and the verb is the action being performed. Subjects and verbs must agree in number; plural subjects get plural verbs, and singular subjects get singular verbs.

Identifying Subjects and Verbs

The first step to addressing a subject-verb agreement error is to correctly identify the subjects and the verbs of the sentence. Follow these steps:

<u>Step One</u>: *Cross out phrases that are contained within sets of commas, parentheses, or dashes.*

Each of the students, including Annabelle, passed the final exam.

<u>Step Two</u>: *Cross out prepositional phrases (phrases that begin with a preposition like of, for, under, etc.).*

Each of the students passed the final exam.

<u>Step Three</u>: *Of the remaining nouns and pronouns, determine which one is performing the action of the sentence.*

Each passed the final exam.

In this sentence, the pronoun "each" is performing the action. "The final exam" is an object rather than a subject.

<u>Step Four</u>: *Identify the action taking place. If there is no action, look for helping verbs like is/are, was/were, or has/have. This is the verb.*

In this sentence, the action is "passed," which is the verb of the sentence.

Common Subject-Verb Agreement Errors

There are several common errors that can create confusion regarding subject-verb agreement. Don't allow yourself to be caught by these errors:

<u>Error #1</u>: *Objects of prepositions can never be the subject of the sentence.*

Incorrect: Each of the students have passed.

Correct: Each of the students has passed.

<u>Error #2</u>: *"Here" and "there" are not subjects. In sentences that begin with these words, the subject usually comes after the verb.*

Incorrect: There is cars parked along both sides of the street.

Correct: There are cars parked along both sides of the street.

Error #3: *Compound subjects connected by "and" take plural verbs.*

Incorrect: Ms. Anderson and Mr. Joel decorates their classrooms with a superhero theme each year.

Correct: Ms. Anderson and Mr. Joel decorate their classrooms with a superhero theme each year.

Error #4: *Compound subjects connected by "nor" or "or" could require either a singular or a plural verb. The subject that is closer to the verb determines whether the verb should be singular or plural.*

Incorrect: The teacher or the students decides on the theme.

Correct: The students or the teacher decides on the theme.

Error Five: *When the subject is an indefinite pronoun, a pronoun that does not refer to specific person, place, or thing, the subject might be singular or plural depending on the context. The chart below identifies indefinite pronouns as singular or plural.*

Singular Indefinite Pronouns		Plural Indefinite Pronouns	Variable Indefinite Pronouns
Somebody	Everybody	Both	Any
Something	Everything	A number	Some
Someone	Everyone	Fewer	More
Anybody	Each	Few	Most
Anything	Neither	Many	All
Anyone	Either	Several	None
Nobody	Much		
No one	One		
Nothing	The number		

TO ANSWER SUBJECT-VERB AGREEMENT QUESTIONS:

Step One: Identify the subject and the verb. Avoid misidentifying objects of prepositions as subjects.

Step Two: Determine whether the subject and the verb agree. Remember that plural subjects get plural verbs, and singular subjects get singular verbs.

Step Three: Eliminate any answer choices that do not provide the correct subject and verb for the sentence.

PRACTICE EXERCISE

Directions: Identify the subject(s) of each sentence, then circle the correct verb(s) in parentheses. Remember that more complex sentences can have more than one subject and/or verb.

1. The most violent storms in nature (IS / ARE) tornadoes.

2. Thunderstorms or a tornado sometimes (CREATES / CREATE) large amounts of damage, but tornadoes (IS / ARE) much more violent weather events.

3. Spawned from a powerful thunderstorm, tornadoes often (CAUSES / CAUSE) fatalities and (DEVASTATES / DEVASTATE) whole communities.

4. There (IS / ARE) different types of tornadoes, but most tornadoes (APPEARS / APPEAR) as rotating, funnel-shaped clouds.

5. Although many tornadoes (IS / ARE) clearly visible, there (IS / ARE) others that are obscured by rain or nearby clouds.

6. A cloud of debris often (MARKS / MARK) the location of a tornado even when the funnel (IS / ARE) not visible.

7. The wind caused by tornadoes (IS / ARE) capable of reaching 300 miles per hour.

8. At times, the area of damage from a tornado (REACHES / REACH) one mile wide and up to fifty miles long.

9. Scientists (HAS / HAVE) spent decades studying tornadoes, yet their research (HAS / HAVE) not resulted in adequate warning systems.

10. Victims of a tornado sometimes (HAS / HAVE) just a few moments to seek shelter.

11. Because of this, there (IS / ARE) few other natural disasters that rival tornadoes for danger.

12. The most record-breaking tornado in the history of the United States (WAS / WERE) the Tri-State Tornado; whole parts of Missouri, Illinois, and Indiana (WAS / WERE) destroyed when this tornado ripped a 219-mile path in 1925.

13. Although the Tri-State Tornado (IS / ARE) among the deadliest tornadoes on record, it (WAS / WERE) surpassed by a tornado in Bangladesh in 1989.

14. Known as the Daultipur-Salturia Tornado, this 1989 storm (IS / ARE) believed to have caused over 1,300 deaths.

15. There (HAS / HAVE) been at least 19 tornadoes in Bangladesh that have killed at least 100 people.

ACT English: Basic Sentence Structure

One of the primary types of usage and mechanics errors tested on the ACT English Test is sentence structure. Among the most common sentence structure errors are those dealing with improperly combined sentences. This includes sentence fragments, run-ons, and comma splices.

Complete sentences must have a subject and a verb, and they must express a complete idea. Sentences that don't meet these requirements are sentence fragments. Sentences that contain multiple subjects and verbs without being properly connected to each other are either run-on sentences or comma splices.

Fragments, Run-ons and Comma Splices

Sentence fragments are incomplete sentences. They are missing a subject or a verb, or they do not express a complete idea. In other words, a sentence fragment is a sentence that is missing an independent clause.

Fragment: Before class starts.

Complete Sentence: Class starts soon.

The sentence fragment and the complete sentence differ by just one word, but that word is enough to make the first sentence a fragment because it creates an incomplete idea.

Run-ons and comma splices represent an opposite error to a sentence fragment. In these errors, too many clauses occur in the sentence without being properly connected.

Run-On: Class starts soon I took my seat.

Comma Splice: Class starts soon, I took my seat.

Correct Sentence: Class starts soon, so I took my seat.

Correcting fragments, run-ons, and comma splices can often be done by combining sentences properly.

Combining Sentences Using Coordination and Subordination

There are several ways to properly combine sentences: Coordination, subordination, semicolons, and colons. In this lesson, we will focus on using coordination and subordination to effectively combine sentences.

COORDINATION

Coordination is used to combine two independent clauses with a comma and a coordinating conjunction. There are seven coordinating conjunctions that you can remember using the acronym **FANBOYS**: **F**or, **A**nd, **N**or, **B**ut, **O**r, **Y**et, **S**o.

Incorrect: Class starts soon, or I took my seat.

Incorrect: Class starts soon so I took my seat.

Correct: Class starts soon, so I took my seat.

There are two common errors when dealing with coordination. The first, as seen above, is to use a conjunction that doesn't properly communicate the relationship between the two clauses. In this case, "or" does not express any logical relationship between the first and second clauses. The second error is to use a coordinating conjunction without a comma; the second incorrect example on the previous page does not include a comma for "so". Coordination requires both a comma and a conjunction.

SUBORDINATION

Subordination is slightly more complicated than coordination. With subordination, one clause becomes a dependent clause while the other remains an independent clause. Dependent clauses can be formed by either omitting the subject or verb or by adding a subordinating conjunction. There are many subordinating conjunctions. Some of the most frequently used subordinating conjunctions include:

Subordinating Conjunctions		
After	Although	As
Because	Before	Even
How	If	In order that
Now that	Once	Provided
Rather than	Since	So that
Than	That	Though
Unless	Until	When
Whenever	Where	Whereas
Wherever	Whether	While

As with coordination, it is important to choose a conjunction that properly expresses the relationship between the two ideas. However, the rules for punctuation with subordination are different from those with coordination. With subordination, we use a comma only when the clause with the subordinating conjunction comes first. If the clause with the subordinating conjunction comes second, no comma is needed.

Incorrect: Although class starts soon I have not yet taken my seat.

Incorrect: I have not yet taken my seat, although class starts soon.

Incorrect: Whether class starts soon, I have not yet taken my seat.

Correct: Although class starts soon, I have not yet taken my seat.

Correct: I have not yet taken my seat although class starts soon.

In the first sentence, the clause containing the subordinating conjunction "although" should have a comma after it. In the second sentence, the clauses should not be divided by a comma because the clause containing the subordinating conjunction comes last. In the third sentence, the subordinating conjunction "whether" does not describe a logical relationship between the two clauses.

Common Sentence Structure Errors

Some common sentence structure errors include:

Fragments: Sentences that do not contain both a subject and a verb or that fail to communicate a complete idea. Can often be solved by combining the fragment with another sentence.

Run-ons or Comma Splices: Multiple sentences that are not properly combined. Can often be solved by following the rules for coordination or subordination.

Subordination Errors: Sentences combined using a subordinating conjunction that does not express a logical relationship between the two ideas or that is improperly punctuated.

Coordination Errors: Sentences combined using a coordinating conjunction that does not express a logical relationship between the two ideas or that is improperly punctuated.

TO ANSWER BASIC SENTENCE STRUCTURE QUESTIONS:

Step One: Identify the error by looking at the underlined portion and the sentences immediately before and after the underlined portion.

Step Two: Eliminate any answer choices that fail to solve the error.

Step Three: Examine the remaining answer choices to ensure that they do not create new errors.

Step Four: Choose the answer that addresses the original error without creating any new errors.

PRACTICE EXERCISE

Part A

<u>Directions</u>: Identify each of the following sentences or pairs of sentences as a fragment, comma splice, or run-on. Then choose the answer choice that best addresses the error.

1. As a bounty of new research on carnivorous plants reveals.

   Error type: _____

   a) New research reveals carnivorous plants.

   b) There is a bounty of revealing new research on carnivorous plants.

   c) A bounty of new research, carnivorous plants reveal.

2. Biologists are still unearthing surprising details about the anatomy, evolution, biochemistry, and hunting tactics of carnivorous plants biologists remain fascinated by these unique specimens.

   Error type: _____

   a) Biologists are still unearthing surprising details about the anatomy, evolution, biochemistry, and hunting tactics of carnivorous plants, they remain fascinated by these unique specimens.

   b) These unique specimens remain fascinating to biologists because unearthing surprising details about the anatomy, evolution, biochemistry, and hunting tactics of carnivorous plants.

   c) Biologists remain fascinated by carnivorous plants as researchers continue to unearth surprising details about the anatomy, evolution, biochemistry, and hunting tactics of these unique specimens.

3. A group of scientists recently determined that one species of pitcher plant supplements its insectivorous diet with bat guano, it attracts bats to roost in a goblet made up of a leaf by tuning its shape to precisely match the bats' echolocating calls.

   Error type: _____

   a) A group of scientists recently determined that one species of pitcher plant supplements its insectivorous diet with bat guano, attracting bats to roost in a goblet made up of a leaf by tuning its shape to precisely match the bats' echolocating calls.

   b) A group of scientists recently determined that one species of pitcher plant supplements its insectivorous diet with bat guano, yet it attracts bats to roost in a goblet made up of a leaf by tuning its shape to precisely match the bats' echolocating calls.

   c) A group of scientists recently determined that one species of pitcher plant supplements its insectivorous diet with bat guano, while it attracts bats to roost in a goblet made up of a leaf by tuning its shape to precisely match the bats' echolocating calls.

4. Another team has nearly decoded the complete DNA sequence of the Venus fly trap its genome is virtually the same size as the human genome.

   Error type: _____

   a) Another team has nearly decoded the complete DNA sequence of the Venus fly trap, whose genome is virtually the same size as the human genome.

   b) Although another team has nearly decoded the complete DNA sequence of the Venus fly trap its genome is virtually the same size as the human genome.

   c) Another team has nearly decoded the complete DNA sequence of the Venus fly trap, virtually the same size as the human genome.

5. Interesting findings, such as the theory that the plant imported genes from its insect prey, gleaned from decoding Venus fly trap DNA.

   Error type: _____

   a) Interesting findings have been gleaned from decoding Venus fly trap DNA, and the theory that the plant imported genes from its insect prey.

   b) Interesting findings, gleaned from decoding Venus fly trap DNA, such as the theory that the plant imported genes from its insect prey.

   c) Interesting findings have been gleaned from decoding Venus fly trap DNA, such as the theory that the plant imported genes from its insect prey.

Part B

Directions: Combine each pair of sentences using subordination.

6. Other researchers compared the proteins and hormones found in the digestive fluids of carnivorous plants with similar molecules active in non-carnivorous plants. They concluded that carnivorous plants used the defense mechanisms of ordinary plants to develop the ability to consume insects.

   _____

   _____

   _____

   _____

   _____

   _____

7. Researchers hope to explore a range of questions by examining carnivorous plants, including how organisms adapt to extreme adversity and scarcity. Such answers could have widespread practical applications.

_____

_____

_____

_____

_____

8. Studies have shown that several enzymes produced by carnivorous plants remained exceptionally stable under extreme heat and acidity that demolished most enzymes. Biologists could learn how to make enzymes more tolerant to extreme conditions by studying these plants.

_____

_____

_____

_____

_____

9. The 590 known species of carnivorous plants are certainly oddities among the plant world. All are legitimate, chlorophyll-carrying members of the kingdom Plantae.

_____

_____

_____

_____

_____

10. Other plants absorb nutrients like nitrogen from the ground. Carnivorous plants colonize habitats with poor soil and acquire such nutrients from insect sources.

_____

_____

_____

_____

_____

Part C

Directions: Combine each pair of sentences using coordination.

11. Carnivorous plants generally feed on insects. Their prey can sometimes include frogs, fish, and even small mammals.

   _____

   _____

   _____

   _____

12. Some carnivorous plants trap insects in a basin or a sticky substance. Perhaps the most impressive snare is the Venus fly trap, which actually moves to catch its prey.

   _____

   _____

   _____

   _____

13. Carnivorous plants evolved to consume live prey. At least one carnivorous plant seems to be evolving to subsist on bat guano instead.

   _____

   _____

   _____

   _____

14. The bat benefits as well. The Hardwicke's woolly bat and a local pitcher plant species have developed a symbiotic relationship.

   _____

   _____

   _____

   _____

15. The pitcher plant consumes the nitrogen-rich guano. The bat gets a perfect place to roost.

   _____

   _____

   _____

   _____

ACT English: Punctuation

One of the most frequent types of errors on the ACT English test is punctuation errors. Although there are a wide variety of possible punctuation errors, understanding the basic rules of punctuation will help you to address these questions.

Nonessential Elements

Nonessential elements are parts of a sentence that are unnecessary to the primary meaning of the sentence. To maintain the clarity of the sentence, nonessential elements have to be set off by punctuation.

COMMAS

To set off nonessential elements, the most commonly used punctuation marks are commas. Commas are generally used to set off information that feels like a natural part of the sentence.

Incorrect: The Food and Drug Administration, also known as the FDA, oversees products that include food, drugs, medical products, and dietary supplements.

Correct: The FDA, established in 1906, enforces a wide variety of federal laws that are intended to protect public health.

In the first sentence, the information inside the commas interrupts the flow of the sentence without adding important information. Since commas are usually used with information that feels like it flows with the sentence, this is an incorrect use of commas to set off a nonessential element. The second sentence is an example of correct use of commas to offset a nonessential element because the information in the commas adds information that feels like a part of the sentence. Note that there are two commas when a nonessential element is in the middle of the sentence, two commas are needed, but when the nonessential element comes at the end of the sentence, only one comma is needed.

PARENTHESES

Parentheses are used to set off something that seems out of place in the sentence or that would otherwise interrupt the flow of the sentence. Parentheses must always be used in pairs.

Incorrect: The book (when read aloud to the class) took on new meaning.

Correct: The authors use of dialect (a regional form of a language) made the book ideal for reading aloud.

In the first sentence, the information inside the parentheses is important to the sentence because it defines a set of circumstances under which the book took on new meaning. In the second sentence, there is a pair of parentheses and the information contained within them simply defines the term "dialect," which is good information but would interrupt the flow of the sentence otherwise.

DASHES

Dashes are often used to add drama or emphasis to the information contained within them. Unlike parentheses, which minimize the information inside them, dashes highlight the information inside them.

Incorrect: My birthday—April 15—is an inauspicious day in history.

Correct: April 15 is the date on which Abraham Lincoln was killed, the *Titanic* sank, and the Boston Marathon was bombed—it's also my birthday.

The first sentence uses dashes incorrectly because the date is not the key piece of information in the sentence. In the second sentence, the information that follows the dash is unexpected, and the dash emphasizes that information. Note that there is only one dash in the second sentence. Only one dash is needed when the parenthetical element is at the end of the sentence; otherwise, two are necessary.

Other Uses of Commas

Commas serve many functions in sentences. In addition to setting off nonessential elements, commas are commonly used to separate clauses within a sentence or to separate items in a series.

COMMAS WITH COORDINATION AND SUBORDINATION

For a thorough overview of coordination and subordination, review the lesson on Basic Sentence Structure. Remember that the rules for comma usage with coordination and subordination are:

Rule One: *When combining clauses using coordination, you must use a comma and a coordinating conjunction.*

Incorrect: The 1938 Federal Food, Drug, and Cosmetic Act established the FDA but it has been amended many times since then.
Correct: The 1938 Federal Food, Drug, and Cosmetic Act established the FDA, but it has been amended many times since then.

Rule Two: *When combining clauses using subordination, use a comma when the subordinating clause comes first.*

Incorrect: Before the FFDCA was passed there were few regulations regarding the safety of new drugs.
Correct: Before the FFDCA was passed, there were few regulations regarding the safety of new drugs.

Rule Three: *When combining clauses using subordination, do NOT use a comma when the subordinating clause comes second.*

Incorrect: The new regulatory act was finally passed, after an improperly prepared medicine caused the deaths of more than 100 people.
Correct: The new regulatory act was finally passed after an improperly prepared medicine caused the deaths of more than 100 people.

ITEMS IN A SERIES

Commas are also used to separate items in a series when those items do not already contain commas. When the items in the series already contain commas or are particularly lengthy, semicolons are used to separate the items. Punctuation within a series of items must be consistent regardless of whether commas or semicolons are used.

Incorrect: On our vacation, we planned to visit London, England, Paris, France, and Berlin, Germany.
Correct: On our vacation, we planned to visit London, England; Paris, France; and Berlin, Germany.

In the first sentence, the items in the series already contain commas. To avoid unnecessary confusion, if even one item in a series already has a comma, all of the items should be separated by semicolons.

Incorrect: On our vacation, we hope to ride a double-decker bus and tour the Tower of London, visit the Louvre and ride to the top of the Eiffel Tower, and see the Brandenburg Gate and tour Museum Island.

Correct: On our vacation, we hope to ride a double-decker bus and tour the Tower of London; visit the Louvre and ride to the top of the Eiffel Tower; and see the Brandenburg Gate and tour Museum Island.

In these sentences, the items in the series are fairly lengthy. Use of semicolons rather than commas helps to clarify the sentence by streamlining the series of items.

Semicolons

In addition to separating items in a series, semicolons can also be used to combine sentences. There are two important rules for combining sentences using semicolons:

<u>Rule One</u>: *Semicolons can be used to combine two independent clauses when those clauses are closely and clearly related to one another.*

> **Incorrect:** We need to pick up some celery and carrots; we're out of apples.
> **Incorrect:** We need to pick up some celery and carrots; because I need them to make soup.
> **Correct:** We need to pick up some celery and carrots; I need them to make soup.

The first sentence is incorrect because the two independent clauses have no relationship with one another. In the second sentence, the clauses are clearly related, but the second clause is a dependent clause, and semicolons are only used to combine independent clauses. The third sentence offers a good example of a correctly used semicolon because both clauses are independent and clearly related.

<u>Rule Two</u>: *Semicolons should not be used with conjunctions, but they can be used with conjunctive adverbs (such as* therefore *or* however*) and with transitional phrases (such as* for example*).*

> **Incorrect:** There are many exceptions to grammar rules; and this makes English grammar difficult to master.
> **Correct:** There are many exceptions to grammar rules; therefore, English grammar is difficult to master.

The first sentence uses the coordinating conjunction "and," making the use of a semicolon incorrect. The second sentence, however, uses a conjunctive adverb, so the use of the semicolon is correct.

Colons

Like semicolons, colons can also be used with items in a series and to combine sentences. Here are the rules for correct colon usage:

<u>Rule One</u>: *Colons are used to introduce items in a series, but only when the clause preceding the colon is an independent clause.*

> **Incorrect:** When you go to the store, please get: apples, milk, and eggs.
> **Correct:** When you go to the store, please pick up these items: apples, milk, and eggs.

<u>Rule Two</u>: *Like semicolons, colons are only used to combine independent clauses, but unlike semicolons, colons are only used to combine sentences when the second sentence clarifies, explains, or otherwise expands upon the first sentence.*

> **Incorrect:** He got what he deserved: he can't wait to tell his wife.
> **Incorrect:** He got what he deserved: because he really worked for that promotion.
> **Correct:** He got what he deserved: he really worked for that promotion.

In the first sentence, the second clause in no way clarifies or expands upon the first clause. In the second sentence, the second clause is a dependent clause. Only the third sentence properly uses a colon to combine two independent clauses.

Punctuation Rules

1. *Nonessential Elements*: Parentheses minimize information, dashes emphasize information, and commas are most commonly used to offset nonessential elements. Parentheses must always come in pairs, but dashes and commas can sometimes be used singly.
2. *Commas*: Use a comma with a coordinating conjunction when combining independent clauses. Only use a comma with a subordinating conjunction when the subordinating clause comes first. Use commas to separate items in a series when those items do not already contain commas.
3. *Semicolons*: Use semicolons to combine sentences when those sentences are clearly related. Semicolons should generally not be used with conjunctions. Semicolons are also used to separate items in a series when those items are lengthy or already contain commas.
4. *Colons*: Use colons to combine sentences when the second sentence expands upon the ideas in the first sentence. Colons can also introduce items in a series, but the clause before the colon must always be an independent clause.

TO ANSWER PUNCTUATION QUESTIONS:

Step One: Identify the punctuation error.

Step Two: Eliminate any answer choices that fail to correct the error.

Step Three: Eliminate answer choices that create new punctuation errors or that create sentence boundary errors.

Step Four: Of the remaining answers, choose the one that best solves the original error.

Step Five: Plug your chosen answer into the sentence to ensure that no new errors are introduced.

PRACTICE EXERCISE

Directions: All of the following sentences are missing correct punctuation. Add the correct punctuation marks to each sentence. Keep in mind that some sentences may include more than one type of missing punctuation.

1. There were several very popular items on the menu figs wrapped in bacon apples stuffed with gruyere and polenta bites.

2. My father the man with the big white hat is the chef at this restaurant.

3. Although I am lactose-intolerant I love to cook with cheese cream and other dairy products.

4. My father cannot prepare shellfish dishes he is so allergic to seafood that even touching it causes a reaction.

5. My favorite dish at the restaurant is chicken under a brick my least favorite is the lobster bisque.

6. Lobster bisque which is a type of soup is very popular in certain regions but is only really good when the lobster is very fresh.

7. Because my dad is the chef at the restaurant I get to eat there for free which is a very nice perk.

8. I work at the restaurant on weekends if it's not too busy I get to help in the kitchen instead of acting as hostess up front since there are fewer guests to welcome.

9. Last night my dad sent me to the store for emergency supplies including eggs potatoes and heavy cream.

10. The restaurant founded in 1902 has been in our family for four generations and it will eventually pass on to me.

11. While most of my classmates are worried about what they will do when they grow up I already know what I will be a chef.

12. Before I take over the restaurant I want to visit the culinary capitals of the world Paris France Rome Italy and Tokyo Japan.

13. These cities have some of the best restaurants in the world so I hope to learn a lot from other chefs especially those who have classical training.

14. One day perhaps I will teach my own children how to prepare a great dish however, if they do not want to be in the restaurant business I will encourage them to pursue their dreams.

15. Although I have always known that I have a responsibility to follow a culinary career in order to keep the restaurant in the family I love to cook so I look forward to running my own kitchen.

ACT English: Pronoun Errors

Pronouns take the place of nouns in sentences to make writing less repetitive. The noun that a pronoun replaces is called its antecedent.

Pronoun-Antecedent Agreement

Just as subjects and verbs must agree with each other, so must pronouns and their antecedents. When a pronoun takes the place of singular noun, the pronoun must be singular; when a pronoun takes the place of a plural noun, the pronoun must be plural.

Incorrect: Each team member is responsible for their own uniform.
Correct: Each team member is responsible for his or her own uniform.

In the sentences above, the incorrect sentence replaces *each team member*, which is singular, with the plural pronoun *their*. The error is corrected in the second sentence, where *each team member* is replaced by *his or her*.

It can be tempting to use *they* or *their* as a singular pronoun because *they* is gender-neutral. Although it might feel awkward to use *he or she* instead, it is more correct to do so because *they* is plural.

Pronoun Cases

The case of a pronoun refers to whether the pronoun is acting as a subject or an object in the sentence. These tables show the different pronouns for each case:

SUBJECT CASE

	Singular	Plural
1st person	I	We
2nd person	You	You
3rd person	He/She/It/One	They

OBJECT CASE

	Singular	Plural
1st person	Me	Us
2nd person	You	You
3rd person	Him/her/it/one	Them

When approaching a pronoun question on the ACT English test, it is important to determine whether the pronoun acts as a subject or an object; this will enable you to determine whether the appropriate pronoun case is being used.

Determining pronoun case is often straightforward, but can be tricky with compound subjects and objects.

Incorrect: My brother and me will finish all of the yard work tomorrow.
Correct: My brother and I will finish all of the yard work tomorrow.

This pair of examples conforms to a rule that many of us have heard before: Always use "so-and-so and I" rather than "so-and-so and me." In this particular pair of examples, the use of "and I" is correct because the pronoun is being used as part of the subject of the sentence; however, there are many instances in which it is grammatically correct to use "and me."

Incorrect: When the yard work is finished, my parents will give my brother and I twenty dollars each.
Correct: When the yard work is finished, my parents will give my brother and me twenty dollars each.

In this example, *my brother and I* is the object of the sentence, so the pronoun should take the object case. In other words, it is actually grammatically correct to use "and me" in this sentence.

The easiest way to decide which pronoun to use in cases like these is to eliminate the first person in the sentence to see which pronoun sounds better. In this example, the sentence would read, "my parents will give I" or "my parents will give me." Since we would say *me* in this case, *me* is the correct pronoun.

Ambiguous Pronoun References

In good writing, it is important that pronouns and their antecedents be clearly related. The reader should be able to easily tell what a pronoun is referring to.

Incorrect: When we toured the Tower of London, the guide told my cousin that he knew a lot about British history.
Correct: When we toured the Tower of London, the guide told my cousin that my cousin knew a lot about British history.

In the first sentence, we have no way of knowing whether the guide said that *my cousin* knew a lot about British history or that *the guide* knew a lot about British history. Although the second sentence seems repetitive, it correctly clarifies who knew a lot about British history.

Another common error with ambiguous pronoun references occurs when there is no antecedent at all.

Incorrect: If you want to work at a history museum, they require that you take a series of history classes.
Correct: If you want to work at a history museum, the management requires that you take a series of history classes.

In the first sentence, the pronoun *they* does not actually refer to anyone at all—it has no antecedent. The sentence must be rewritten to clarify who *they* are.

Pronoun Rules

1. Pronouns must agree with their antecedents in number—plural antecedents get plural pronouns, and singular antecedents get singular pronouns.
2. Pronouns must be in the correct case. Pronouns that act as subjects should be in the subject case, and pronouns that act as objects should be in the object case.
3. Pronouns must have clear antecedents.

TO ANSWER PRONOUN QUESTIONS:

Step One: If the underlined portion of the sentence contains either a pronoun or an antecedent, identify any pronoun errors in the sentence.

Step Two: Eliminate answer choices that fail to correct the pronoun error.

Step Three: Eliminate answer choices that create new pronoun errors or that fail to identify a clear relationship between the pronoun and antecedent.

Step Four: Choose the answer that corrects the original error without introducing any new errors.

PRACTICE EXERCISE

Directions: Each of the following sentences includes a pronoun error. Underline all of the pronouns in the original sentence, and then rewrite each sentence to correct the error.

1. Each of the boys has his or her own savings account.

   _____

   _____

2. Neither Bill nor Alexandra could find their jacket.

   _____

   _____

3. Mike thought that his brother should see his doctor.

   _____

   _____

4. After the big boxing match between Alex and Rodriguez, he ran around the ring in a victory lap.

   _____

   _____

5. When I tried to pick up the dog's food dish, it bit me.

   _____

   _____

6. Her and Chris will be going to the store later today.

   _____

   _____

7. Hannah and Grace turned in her report on time, but neither Alison nor Elise turned theirs in.

   _____

   _____

8. He is a better baseball player than myself.

   _____

   _____

9. The candidate informed his assistant that he was leaving on the next flight.

   _____

   _____

10. Matthew brought Jenna and I fresh bottles of water.

    _____

    _____

11. Everyone will receive his or her final grades in the mail.

_____

_____

12. Nobody plays their best when the temperature is so high.

_____

_____

13. It was difficult because my brother and me were both running for class treasurer.

_____

_____

14. When the eggs were served to the customers, they often looked a bit green.

_____

_____

15. I dropped the mirror on my foot and broke it.

_____

_____

ACT English: Verb Errors

Verb Tense, Mood, and Voice

In addition to testing subject-verb agreement, the ACT English Test will also include errors in verb tense, mood, and voice. A verb's tense tells us when an action occurs. A verb's mood tells us the attitude of the speaker. Finally, a verb's voice tells us the relationship between the verb and the participants in the action described by the verb.

VERB TENSES

Tenses tell us when the action of a verb occurs—past, present, or future. See the chart below for a detailed description of various verb tenses.

Past	Present	Future
Simple Past: Actions that took place at a specific time in the past. *I **drove** to practice on Monday.*	Simple Present: Actions that take place at the present moment. *I **drive** to practice every day.*	Simple Future: Actions that will happen at a point in time in the future. *I **will drive** to practice on Thursday.*
Past Progressive: Actions that occurred over a period of time in the past and were interrupted by another action. *I **was driving** to practice when I hit a deer.*	Present Progressive: Actions that occur over a period of time that includes the present moment. *I **am driving** to practice.*	Future Progressive: Actions that will occur over a period of time in the future. *I **will be driving** to practice every day this season.*
Past Perfect: Actions that occurred before another event in the past. *I **had been driving** to practice until my car broke down.*	Present Perfect: Actions that occurred in the past and include the present moment. *I **have been driving** to practice all season.*	Future Present: Actions that will occur in the future but before another event in the future. *By the time the season ends, I **will have been driving** to practice for four months.*

On the ACT English Test, it will be important to use context clues from the passage to determine the correct verb tense for a given sentence. Remember that sometimes the clues might come from sentences that come before or after the sentence in which the error has been underlined.

To address verb tense errors, follow these steps:

<u>Step One</u>: *Identify the time at which the action takes place and determine whether there are other actions or events that might affect the verb tense.*

<u>Step Two</u>: *Eliminate answer choices that clearly provide the wrong verb tense.*

<u>Step Three</u>: *Select the answer that best identifies the time at which the action takes place.*

VERB MOODS

Most sentences use the *indicative mood*, including questions and statements of fact or opinion. The *imperative mood* is used to give commands. In these sentences, the subject is usually assumed to be "you," or the person being addressed by the sentence. Finally, the *subjunctive mood* expresses states of unreality, such as hypothetical situations, requests, hopes, and wishes. Sentences that use the subjunctive mood will often include some form of the verb *to be*—either *was* or *were*. When a sentence is expressing something that isn't true, the sentence should use *were*. Such sentences will often begin with the word "if," as in, "If I were a super hero…"

Indicative Mood: I **will dress** as a super hero for the costume party.

Imperative Mood: Please **go buy** a super hero costume for me.

Subjunctive Mood: I wish I **were** a super hero in real life.

VERB VOICE

Verb voice can be either passive or active. A verb is in the active voice if the action is being performed by the subject. A verb is in the passive voice if a party other than the subject is performing the action.

Active Voice: I **finished** my book last night.

Passive Voice: My book **was finished** last night.

A fun way to test for passive voice is to add a phrase like "by gorillas" or "by zombies" after the verb. If the resulting sentence still makes sense, it's in the passive voice. Let's use this trick with the sentences above:

Active Voice: I finished *by gorillas* my book last night.

Passive Voice: My book was finished *by gorillas* last night.

Setting aside the realism of book-reading gorillas, we can see that the addition of the phrase "by gorillas" still makes grammatical sense in the passive voice sentence.

Generally, active voice is considered to be more correct for stylistic reasons. The only exceptions to this rule are when the thing being acted upon is more important in the sentence than the actor or when the author does not know who performed the action. This is rare, so it is usually best to choose active voice over passive voice when selecting the best answer on the ACT English Test.

Verb Errors

Verb tense, mood, and voice questions will always include a verb in the underlined portion of the sentence. If the underlined portion of the question and the answer choices include verbs, examine the rest of the sentence to determine whether there is an error in verb tense, mood, or voice.

TO ANSWER VERB ERROR QUESTIONS:

Step One: If the underlined portion of the sentence includes verbs, examine the sentence to identify a possible verb error. Remember to check the verb's tense, mood, and voice.

Step Two: Eliminate any answer choices that do not use the correct verb tense.

Step Three: Eliminate any answer choices that do not use the correct verb mood.

Step Four: If multiple answer choices remain, eliminate any that are in the passive voice.

Step Five: Select the answer that best completes the sentence without introducing new errors.

PRACTICE EXERCISE

Directions: Each of the following sentences contains at least one error in verb tense, mood, or voice. Underline the verbs in each sentence, and then rewrite the sentence to correct the error.

1. I suggest that she seeks extra practice in math.

   _____

   _____

2. Concerts are often performed by stars to raise money for charities.

   _____

   _____

3. As Beebee looks for her glasses, her cell phone rang.

   _____

   _____

4. If we played better in the second half, we scored four additional baskets and won the game.

   _____

   _____

5. Tens of thousands of people have seen the exhibition before the museum closes.

   _____

   _____

6. The doctor recommended bed rest for the patient, who suffers from a bad cold.

   _____

   _____

7. I wish she spends more time cleaning and less time complaining.

   _____

   _____

8. If people walk on Mars, they would have weighed about one-third of what they would have weighed on Earth.

   _____

   _____

9. Lives are saved since the development of advanced tornado warnings.

   _____

   _____

10. By the time negotiations begun, many politicians had expressed doubt about them.

   _____

   _____

11. Everyone hopes the plan would work.

_____

_____

12. Her teacher recommends that she spent more time on math than on English.

_____

_____

13. I was terribly disappointed with my test score because I studied really hard.

_____

_____

14. The boy insists he will have paid for the candy bars.

_____

_____

15. After Alice played croquet with the queen, she is sentenced to death.

_____

_____

ACT English: Adjectives and Adverbs

At least one or two questions on the ACT English Test will examine your ability to properly use adjectives and adverbs in context. This includes understanding when to use adjectives versus adverbs and how to properly use the comparative forms of adjectives and adverbs.

Adjectives vs. Adverbs

The most important rule to know regarding adjectives and adverbs is that adjectives can only be used to describe nouns and pronouns while adverbs describe verbs, adjectives, and other adverbs.

Incorrect: Last night's game was well.
Correct: Last night's game was good.

In this example, the descriptor is describing *game*. Since *game* is a noun, we have to use the adjectival form, *good*, rather than the adverbial *well*.

Incorrect: Last night's game was played good.
Correct: Last night's game was played well.

Here we have the opposite situation. In this case, the descriptor is describing the verb *played*, so we need to use the adverbial *well* rather than the adjectival *good*.

Sometimes choosing between an adjective and an adverb is easy because one will simply sound wrong. However, since adjective and adverb errors are common in everyday speech, it is important not to rely on your ear when addressing these questions. Take the time to identify the descriptor and the word being described to be sure that you select the correct word.

Comparisons with Adjectives and Adverbs

There are two forms of adjectives and adverbs when we are making comparisons: The comparative form is used when two items are being compared, and the superlative form is used when three or more items are being compared. Use this chart to help determine the correct forms for comparative and superlative adjectives and adverbs:

	Comparative	Superlative
Short adjectives and one-syllable adverbs	**Add -er**	**Add -est**
Short	Shorter	Shortest
Pretty	Prettier	Prettiest
Simple	Simpler	Simplest
Fast	Faster	Fastest
Longer adjectives and adverbs ending in -ly	**Add more**	**Add most**
Intelligent	More intelligent	Most intelligent
Carefully	More carefully	Most carefully
Dangerous	More dangerous	Most dangerous
Irregular forms	**Examples**	**Examples**
Good	Better	Best
Bad	Worse	Worst
Much/Many	More	Most
Well	Better	Best
Badly	Worse	Worse

One important rule regarding use of comparative and superlative adjectives and adverbs is to *never* combine the -er or -est forms with more or most.

Incorrect: This method is more quicker than the other method.
Correct: This method is quicker than the other method.

TO ANSWER ADJECTIVE AND ADVERB QUESTIONS:

Step One: If the underlined portion of the sentence includes an adjective or an adverb, look for an adjective or adverb error by identifying the descriptor and the word being described.

Step Two: If the descriptor is an adjective, it must describe a noun or pronoun; if the descriptor is an adverb, it must describe a verb, adjective, or adverb. Eliminate any answer choices that fail to adhere to this rule.

Step Three: Determine whether a comparison is being made. If so, determine whether the comparative form should be used (when comparing two items) or the superlative form should be used (when comparing three or more items). Eliminate any answer choices that fail to use the proper form.

Step Four: Of the remaining answer choices, select the one that best suits the context of the sentence.

PRACTICE EXERCISE

Directions: Each of the following sentences contains an adjective or adverb error. Underline the adjective or adverb errors in each sentence, and then rewrite the sentence to correct the error.

1. Unfortunately, the lead singer in the musical is an amazingly poorly singer.

    _____

    _____

2. The powerfully summer sun beat down on the campers.

    _____

    _____

3. All birds that fly have ten primary flight feathers, each one shaped slight different.

    _____

    _____

4. Of all computer brands, Macs are easier to use.

    _____

    _____

5. Between Alan and Margaret, Alan is the quietest.

    _____

    _____

6. The two types of kayaks are the easily maneuverable white-water kayak and the largest sea kayak.

    _____

    _____

7. Of the three boys who competed at the science fair, Rob had the more interesting project.

    _____

    _____

8. Despite the chaos, the nurse examined the patient calmly and careful.

    _____

    _____

9. Of the many flower choices, petunias are the less interesting option.

    _____

    _____

10. It was an extreme cold winter day.

    _____

    _____

11. Richard's comments were carelessly.

_____

_____

12. She did real well on that test.

_____

_____

13. The milk smells rottenly.

_____

_____

14. Although we looked at a lot of houses, they all seemed to be of similarly quality.

_____

_____

15. There are 20 students in the class, each performing similar.

_____

_____

ACT English: Commonly Confused Words

Commonly Confused Words

The ACT will test your knowledge of pairs or groups of words that are commonly confused. The following is a list of some of the most commonly confused words that might appear on the ACT:

accede **exceed**	**Accede** means "to agree or allow": The county *acceded* to our request for speed bumps on our road. **Exceed** means "to go beyond": My perfect test score *exceeded* my expectations.
accept **except**	**Accept** means "to take willingly": I had to sign in order to *accept* the package. **Except** means "excluding": The package contained everything *except* batteries.
adapt **adept** **adopt**	**Adapt** means "to adjust": You must float fish in the tank before releasing them in order to allow them to *adapt* to the water temperature. **Adept** means "skilled": Fish are *adept* at swimming. **Adopt** means "to accept as your own": Though I was nervous, I *adopted* a self-assured posture.
adverse **averse**	**Adverse** means "unfavorable": A low test score will *adversely* affect your grade. **Averse** means "unwilling": I am *averse* to jumping from high heights.
advice **advise**	**Advice** means "an opinion intended to be helpful": My sister loves to give me *advice* about my clothes. **Advise** means "to give advice": My sister loves to *advise* me about my clothes.
affect **effect**	**Affect** means "to influence": The temperature can *affect* the growth rate of plants. **Effect** is usually a noun meaning "a result": The temperature can have an *effect* on the growth rate of plants.
assure **ensure** **insure**	**Assure** means "to guarantee": The doctor *assured* me that it was just a cold. **Ensure** means "to make sure": The medicine will *ensure* that I get over the cold quickly. **Insure** means "to provide insurance against loss or injury": Luckily, I am *insured*, so the doctor's bill will be small.
bare **bear**	**Bare** usually means "to reveal": When his private emails were leaked, the Senator was forced to *bare* his secrets to the world. **Bear** usually means "to carry": Now he must *bear* the burden of public shame.
breadth **breath** **breathe**	**Breadth** means "width" or "extent": The *breadth* of the damage was irreversible. **Breath** means "the air that you breathe": I ran until I had no more *breath*. **Breathe** means "to take air into your lungs": He couldn't *breathe* when the rock fell on his chest.
censor **sensor** **censure**	**Censor** is "to prohibit free expression": It is wrong to *censor* the press. A **sensor** is "something that interprets stimulation": Our security system includes a motion *sensor*. **Censure** means "to harshly criticize": They will *censure* the lawyer for his misbehavior.
complement **compliment**	**Complement** means "to make complete" or "to supplement": The upholstery *complements* the wall color by making it seem richer. **Compliment** means "to express admiration": My mom *compliments* my speaking abilities after every debate tournament.

conscience **conscious**	**Conscience** means "knowing right from wrong": The lie weighed on my *conscience*. **Conscious** means "being awake or aware": I became *conscious* when Bobby dumped ice water on my face.
device **devise**	A **device** is "an instrument used to complete a task": I need a sharp *device* to open the box. To **devise** is "to create": I will *devise* a way to open the box.
disinterested **uninterested**	**Disinterested** means "unbiased or impartial": The judge serves as a *disinterested* party. **Uninterested** means "not interested": Harry was *uninterested* in the movie, so he spent the whole time reading a book.
elicit **illicit**	**Elicit** means "to draw out": The knock on the door did not *elicit* a response. **Illicit** means "illegal or illegitimate": The locker search turned up no *illicit* materials.
emanate **eminent** **imminent**	**Emanate** means "to issue or spread": The old, rotting broccoli caused a stench to *emanate* from the fridge. **Eminent** means "prestigious": An *eminent* attorney spoke at the graduation ceremony. **Imminent** means "about to happen": The thunder suggests that the storm is *imminent*.
explicit **implicit**	**Explicit** means "clear and direct": The teacher's detailed instructions were *explicit*. **Implicit** means "indirectly" or "implied": Her tone of voice suggested an *implicit* meaning hidden in her words.
fewer **less**	**Fewer** refers to "things that can be counted": There were *fewer* books available. **Less** refers to "things that cannot be counted": He has *less* interest than she does.
peek **pique** **peak**	**Peek** means "to look quickly without someone knowing": A *peek* through the curtains revealed an eerie sight. **Pique** can either mean "to provoke" or "resentment": Any noise outside will *pique* my curiosity. OR I am in a state of *pique* over the loud noises my neighbors make. **Peak** means "the highest point": The mountain's *peak* offered a fantastic view.
perspective **prospective**	A **perspective** is "a point of view": My sister shares my *perspective* on curfews. **Prospective** means "possible or likely to happen": I am going to visit my *prospective* colleges.
precede **proceed**	**Precede** means "to come before": Studying should *precede* test day. **Proceed** means "to move forward": Once you read the directions, you may *proceed*.
restive **restful**	**Restive** means "impatient, nervous, or restless": Sally is *restive* when she sits still too long. **Restful** means "full of rest, calm, quiet": The week after graduation promises to be *restful*.
than **then**	**Than** is used "to compare": This test is harder *than* any other test I've taken. **Then** is used "to describe a time that is not now": Sharpen your pencil and *then* begin the test.

By becoming familiar with the words in this chart, you will be better able to recognize commonly confused words on the ACT English Test. Whenever you see answer choices that are spelled or pronounced very similarly, the question is likely a commonly confused words question, and you should pay careful attention to the minute differences between the answer choices.

Possessive Determiners

Another category of commonly confused words is possessive determiners. Possessive determiners tell us who possesses something. Examples include *my* and *her*. Some possessive determiners, like *your, their,* and *its* fall under the category of commonly confused words that might appear on the ACT.

Your vs. You're: "Your" is a possessive determiner, as in, "Your hair looks nice today." "You're" is a contraction that means "you are," as in, "You're going to the store."

Their vs. There vs. They're: "Their" is a possessive determiner, as in, "Their dog ran away." "There" is most commonly used to show the existence or position of something, as in, "There is a dog over there." "They're" is a contraction that means "they are," as in, "They're going on vacation."

Its vs. It's: "Its" is a possessive determiner, as in "The dog licked its injured foot." "It's" is a contraction that means "it is," as in, "It's cold in here." Note that "its'" is never correct.

TO ANSWER COMMONLY CONFUSED WORDS QUESTIONS:

Step One: Look for answer choices that are spelled or pronounced similarly.

Step Two: Carefully examine the context of the sentence to identify the correct word choice.

PRACTICE EXERCISE

<u>Directions</u>: Each of the following sentences includes a misused commonly confused word. Underline the incorrect word and write the correct word on the line provided.

1. There were less customers than anticipated.

   _____

2. There going to the amusement park on Saturday.

   _____

3. The chemical is terrible for the environment because it leeches into the ground.

   _____

4. My brother hurt his hand when he hit the wall in a fit of peak.

   _____

5. The dog keeps shaking its' head.

   _____

6. He chose to attend Harvard because it was the most imminent university that had accepted him.

   _____

7. The affect of your test scores cannot be understated.

   _____

8. After he takes attendance, the teacher precedes with his lesson.

   _____

9. It is important to weatherproof windows in order to insure that cold air does not leak in during the winter.

   _____

10. The perspective employee waited for his interview nervously.

    _____

11. You're new shirt already has a stain on it.

    _____

12. Please except my apology for my tardiness.

    _____

13. He provided her with some valuable advise about the job market.

    _____

14. Never go to a doctor who's office plants have died.

    _____

15. Elizabeth's room is cleaner then yours.

    _____

ACT English: Idioms

Idioms are expressions or phrasings that are peculiar to a certain language. They include expressions like "barking up the wrong tree" or "last straw," but the ACT English Test will (luckily) not test these seemingly nonsensical idiomatic expressions. Instead, the idioms tested on the ACT are idioms with prepositions and two-part idioms.

Idioms with Prepositions

Most idiom questions will ask you to identify the correct preposition in a certain expression. These questions can be difficult because there are no real rules governing such use of prepositions. Those who feel comfortable with their ear for English usage can often rely on instinct to determine the correct preposition for a certain context; others will need to memorize the correct preposition for commonly used expressions.

> **Incorrect:** He was accused for stealing from the classroom.
> **Correct:** He was accused of stealing from the classroom.

As you can see in this example, the only difference is the use of the preposition *for* versus *of*. Unfortunately, there is no real reason why *of* is more correct.

Be sure to review the following chart, which contains some of the most common idiomatic prepositional phrases. Take special care to familiarize yourself with any expressions that you are not yet familiar with. Keep in mind that this chart is by no means a comprehensive list of all idiomatic prepositional phrases. You should take note of new prepositional phrases that you come across in your reading or studies.

Phrase	Example
Accused of	She was accused of cheating on the exam.
Acquainted with	He is well acquainted with the rules.
Agreed to	They all agreed to follow the rules.
Afraid of	My brother is deathly afraid of ghosts.
Apologized for	My sister apologized for swiping my favorite hairbrush.
Arrived at	We arrived at school an hour late.
Aware of	Are you aware of the rules?
Believe in	Do you believe in fairies?
Capable of	He is not capable of hurting others.
Committed to	I am committed to excellence.
Depend on	You can't depend on the weather forecast.
Differ from	My study schedule does not differ from his study schedule.
Difference between	What is the difference between an adjective and an adverb?
Encouraged by	I am encouraged by your dedication.
Fond of	She is fond of chocolate ice cream.
Fondness for	She has a fondness for chocolate ice cream.
Guilty of	He is guilty of nothing more than trying too hard.
Hint at	The rule changes hint at a conspiracy.
Interested in	I am very interested in applying to Harvard.
Limited to	My experience is limited to volunteer work.
Opposed to	I am opposed to the proposed rule change.
Participate in	We will participate in the fundraiser.
Proud of	I am so proud of my little brother's great grades.

Provide with	They will provide us with pencils.
Similar to	Mrs. Jones's class is similar to Mr. Smith's class.
Substitute for	Synthetic fabrics are no substitute for natural cotton.
Tired of	I'm tired of always being last in line.
Worried about	I'm worried about my exam grade.

Two-part Idioms

The other form of idiomatic phrase that may appear on the ACT English Test is the two-part idiom. These are certain phrases that must always contain two parts, including:

Either...or/Neither...nor

> **Incorrect:** Either my brother nor my sister will drive to the park.
> **Correct:** Either my brother or my sister will drive to the park.
> **Correct:** Neither my brother nor my sister will drive to the park.

These words must work together. *Either* can only be used with *or*, never with *nor*. *Neither* must be used with *nor*, never with *or*.

Between...and

> **Incorrect:** Between math or English, I prefer math.
> **Correct:** Between math and English, I prefer math.

When using the word *between* to establish a comparison, always use *and*.

As...as

> **Incorrect:** Her dress is not as pretty than Julie's dress.
> **Correct:** Her dress is not as pretty as Julie's dress.

When using *as* to set up a comparison, use *as* rather than *than* to complete the comparison.

Not only...but also

> **Incorrect:** Not only did he write four novels, but he authored a volume of poetry.
> **Correct:** Not only did he write four novels, but also he authored a volume of poetry.
> **Correct:** Not only did he write four novels, but he also authored a volume of poetry.

When a sentence includes *not only*, it must also include *but also*.

Whenever you see the beginning of a two-part idiom, be sure the other half is also included.

TO ANSWER IDIOM QUESTIONS:

Step One: If the underlined portion of the sentence includes a preposition and you cannot immediately spot another type of error, read the sentence closely to determine whether there is an idiomatic preposition error.

Step Two: If there is an idiomatic preposition error, select the answer choice that best corrects this error without introducing new errors.

Step Three: If the sentence includes part of a two-part idiom, check to see if the second part of the idiom is present.

Step Four: If the second part of the idiom is missing or inaccurate, select the answer choice that best corrects this error without introducing new errors.

PRACTICE EXERCISE

Directions: Each of the following sentences contains an idiom error. Rewrite each sentence to correct the error.

1. When Chris ruined Kelly's science project, everyone was outraged for his behavior.

2. I sat across the aisle with a woman who had her music volume too high.

3. The students argued that they had a right for wearing whatever they wanted.

4. He was curious on whether the teacher would give a lot of homework this weekend.

5. Neither Alice or Gina could understand the lesson.

6. The defendant was found guilty for burning down the house.

7. I sometimes use applesauce as a substitute of oil in baking recipes.

8. Her taste in clothing differs between mine.

9. I'm worried for my brother's driving test results.

10. She needed to decide between taking European history or Asian history.

11. Jenna arrived to the party fifteen minutes early.

_____

_____

12. He not only broke Mom's favorite vase, but he lied about it.

_____

_____

13. Michael says he is opposed against the new dress code.

_____

_____

14. The dog has a fondness of my favorite shoes.

_____

_____

15. The ACT consists in four sections: English, Reading, Math, and Science.

_____

_____

ACT English: Parallelism and Modifiers

Parallelism

Parallelism requires that elements in a sentence (or in related sentences) share the same form. This creates a better overall writing style by making the sentence clearer and preventing awkwardness.

PARALLELISM WITH COORDINATING CONJUNCTIONS

When elements of a sentence are joined by a coordinating conjunction, those elements must be in the same form.

> **Incorrect:** I love to travel and writing about my travels.
> **Correct:** I love to travel and to write about my travels.
> **Correct:** I love travelling and writing about my travels.

In the first sentence, "to travel" and "writing" serve the same purpose, so they need to be in the same form. The second and third sentences correct this error.

PARALLELISM WITH ITEMS IN A SERIES

The same rule applies to items in a series: items in a series must be in the same form.

> **Incorrect:** Tomorrow I will finish my homework, study for my history test, and practicing the piano.
> **Correct:** Tomorrow I will finish my homework, study for my history test, and practice the piano.

In the first sentence, the final item in the series "practicing the piano" is in a different verb form than the verb forms for other two items. To correct the error, the item must have the same form of the other items.

PARALLELISM IN COMPARISONS

When two things are being compared, both items must be in the same form.

> **Incorrect:** Driving across the country takes more time than to fly.
> **Correct:** Driving across the country takes more time than flying.

In the first sentence, the verbs *driving* and *to fly* are not in the same form. This error is corrected in the second and third sentences.

TO ANSWER PARALLELISM QUESTIONS:

Step One: Examine the entire sentence – not just the underlined portion – to identify sentence elements that are not in the same form.

Step Two: Eliminate any answer choices that fail to correct the parallelism error or that introduce new parallelism errors.

Step Three: Eliminate answer choices that introduce new errors or create awkward phrasing.

Step Four: Choose the answer that best solves the parallelism error without introducing new errors.

Modifier Errors

A modifier is a word or phrase that describes, clarifies, or otherwise modifies something else in a sentence. Modifier errors typically occur when the object being modified is either missing or does not appear immediately before or after the modifier. The ACT English Test will test your ability to identify and correct modifier errors.

MISPLACED MODIFIERS

If you suspect that a question might contain a misplaced modifier, the first step is identifying the modifying word or phrase. Modifiers are usually adjectives, adverbs, or phrases such as prepositional phrases. They are often, but certainly not always, set apart by commas. In the sample sentences below, the modifiers are underlined:

> **Sample 1:** The woman <u>with brown hair</u> walked to her car.
> **Sample 2:** Her <u>brand-new</u> car was cherry red.
> **Sample 3:** <u>Parked crookedly</u>, the car was <u>already</u> dented.

In the first sentence, *with brown hair* modifies *woman*. In the second sentence, *brand-new* modifies car. And in the final sentence, *parked crookedly* modifies *car* and *already* modifies *dented*.

The placement of modifiers can change the meaning of a sentence. Look at these sample sentences:

> **Sample 1:** Miss Jones waved at Evan <u>just</u> as she came in.
> **Sample 2:** Miss Jones waved <u>just</u> at Evan as she came in.
> **Sample 3:** Miss Jones <u>just</u> waved at Evan as she came in.

These sentences are all virtually identical with the exception of the placement of *just*. By placing this modifier in different parts of the sentence, we can change the sentence's meaning. In the first sentence, the modifier tells us when Miss Jones waved at Evan because it modifies *as she came in*. In the second sentence, the modifier tells us that Miss Jones did not wave at anyone except for Evan because it modifies *at Evan*. And in the third sentence, the modifier tells us that Miss Jones only waved at Evan and did not greet him in any other way because it modifies *waved at*.

Since the placement of a modifier can change a sentence's meaning, misplaced modifiers can create unintended meanings. For example:

> **Incorrect:** Thundering down the hill, Isaac was worried that the rocks would land on his campsite.
> **Correct:** Isaac was worried that the rocks, which were thundering down the hill, would land on his campsite.

The incorrect sentence includes a misplaced modifier. *Thundering down the hill* is modifying Isaac. This makes little sense – why would Isaac be worried about rocks landing on his campsite if he was the one thundering down the hill? The corrected sentence ensures that *thundering down the hill* modifies rocks. This sentence makes much more sense.

The best way to fix a misplaced modifier is to ensure that the modifier is located as close to the intended object as possible.

DANGLING MODIFIERS

A similar type of error occurs when a modifier describes something that isn't actually mentioned in a sentence – this is called a dangling modifier. As with misplaced modifiers, it's important to first identify the modifier and then identify the thing being modified. Let's look at an example:

<u>Walking near the river</u>, the fish jumped.

In this sentence, the modifier, *walking near the river*, is modifying *fish*. This doesn't make logical sense. As a reader, we know that it is highly unlikely that the fish jumped while they were walking near the river; we can assume that the actual subject of the sentence is a person who was walking near the river. However, good writing never makes the reader assume something like that. To fix this dangling modifier, we need to rewrite the sentence to include the proper subject:

<u>Walking near the river</u>, *I watched as* the fish jumped.

In this corrected version of the sentence, the modifier clearly describes *I*. The sentence makes more sense and the modifier error is solved.

TO ANSWER MODIFIER QUESTIONS:

Step One: Identify the modifier.

Step Two: Identify the word/phrase being modified.

Step Three: Decide what word/phrase should be modified. If this word/phrase is not the same as the word/phrase identified in step two, the error is a misplaced modifier. If it is missing, the error is a dangling modifier.

Step Four: Eliminate answer choices that fail to solve the modifier error or that create new errors. Pay particular attention to those that create misplaced modifiers.

Step Five: Of the remaining answers, choose the one that creates the most logical relationship between the modifier and the word/phrase that should be modified.

PRACTICE EXERCISE

Part A

<u>Directions</u>: Each of the following sentences contains a parallelism error. Rewrite the sentence to correct the error.

1. As the best player on his team, James often dunks, steals, and blocking the basketball.

    _____

    _____

2. Martin Luther King, Jr. is admired for his courage, his dedication, and being intelligent.

    _____

    _____

3. The ACT English section challenges students and frustration is found in them.

    _____

    _____

4. Alexander displays both a disregard for the rules and disrespecting his teachers.

    _____

    _____

5. The painter was complimented not only for his use of color but also about his technique.

    _____

    _____

6. The diligent student completed his homework punctually, studied the material thoroughly, and his presentations were well delivered.

    _____

    _____

7. Since Valentino hasn't been getting enough sleep, he is having trouble staying awake and focus in class.

    _____

    _____

8. The neutral countries in World War I included Denmark, Argentina, Norway, and the Spanish.

    _____

    _____

9. Tommy was a good skater, but Billy danced better.

    _____

    _____

10. When her favorite scarf went missing, Sue looked under the couch, the bed, and in her closet.

_____

_____

Part B

Directions: Each of the following sentences contains a modifier error. Rewrite the sentence to correct the error.

11. Weighing more than 15,000 tons each, workers used massive tunnel boring machines to dig the tunnel.

_____

_____

12. Appointed as the nation's sole provider of telecommunications, widespread criticism about the Bell System proliferated.

_____

_____

13. Originally wanting to study biology, mathematics was the field in which she truly excelled.

_____

_____

14. Having finished his introduction, the slideshow was the first thing the presenter showed to the class.

_____

_____

15. Hiding in the dark, the cat's eyes glowed.

_____

_____

16. The robot was for sale by the woman across the street with a remote control.

_____

_____

17. While out of town, Jessica sent long letters to her friend filled with tales about her travels.

_____

_____

18. Edgar Allan Poe is revered for his frightening tales by critics.

_____

_____

19. The artist was sketching in the flowing scarf with colored pencils.

_____

_____

20. The woman walked her dog in high heels.

_____

_____

ACT English: Transitions and Organization

Organization

The ACT English Test has several types of questions that test your ability to improve the organization of a sentence, paragraph, or passage. These include questions that ask you to determine the most logical sequence of phrases within a sentence, sentences within a paragraph, or paragraphs within a passage; questions that ask you to add a sentence that suits the passage or that accomplishes a particular goal; and questions that ask you to improve the transitions or transitional sentences in the passage.

Logical Sequence

One of the most common logical sequence/organization questions involves modifier placement. Up to half of the organization questions on the ACT English Test will involve misplaced or dangling modifiers, so be sure to review the lesson on Parallelism and Modifiers.

Other logical sequence questions will ask you to put ideas in the most logical order, whether by rearranging sentences within a paragraph, deciding the most appropriate place to add a sentence, or rearranging paragraphs within a passage. Answering logical sequence questions requires close attention to context, relationships between ideas, and use of transitions in order to determine the most logical order of ideas.

LOGICAL SEQUENCE OF SENTENCES

Logical sequence questions that focus on sentences will either require that you rearrange the sentences within a paragraph or add a sentence in the most appropriate place in a paragraph. The most logical order of sentences in any given paragraph depends on the content of the individual sentences, so these questions require much closer reading than many other writing questions.

Concepts that are closely related to one another should appear close together in the paragraph, and if there is a cause and effect relationship within the paragraph, the cause usually should come before the effect. Pay close attention to transitional words and phrases because these can often provide clues to help determine the most logical sequence of sentences.

TO ANSWER LOGICAL SEQUENCE OF SENTENCES QUESTIONS:

Step One: Look for transitional words or phrases that don't seem to make sense. Eliminate any answer choices that don't address these illogical transitions.

Step Two: Look for sentences that contain closely related ideas, but that are not placed close together in the paragraph. Eliminate any answer choices that do not place closely related ideas together.

Step Three: Look for sentences that relate to the paragraph immediately preceding or following the paragraph in question. Eliminate answer choices that do not place these sentences nearest this paragraph.

Step Four: Of the remaining answer choices, choose the one that seems to place the sentences in the most logical order. Reread the paragraph as it should be based on the answer choice you selected. If the paragraph now makes logical sense, move on to the next question.

LOGICAL SEQUENCE OF PARAGRAPHS

Logical sequence questions that focus on paragraphs require that you arrange the paragraphs within the passage in the most logical order. Often, these questions ask where a certain paragraph should be placed.

Understanding the basic structure of a well-written passage is helpful when answering these questions. Remember that the first paragraph usually serves as an introduction and the final paragraph usually serves as a conclusion. The body paragraphs provide supporting information and should flow logically from one idea to the next. As with logical sequence of sentences questions, transitions can be very helpful in determining the best order of the paragraphs.

TO ANSWER LOGICAL SEQUENCE OF PARAGRAPHS QUESTIONS:

Step One: Look for transitional words, phrases, or sentences that seem out of place. Eliminate any answer choices that fail to solve this problem.

Step Two: Look for paragraphs that contain closely related ideas that are not placed near each other. Eliminate any answer choices that do not place closely related paragraphs near one another.

Step Three: Of the remaining answer choices, choose the one that seems to place the paragraphs in the most logical order.

Step Four: Quickly skim the passage with the paragraphs in the order indicated by the answer you selected. If the new version of the passage makes sense, move on to the next question.

Transitions

Transition questions require that you use appropriate transitions to express the logical order of ideas within a paragraph or passage. The following is a table containing frequently used transitions and transitional phrases and the relationships they demonstrate:

FUNCTION	TRANSITIONAL WORDS AND PHRASES			
Sequence	First Second Third Next Then	Finally After Afterward At last Before	Currently During Earlier Immediately Later	Meanwhile Now Recently Simultaneously Subsequently
Conclusion	Finally In a word In brief In conclusion	In the end In the final analysis On the whole	Thus To conclude To summarize	In sum To sum up In summary
Example	For example To illustrate	For instance	Namely	Specifically
Position	Above Adjacent Below	Beyond Here	In front In back	Nearby There
Cause/Effect	Therefore Accordingly	Consequently Thus	Hence	So
Emphasis	Even Truly	Indeed	In fact	Of course
Similarity	Also Just as	In the same way Similarly	Likewise	Much as
Contrast	But Nonetheless Still	However Notwithstanding Yet	In spite of In contrast	Nevertheless On the contrary

It is important to know the functions of different transitions in order to identify the best transition to use in the context of the passage. For example:

Incorrect: Animal welfare and human welfare are closely connected. *Nevertheless,* failure to embrace spay and neuter programs has led to animal overpopulation in many communities, causing the spread of certain diseases and a rise in minor car accidents.

Correct: Animal welfare and human welfare are closely connected. *For example,* failure to embrace spay and neuter programs has led to animal overpopulation in many communities, causing the spread of certain diseases and a rise in minor car accidents.

The transition used in the first example incorrectly identifies the relationship between the two sentences as a contrasting relationship. But the information in the second sentence doesn't contrast with the information in the first sentence; instead it clarifies the information by providing an example. *For example* provides a transition that properly identifies this relationship.

TO ANSWER TRANSITION QUESTIONS:

Step One: Read the sentence containing the transition as well as the sentences immediately before and after. Determine which two sentences are connected by the transition.

Step Two: Identify the relationship between the two sentences. Eliminate any answer choices that don't reflect that relationship.

Step Three: Of the remaining choices, choose the one that best reflects the relationship between the two sentences.

PRACTICE EXERCISE

<u>Directions</u>: Read the following passage and answer the accompanying questions.

[1]

In the United States, political primaries are the dominant method by which a party determines its nominees for office. They serve a powerful filtering function, screening out many potential candidates in favor of just one.

[2]

Of those dozens of candidates, just two will have any real chance of becoming president, **(1)** <u>so</u> very few Americans are truly a part of the process that determines who those two will be. A few hundred thousand partisans in Iowa and New Hampshire exert an outsized influence on making these decisions on behalf of the rest of us, but, in the end, just a few thousand party insiders effectively make these choices.

[3]

[1] **(2)** <u>Despite</u> this markedly undemocratic process, the original point of primaries was actually to make party decisions more democratic. [2] Before the days of primaries, parties typically chose their nominees through conventions guided by just one or two party bosses. [3] Consider, for example, the infamous Boss Tweed, who all but ran New York City during the 1860s and 1870s through his role as the head of the Democratic General Committee. [4] His corruption serves as a perfect illustration of why primaries came about. [5] In this role, Tweed not only enjoyed substantial financial benefits, but also held incredible power as the gatekeeper to New York politics. [6] Primaries were intended to allow rank-and-file party members, rather than just party bosses, to make the key decision of which candidates the party nominated. {3}

1. A) NO CHANGE
   B) yet
   C) and
   D) for

2. A) NO CHANGE
   B) Because of
   B) In addition to
   D) With

3. To improve the organization of the this paragraph, sentence 5 would best be placed:

   A) where it is now.
   B) before sentence 3.
   C) before sentence 4.
   D) after sentence 6.

[4]

In fact, we have never had that right, **(4)** <u>or</u> have we ever really had that ability. In truth, despite the "democratization" of the primary process, party elites still hold all the cards. Modern party bosses have such influence over fundraising, endorsements, and media exposure that most party primaries are decided long before voters head to the polls. In the end, most party primaries are really little more than a show put on to convince the masses of the democratic principles of our election system. {5}

[5]

(6) <u>Although</u> democratic parties might sound like a good idea on the surface, the concept doesn't make sense upon further consideration. **(7)** <u>In spite of this</u>, political parties are hardly membership organizations. We might call ourselves Democrats or Republicans, but we don't need to pay dues or vote for the right candidates to do so. Given this fact, what gives us the right to control political parties that we have no real loyalty to?

4. A) NO CHANGE
    B) so
    C) and
    D) nor

5. To improve the organization of the passage, the fourth paragraph would best be placed:

    A) where it is now.
    B) at the beginning of the passage.
    C) after the second paragraph.
    D) after the fifth paragraph.

6. A) NO CHANGE
    B) Despite
    C) Because
    D) Whether

7. A) NO CHANGE
    B) In the present
    C) After all
    D) As a result of this

8. The writer wishes to include the following sentence in the essay:

    Just at the presidential level, there are typically one to two dozen candidates who run in the primaries.

    That sentence will fit most smoothly and logically into Paragraph:

    A) 1, before the first sentence.
    B) 1, after the last sentence.
    C) 2, before the first sentence.
    D) 3, before the first sentence.

ACT English: Author's Intent

Author's Intent

The ACT English Test goes beyond the mechanics of writing to examine your grasp of strong content. After all, good writing requires more than an understanding of *how* to write; you must also know *what* to write.

Purpose Questions

Purpose questions ask you to determine how best to accomplish a particular goal. Like some other types of questions on the ACT English Test, purpose questions can come in more than one form. Nearly all purpose questions will include a specific question, but some purpose questions will focus on a single underlined phrase while others may ask you to change or add an entire sentence.

For example:

{1} The process of firing a piece of pottery in a kiln converts weak clay into a strong, durable, glasslike form. When a potter is ready to fire his work, he must first allow the kiln to reach the right temperature. Traditional potters rely on the same fire-based kilns used in past centuries. First, the potter must build a fire in the kiln and allow it to grow. By nightfall **(2)** a controlled inferno roars in the kiln. At this point, the pottery is ready to be carefully placed inside.

1. The author wishes to begin the paragraph with a topic sentence that establishes the importance of firing pottery. Which would be the best choice?

   A) Firing pottery involves exposing the clay to extremely high temperatures to create a more durable final product.
   B) Firing is a vital part of the ceramics process because it is the one step that makes the clay durable.
   C) Traditional kilns are still popular, but electric kilns are more environmentally friendly.
   D) Without firing pottery, the clay remains weak.

2. The author would like to indicate that the fire is extremely intense. Given that all choices are true, which one best accomplishes the author's goal?

   A) NO CHANGE
   B) the fire is stronger than ever
   C) there is more heat being produced
   D) a kind of intense blaze takes place

The first question is an example of a question that asks us to add a sentence in order to suit the author's purpose; the second question is an example of a question that focuses on changing a single phrase.

ANSWERING PURPOSE QUESTIONS

First, it is important to determine exactly what the question is asking. If we use the first question as our example, we see that the question asks for a topic sentence (a sentence that encapsulates the main idea of the paragraph) that focuses on the importance of firing.

Next, we eliminate any answer choices that are clearly wrong. We know that the main idea of the paragraph is an explanation of firing. All of the answer choices except for choice C could potentially relate to an explanation of firing, so we can eliminate choice C. We must also look for an answer choice that emphasizes the important of firing. Choice A explains the effect of firing clay without explaining why that effect is important. Choice B seems to most clearly emphasize the importance of firing, but since Choice D also suggests the reason for why firing is important, we shouldn't eliminate it yet.

Our third step is to consider remaining the answer choices in the context of the paragraph, looking at both tone and conciseness. When we do this, we can eliminate choice D because it is repetitive when read along with the next sentence in the paragraph.

This leaves us with choice B as the correct answer.

TO ANSWER PURPOSE QUESTIONS:

Step One: Determine exactly what the question is looking for.

Step Two: Eliminate answer choices that are clearly wrong.

Step Three: Consider the remaining answer choices in the context of the paragraph. Eliminate answer choices that do not suit the tone of the paragraph, that introduce redundancy, or that are overly wordy.

Step Four: Of the remaining answer choices, choose the one that best accomplishes the goal set forth by the question and that suits the overall tone of the paragraph.

Big Picture Questions

Each ACT English Test is likely to include at least one big picture question. These questions always come at the end of a passage. They ask you to examine the passage as a whole in order to identify the passage's main point, intended purpose, or intended audience.

Because they come at the end of the passage, big picture questions are easy to spot. They are made all the easier to identify because the answer choices will include two "No" answers and two "Yes" answers. For example:

> If the writer had intended to write an essay explaining the development of the British novel throughout the 19th and early 20th centuries, would this passage successfully accomplish this goal?
>
> A) No, because the essay omits mention of famous poets.
> B) No, because the essay restricts its focus to the American novel from 1850 to 1945.
> C) Yes, because the essay describes the evolution of novel writing from 1799 to 1945.
> D) Yes, because the essay focuses on the novel's birth in the 19th century.

ANSWERING BIG PICTURE QUESTIONS

The first step to answering big picture questions is to eliminate obviously wrong answer choices. Even without having read the passage that accompanies our sample question, you can likely eliminate some of the answer choices. For example, choice A can be eliminated because mention of famous poets would have nothing to do with the development of the British novel. Likewise, choice D can be eliminated because a focus on the novel's birth in the 19th century (even if we were to accept the false assertion that the novel was born that late) would fail to explain the development of the British novel throughout the 19th and 20th centuries. In other words, without even seeing the passage, we have successfully eliminated half of the answer choices.

Next, examine the remaining answer choices in the context of the passage. For instance, in our example, if the passage did indeed focus on the American novel, then choice B would be correct. If, however, the passage described the evolution of novel writing from 1799 to 1945, then choice C would be correct.

TO ANSWER BIG PICTURE QUESTIONS:

Step One: Without looking at the passage, eliminate answer choices that are illogical or clearly wrong.

Step Two: Examine the remaining answer choices within the context of the passage. Eliminate answer choices that do not reflect the content of the passage.

Step Three: Of the remaining answer choices, choose the one that best reflects the passage's main idea, intended purpose, or intended audience.

PRACTICE EXERCISE

Directions: Read the following passage and answer the accompanying questions.

{1} The innermost of Jupiter's moons, Io, is a volcanic powerhouse with constant eruptions and seismic shifts that constantly reshape the moon's surface. In recent months, however, scientists have gotten a clear and close look at Io's volcanic activity, especially in one spot.

The Large Binocular Telescope Interferometer, **(2)** <u>a technologically advanced telescope</u>, has given scientists a hi-definition look at Io. The image is not crystal clear, but what makes it impressive is the distance at which these photographs have been taken: 600 million kilometers away. Each pixel in the pictures this telescope takes is the rough equivalent of 100 square kilometers.

1. The author wishes to introduce the passage with a sentence that contrasts a relatively unknown moon with a familiar moon. Which of the following best accomplishes this goal?

   A) The moons of Jupiter vary widely in terms of geography, geology, and climate.
   B) There are a wide variety of moons throughout our solar system.
   C) Io, one of Jupiter's moons, is very similar to several of Saturn's sixty-two moons, some of which have yet to be officially named.
   D) When we think of our moon, we think of a dead, cratered planetoid without an atmosphere, yet other moons in our solar system can be very different.

2. The author wishes to indicate that the telescope is extremely powerful. Assuming each of the following is true, which choice best accomplishes this goal?

   A) NO CHANGE
   B) a telescope capable of producing higher resolution images than any other type of telescope
   C) a telescope that uses electromagnetic waves to compose an image
   D) a relatively recently invented type of telescope

{3} They named this volcanic spot "Loki" after the Norse trickster god. Over 200 km – or 120 miles – in diameter, the "Loki" spot is what is known as a patera. A patera is an entire lake of lava, covered by a solidified lava crust. As the lake fills with lava, this crust periodically sinks into the lava below, and then as the lake cools, the crust becomes solid again. These cycles are what the scientists are able to spot from Earth. Before the use of the Large Binocular Telescope Interferometer, all they could see was a single spot. Now, astronomers can tell that almost all of the 200 km area is subject to a great deal of seismic activity. Not only that, they also spotted two other areas of heavy volcanic activity. {4}.

3. Assuming each of the following is true, which choice would best serve as this topic sentence for this paragraph if added here?

A) One particular spot on Io is heavily volcanic and has long been known to scientists.
B) Scientists have exclusively studied a particularly volcanic spot on Io.
C) Io is hardly the only volcanic moon that scientists have studied.
D) The entire moon of Io is not volcanic; instead, there is one very large spot that is particularly volcanic.

4. The author wishes to add a sentence that clarifies the significance of the findings of the Large Binocular Telescope. Assuming all of the following are true, which choice would best accomplish this goal?

A) It turns out that Io is less active than scientists had previously believed.
B) Io is, perhaps, more active than scientists could have guessed.
C) One can only imagine how much more seismic activity might be identified on Io with future telescopes.
D) Io is clearly more active than any other moon.

Yet some have asked, "What benefit does the study of a moon of Jupiter allow?" Scientists argue that by studying volcanism on worlds other than Earth, **(5)** astronauts can be better informed when they travel to other planets. "It's becoming clear," said one researcher, "that volcanism on the Earth is part and parcel of what makes it a habitable planet, and so understanding how these processes work off-world helps us address a number of issues in exoplanetary science." Understanding how Io's seismic properties work, the researcher added, could also aid our understanding of what makes a planet livable. The accepted idea of habitable planets posits that they must be in a "Goldilocks zone" – not too hot, not too cold. {6} {7}

5. The author would like to communicate the Earth-bound applications of studying volcanism on a place like Io. Which of the following would best accomplish this goal?

A) NO CHANGE
B) astronomers can discover new worlds with volcanic activity
C) they can better understand how it works here
D) they can figure out how volcanic activity might contribute to the development of life on other planets

6. The author would like to add a concluding sentence that effectively explains the significance of Io's volcanoes in the context of the final paragraph. Which of the following best accomplishes this goal?

A) Io's volcanoes offer another theory: livable planets must be seismically active.
B) Io's volcanoes prove that volcanoes are what make planets part of the "Goldilocks zone."
C) Io's volcanoes will likely help us to identify other volcanic planets.
D) Io's volcanoes obviously disprove this theory since if planets other than Earth have volcanoes, clearly they must also have life.

7. If the author had intended to write an essay explaining the history of scientific observation of Io, would this passage accomplish this goal?

A) No, because the essay focuses on the observation of a single spot on Io.
B) No, because the essay focuses on the impacts of a recent observation of Io.
C) Yes, because the essay discusses the evolution of observations of Io's volcanic activity.
D) Yes, because the essay links observations of volcanic activity on Io with potential future findings.

ACT English: Relevance

One key to good writing is to ensure that there isn't any extraneous or unnecessary information. The ACT English Test will examine your ability to determine what information is and isn't necessary through relevance questions. These questions will ask you whether certain phrases or sentences are extraneous.

Recognizing Relevance Questions

Some relevance questions will be fairly obvious because they will include an actual question asking whether the author ought to add a given sentence. Since such questions deviate from the usual ACT English question format, they are the easiest relevance questions to find. Here are some examples of such questions:

> The author wishes to add the following sentence at this point in the passage:
>
> *This particular writing style is now considered outdated and overly formal.*
>
> Should the author make this addition?
>
> A) No, because it does not meaningfully develop the main idea of the paragraph.
> B) No, because it is unrelated to the main idea of the paragraph.
> C) Yes, because it develops the author's argument by providing additional evidence.
> D) Yes, because it clarifies an important point made earlier in the paragraph.
>
> The author wishes to add information here that will further support the point made in the preceding paragraph. Which of the following sentences best accomplishes this goal?
>
> A) Today, this style is not as popular as it once was.
> B) However, there are many 19th century works not written in this style.
> C) For example, Smith's inaugural work was written in this style.
> D) Although not widely read, Jones's early works were written in a different style.

As you can see, although these questions are worded differently, both clearly ask you to determine whether or what information ought to be added to a given passage. Other relevance questions can be a bit more difficult to spot because they blend in with the standard ACT question format. When there is a question that uses the standard underlined portion with four answer choices, and when that question does not seem to contain any grammar or usage errors, it might be a relevance question. Look for standard format questions in which some of the answers are significantly longer than others and in which some answer choices include information that does not appear elsewhere in the passage. For example:

(1) The Navajo developed and memorized the code. Since their language did not have words for common U.S. military equipment, they turned to nature...

1. A) NO CHANGE
   B) The Navajo, who were various heights and weights,
   C) Being of different sizes, the Navajo
   D) The Navajo, who were all quite young,

There is nothing grammatically incorrect with any of the answer choices. This could suggest that the question is a wordiness question, but before making that decision, it's important to look at whether the information contained in these extra words is relevant. In this question, we can see that the information is not redundant since it doesn't appear elsewhere, but it also isn't relevant.

What Information is Relevant?

It is important to note that more information is not necessarily better. For instance, if we consider the example question about the Navajo, we can see that answer choices B, C, and D would introduce new information, but the information doesn't seem to have any relation to the passage. After all, what does the Navajo's size or age have to do with developing a code?

When determining whether information is relevant, consider two questions:

- Does the sentence or paragraph make logical sense without the added information? In other words, is the information necessary?
- Is the information relevant to the main idea of the sentence or paragraph? In other words, does the information serve a purpose?

If the answer to the first question is "no," then the information is most definitely relevant. After all, if the paragraph doesn't make sense without the information, clearly that information is necessary.

If the answer to the first question is "yes," then consider whether the information meaningfully develops the main idea of the sentence or paragraph. Information that adds nothing meaningful to the main idea or argument of the paragraph is just useless information.

This means that relevant information must be necessary and/or serve a clear purpose.

TO ANSWER RELEVANCE QUESTIONS:

Step One: Identify the question as a relevance question.

Step Two: Consider whether the additional information is necessary to the logic of the sentence or paragraph. If it is necessary, the information is relevant. Eliminate any answer choices that do not reflect this.

Step Three: If the information is not necessary to the logic of the sentence or paragraph, consider whether the additional information serves a clear purpose within the context of the paragraph. If the information develops the main idea, it is relevant. Eliminate any answer choices that do not reflect this.

Step Four: Of the remaining choices, choose the one that best reflects the purpose of the sentence or paragraph.

PRACTICE EXERCISE

Directions: Read the following passage and answer the accompanying questions.

We've all heard that people tend to favor those similar to them and discriminate against out-groups, but that's a simplistic view of prejudice, says **(1)** Amy Cuddy. Cuddy has joined psychologists Susan Fiske of Princeton University and Peter Glick of Lawrence University in studying the nature of prejudice, and they have found that in every corner of the world, people judge others on two main qualities: warmth and competence.

First impressions are a fact of life – we don't necessarily decide to judge someone, but we do it anyway. When we meet someone, we immediately and often unconsciously assess him for warmth and competence. Interestingly, though we obviously admire those who are warm and competent and feel contempt for those who are cold and incompetent, we respond somewhat unpredictably toward other mixes of the two traits. People who are judged to be competent but cold provoke envy and a desire to harm. {2} By contrast, groups that are stereotyped as warm but incompetent, such as mothers and the elderly, elicit pity and benign neglect.

New research is revealing that these split-second judgments are, unsurprisingly, often wrong. They rely on crude stereotypes and other mental shortcuts, leading to inaccurate conclusions. A few years ago, psychologist Nicolas Kervyn and his colleagues published studies that showed we often jump to conclusions about people's competence based on their warmth and vice versa. When participants were shown facts about two groups of people, one warm and one cold, they assumed that the warm group was less competent than the cold group; similarly, when participants were told that one group was competent and the other was not, they assumed that the competent group was cold and the other was warm. {3}

1. A) NO CHANGE
   B) Amy Cuddy, a professor at Harvard Business School who studies how we judge others
   C) Amy Cuddy, who is interested in studying how we judge others
   D) Amy Cuddy, who works at Harvard Business School

2. The author wishes to add an example that will help to illustrate the idea presented in the previous sentence. Assuming all answer choices are true, which of the following would best accomplish this goal?

   A) Consider, for instance, the widespread prejudice against the poor, who are often painted as being lazy or incompetent.
   B) For example, consider American ambivalence toward Canadians and widespread prejudice toward Mexicans.
   C) For instance, in modern politics, some politicians revere the wealthy for being competent while others denigrate the wealthy for being greedy.
   D) Consider, for example, the stereotypes of Asians, the Jewish, and the wealthy; each of these groups has experienced violence as a result of such judgment.

3. The author wishes to add the following sentence at this point:

   In other words, when a person is judged higher in one category, he tends to lose in the other.

   Should the author make this addition?

   A) No, because it is redundant.
   B) No, because it describes the findings of a different study.
   C) Yes, because it clarifies the findings of the study.
   D) Yes, because it explains the findings of a study discussed in the next paragraph.

This so-called compensation effect occurs when we compare people rather than evaluating individuals; interestingly, this effect runs counter to the well-known **(4)** <u>halo effect, in which someone scoring high on one quality gets higher ratings on other traits</u>. Both effects are examples of the types of mistakes we make in snap judgments. For example, we see high-status individuals as competent even if their status was an accident of birth, yet we see those in competition with us as bad people.

Whether or not we should judge others is irrelevant – we do it whether we like it or not. But with a better understanding of how these judgments work, perhaps we can avoid letting first impressions dictate our behavior.

4. A) NO CHANGE
    B) halo effect
    C) halo effect, which has been supported by other studies.
    D) halo effect, another standard of judgment.

ACT English: Conciseness

Conciseness questions require a thorough understanding of a couple of concepts: wordiness and redundancy.

Wordiness

When answering a conciseness question, you will usually choose the answer that includes the fewest words without losing any meaning. The most common mistakes that lead to wordiness include:

PASSIVE VOICE

It is usually best to use active voice in writing, in part due to the wordiness created by passive voice. For example:

Passive: The race was won by the driver in the red car.

Active: The driver in the red car won the race.

For more on passive voice, review the lesson on Verb Errors.

"THERE IS," "THERE ARE," AND "IT IS"

These often unnecessary phrases simply add word count. For example:

Wordy: There is a problem with this house.

Concise: This house has a problem.

THIS AND THAT

Sentences can often be combined or shortened to reduce wordiness by eliminating words like "this," "that," and "which." For example:

Wordy: I like to go fishing, which is because I like being on the water.

Concise: I like to go fishing because I like being on the water.

Redundancy

Redundancy occurs when there is needless repetition of words, phrases, or ideas within a given sentence or paragraph. For example:

Redundant: Many uneducated citizens who *never graduated from school* continue to vote for education improvements.

Concise: Many uneducated citizens continue to vote for education improvements.

TO ANSWER CONCISENESS QUESTIONS:

Step One: Read the sentence containing the underlined portion and the surrounding sentences. Identify any redundancies in the underlined portion.

Step Two: Examine the answer choices. Eliminate any answer choices that are overly lengthy or redundant.

Step Three: Eliminate any answer choices that lose important meaning by cutting out too many words.

Step Four: Of the remaining choices, choose the one that conveys the same information in the fewest words. Reread the sentence with your chosen answer to ensure that no new redundancies are created.

PRACTICE EXERCISE

<u>Directions</u>: Rewrite each sentence to eliminate wordiness or redundancy.

1. Trouble is caused when people disobey rules that have been established for the safety of all.

   _____

   _____

2. Angelina took me to a party that was a very fun time.

   _____

3. He has an affinity for *The New York Times*, this being the publication in which most of his early exposes had appeared.

   _____

   _____

4. She worked for thirty-three years as a teacher and librarian in the field of education in Los Angeles public schools.

   _____

   _____

5. Over several months, as time went by, his test scores improved.

   _____

   _____

6. This article offers pertinent information that provides relevant facts for conserving water.

   _____

   _____

7. I think maybe I might possibly have finished all of those worksheets.

   _____

   _____

8. The senator spoke consecutively for fifteen hours straight while filibustering the bill.

   _____

   _____

9. The accountant reviewed the annual tables of yearly sets of data regarding the company's expenditures.

   _____

   _____

10. Louis spent so many hours studying that his social life was minimal and not abundant at all.

_____

_____

11. There are several rules that govern noise pollution.

_____

_____

12. It is expected that a new schedule will be announced by the bus company.

_____

_____

13. The students were given a series of quizzes by the teacher.

_____

_____

14. This is an excellent book that is extremely fun and helpful to read.

_____

_____

15. The couch was moved to the center of the room by Cory.

_____

_____

ACT English: Style and Tone

Tone is an author's attitude toward his or her audience. Any correct answer on the ACT English Test should suit the overall tone of the passage. By examining the author's purpose and word choice, you can determine tone.

Purpose

As we mentioned in our very first ACT English lesson, it's important to quickly read through the entire passage before beginning to answer the questions. This strategy will help you to determine the author's purpose, which will provide important clues to determining the author's tone.

As you read, consider whether the author intends to inform, persuade, or narrate. Based on the author's purpose, you can narrow down the possibilities for tone. For example, if the author is writing to persuade, his tone is more likely to be enthusiastic, passionate, determined, or argumentative. By contrast, if the author is writing to inform, the tone is more likely to be objective, dispassionate, and instructive. Narrative tone will depend more on the subject matter since authors may display a wider range of emotion when telling a story.

After you finish reading each passage, jot down a very brief summary of the author's purpose. For example, the purpose of a persuasive passage might be described as "to persuade to support animal rights."

Word Choice

To further define the author's tone, examine his or her word choice. Is the word choice formal or informal?

Does the author rely on high-level vocabulary and avoid slang? If so, the author is using a more formal writing style that indicates a serious tone. This is the way that you would speak during a job interview or when giving a presentation. Any correct answer choices should match this formal and serious tone.

Does the author utilize colloquialisms and casual contractions? If so, the author is using a more informal writing style that indicates a more familiar tone. This is the way that you might speak to a friend or acquaintance. Any correct answer choices should match this informal and casual tone.

After you finish reading each passage, jot down two or three words that describe the author's word choices. Such descriptors might include words like formal, informal, passionate, dispassionate, biased, unbiased, instructive, or argumentative.

Style and Tone Questions

While the ACT English Test will likely include a small number of questions that focus exclusively on style and tone, this information is more likely to help you to eliminate answer choices for other question types.

Questions that exclusively focus on style and tone will, like most other ACT English questions, simply include an underlined portion of the sentence and several alternative options. These questions will not contain any grammar or usage errors; instead, the differences in answer choices will primarily be in the choices' style or tone.

Although style and tone will only be exclusively tested in a handful of questions, understanding style and tone will help you when answering almost all questions on the ACT English Test. Once you have eliminated obviously incorrect answer choices, you can focus on the passage's style and tone to further narrow down your choices.

TO ANSWER STYLE AND TONE QUESTIONS:

Step One: Quickly read through the passage.

Step Two: Write a very brief summary of the author's purpose. Jot down two or three words describing the author's tone based on his or her word choice.

Step Three: If the question contains grammar or usage errors, eliminate any obviously incorrect answers.

Step Four: Eliminate any answer choices that do not accomplish the author's intended purpose.

Step Five: Eliminate any answer choices that fail to match the author's word choice.

PRACTICE EXERCISE

<u>Directions</u>: Rewrite each sentence to accomplish the style/tone identified in parentheses.

1. The *Mona Lisa* looks weird when you're basically standing right on top of it. (formal)

   _____

   _____

   _____

   _____

2. It is vital to fully comprehend the text one must read while developing a thesis. (informal)

   _____

   _____

   _____

3. Long regarded as "the newspaper of record," the *New York Times* has the largest circulation of any metropolitan paper in the U.S. (persuasive)

   _____

   _____

   _____

   _____

4. It's ridiculous to spend money on pricey pet food because the terms used to tout fancy pet food are largely meaningless and unregulated. (informative)

   _____

   _____

   _____

   _____

5. In 2015, the EPA accused Volkswagen of cheating on emissions tests, and after lying for more than a year, Volkswagen finally admitted its evil deeds. (objective)

   _____

   _____

   _____

   _____

6. Augustinian friar Martin Luther rejected many of the teachings of the Catholic Church, particularly the notion that one could purchase freedom from punishment for sins. (passionate)

_____

_____

_____

_____

7. According to legend, outlaw Billy the Kid killed 22 men, but it is now generally believed that this number is only 8. (informal)

_____

_____

_____

_____

8. The sombrero isn't just a silly fashion statement – it's also great sun protection. (formal)

_____

_____

_____

_____

9. Australia is a pretty cool country because, even though it's pretty wealthy now, it was originally settled by a bunch of British criminals. (formal)

_____

_____

_____

_____

10. Although American Samoa is noted for having the highest rate of military enlistment of any U.S. state or territory, American Samoans do not have the right to vote in U.S. elections. (persuasive)

_____

_____

_____

_____

PRACTICE EXERCISE 1

Directions: Read the following passage and answer the accompanying questions.

Biomedical research is one of the most difficult processes in the research field. Tens of thousands of atoms comprise the billions of molecules contained in each of the trillions of cells in the human body. The human body is such a complex **(1)** machine working vigorously at molecular levels **(2)** to perform tasks precisely and in tandem within the body with all of the moving parts. {3} There have been advancements in investigative tools available to researchers in the last century or so. These instruments are powerful tools against the war on disease and **(4)** ignorance so none of them can duplicate the exact intricacies of a living organism.

1. A) NO CHANGE
   B) machine, and working
   C) machine; working
   D) machine, working

2. A) NO CHANGE
   B) to perform tasks precisely and within the body in tandem with all of the moving parts
   C) in tandem and to perform tasks precisely with all of the moving parts within the body
   D) to perform tasks precisely and in tandem with all of the moving parts within the body

3. The author is considering adding the following sentence at this point:

   In order to further their research, biomedical researchers need tools that have the ability to mirror this level of intricacy.

   Should this addition be made?

   A) No, because it would create an abrupt change in tone that clashes with the rest of the passage.
   B) No, because it introduces a line of discussion that is unrelated to any of the main ideas in the passage.
   C) Yes, because it effectively transitions to a discussion of overcoming the challenges of biomedical research.
   D) Yes, because it provides an important counterpoint that will be addressed later in the essay.

4. A) NO CHANGE
   B) ignorance, but none
   C) ignorance but none
   D) ignorance, for none

The ability to use animals in research allows scientists to work on living organisms. Without animal research, scientists' efforts would be hindered **(5)** in not only the development of new treatments, but in the aspects of fundamental research that reinforces all biomedical knowledge. **(6)** Many famous discoveries, such as knowledge of the functions of the nervous system, were only possible through work done on animals and living organisms. Without this type of research, we would know much less about our own bodies and how to treat incorrect functions.

There is no denying the fact that there are considerable biological differences between species, but researchers incorporate these variations into their work and **(7)** are selecting suitable model organisms to replicate the system that is being researched. **(8)** Unfortunately, scientists have constructed many routes of reducing inter-species variation. One way is by using transgenic **(9)** animals; animals that have been genetically modified to more closely reflect human physiology. Transgenic animals have additional benefits such as a **(10)** more shorter generation-span, which allows scientists to conduct experiments that would be impossible using humans (ignoring ethical concerns).

5. A) NO CHANGE
   B) in not the development of new treatments, but in
   C) in not only the development of new treatments, but also in
   D) in only the development of new treatments, also in

6. A) NO CHANGE
   B) One famous discovery, the functions of the nervous system,
   C) Many famous discoveries, such as the invention of dynamite,
   D) Many famous discoveries

7. A) NO CHANGE
   B) may be selecting
   C) were selective of
   D) select

8. A) NO CHANGE
   B) Specifically
   C) Luckily
   D) Nonetheless

9. A) NO CHANGE
   B) animals, and animals
   C) animals, animals
   D) animals; however, animals

10. A) NO CHANGE
    B) shorter
    C) shortest
    D) shortly

{11} However, (12) <u>none currently exists,</u> and the process of developing such non-animal methods still lies in the realms of science fiction. People can proclaim that exclusively non-animal methods of testing can lead to the same medical discoveries, but until (13) <u>one</u> can propose realistic substitutes to animal testing, these claims are meaningless.

11. The author would like to add a topic sentence that introduces the counterpoint argued in this paragraph. Which of the following best accomplishes this goal?

A) Many people are against the idea of animal testing and want a method that will "eliminate the risk of species differences."
B) Unless we can somehow bring science fiction tales to life, there is simply no feasible means of eliminating animal testing.
C) Those who oppose animal testing often point to ethical issues surrounding cruelty and animal rights.
D) Animal testing introduces a variety of ethical questions regarding research methods.

12. A) NO CHANGE
B) none currently exist
C) none currently existed
D) none currently will exist

13. A) NO CHANGE
B) he or she
C) they
D) I

There are many proposed alternatives such as microfluidics and microdosing, but **(14)** these alternative methods do not produce the same level of detailed results needed for researches to make the proper conclusions as animal testing, which produces more detailed results to allow for better accuracy. People continue to ignore the most crucial use of animals in science – basic research. Access to live organisms is the only reason we know about the functions of the cardiovascular system, digestive system, hormonal interactions, and many more functions of our complex bodies. {15}

14. A) NO CHANGE
B) these alternative methods do not produce the same level of detailed results needed for researchers to make the proper conclusions as animal testing does
C) these alternative methods do not allow for proper conclusions, unlike animal testing
D) these alternative methods produce less detailed results than the conclusions allowed by animal testing

15. The author wishes to add the following sentence:

If medical knowledge and discovery is a priority, then animal research is essential.

Where would this sentence best be placed?

A) At the end of the fifth paragraph
B) At the end of the fourth paragraph
C) At the beginning of the third paragraph
D) At the beginning of the first paragraph

PRACTICE EXERCISE 2

<u>Directions</u>: Read the following passage and answer the accompanying questions.

[1]

(1) <u>NASA has started a field campaign to study, in a wide effort to observe the environmental and societal impacts of climate change, the ecological impacts</u> of the **(2)** <u>quickly</u> changing climate of the North Western Hemisphere. The Arctic Boreal Vulnerability Experiment (ABoVE) will combine on-the-ground research in Alaska and northwestern Canada with a wide range of data collected by **(3)** <u>NASA airborne instruments; satellites; and other NASA programs.</u>

[2]

Scientists from NASA, as well as other public and private organizations, **(4)** <u>plans</u> to examine the tremendous 2.5 million square mile region over the next decade in search of answers regarding the effects of climate change.

[3]

ABoVE **(5)** <u>has incorporated</u> three project phases as well as two seasons of thorough airborne surveys; there are 21 projects chosen for the first **(6)** <u>phase, and which</u> will gather information on such topics as the impacts of wildfire and insect outbreaks.

1. A) NO CHANGE
   B) NASA, in a wide effort to observe the environmental and societal impacts of climate change, has started a field campaign to study the ecological impacts
   C) NASA has started a field campaign to study the ecological impacts, in a wide effort to observe the environmental and societal impacts of climate change,
   D) NASA, in a wide effort, has started a field campaign to study, to observe the environmental and societal impacts of climate change, the ecological impacts

2. A) NO CHANGE
   B) fastest
   C) fast
   D) most quickly

3. A) NO CHANGE
   B) NASA: airborne instruments; satellites; and other NASA programs
   C) NASA: airborne instruments, satellites, and other NASA programs
   D) NASA airborne instruments, satellites, and other NASA programs

4. A) NO CHANGE
   B) plan
   C) was planning
   D) were planning

5. A) NO CHANGE
   B) incorporated
   C) will have incorporated
   D) will incorporate

6. A) NO CHANGE
   B) phase, and
   C) phase; which
   D) phase, which

[4]

"Boreal forests and tundra are critical for understanding the ecological impacts of Earth's changing climate," said Jack Kaye, associate director for research in NASA's Earth Science Division in **(7)** Washington, "these ecosystems hold a third of the carbon stored on land — in trees, shrubs and the frozen ground of the permafrost. That's a lot of potential greenhouse gases in play. We need to better understand these ecosystems, and how a warming climate will affect forests, wildlife, and communities both regionally and globally." {8}

[5]

To better determine the amount of carbon stored in remote regions, **(9)** Alaska's interior forests will be surveyed by ABoVE researchers who will examine the extent and thawing rate of permafrost. {10}

7. A) NO CHANGE
   B) Washington "these
   C) Washington. "These
   D) Washington: "These

8. The preceding paragraph would best be placed:

   A) Where it is now.
   B) After Paragraph 2.
   C) After Paragraph 1.
   D) At the end of the passage.

9. A) NO CHANGE
   B) Alaska's interior forsts will be surveyed and examined by ABoVE researchers who will determine
   C) ABoVE researchers will survey Alaska's interior forests by examining
   D) ABoVE researchers will survey and examine Alaska's interior forests in order to determine

10. The author is considering adding the following sentence:

    Permafrost is soil that has been kept frozen for thousands of years, preserving the carbon-rich plant and organic matter.

    Should this sentence be added here?

    A) No, because it is redundant.
    B) No, because it clarifies a term that is widely known without adding any useful information.
    C) Yes, because it clarifies an important term and explains its significance within the context of the passage.
    D) Yes, because it introduces an important argument regarding climate change.

[6]

"[1] Warming air temperatures can thaw permafrost, which acts like unplugging a deep freezer," said Peter Griffith, ABoVE chief support scientist at NASA's Goddard Space Flight Center in Greenbelt, Maryland. "[2] This increase in greenhouse gases further warms air temperatures, perpetuating the cycle by causing more thawing and more greenhouse gas release. [3] The vegetation and carbon previously frozen in the soil start to rot and decay — like food in an unplugged freezer — releasing methane and carbon dioxide into the atmosphere." {11}

[7]

(12) This project will also investigate the effects of climate change on the wildlife of the area, as well as their habitat and migration changes. (13) A significant amount of focus of the campaign will be centered on the socio-ecological impacts of climate change. For example, the Dall sheep study will explore the (14) consequences from the changing climate and ecosystem on subsistence hunting and tourism. By working with village residents in the Yukon-Kuskokwim River Delta of western Alaska, another research group can log changes in vegetation, permafrost, fires, and bodies of water. {15}

11. In the preceding paragraph, sentence 2 would best be:

A) OMITTED.
B) Placed before the first sentence.
C) Placed after the third sentence.
D) Placed at the beginning of the next paragraph.

12. This sentence would best be:

A) OMITTED.
B) Placed at the end of the preceding paragraph.
C) Placed at the end of the passage.
D) Allowed to function as its own paragraph between paragraphs 6 and 7.

13. A) NO CHANGE
B) A significant amount of the campaign's focus
C) The campaign's sole focus
D) A significant amount of the central focus of the campaign

14. A) NO CHANGE
B) consequences on
C) consequences about
D) consequences of

15. The author wishes to add a sentence to conclude the passage as a whole. Assuming all of the following are true, which best accomplishes this goal?

A) This study will be able to definitively prove the existence of climate change.
B) Such widespread studies will provide a more comprehensive understanding of the impacts of climate change.
C) Understanding the human impacts of climate change will encourage action on environmental issues.
D) Many believe that this study is a waste of resources.

PRACTICE EXERCISE 3

<u>Directions</u>: Read the following passage and answer the accompanying questions.

The decree by the restaurant chain Chipotle that they will discontinue the use of genetically modified foods **(1)** <u>are</u> the **(2)** <u>lateliest</u> instance highlighting the effects of public concerns regarding scientifically altered foods. This decision was expected: Once the industry persuaded the Food and Drug Administration that GMOs **(3)** <u>– genetically modified organisms –</u> should not necessitate labeling, public backlash was only a matter of time. I am only amazed that it took 20 years for this to happen.

I was a part of the FDA Food Advisory Committee when the organization first permitted GMOs in the food supply in 1994. At the time, consumer opinion surveys **(4)** <u>indicate</u> that approximately 90% of respondents wanted genetically modified foods to be labeled. Consumer representatives on the committee, such as myself, contended that labeling was crucial for public support. Without labels, people might speculate that the industry was attempting to hide something and **(5)** <u>lose</u> trust in the FDA. {6}

1. A) NO CHANGE
    B) will be
    C) is
    D) were

2. A) NO CHANGE
    B) lately
    C) latest
    D) later

3. A) NO CHANGE
    B) – genetically modified organisms
    C) genetically modified organisms,
    D) (genetically modified organisms)

4. A) NO CHANGE
    B) indicated
    C) have indicated
    D) will indicate

5. A) NO CHANGE
    B) losing
    C) lost
    D) had lost

6. The author would like to add a sentence that supports the argument made in this paragraph and effectively transitions into the idea presented in the first sentence of the next paragraph. Assuming all are true, which of the following best accomplishes this goal?

    A) The FDA rarely mandates special labeling of food manufacturing processes.
    B) The FDA mandated labeling of other processes, such as "made from concentrate" and "irradiated," so there was no reason to vary from precedent in this case.
    C) The FDA has mandated labeling of other processes, such as "made from concentrate" and "irradiated," but not of GMOs.
    D) A loss of public trust in the FDA would be concerning but not devastating since the organization has little public interaction.

Yet the FDA determined that genetic modification was a practice that required no special labeling. **(7)** <u>The industry made the silly claim that genetic modification doesn't matter because DNA is DNA no matter what.</u> Labels, the FDA said, could distort the public's perception, causing them to view genetically modified foods as different from conventional foods.

(8) <u>After all</u>, GMOs are essentially different – DNA transfers are occasionally derived from totally different organisms – and the public feels they have the right to be **(9)** <u>aware for</u> these types of changes.

The GMO controversy is not simply an unease about food safety, but it is also about much more. Chipotle is reacting to public apprehension about the safety of GMO crops, but it is also acknowledging the angst about **(10)** <u>corporate control of the food supply, the absence of transparency, and the massive amount of money being spent</u> by the industry and its trade associations to crush GMO-labeling proposals.

(11) <u>There is a necessity for enhanced criteria for labeling that is demonstrated by the sudden, widespread rise of products branded "GMO-free."</u> The specifics of recommended labeling initiatives are muddled and complex, but they are not impossible.

7. A) NO CHANGE
   B) The industry, concerned with protecting its precious image, claimed that genetic modification was not "material" to food safety since DNA is DNA regardless of whether it's been messed with.
   C) The industry erroneously claimed that genetic modification didn't matter because DNA is DNA whether it's genetically modified or not.
   D) The industry argued that genetic modification was immaterial to food safety since the origins of DNA does not change the basic nature of DNA.

8. A) NO CHANGE
   B) For example
   C) Nevertheless
   D) Similarly

9. A) NO CHANGE
   B) aware about
   C) aware of
   D) aware on

10. A) NO CHANGE
    B) corporate control of the food supply, lacking transparency, and spending massive amounts of money
    C) corporate controlling of the food supply, transparency being absent, and the massive amount of money spent
    D) corporations controlling the food supply, the absence of transparency, and the massive amount of money being spent

11. A) NO CHANGE
    B) Enhanced criteria for labeling is a necessity demonstrated by the sudden and widespread rise of products branded "GMO-free," a label that has become more and more common.
    C) "GMO-free" labels provide the need for better labeling.
    D) The sudden, widespread rise of products branded "GMO-free" demonstrates a necessity for enhanced criteria for labeling.

(12) Vermont passed a law that indicates future change. Whether this exact law endures court challenges is irrelevant. The Grocery Manufacturers Association has recognized the warning signs and is now petitioning for a national GMO labeling law that will prevent states from passing their own laws. This national law would likely allow the use of the word "natural" in advertising GMOs. **(13)** This is a lapse in judging public opinion. Most Americans do not deem GMOs as "natural," just as they do not believe GMOs are organic.

[1] If genetically modified foods are labeled, will people stop purchasing them? [2] Regardless, this industry brought the present situation upon itself and should now accept the consequences. [3] Some people will, but others will not care. [4] Requiring labeling may come too late to resolve public apprehensions about GMOs, but it is an essential first phase in moving these debates to a less contentious level. {14} {15}

12. A) NO CHANGE
    B) Vermont passed a GMO-labeling law that indicates changes to come.
    C) Vermont's laws indicate future change.
    D) Vermont passed a GMO-labeling law.

13. A) NO CHANGE
    B) This is ridiculous.
    C) Public opinion does not support such a move.
    D) This is a really dumb lapse in judging public opinion.

14. To improve the organization of this paragraph, in which order should the sentences be placed?

    A) 4, 1, 2, 3
    B) 1, 3, 4, 2
    C) 1, 3, 2, 4
    D) 3, 2, 1, 4

15. If the writer had intended to write an informative piece about FDA labeling practices, would this essay accomplish this goal?

    A) No, because the essay informs readers about the dangers of GMOs.
    B) No, because the essay primarily advocates labeling GMOs.
    C) Yes, because FDA labeling practices are discussed throughout the passage.
    D) Yes, because the essay discusses several types of FDA labels.

PRACTICE EXERCISE 4

<u>Directions</u>: Read the following passage and answer the accompanying questions.

August 2, 2008 was one of the deadliest days in mountain climbing history. All around the world, headlines repeated the same story of the fatal events on **(1)** <u>the mountain, K2.</u> **(2)** <u>K2 is located in the Karakoram Range of northern Pakistan and is known as one of the most difficult climbs in the world, suitable for only the world's most skilled climbers.</u> Eleven fatalities were recorded as K2 lived up to its lethal reputation with unimaginable, and sometimes conflicting, stories of heroics and folly. Books, movies, documentaries, and interviews followed this event.

1. The author wishes to indicate the significance of attempting to climb K2. Which of the following best accomplishes this goal?

A) NO CHANGE
B) Pakistan's K2
C) popular climbing locale, K2
D) the world's second-highest mountain, K2

2. A) NO CHANGE
B) Located in the Karakoram Range of northern Pakistan, K2 is known as one of the most difficult climbs in the world.
C) The Karakoram Range of northern Pakistan contains K2, which is known as one of the most difficult climbs in the world and is suitable only for the world's most skilled climbers.
D) K2 is located in Pakistan, is known as one of the most difficult climbs in the world, and is suitable only for skilled climbers.

Initially, I was suspicious of the book *No Way Down: Life and Death on K2*, written by New York Times reporter Graham Bowley. {3} Surprisingly, Bowley's account **(4)** is assembling very diligently, respectfully, and as accurately as possible through ample study of events and interviews to piece together the brutal events of that day. Fatality by fatality.

3. The author is considering adding the following sentence:

   How could someone who does not climb and was not present during this tragic event properly record the story?

   Should this addition be made?

   A) No, because this question is rhetorical and therefore serves no purpose in the passage.
   B) No, because this sentence calls into question the author's authority on the subject matter.
   C) Yes, because this question clarifies the author's suspicions.
   D) Yes, because this question represents the primary query answered by the passage.

4. A) NO CHANGE
   B) was assembled
   C) had been assembled
   D) will have been assembled

Loosely coordinated, a field of climbers set out for the summit on August 1. **(5)** The group consisted of sponsored Koreans; an independent Basque and professional Sherpas; young Serbs; and Americans, as well as a wide range of language barriers, differing equipment, and clashing styles. **(6)** Nonetheless, they sensed safety in numbers that morning as they "felt a sort of inner transcendence…Now at last, after weeks, months, years of preparation and toil, they were closing in." Although there were a few missteps early on in the climb, leading to two fatalities, 19 of the remaining climbers made the calamitous "groupthink" decision to continue to the peak, **(7)** which, in retrospect, was really dumb.

[1] Many of the climbers made it to the top, euphorically posing for photos and calling their loved ones from K2's 28,251-foot summit. [2] Around the same time, a giant sérac gave way, wiping out the fixed ladders and ropes below, which not only **(8)** changed the terrain but also made the area – which was already volatile – very susceptible to avalanches. [3] Bad decisions mingled with small errors throughout the day essentially **(9)** set the stage for an all-out disaster, turning the already risky descent into a very lethal one. [4] Their path for descent was now gone. {10}

5. A) NO CHANGE
   B) The group consisted of: sponsored Koreans, an independent Basque, professional Sherpas, young Serbs, and Americans
   C) The group consisted of sponsored Koreans; an independent Basque; professional Sherpas; young Serbs; and Americans
   D) The group consisted of sponsored Koreans, an independent Basque, professional Sherpas, young Serbs, and Americans

6. A) NO CHANGE
   B) As a result
   C) Similarly
   D) Interestingly

7. A) NO CHANGE
   B) resulting in a couple of really dumb climbing mistakes, including a late summit assault and a dark descent
   C) a clear violation of two vital climbing rules that dictate that one ought never to ascend a summit late in the day nor descend in the dark
   D) perpetrating the two climbing sins of a late summit assault and a dark descent

8. A) NO CHANGE
   B) causes the terrain to change
   C) would have changed the terrain
   D) changes the terrain

9. A) NO CHANGE
   B) sets
   C) were setting
   D) was setting

10. To improve the logical organization of the preceding paragraph, in which order should the sentences be arranged?

    A) NO CHANGE
    B) 1, 2, 4, 3
    C) 3, 1, 4, 2
    D) 1, 4, 2, 3

The details of the (11) horrifically descent – whether by avalanche, slip, or heroic rescue attempt – make the climbers' deaths all the more crushing. Three climbers were dangled upside down for 24 freezing hours, tangled in (12) his or her ropes, only to be swept away by an avalanche once freed from the agonizing situation. Several others were also avalanched on while climbing back up to save suspended climbers. The details of the manner in which many were taken from the mountain cannot be verified, (13) nor can the heroic survival stories that were told by those who survived.

(14) Rather than concluding the story on the glacial slopes that enshrine the bodies of countless climbers Bowley ends this story with the confused and devastated families and with the survivors, spread out around the world in different stages of mourning and grief, leaving the readers and interviewees in contemplation of the disaster on K2. {15}

11. A) NO CHANGE
    B) horrifically descending
    C) horrific descent
    D) horrific descending

12. A) NO CHANGE
    B) one's
    C) their
    D) they're

13. A) NO CHANGE
    B) nor the stories of survivors
    C) nor can the heroic stories that were told by those who survived the climb
    D) nor can the heroic stories told by the survivors

14. A) NO CHANGE
    B) Rather than concluding the story on the glacial slopes that enshrine the bodies of countless climbers, Bowley
    C) Despite concluding the story on the glacial slopes that enshrine the bodies of countless climbers, Bowley
    D) Despite concluding the story on the glacial slopes that enshrine the bodies of countless climbers Bowley

15. If the writer had intended to write a critical review of Bowley's book, would this essay accomplish that goal?

    A) No, because the essay provides a firsthand account of the events described in Bowley's book.
    B) No, because the essay primarily summarizes Bowley's account rather than critiquing it.
    C) Yes, because the author questions the accuracy of Bowley's account.
    D) Yes, because the essay shares a biased and heavily positive view of Bowley's book.

PRACTICE EXERCISE 5

Directions: Read the following passage and answer the accompanying questions.

[1]

Where is philosophy? This is no misprint. *What* is philosophy is a frequent query, but rarely do we ponder where philosophy occurs. {1}

[2]

Philosophy is normally portrayed as an isolated activity accomplished in secluded natural surroundings: **(2)** a clearing in the heart of a forest, a cave on the side of a mountain, or a rocking chair on a porch overlooking a field. One notable thinker **(3)** borne a significant amount of responsibility for encouraging this countrified ethos.

1. The author is considering adding the following two sentences at the end of the paragraph:

   Visualize a philosopher at work. Where does this scene take place?

   Should the author make this addition?

   A) No, because this pair of sentences poses a question that is not relevant to the overall argument of the passage.
   B) No, because this pair of sentences is redundant.
   C) Yes, because this pair of sentences clarifies a confusing concept introduced in the introduction.
   D) Yes, because this pair of sentences provides powerful imagery that is vital to the overall argument of the passage.

2. The author wishes to provide imagery to clarify the preceding clause. Which of the following would best accomplish this goal?

   A) NO CHANGE
   B) a quiet library filled with dusty tomes, a bench in a corner of Central Park, or a ship rocking on the sea
   C) a small row boat bobbing on a pond, an empty classroom devoid of the buzz of conversation, or a quiet office furnished in leather and polished wood
   D) a crowded beach where the waves drown out the sound of swimmers, a park bench near a play ground, or dock on a busy river

3. A) NO CHANGE
   B) bores
   C) bares
   D) bears

[3]

In the 18th century, as Paris was starting to take shape as the capital of the world, it also cultivated the person who would become **(4)** it most fervent critic. Jean-Jacques Rousseau went there as a young man **(5)** without: money, status, education, or reputation. {6} During the few years that he resided in Paris, his philosophical prominence **(7)** grows.

[4]

With Rousseau's renown also arose his deep loathing of the city. In a letter to fellow philosopher Denis Diderot, Rousseau concludes: "It is in the country that men learn how to love and serve humanity; all they learn in cities is to despise it." Given Diderot's urbanite tendencies, **(8)** it's not exactly shocking that Diderot broke up with Rousseau after getting the letter.

4. A) NO CHANGE
   B) it's
   C) its
   D) its'

5. A) NO CHANGE
   B) without money, status, education, or reputation
   C) without money; status; education; or reputation
   D) without: money; status; education; or reputation

6. The author wishes to add a sentence that illustrates the process of the growth of Rousseau's renown. Assuming all are true, which of the following best accomplishes this goal?

   A) Despite this, he soon began to garner solicitations to Paris's trendiest salons, where he befriended some of the most prominent intellectuals of his time.
   B) As a result, he struggled to find a foothold in the intellectual circles of Parisian society.
   C) Since Rousseau disliked Paris, he chose not to stay long enough to establish himself as a widely known philosopher.
   D) In a relatively short period of time, Rousseau became a fairly well-known philosopher in certain circles.

7. A) NO CHANGE
   B) grew
   C) had grown
   D) has grown

8. A) NO CHANGE
   B) it's not surprising that Diderot started hating Rousseau so much that they stopped being friends
   C) it is perhaps unsurprising that the letter resulted in the termination of their friendship
   D) Roussea was silly for thinking his letter wouldn't cause problems

[5]

Everybody knew to **(9)** <u>who</u> Diderot was alluding when he subsequently wrote that "only the wicked lives alone." Rousseau ultimately got the final word following the death of both men. Diderot and his fellow French philosophers, who **(10)** <u>is</u> apt to revere their flourishing city, eventually lost the intellectual skirmish to the German Romantics.

[6]

Led by the philosopher and poet Johann Gottfried Herder, the Romantics maintained Rousseau's **(11)** <u>legacy, regarding</u> the countryside as the promised land that would rescue humanity from the nightmare of urban existence. The lone intellectual was seen as the savior of the masses.

[7]

The term "urban philosophy" is somewhat deceptive, or redundant. Isn't philosophy always urban? Urban philosophy implies that there are types of philosophy that are not urban, or that it is itself a branch within the larger field. {12}

[8]

(13) <u>Consequently,</u> a cursory understanding of the history of Western philosophy reveals that the city is necessary for doing theoretical work, which could then be continued in less chaotic locations. To appreciate the significance of the city to philosophy, **(14)** <u>one of the most basic pragmatist principles must first be accepted by us</u>: ideas do not operate in a void. They depend on human beings in specific circumstances. Ideas occur not due to their indisputable logic but because they are entrenched in the social environment.

[9]

When the necessity to refer to two things as if they were one arises, we commonly develop amalgams — words like frenemies or Brangelina. Maybe the term metrosophy can better articulate the connection between the metropolitan and philosophical experiences. This terminology could serve to aid us in viewing cities **(15)** <u>not only as hubs of economic activities but as</u> springs of abstract meditations.

9. A) NO CHANGE
    B) whose
    C) whom
    D) who's

10. A) NO CHANGE
    B) are
    C) was
    D) were

11. A) NO CHANGE
    B) legacy, and regarding
    C) legacy, since they regarded
    D) legacy; regarding

12. To improve the logical flow of the passage, paragraph 7 would best be placed:

    A) At the beginning of the passage
    B) Between paragraphs 5 and 6
    C) Between paragraphs 8 and 9
    D) At the end of the passage

13. A) NO CHANGE
    B) Similarly
    C) However
    D) Indeed

14. A) NO CHANGE
    B) we must first accept one of the most basic pragmatist principles
    C) first acceptance by us of one of the most basic pragmatist principles is necessary
    D) we must first and foremost accept pragmatist principles of the most basic nature

15. A) NO CHANGE
    B) not only as hubs of economic activities but also as
    C) not as hubs of economic activities but as
    D) not as hubs of economic activities but also as

PRACTICE EXERCISE 6

Directions: Read the following passage and answer the accompanying questions.

The winter of 1944 was the coldest in countless decades in the Red River Delta of Vietnam. Due to record low temperatures and a harsh north **(1)** wind, the winter harvest was the worst catastrophe in a century. Rice production in certain villages was less than 30 percent of a typical crop in various fields. Even children my age recognized that a serious food shortage was **(2)** emanate.

After **(3)** Tet, famished peasants in the overpopulated neighborhoods of my province began relocating to other areas, where they anticipated they would find food. Before departing, they **(4)** will have sold everything they owned. A thatch roof could be sold as tinder for a few cents. In countless hamlets south of my village, portions of impoverished neighborhoods began to **(5)** disappear, only earthen walls remained. Some villages in which live bamboo fences had once flourished were devastated. **(6)** Emaciated bodies in rags roamed the country roads and city streets.

1. A) NO CHANGE
    B) wind; the
    C) wind the
    D) wind, so the

2. A) NO CHANGE
    B) imminent
    C) eminent
    D) emanating

3. A) NO CHANGE
    B) the Tet Offensive of 1968
    C) the Tet Offensive
    D) the Tet Offensive, one of the largest military campaigns of the Vietnam War,

4. A) NO CHANGE
    B) have sold
    C) sold
    D) are selling

5. A) NO CHANGE
    B) disappear and only
    C) disappear; only
    D) disappear, since only

6. The author would like to provide imagery that emphasizes the terrible plight of the villagers. Which of the following best accomplishes that goal?

    A) NO CHANGE
    B) Hungry people with few possessions strode
    C) Displaced villagers took to
    D) The plight of the villages was seen on

Groups of starving men and women with babies in their arms and other children at their sides overran every nearby field and garden in search of anything that might be **(7)** edible green bananas, core and bulbs of banana trees, and bamboo shoots. In desperation, they began eating oilcakes, typically used for fertilizer, resulting in many deaths. Our fellow villagers had to guard their land by force. **(8)** Trespassers were warded off of fields that were patrolled by strong men each night. Occasionally, there were quarrels that resulted in injuries. Ravenous mobs attacked rich landlords' homes and plundered their granaries. In most cases, law and order was not enforced.

One day, my three-year-old sister was eating a rice cake at the front door, approximately ten yards from the gate that opened to the street. She held the majority of the cake in her right hand. **(9)** A rude young man paused at our gate. With one leap, he reached the doorstep. His left hand forced my sister's mouth open, and his right hand scooped the bite of cake from her mouth and crammed it into his own. Then he jerked the rest of the cake from her hand and bolted in an instant. My mother and I stood there flabbergasted. My mother pacified my sister without a word, but I could see the tears running down **(10)** her cheeks as she mourned the situation that forced men to such actions.

[1] All of the middle-class families in my neighborhood did the same. [2] The other seven members of my family only had two bowls of rice in two meals a day—opposed to the typical six—to save rice for starving people, a dozen of whom could be seen on our street at any given time. [3] My little sister and I did not experience this famine as others did because we were the only two in our family who were fully fed. {11}

By the summer, a good harvest brought hope. The new rice was reaped **(12)** slightly early than usual and saved many people on the brink of collapse. Even so, a dozen people in the area perished, not from starvation but from binging after gathering the first few bushels of rice.

7. A) NO CHANGE
   B) edible, green bananas; core and bulbs of banana trees; and bamboo shoots
   C) edible: green bananas; core and bulbs of banana trees; and bamboo shoots
   D) edible: green bananas, core and bulbs of banana trees, and bamboo shoots

8. A) NO CHANGE
   B) Each night, strong men patrolled the fields to ward off trespassers.
   C) The fields were patrolled by strong men each night so that they could ward off trespassers.
   D) Trespassers were warded off by strong men.

9. A) NO CHANGE
   B) A skinny, lanky man eyed my sister as he
   C) A gaunt young man, little more than a ghost in tattered clothes,
   D) Some guy who looked pretty hungry

10. A) NO CHANGE
    B) my mother's
    C) my sister's
    D) their

11. In order to improve the logical organization of the preceding paragraph, the sentences should be arranged in which of the following orders?

    A) NO CHANGE
    B) 2, 1, 3
    C) 3, 1, 2
    D) 3, 2, 1

12. A) NO CHANGE
    B) slight early
    C) slight earlier
    D) slightly earlier

Even as I got older, I never forgot **(13)** the faces of the emaciated victims of that famine. I would eventually discover that between 2 to 3 million peasants perished during this time in 1945. {14} {15}

13. A) NO CHANGE
    B) the faces of the victims of that emaciated famine
    C) the emaciated victims and their faces of that famine
    D) that famine of emaciated victims and their faces

14. The author would like to add the following concluding sentence:

    While I am thankful that my family was spared, I still mourn those who did not make it.

    Would this sentence reflect the author's perspective as presented in this passage?

    A) No, because it does not suit the persuasive nature of the essay.
    B) No, because it does not adequately reflect the suffering felt by the author's family.
    C) Yes, because it summarizes the author's attitude of pitying those less fortunate than himself.
    D) Yes, because it effectively summarizes the events discussed in the essay.

15. If the writer had intended to write a caustic essay critical of the government's handling of a famine, would this essay suit that purpose?

    A) No, because it does not express judgment of any particular party.
    B) No, because it is largely supportive of the government's response.
    C) Yes, because it focuses on the suffering caused by government inaction.
    D) Yes, because it is written by a former government official who is unhappy with his role in the tragedy.

PRACTICE EXERCISE 7

Directions: Read the following passage and answer the accompanying questions.

For most rockers and aging hippies, Woodstock's 40th anniversary was time to reminisce, evoking fond memories of peace, love, and rock 'n' roll. For the rock 'n' roll industry itself, the anniversary **(1)** will provoke mixed feelings. Why?

In 1969, the three-day concert, which drew over 350,000 people, was originally a financial catastrophe for its producers. You might be wondering how this is the **(2)** case. Consider the arithmetic of Woodstock. For a ticket to all three days of the festival, the promoters, Woodstock Ventures, charged just $18 in advance. **(3)** Adjusted for inflation, those who purchase advance tickets paid about $106 in today's dollars.

(4) As a result of this, only a tenth of those who attended Woodstock actually paid to get in according to the event's promoters. To make matters **(5)** bad, as many as 18,000 of those who had advance tickets later requested their money **(6)** back, since they had been unable to get to the concert grounds on Max Yasgur's farm following road closures. With festival costs of $3.4 million – including Mr. Jimmy Hendrix's moderate $18,000 fee – Woodstock Ventures ultimately ended up $1.6 million in debt after all was said and done.

1. A) NO CHANGE
   B) provoked
   C) had provoked
   D) is provoking

2. A) NO CHANGE
   B) case?
   C) case!
   D) case:

3. The author is considering deleting this sentence. Should this change be made?

   A) No, because this sentence eases the transition from this paragraph into the next paragraph.
   B) No, because without this information a comparison between Woodstock and modern music festivals could not be made.
   C) Yes, because this sentence adds no meaningful information to develop the main ideas of the paragraph.
   D) Yes, because the information is irrelevant to a discussion of Woodstock's financials.

4. A) NO CHANGE
   B) Conversely
   C) Specifically
   D) In addition

5. A) NO CHANGE
   B) badly
   C) worst
   D) worse

6. A) NO CHANGE
   B) back; they
   C) back since they
   D) back, but they

Now compare that to the arithmetic of the major yearly music festivals of today, **(7)** which are widely attended by young audiences. For one person to attend the entirety of one of these events, general admission passes start at $250, and VIP passes start at around $700. **(8)** There are approximately 100,000 people attending each event, and modern security allows very few, if any, non-paying attendees. Moreover, all of these festivals attract rich sponsors looking to reach a young and hip clientele.

[1] Nevertheless, Woodstock was not entirely a loss for Woodstock Ventures. [2] Here's where the entertainment industry pounced on an opportunity. [3] Warner Brothers obtained exclusive distribution rights to the Woodstock documentary. [4] In exchange for the rights, Woodstock Ventures took a $1 million one-time fee, plus a small percentage of the back end. [5] Inside a decade, the film netted more than $50 million at the box office, of which Woodstock Ventures received $16.4 million. {9}

Then there was Woodstock, the album. A year after the festival, Atlantic Records released a $14.98 three-record collection that sold over two million copies that year and **(10)** topped Billboard's pop album chart. The next year saw the release of a follow-up compilation that immediately went platinum.

Today, the economics of rock music are reversed. In an age of smart phones and digital recording devices, concertgoers no longer demand professionally produced recordings of their musical experiences. **(11)** Thanks to YouTube, freeloaders don't have to go to concerts to see their favorite bands.

All of this has contrived to force more of the financial pie to the concert itself. That helps explain why major music groups, such as Warner Music, have been procuring stakes in companies that offer a wider range of services to artists than those customarily provided by record labels.

7. The author would like to provide additional context to help modern readers develop a more accurate comparison between Woodstock and today's music festivals. Which of the following would best accomplish that goal?

   A) NO CHANGE
   B) which are not like regular concerts given by single acts.
   C) including such well-known and widely attended festivals as Bonnaroo, Lollapalooza, or Coachella.
   D) including small, local festivals like England's Deer Fest.

8. A) NO CHANGE
   B) Approximately 100,000 people attend each event
   C) Each event is attended by approximately 100,000 people
   D) Attended by approximately 100,000 people

9. In order to improve the logical organization of the preceding paragraph, in which order should the sentences be arranged?

   A) NO CHANGE
   B) 2, 3, 5, 4, 1
   C) 2, 3, 1, 5, 4
   D) 1, 5, 2, 3, 4

10. A) NO CHANGE
    B) will have topped
    C) topping
    D) having topped

11. A) NO CHANGE
    B) Anyone who wishes to experience a concert can watch free versions of many events on YouTube.
    C) Fans who can't afford concerts don't have to anymore since YouTube gives free access.
    D) Social media allows concert-goers to upload digital files containing recordings of musical acts, in turn providing free access to musical events for those who did not or could not attend.

It is also the motive behind the Ticketmaster and Live Nation attempted merger, which would create a vertically integrated concert promoter, ticketing service, and artist management group. Of course, as more companies attempt to create monopolies in the music (12) business: vehement opposition from legislators, music industry rivals, and even artists like Bruce Springsteen (13) work fervently in an effort to protect the rights of the artists and consumers. The fact remains that no matter the circumstances, the music industry will find a means of making money. {14} {15}

12. A) NO CHANGE
    B) business: vehement opposition from legislators; music industry rivals; and
    C) business, vehement opposition from legislators; music industry rivals; and
    D) business, vehement opposition from legislators, music industry rivals, and

13. A) NO CHANGE
    B) works
    C) was working
    D) were working

14. The author wishes to add a concluding sentence that ties the end of the essay back to the beginning of the essay while still articulating the author's opinion of the music industry. Which of the following best accomplishes that goal?

    A) After all, even Woodstock was nothing more than a means of turning a huge profit.
    B) The rock 'n' roll industry should have mixed feelings about Woodstock after all.
    C) Thus, the peace, love, and rock 'n' roll that Woodstock represents lives on in the modern music industry.
    D) Thus, the peace, love, and rock 'n' roll that Woodstock represents is likely more illusion than reality.

15. If the writer had intended to write an informative piece about the history of rock 'n' roll, would this essay accomplish this goal?

    A) No, because the essay presents a biased argument about the nature of the rock 'n' roll industry.
    B) No, because the essay primarily focuses solely on the history of Woodstock.
    C) Yes, because the essay examines the history of musical events.
    D) Yes, because the essay begins with the story of Woodstock and continues through modern festivals.

PRACTICE EXERCISE 8

Directions: Read the following passage and answer the accompanying questions.

[1]

Occasionally when I'm having difficulty as I am working on a picture, I spread out copies of the 306 *Post* covers I have painted, pace around them, and attempt to determine if my work **(1)** will have improved over the years. If it has not, I will conclude that I am washed up.

[2]

However, I am never able to resolve this dilemma because my memories keep interfering. Gazing at all the covers, I remember their history: **(2)** the models I used, struggling to get the original idea, and the public response. Nearly everything I have ever seen or done has made it into my pictures in some form. My autobiography is actually the story of my pictures and their creation.

[3]

[1] **(3)** He was a prosperous old gentleman who in his adolescence had been something of a scientist and inventor. [2] Take my uncle Gil Waughlum. [3] In my family, the story of how Uncle Gil had flown the great Gil Waughlum kite from a building on Washington Square in New York as one of his experiments was recounted with pride. [4] I am not sure of the point of the experiment – something about Benjamin Franklin and electricity, I think – but I do know that Gil Waughlum and the great Gil Waughlum kite were well known by my elders. **{4}**

1. A) NO CHANGE
    B) is improving
    C) will improve
    D) has improved

2. A) NO CHANGE
    B) using models, struggling to get the original idea, and how the public responded
    C) the models I used, struggling to get the original idea, and how the public responded
    D) the models I used, the struggle to get the original idea, and the public response

3. A) NO CHANGE
    B) In his adolescence he was a prosperous old gentleman who had been something of a scientist and inventor.
    C) He was a prosperous old gentleman in his adolescence who had been something of a scientist and inventor.
    D) He was a prosperous old gentleman who had been something of a scientist in his adolescence and inventor.

4. In order to improve the logical organization of the preceding paragraph, in which order should the sentences be placed?

    A) NO CHANGE
    B) 2, 1, 3, 4
    C) 2, 3, 4, 1
    D) 2, 4, 3, 1

[4]

On Christmas Day, as snow was falling outside, Uncle Gil would show up with firecrackers to celebrate the Fourth of July. On Easter, he would give us Christmas presents; on Thanksgiving, he brought chocolate rabbits. {5} We never knew what the next holiday would bring. I could not help pondering how he acquired firecrackers in December or Christmas cards in April. I can only surmise that the vendors in Yonkers, his home town, **(6)** <u>have understood</u> his issue. {7}

[5]

By the time I can recall knowing him, he had given up science. A **(8)** <u>resolutely elderly</u> gentleman with pink cheeks and a bald head, he was constantly chuckling and prodding my brother Jarvis and **(9)** <u>I</u> to ensure that we were cheerful. Of all the things I remember about Uncle Gil, one distinct eccentricity always comes to mind **(10)** <u>first: he</u> had a propensity to get holidays mixed up.

5. The author is considering adding the following sentence at this point:

The subsequent year he brought firecrackers for my birthday and chocolate rabbits for Christmas.

Would this addition be appropriate?

A) No, because contradicts the information presented in the previous sentence.
B) No, because it is unrelated to the main idea of the paragraph.
C) Yes, because it presents new information that meaningfully develops the main idea of the paragraph.
D) Yes, because it further illustrates the idiosyncrasy discussed in the paragraph.

6. A) NO CHANGE
   B) understood
   C) will have understood
   D) are understanding

7. The preceding paragraph would best be placed:

   A) Where it is now.
   B) After paragraph 2.
   C) After paragraph 5.
   D) After paragraph 6.

8. A) NO CHANGE
   B) resolute elder
   C) resolute elderly
   D) resolutely elder

9. A) NO CHANGE
   B) me
   C) us
   D) him

10. A) NO CHANGE
    B) first – he
    C) first, he
    D) first and he

[6]

When he did bring us gifts, he would sneak into the house and hide them – under pillows, behind the couch in the parlor, in dresser drawers – so that receiving gifts from him was more akin to an Easter egg hunt. As I neared a hidden present, he would **(11)** shout "Warm, Norman. Warm!" When I found one, he let out a loud "Hurrah!" {12}

[7]

Obviously, I am not asserting that I put on canvas 66 **(13)** years' worth of people, places, and events. **(14)** Above all, I stockpiled things in my brain, and every time I am in search of an additional element for a picture – a feeling, a character, a wry smile – there it is, ready to be painted. {15}

11. A) NO CHANGE
    B) shout: Warm, Norman
    C) shout, "Warm, Norman
    D) shout, "Warm Norman

12. The author wishes to add an example that links the stories about Uncle Gil and the main idea of the passage as presented in Paragraph 2. Which of the following best accomplishes this goal?

    A) My warm relationship with Uncle Gil helped to inspire my decision to pursue a painting career.
    B) Uncle Gil was a vivid character who inspired a great many of the stories behind my paintings.
    C) In 1936, when I painted a cover of a boy probing the pockets of his grandfather's overcoat for a gift, I was really painting my Uncle Gil.
    D) Whenever I painted a cover that included a grandfatherly figure, it was likely inspired by Uncle Gil.

13. A) NO CHANGE
    B) year's
    C) years
    D) year is

14. A) NO CHANGE
    B) Rather
    C) However
    D) Either way

15. If the writer had intended to write an autobiographical piece about his career, would this essay accomplish this goal?

    A) No, because it focuses solely on the author's family life rather than on his painting.
    B) No, because it is written in the third person about another painter's career.
    C) Yes, because it is a chronological account of the author's magazine career.
    D) Yes, because it is a first-person reflection of the author's lengthy painting career.

PRACTICE EXERCISE 9

Directions: Read the following passage and answer the accompanying questions.

The Republican and Democratic primary elections **(1)** creates some odd bed fellows. 2015 has certainly not been an exception. Why else has Donald Trump, billionaire political chameleon, pledged his loyalty to the eventual Republican nominee? Why else has the self-identified "democratic socialist" Bernie Sanders decided to run for the Democratic nomination despite the party's continued admiration of an economic system that Sanders disagrees with?

The simple answer is America's two-party duopoly, the strange yet enduring system that **(2)** has been muting political competition from outside influences for over a century. **(3)** It is not surprising that nonconformist politicians like Trump and Sanders would choose to identify and run as Republicans or Democrats, even though their beliefs and standards are outside of the parameters specific to each party. Laws passed by Democrats and Republicans, upheld by the courts, have caused third-party candidates to **(4)** face biased ballot access, jump through hurdles to finance campaigns, manipulation and rigging, omission from televised national debates, and media censorship.

1. A) NO CHANGE
   B) is creating
   C) create
   D) are creating

2. A) NO CHANGE
   B) will have muted
   C) has muted
   D) muted

3. The author is considering deleting the underlined sentence. Should this change be made?

   A) No, because this sentence makes the passage's main ideas relevant to modern history.
   B) No, because this sentence links the introductory paragraph to the rest of the passage.
   C) Yes, because this sentence fails to develop the main idea of the paragraph.
   D) Yes, because this sentence renders the paragraph confusing by introducing unrelated information.

4. A) NO CHANGE
   B) face biased ballot access, hurdles to finance campaigns, manipulation and rigging
   C) biased ballot access, hurdles to finance campaigns, manipulation and rigging
   D) face biased ballot access, jump through hurdles to finance campaigns, deal with manipulation and rigging

As frustrating as **(5)** it may be for the candidates, the American voters are even more exasperated by the absence of a range of political choices. Our political system **(6)** will deteriorate into a delicate gridlock that seems to benefit only the major party incumbents. Those who receive these **(7)** benefits wallow in the finger-pointing and blaming of the opposite party for any instance that hinders the ability of the country to move forward, all while colluding to keep out any newcomers.

5. A) NO CHANGE
   B) such exclusionary policies
   C) exasperation
   D) media censorship

6. A) NO CHANGE
   B) had been deteriorating
   C) was deteriorating
   D) is deteriorating

7. A) NO CHANGE
   B) benefits of the opposite party wallow in the finger-pointing and blaming for any instance that hinders the ability of the country
   C) benefits wallow in the finger-pointing of the opposite party and blaming for any instance that hinders the ability of the country
   D) benefits wallow in the finger-pointing and blaming for any instance that hinders the ability of the opposite party of the country

Nothing in the Constitution **(8)** <u>was dictating</u> that the country must be run on a two-party system; in fact, there is nothing in the Constitution about parties at all. Yes, America had a primarily two party system at the federal and state levels for the first hundred years of **(9)** <u>its</u> existence, but at that time minor candidates were able to challenge the two prevailing parties more freely. For much of the nation's early decades, **(10)** <u>leaders in their communal favor of the dominant parties made moves to gain control of access to the ballot.</u> **(11)** <u>After the dominant parties established the two-party system,</u> Abraham Lincoln was chosen as the face of an upstart political party, the Republican Party.

8. A) NO CHANGE
    B) were dictating
    C) dictate
    D) dictates

9. A) NO CHANGE
    B) their
    C) your
    D) us

10. A) NO CHANGE
    B) leaders of the dominant parties made moves to gain control of access to the ballot in their communal favor
    C) leaders of the dominant parties in their communal favor made moves to gain control of access to the ballot
    D) leaders of the dominant parties made moves to gain control of access in their communal favor to the ballot

11. A) NO CHANGE
    B) Before they were able to establish a truly closed off two-party system
    C) As a result of party leaders establishing a closed off two-party system
    D) Instead of party leaders establishing a closed off two-party system

[1] Throughout American history, third-parties have advocated new **(12)** <u>ideas that challenged the status quo.</u> [2] In recent times, the Seattle city councilor, Kshama Sawant of the Socialist Alternative party, was elected to office by riding on the wave of advocacy for a $15 minimum wage. [3] Lincoln's victory is a prime example of why American politics needs major shakeups and new faces to renew competition. [4] The movement is now mainstream and many cities are following their lead. {**13**}

12. A) NO CHANGE
    B) ideas that challenged the status quo, with the exception of Teddy Roosevelt's failed third-party run for president, which was prompted largely by personal animosity
    C) ideas that challenged the status quo, ideas and movements that include women's suffrage, unemployment compensation, and the direct election of senators
    D) ideas that challenged the status quo and introduced new political goals and ideals.

13. In order to improve the logical flow of the paragraph, in which order should the sentences be placed?

    A) NO CHANGE
    B) 1, 2, 4, 3
    C) 4, 2, 1, 3
    D) 3, 1, 2, 4

Third-party movements drive change in America, keeping us from stagnating during crucial times. {14} {15}

14. The author wishes to add a concluding sentence that links the introduction to the conclusion while maintaining the author's view of third-parties. Which of the following best accomplishes this goal?

    A) Until a successful third-party can be developed, American voters will have to be satisfied with so-called outsiders like Trump and Sanders running within the two-party system.
    B) A third-party movement may develop in the 2016 election if Trump or Sanders chooses to run as a third-party candidate, but third-party candidates rarely succeed.
    C) Sadly, neither Trump nor Sanders currently shows signs of separating from the strict-party system by establishing a third party.
    D) Rather than strong-arming outliers like Trump and Sanders into the strict two-party forum, American politics should embrace the birth of new political parties.

15. If the writer had intended to write an informative article about the development of the two-party system, would this essay accomplish that goal?

    A) No, because it takes a persuasive tone advocating a multi-party system.
    B) No, because it primarily focuses on the history of third-party runs.
    C) Yes, because it focuses on how the two-party system evolved in the first 100 years of the nation's history.
    D) Yes, because it discusses Lincoln's role in establishing the dominance of the two primary parties.

PRACTICE EXERCISE 10

<u>Directions</u>: Read the following passage and answer the accompanying questions.

[1]

(1) <u>Abraham Lincoln wasn't a huge fan of Thomas Jefferson.</u> Even though a president criticizing other presidents is nothing new, Lincoln's disapproval of Jefferson is surprising. These two heroic, resilient, and composed legends are affixed on Mount Rushmore for a reason, and any suggestion of bitterness seems in some way a criticism of America **(2)** <u>ourselves.</u>

[2]

(3) <u>Above all,</u> sources corroborate Lincoln's sentiments towards Jefferson. "Mr. Lincoln reviled Thomas Jefferson as a man and as a politician," wrote **(4)** <u>William Henry Herndon.</u> In truth, Thomas Jefferson had not always been an endearing figure, even in his own time. His contemporaries viewed Jefferson as "one of the most artful, intriguing, industrious, and double-faced politicians in all of America."

1. The author wishes to include an introductory sentence that grabs the reader's attention while maintaining the style and tone of the passage. Which of the following best accomplishes this goal?

   A) NO CHANGE
   B) Decades separate the presidencies of Abraham Lincoln and Thomas Jefferson.
   C) Abraham Lincoln disagreed with many of Thomas Jefferson's viewpoints.
   D) Abraham Lincoln loathed Thomas Jefferson.

2. A) NO CHANGE
   B) themselves
   C) itself
   D) myself

3. A) NO CHANGE
   B) Conversely
   C) In any case
   D) Nevertheless

4. A) NO CHANGE
   B) Herndon
   C) William Henry Herndon, a man who knew Lincoln
   D) William Henry Herndon, Lincoln's law partner of 14 years

[3]

{5} Jefferson would've hated Lincoln, too. These two men approached the world with wildly dissimilar points of view, resulting in opposing political goals. Having grown up on a farm, Lincoln saw nothing but blatant misconduct and tiresome labor under the rule of his uncouth and uneducated father. Once he turned 21, he escaped from the farm and become a storeowner. After the store failed, he went into law. When he eventually became an Illinois state legislator, Lincoln endorsed a state banking system and public funding for canals and bridges. As a lawyer, Lincoln was not resistant to representing a great soulless corporation – especially railroads. As president, he instituted a national banking system, protective tariffs for American manufacturing, and government guarantees for building a transcontinental railroad. {6}

[4]

Lincoln **(7)** disliked the personal contradiction of Jefferson as a man. Lincoln was acutely aware of Jefferson's abhorrent relationship with his **(8)** slave, Sally Hemings, which occurred while Jefferson was "puling about liberty, equality, and the degrading curse of slavery." **(9)** However, this was not the only way in which Lincoln was disenchanted with Jefferson.

5. The author would like to include a topic sentence that effectively illustrates the main idea of the paragraph. Which of the following best accomplishes this goal?

A) NO CHANGE
B) Jefferson would not have liked Lincoln any more than Lincoln liked Jefferson.
C) Jefferson grew up wealthy and enjoyed a world-class education.
D) Lincoln and Jefferson disagreed on many things.

6. The preceding paragraph would best be placed:

A) Where it is now.
B) After paragraph 4.
C) After paragraph 5.
D) After paragraph 6.

7. The author wishes to express the vehemence of Lincoln's dislike toward Jefferson. Which of the following best accomplishes this goal?

A) NO CHANGE
B) despised
C) disdained
D) spurned

8. A) NO CHANGE
B) slave – Sally Hemings – which
C) slave, Sally Hemings which
D) slave Sally Hemings which

9. Which of the following provides the strongest transition between this paragraph and paragraph 5?

A) NO CHANGE
B) Accordingly, Lincoln disagreed with Jefferson's view of wealth.
C) Despite this, Jefferson remains enshrined as a patriotic hero in the collective national memory.
D) Incidentally, Lincoln is known for emancipation of the slaves.

[5]

Jefferson thought that the only genuine wealth was **(10)** <u>land, and, that</u> the only proper occupation of righteous and sovereign citizens in a republic **(11)** <u>is</u> farming. He detested "the selfish spirit of commerce" for desiring "no passion or principle but that of gain." **(12)** <u>Furthermore, he viewed banks as the cradle of all commercial corruption.</u> In Jefferson's mind, banks served only to promote "paper speculation," and nurture "the spirit of gambling in paper, in lands, in canal schemes, town lot schemes, manufacturing schemes, and whatever could hit the madness of the day."

10. A) NO CHANGE
 B) land, and that
 C) land and that
 D) land and, that

11. A) NO CHANGE
 B) are
 C) was
 D) were

12. A) NO CHANGE
 B) Furthermore, banks were viewed by Jefferson as the cradle of all commercial corruption.
 C) Furthermore, the cradle of all commercial corruption was considered by be banks by Jefferson.
 D) Furthermore, he viewed the cradle of all commercial corruption to be banks.

[6]

(13) Despite the differences between the two men, Lincoln recognized Jefferson as the man who still succeeded in his expression of certain universal truths, for all his imperfections and compulsions. Lincoln appreciated that Jefferson's words shaped "the definitions and axioms of free society." During the Civil War when told to disregard the Constitution's restraints on presidential power, Lincoln **(14)** will have reiterated Jefferson's warning against taking "possession of a boundless field of power." Lincoln recognized Jefferson for **(15)** having the composure, using foresight, and aptitude to establish in the Declaration of Independence the abstract truth that all men are created equal, so that it would forestall anyone who intended to reestablish tyranny and oppression.

[7]

History is neither a political allegory in which all men are heroic and all women are virtuous, nor a scandalous exposé, full of corruptions and gaffes. Lincoln recognized both the greatness and the limits of Thomas Jefferson and still managed to embrace the American experiment for "giving liberty, not alone to the people of this country, but hope to the world for all future time." We should do the same.

13. A) NO CHANGE
    B) Despite the differences between the two men, Lincoln recognized Jefferson as the man, for all his imperfections and compulsions, who still succeeded in his expression of certain universal truths.
    C) Despite the differences between the two men, for all his imperfections and compulsions, Lincoln recognized Jefferson as the man who still succeeded in his expression of certain universal truths.
    D) Despite the differences between the two men, Lincoln recognized Jefferson as the man who, for all his imperfections and compulsions, still succeeded in his expression of certain universal truths.

14. A) NO CHANGE
    B) reiterated
    C) has reiterated
    D) would have reiterated

15. A) NO CHANGE
    B) having the composure, foresight, and aptitude
    C) having the composure, using the foresight, and the aptitude
    D) having the composure, foresight, and having the aptitude

English Practice Exercises Answer Key

Subjects and Verbs

1. ARE
2. CREATES, ARE
3. CAUSE, DEVASTATE
4. ARE, APPEAR
5. ARE, ARE
6. MARKS, IS
7. IS
8. REACHES
9. HAVE, HAS
10. HAVE
11. ARE
12. WAS, WERE
13. IS, WAS
14. IS
15. HAVE

Basic Sentence Structure

Part A

1. Error Type: Fragment, b)
2. Error Type: Run-on, c)
3. Error Type: Comma splice, a)
4. Error Type: Run-on, a)
5. Error Type: Fragment, c)

Part B

6. By comparing the proteins and hormones found in the digestive fluids of carnivorous plants with similar molecules active in noncarnivorous plants, other researchers concluded that carnivorous plants used the defense mechanisms of ordinary plants to develop he ability to consume insects.
7. Researchers hope to explore a range of questions by examining carnivorous plants, including how organisms adapt to extreme adversity and scarcity, as such answers could have widespread practical applications.
8. Since studies have shown that several enzymes produced by carnivorous plants remained exceptionally stable under extreme heat and acidity that demolished most enzymes, biologists could learn how to make enzymes more tolerant to extreme conditions by studying these plants.
9. Although 590 known species of carnivorous plants are certainly oddities among the plant world, all are legitimate, chlorophyll-carrying members of the kingdom Plantae.
10. While other plants absorb nutrients like nitrogen from the ground, carnivorous plants colonize habitats with poor soil and acquire such nutrients from insect sources.

Part C

11. Carnivorous plants generally feed on insects, but their prey can sometimes include frogs, fish, and even small mammals.
12. Some carnivorous plants trap insects in a basin or a sticky substance, but perhaps the most impressive snare is the Venus fly trap, which actually moves to catch its prey.
13. Carnivorous plants evolved to consume live prey, yet at least one carnivorous plant seems to be evolving to subsist on bat guano instead.
14. The bat benefits as well, so the Hardwicke's woolly bat and a local pitcher plant species have developed a symbiotic relationship.
15. The pitcher plant consumes the nitrogen-rich guano, and the bat gets a perfect place to roost.

Punctuation

1. Insert a colon between "menu" and "figs".
2. Insert commas after "father" and "hat".
3. Insert commas after "lactose-intolerant", "cheese", and "cream".

4. Insert a colon or semicolon after "dishes".
5. Insert a semicolon after "brick".
6. Enclose "which is a type of soup" in parentheses or insert commas before and after the phrase. Also, insert a comma after "regions" before "but".
7. Insert commas after "restaurant" and "free".
8. Insert a semicolon after "weekends" and a comma after "free".
9. Insert commas after "supplies", "eggs", and "potatoes".
10. Insert commas after "restaurant", "1902, and "generations".
11. Insert a commas after "up" and a colon or a long dash after "be".
12. Insert commas after "restaurant", "Paris", "Rome", and "Tokyo", and insert semicolons after "France", and "Italy". Also, insert a colon after "world".
13. Insert commas after "world" and "chefs".
14. Insert a semicolon after "dish" and a comma after "business".
15. Insert commas after "family" and "cook".

Pronoun Errors – Corrected Sentences

1. Each of the boys has his own savings account.
2. Neither Bill nor Alexandra could find his or her jacket.
3. Mike thought that his brother should see Mike's doctor/his brother's doctor.
4. After the big boxing match between Alex and Rodriguez, Alex/Rodriguez/the winner ran around the ring in a victory lap.
5. When I tried to pick up the dog's food dish, the dog bit me.
6. She and Chris will be going to the store later today.
7. Hannah and grace turned in their reports on time, but neither Alison nor Elise turned hers in.
8. He is a better baseball player than I.
9. The candidate informed his assistant that the candidate/his assistant was leaving on the next flight.
10. Matthew brought Jenna and me fresh bottles of water.
11. Everyone will receive their final grades in the mail.
12. Nobody plays his or her best when the temperature is so high.
13. It was difficult because my brother and I were both running for class treasurer.
14. When the eggs were served to the customers, the eggs often looked green.
15. I dropped my mirror on my foot and broke the mirror/my foot.

Verb Errors – Corrected Sentences

1. I suggest that she seek/should seek extra practice in math.
2. Stars often perform concerts to raise money for charities.
3. As Beebee looks for her glasses, her cell phone rings OR As Beebee looked for her glasses, her cell phone rang.
4. If we had played better in the second half, we would have scored four additional baskets and won the game.
5. Tens of thousands of people will have seen the exhibition before the museum closes OR Tens of thousands of people had seen the exhibition before the museum closed.

6. The doctor recommends bed rest for the patient, who suffers from a bad cold OR The doctor recommended bed rest for the patient, who suffered from a bad cold.
7. I wish she would spend more time cleaning and less time complaining.
8. If people were to walk on Mars, they would weigh about one-third of what they weigh on Earth.
9. Lives have been saved since the development of advanced tornado warnings.
10. By the time negotiations had begun, many politicians had expressed doubt about them OR By the time negotiations began, many politicians had expressed doubt about then.
11. Everyone hopes the plan will work OR Everyone hoped the plan would work.
12. Her teacher recommends that she spend more time on math than on English.
13. I was terribly disappointed with my test score because I had studied hard.
14. The boy insists/insisted that he would have paid for the candy bars OR The boy insists he paid for the candy bars.
15. After Alice played croquet with the queen, she was sentenced to death.

Adjective and Adverbs – Corrected Sentences

1. Unfortunately, the lead singer in the musical is an amazingly poor singer.
2. The powerful summer sun beat down on the campers.
3. All birds that fly have ten primary flight feathers, each one shaped slightly differently.
4. Of all computer brands, Macs are the easiest to use.
5. Between Alan and Margaret, Alan is quieter.
6. The two types of kayaks are the easily maneuverable white-water kayak and the larger sea kayak.
7. Of the three boys who competed at the science fair, Rob had the most interesting project.
8. Despite the chaos, the nurse examined the patient calmly and carefully..
9. Of the many flower choices, petunias are the least interesting option.
10. It was an extremely cold winter day.
11. Richard's comments were careless.
12. She did really well on that test.
13. The milk smells rotten.
14. Although we looked at a lot of houses, they all seemed to be of similar quality.
15. There are 20 students in the class, each performing similarly.

Commonly Confused Words

1. Replace "less" with "fewer".
2. Replace "there" with "they're".
3. Replace "leeches" with "leaches".
4. Replace "peak" with "pique".
5. Replace "its'" with "its".
6. Replace "imminent" with "eminent".
7. Replace "affect" with "effect".
8. Replace "precedes" with "proceeds".
9. Replace "insure" with "ensure".
10. Replace "perspective" with "prospective".
11. Replace "you're" with "your".
12. Replace "except" with "accept".

13. Replace "advise" with "advice".
14. Replace "who's" with "whose".
15. Replace "then" with "than".

Idioms

1. Replace "outraged for" with "outraged by".
2. Replace "across the aisle with" with "across the aisle from".
3. Replace "had a right for wearing" with "had a right to wear".
4. Replace "curious on" with "curious about".
5. Replace "Neither Alice or Gina" with "Neither Alice nor Gina".
6. Replace "found guilty for" with "found guilty of".
7. Replace "substitute of" with "substitute for".
8. Replace "differs between" with "differs from".
9. Replace "worried for" with "worried about".
10. Replace "or" with "and".
11. Replace "arrived to" with "arrived at".
12. Replace "but" with "but also".
13. Replace "opposed against" with "opposed to".
14. Replace "fondness of" with "fondness for".
15. Replace "consists in" with "consists of".

Parallelism and Modifiers
Part A

1. Change "blocking" to "blocks".
2. Change "being intelligent" to "his intelligence".
3. Change "challenges students and frustration is found in them" to "challenges and frustrated students".
4. Change "disrespecting" to "disrespect".
5. Change "about his technique" to "for his technique".
6. Change "his presentations were well delivered" to "delivered his presentations well".
7. Change "focus" to "focusing".
8. Change "the Spanish" to "Spain".
9. Change "was a good skater" to "skated better" OR Change "danced better" to "was a better dancer".
10. Change "the bed" to "beneath the bed".

Part B (Answers may vary)

11. Workers used massive tunnel boring machines weighing more than 15,000 tons each to dig the tunnel.
12. Appointed as the nation's sole provider of telecommunications, the Bell System was widely criticized.
13. Originally wanted to study biology, she found that she truly excelled in mathematics.
14. Having finished his introduction, the presenter showed the slideshow to the class first.
15. Hiding in the dark, the cat had glowing eyes.
16. The robot with the remote control was for sale by the woman across the street.

17. While out of town, Jessica sent long letters filled with tales about her travels to her friend.
18. Edgar Allen Poe si revered by critics for his frightening tales.
19. The artist in the flowering scarf was sketching with colored pencils.
20. The woman in high heels walked her dog.

Transitions and Organization	Author's Intent	Relevance
1. B	1. D	1. B
2. A	2. B	2. D
3. C	3. A	3. C
4. D	4. B	4. A
5. D	5. C	
6. A	6. A	
7. C	7. B	
8. C		

Conciseness (Answers may vary)
1. People who disobey rules that have been established for the safety of all cause trouble.
2. I had a very fun time at the party Angelina took me to.
3. He has an affinity for *The New York Times*, which published most of his early exposes.
4. She worked for thirty-three years as a teacher and librarian in Los Angeles public schools.
5. Over several months, his test scores improved.
6. This article offers pertinent information for conserving water.
7. I think I finished all of those worksheets.
8. The senator spoke for fifteen consecutive hours during the filibuster.
9. The accountant reviewed the annual data regarding the company's expenditures.
10. Louis spent so many hours studying that his social life was minimal.
11. Several rules govern noise pollution.
12. The bus company is expected to announce a new schedule.
13. The teacher gave a series of quizzes.
14. This book is extremely fun and helpful.
15. Cory moved to the couch to the center of the room.

Style and Tone (Answers may vary)
1. When examined up close, *The Mona Lisa* is not what one would expect.
2. You've got to understand what you're reading when you write your thesis.
3. *The New York Times*, which has the largest circulation of any metropolitan paper in the U.S. and is known as "the newspaper of record," is the most highly regarded paper in the country.
4. Because the terms used to advertise fancy pet food are largely meaningless and unregulated, some believe that the higher prices are unjustified.
5. In 2015, when the EPA alleged that Volkswagen had cheated on emissions tests, the company reversed its year-long official position and admitted to the charges.
6. Augustinian friar Martin Luther inspired an entirely new branch of religion when he bravely called out the Catholic Church for corrupt practices such as selling absolution.

7. Legend has it that Billy the Kid killed 22 men, but that's overblown since he really only kill 8.
8. The sombrero serves an incredibly useful purpose by providing much needed sun protection.
9. Australia is a unique nation given that it has evolved from a British penal colony to one of the wealthiest nations in the world.
10. American Samoa has the highest rate of military enlistment of any U.S. state or territory, a reflection of patriotism that ought to be rewarded with the right to vote in U.S. elections.

Practice Exercise 1
1. D
2. D
3. C
4. B
5. C
6. A
7. D
8. C
9. C
10. B
11. A
12. B
13. C
14. B
15. A

Practice Exercise 3
1. C
2. C
3. D
4. B
5. A
6. B
7. D
8. C
9. C
10. A
11. D
12. B
13. A
14. C
15. B

Practice Exercise 5
1. C
2. A
3. D
4. C
5. B
6. A
7. B
8. C
9. C
10. D
11. A
12. C
13. B
14. B
15. C

Practice Exercise 2
1. B
2. A
3. D
4. B
5. D
6. D
7. C
8. B
9. C
10. C
11. C
12. A
13. B
14. D
15. B

Practice Exercise 4
1. D
2. B
3. C
4. B
5. D
6. A
7. D
8. A
9. A
10. B
11. C
12. C
13. D
14. B
15. B

Practice Exercise 6
1. A
2. B
3. D
4. C
5. C
6. A
7. D
8. B
9. C
10. B
11. D
12. D
13. A
14. C
15. A

Practice Exercise 7

1. B
2. A
3. B
4. D
5. D
6. C
7. C
8. B
9. A
10. A
11. B
12. D
13. B
14. D
15. A

Practice Exercise 8

1. D
2. D
3. A
4. B
5. D
6. B
7. C
8. C
9. B
10. A
11. C
12. C
13. A
14. B
15. D

Practice Exercise 9

1. C
2. A
3. B
4. B
5. B
6. D
7. A
8. D
9. A
10. B
11. B
12. C
13. D
14. D
15. A

Practice Exercise 10

1. D
2. C
3. D
4. D
5. B
6. C
7. B
8. A
9. A
10. C
11. C
12. A
13. D
14. B
15. B

ACT Math: Pre-Algebra Review

Operations on Integers

- Instead of subtracting two numbers, change the subtraction sign to an addition sign and then change the sign of the second number: $7 - (-3) = 7 + +3 = 10$
- When multiplying or dividing two numbers with the same signs, you will get a positive answer: $-6 \times -5 = 30$
- When multiplying or dividing two numbers with different signs, you will get a negative answer: $-7 \times 3 = -21$

Fractions

- To add or subtract fractions, you must have a common denominator:
$$\frac{1}{6} + \left(-\frac{3}{5}\right) = \frac{5}{30} - \frac{18}{30} = -\frac{13}{30}$$
- You do not need a common denominator to multiply fractions: $\frac{2}{3} \times \frac{5}{8} = \frac{10}{24} = \frac{5}{12}$
- To divide one fraction by another, change the division sign to a multiplication sign and then take the reciprocal of the second number: $\frac{3}{4} \div \frac{1}{3} = \frac{3}{4} \times \frac{3}{1} = \frac{9}{4}$

Decimals

- To change a decimal to a percentage, move the decimal point two places to the right (or multiply it by 100) and add a percent sign: $0.75 = 75\%$
- To change a percentage to a decimal, move the decimal point two places to the left (or divide it by 100) and remove the percent sign: $135\% = 1.35$
- To change a fraction into a decimal, divide the numerator by the denominator: $\frac{5}{8} = 0.625$

Place Value

- Look at the chart below for a review of the place value designations of the number 1376.243:

Thousands	Hundreds	Tens	Ones (or Units)	Tenths	Hundredths	Thousandths
1	3	7	6.	2	4	3

- To round to a certain place value, look at the next smaller place value. If that number is 5 or greater, round up. Otherwise, round down. For example, if rounding 1376.243 to the tenth place, round down since the next smaller place value (the hundredths place) shows a 4. Thus, our answer is 1376.2.

Numerical Order

- To order numbers, such as whole numbers and fractions, from least to greatest (or greatest to least), first make sure all numbers are represented as decimals. Use your calculator to turn any fractions into decimals first:

  Place the numbers $3\frac{3}{4}$, 3.6, and $3\frac{5}{8}$ in order from least to greatest:
  $$3\frac{3}{4} = 3.75, \, 3.6 = 3.6, \text{ and } 3\frac{5}{8} = 3.625$$

- Next, line up the numbers in a chart so that each number's decimal point lines up.

3	.	7	5	
3	.	6		
3	.	6	2	5

- Finally, compare the entries for each number in the chart from left to right. If the value of one row of the left-most column is higher than the values of the other rows of that column, that number is greatest. If all the values in that column are equal, move to the next column to the right, then repeat the process:

  All three numbers have equivalent values in the left-most column (3), so let's move to the 2nd column. Here, the top number (7) is greater than other two (both 6), so we know that 3.75 is greatest. Since the other two numbers both have the value 6 in the 2nd column, move to the next column to the right. Here, 2 is greater than the blank, or 0, value. So 3.625 is the next greatest, and 3.6 is smallest. Thus the answer is 3.6, $3\frac{5}{8}$, $3\frac{3}{4}$.

Exponents

- An exponent is like a repeated multiplication: $x^4 = x \times x \times x \times x \times x$
- When multiplying exponents, add the powers: $c^2 \times c^4 = c^6$
- When dividing exponents, subtract the powers: $\frac{f^5}{f^2} = f^3$
- When raising an exponent to a power, multiply the powers: $(a^3)^4 = a^{12}$
- Any number raised to the first power is equal to itself: $s^1 = s$
- Any number raised to the zero power is equal to 1: $s^0 = 1$
- A number raised to a negative power is equivalent to the reciprocal of that number: $v^{-1} = \frac{1}{v}$
- The product of two or more numbers, each raised to the same power, is equivalent to the product of those numbers, raised as a collective to that power: $a^c b^c = (ab)^c$

Scientific Notation

- Scientific notation is a means of rewriting very large or very small numbers.
- A number written in scientific notation consists of two parts: 4.356×10^3

- The first part of the number must always be between 1 and 10, inclusive.
- The second part of the number is always a power of 10.
- To change a number smaller than 1 into scientific notation, move the decimal to the right until it is exactly to the right of the first non-zero number. The power of the scientific notation will be negative and equivalent to the number of places you moved the decimal:
$$0.0000436 = 4.36 \times 10^{-5}$$
- To change a number larger than 1 into scientific notation, move the decimal to the left until it is exactly to the right of the first non-zero number. The power of the scientific notation will be positive and equivalent to the number of places you moved the decimal:
$$345,316,254 = 345,316,254.0 = 3.45316254 \times 10^{8}$$
- Operations on numbers in scientific notation can most easily be performed by using your calculator.

Radicals

- The square root of a number is written as follows: $\sqrt{25}$. To simplify $\sqrt{25}$, ask yourself this: "What number times itself equals 25?" $\sqrt{25} = 5$
- Radicals may have degrees higher than the square root (degree 2). For example, the cube root of 8, $\sqrt[3]{8}$, asks "Three of what number, all multiplied together, equals 8?" $\sqrt[3]{8} = 2$
- Fractional exponents can be rewritten as follows: $\sqrt[7]{y^4} = y^{\left(\frac{4}{7}\right)}$
- Some radicals should be solved based on your knowledge of basic multiplication. Other radicals are simplified most easily with your calculator.

Order of Operations

- **PEMDAS** is a useful acronym to memorize the order of operations:
  Parentheses, **E**xponents, **M**ultiply / **D**ivide, **A**dd / **S**ubtract

  To evaluate an expression like $5(3 - 1)^2 - 2(5 - 2)$:

  First simplify expressions inside the parentheses: $5(2)^2 - 2(3)$
  Next, apply any exponents: $5(4) - 2(3)$
  Then, do your multiplication: $20 - 6$
  Finally, we can subtract: $20 - 6 = 14$

Absolute Value

- Treat absolute value bars as parentheses for the purpose of PEMDAS.
- After performing all of the operations inside the absolute value bars, make the final numerical values inside the absolute value bars positive and remove the bars. Make sure any signs and values outside of absolute value bars keep their signs: $|2 - 7| = |-5| = 5$

Reference Formulas and Information

The following formulas and information will be given to you on the ACT. While you don't necessarily have to memorize this, the more of it you know by heart, the better you will do:

DIRECTIONS: Solve each problem, choose the correct answer, and then fill in the corresponding oval on your answer document.

Do not linger over problems that take too much time. Solve as many as you can; then return to the others in the time you have left for the test.

You are permitted to use a calculator on this test. You may use your calculator for any problems you choose, but some of the problems may best be done without using a calculator.

Note: Unless otherwise stated, all of the following should be assumed.

1. Illustrative figures are NOT necessarily drawn to scale.
2. Geometric figures lie in a plane.
3. The word *line* indicates a straight line.
4. The word *average* indicates arithmetic mean.

Since this is all the information you get, you are responsible for memorizing any important formulas and equations you may need!

PRACTICE EXERCISE

1. For 2 consecutive integers, the result of adding twice the smaller integer to the larger integer is 46. What are the two integers?
   A) 12, 13
   B) 13, 14
   C) 14, 15
   D) 15, 16
   E) 16, 17

2. $|2 - 7| + |7 - 2| = ?$
   A) −10
   B) −5
   C) 0
   D) 5
   E) 10

    $5 + 5 = 10$

3. What is the largest integer less than $\sqrt{63}$?
   A) 3
   B) 7
   C) 8
   D) 9
   E) 31

4. What number is halfway between $\frac{1}{6}$ and $\frac{1}{4}$?
   A) $\frac{1}{10}$
   B) $\frac{1}{5}$
   C) $\frac{5}{24}$
   D) $\frac{1}{2}$
   E) $\frac{2}{3}$

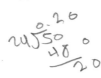
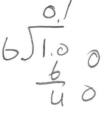

5. What is the least common denominator for adding the fractions $\frac{1}{6}$, $\frac{3}{5}$, and $\frac{11}{12}$?
   A) 30
   B) 60
   C) 120
   D) 240
   E) 360

Page 117

6. $\left|\dfrac{28}{50} - \left(\dfrac{3}{5}\right)^2\right| = ?$

   A) $\dfrac{19}{25}$

   B) $\dfrac{19}{50}$

   C) $\dfrac{1}{5}$

   D) $\dfrac{2}{25}$

   E) $\dfrac{1}{25}$

7. $4.25 \times 10^5 + 1.23 \times 10^6 = ?$

   A) 5.48×10^{11}

   B) 1.655×10^{11}

   C) 5.48×10^6

   D) 1.655×10^6

   E) 4.373×10^5

8. Which of the following lists the numbers 5.235, $5\dfrac{1}{4}$, $\dfrac{26}{5}$, and $\left(\dfrac{5}{2}\right)^2$ in ascending order?

   A) $\dfrac{26}{5}, 5.235, 5\dfrac{1}{4}, \left(\dfrac{5}{2}\right)^2$

   B) $\dfrac{26}{5}, 5\dfrac{1}{4}, 5.235, \left(\dfrac{5}{2}\right)^2$

   C) $\left(\dfrac{5}{2}\right)^2, \dfrac{26}{5}, 5.235, 5\dfrac{1}{4}$

   D) $\left(\dfrac{5}{2}\right)^2, 5.235, 5\dfrac{1}{4}, \dfrac{26}{5}$

   E) $\left(\dfrac{5}{2}\right)^2, 5\dfrac{1}{4}, 5.235, \dfrac{26}{5}$

9. Which of the following shows -3.749 rounded to the hundredths place?

   A) -3.70

   B) -3.74

   C) -3.75

   D) -3.80

   E) -4.00

10. Bob and Jared ordered a pizza to split. If Bob eats $\frac{1}{3}$ of the pizza and Jared eats $\frac{2}{5}$ of what Bob doesn't eat, how much of the pizza is left for them to take home?

   A) $\frac{1}{5}$

   B) $\frac{4}{15}$

   C) $\frac{2}{5}$

   D) $\frac{3}{5}$

   E) $\frac{11}{15}$

$2/3$

$\frac{2}{3} \cdot \frac{2}{5} = \frac{4}{15}$

$\frac{2}{3}$

$\frac{10}{15}$

$.66$

$\frac{6}{15} = \frac{4}{5}$

11. $3.2 \times 10^3 \div 1.6 \times 10^2 = ?$

   A) 0.02

   B) 0.20

   C) 2.00

   D) 20.00

   E) 200.00

10^5

$3.30\phi \div 1.6\phi$

20

$16 \overline{)320}$

$\underline{32}$

00

12. $|3 - 6(2)|^2 + |-5 - 9| = ?$

   A) 18

   B) 50

   C) 67

   D) 95

   E) 239

$3 - 12$

$81 + 14 =$

13. What is the smallest integer greater than $\sqrt{96}$?

   A) 7

   B) 8

   C) 9

   D) 10

   E) 11

14. What fraction is equivalent to $\sqrt{\frac{16}{9}}$?

   A) $\frac{80}{45}$

   B) $\frac{3}{4}$

   C) $\frac{4}{3}$

   D) $\frac{32}{18}$

   E) $\frac{256}{81}$

$\frac{4}{3}$

15. What is the product of $\frac{3}{8}$, $\frac{5}{6}$, and $\frac{9}{5}$?

    A) $\frac{25}{144}$

    B) $\frac{3}{8}$

    C) $\frac{1}{2}$

    D) $\frac{9}{16}$

    E) $\frac{11}{12}$

$\begin{array}{r} 15 \\ 4\,\underline{9} \\ 135 \end{array}$

$\frac{15}{48} \cdot \frac{9}{5} = \frac{135}{240}$

$\begin{array}{r} 48 \\ 4\,\underline{5} \\ 240 \end{array}$

$\begin{array}{r} 48 \\ 5\overline{)240} \\ 20 \\ \underline{40} \end{array}$

$\begin{array}{r} 27 \\ 5\overline{)135} \\ \underline{10} \\ 35 \end{array}$

$\frac{27}{48}$

$\frac{9}{16}$

ACT Math: Number Properties

Types of Numbers

- **Natural numbers** are positive numbers: 1, 2, 3, …
- **Whole numbers** are the natural numbers with the addition of 0: 0, 1, 2, 3, …
- **Integers** are the whole numbers with the addition of the negative values of those numbers: …, −3, −2, −1, 0, 1, 2, 3, …
- **Rational numbers** are the numbers that can be written as the ratio of two integers. This includes repeating decimals and integers: $\frac{1}{6}$, 3, $-\frac{4}{5}$, …
- **Irrational numbers** are the numbers that cannot be written as the ratio of two integers. This includes the square roots of many numbers and some other special numbers: $\sqrt{29}, e, \pi$

Multiples and Factors

- **Multiples** of a number are the numbers that can be divided evenly by that number. 0, 3, 6, and −12 are all multiples of 3 (0 is a multiple of every number).
- The **least common multiple** of two (or more) numbers is the smallest integer (greater than zero) that is a multiple of those numbers. To find the least common multiple of two numbers, list out multiples until you find the same multiple in both lists:
  Multiples of 18: 18, 36, 54, <u>72</u>, 90
  Multiples of 24: 24, 48, <u>72</u>, 96
  The least common multiple of 18 and 24 is 72.
- **Factors** of a number are integers that will divide evenly into that number:
  The factors of 24 are 1, 2, 3, 4, 6, 8, 12, and 24.
- The **greatest common factor** of two (or more) numbers is the largest number that is a factor of those numbers.
  Factors of 18: 1, <u>2</u>, 3, 6, 9, 18
  Factors of 32: 1, <u>2</u>, 4, 8, 16, 32
  The greatest common factor of 18 and 32 is 2.

Even and Odd Numbers

- Each integer that is a multiple of 2 is an **even number**. −8, 2, 6, and 0 are all even.
- Each integer that is not a multiple of 2 is an **odd number**. −7, −1, and 3 are all odd.

Prime and Composite Numbers

- A number is **prime** if it is a natural number greater than 1 with only two factors: 1 and itself. 0, 1, and negative numbers are never prime.
- The only even prime number is 2.
- **Composite numbers** are natural numbers greater than 1 that have more than two factors.

Prime Factorization

- **Prime factorization**, or **prime decomposition**, is the determination of the set of prime numbers which multiply together to get an integer.
- To find the prime factorization of an integer, first figure out two numbers that multiply together to get that integer. Continue this process with each successive integer until you're left with only prime integers. Let's look at the prime factorization of 48:

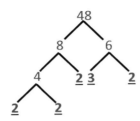

So, the prime factorization of 48 is $2^4 \times 3$.

PRACTICE EXERCISE

1. What is the least common multiple of 30, 40, and 50?
   A) 60
   B) 120
   C) 600
   D) 6,000
   E) 60,000

2. Which of the following is a rational number?
   A) $\sqrt{3.6}$
   B) $\sqrt{3}$
   C) $\sqrt{0.36}$
   D) $\sqrt{0.036}$
   E) $\sqrt{0.03}$

3. Which of the following lists all the positive factors of 36?
   A) 1, 36
   B) 1, 6, 36
   C) 2, 3, 6, 36
   D) 1, 2, 3, 6, 12, 18, 36
   E) 1, 2, 3, 4, 6, 9, 12, 18, 36

4. What is the greatest common factor of 184 and 96?
   A) 2
   B) 4
   C) 8
   D) 12
   E) 16

5. Which of the following is true for all consecutive even integers x and y such that $x < y$?
   A) $x - \frac{y}{2}$ is odd
   B) $x + \frac{y}{2}$ is even
   C) $x^2 + \frac{y^2}{2}$ is even
   D) $x^2 - \frac{y^2}{2}$ is odd
   E) $x^2 + y^2$ is odd

Page 123

6. What is the smallest prime number that is a factor of 420?

  A) 1
  B) 2
  C) 3
  D) 5
  E) 7

7. 18, 24, and 36 are all multiples of which of the following number?

  A) 4
  B) 6
  C) 9
  D) 12
  E) 18

8. Which of the following lists the prime factorization of 144?

  A) $2^2 \times 3^4$
  B) $2^3 \times 3^2$
  C) $2^4 \times 3^2$
  D) $2^4 \times 3^3$
  E) $3^1 \times 4^2$

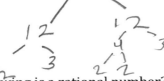

9. Which of the following is a rational number?

  A) $0.\overline{11}$
  B) $0.\overline{45}$
  C) $0.\overline{142857}$
  D) $0.\overline{33}$
  E) All of the above are rational numbers.

10. Which of the following is not a prime number?

  A) 71
  B) 73
  C) 79
  D) 81
  E) 83

11. What is the least common multiple of 26 and 42?

  A) 2
  B) 3
  C) 14
  D) 546
  E) 1,092

12. What is the largest prime number that is a factor of 30?
    A) 2
    B) 3
    C) 5
    ~~D) 10~~
    ~~E) 15~~

13. Which of the following is the greatest common factor of 12 and 15?
    A) 3
    B) 6
    C) 30
    D) 60
    E) 180

14. If k is an even prime number, which of the following could be the value of $k^2 + 1$?
    A) 1
    B) 5
    C) 10
    D) 17
    E) 26

$4 + 1) = 5$

15. If x is a prime number larger than 2, which of the following must be true about $x + 1$?
    A) $x + 1$ is odd.
    B) $x + 1$ is even.
    C) $x + 1$ may be odd or even.
    D) $x + 1$ is also prime.
    E) $x + 1$ is never a rational number.

$3 + 1 = 4$

ACT Math: Ratios, Rates, and Percent

Solving Ratio, Proportion, and Rate Problems

- A **ratio** is a relationship between two or more values and can be written as a fraction:

  3 red marbles for every 4 blue marbles = 3 red:4 blue = $\frac{3 \text{ red}}{4 \text{ blue}}$

- **Proportions** occur when ratios are set equal to each other. Proportions can be solved by cross multiplying:

  $$\frac{3}{7} = \frac{12}{x} \rightarrow 3x = 84 \rightarrow x = 28$$

- Many rate questions involve the equation below:

  $$\text{Distance} = \text{Rate} \times \text{Time}$$

- **Rates** are used to show a "distance" that happens over a period of time, such as miles per hour. Note, however, that the distance does not have to be a physical distance. A pay rate, such as dollars per hour, is another commonly used rate.

Example 1

A copy machine makes 60 copies per minute. A second copy machine makes 80 copies per minute. The second machine starts making copies 2 minutes after the first machine starts. Both machines stop making copies 8 minutes after the first machine started. Together, how many copies did the 2 machines make?

A) 480
B) 600
C) 680
D) 720
E) 960

Let's calculate how many copies the first machine makes. Since it copies at a rate of 60 copies per minute, and works for 8 minutes, it creates:

$$\frac{60 \text{ copies}}{\text{minute}} \times 8 \text{ minutes} = 480 \text{ copies}$$

Since the second copy machine starts 2 minutes after the first, it only copies for 6 minutes:

$$\frac{80 \text{ copies}}{\text{minute}} \times 6 \text{ minutes} = 480 \text{ copies}$$
$$480 \text{ copies} + 480 \text{ copies} = 960 \text{ copies}$$

So, our answer must be **E**.

Solving Percentage Problems

- **Percentage**, or **percent**, $= \frac{\text{part}}{\text{whole}} \times 100$
- $\frac{\text{final}-\text{initial}}{\text{initial}} \times 100\% = $ **percent increase** (positive answer) or **percent decrease** (negative answer)
- The most common types of percentage problems on the ACT will be word problems:

  The price of a $160 bookshelf has decreased by 4%. What is the new price of the bookshelf?

  $$\$160.00 \times 0.04 = \$24.50$$
  $$\$160.00 - \$24.50 = \$135.50$$

- **Tax** is a percentage added to the cost of a purchase – it works the same as a percent increase:

  A $24.00 shirt is purchased in a state with a 5% sales tax rate. How much is the shirt after tax?
  $$\$24.00 \times 0.05 = \$1.20$$
  $$\$24.00 + \$1.20 = \$25.20$$

- **Commission** is a percentage used in calculating how much money salespeople make from sales. A 15% commission means that 15% of a salesperson's sales will be added on to his or her salary:

  Robi made $20,000 in sales this month. If Robi gets 9.5% commission on all of his sales, how much money does he make through commission?

  $$\$20,000.00 \times 0.095 = \$1,900$$

Example 2

If 40% of a given number is 8, then what is 15% of the given number?

A) 1.2
B) 1.8
C) 3.0
D) 5.0
E) 6.5

Since 40% of a number (we'll call the number x) is equal to 8, let's set up an equation:

$$0.4 \times x = 8$$
$$x = 20$$

Now we just need to calculate 15% of 20: $0.15 \times 20 = 3$. So, the answer must be **C**.

PRACTICE EXERCISE

1. A truck averages 15 miles per gallon of gasoline, and a car averages 32 miles per gallon of gasoline. At these rates, how many more gallons of gasoline does the truck need than the car to make a 960-mile trip?
   A) 2
   B) 30
   C) 34
   D) 64
   E) 94

Use the following information to answer questions 2–4.

A poll of 300 registered voters was taken before the election for police chief of Midtown. All 300 voters indicated which 1 of the 4 candidates they would vote for. The results of the poll are given in the table below.

Candidate	Number of voters
Kim	60
Johnson	80
Dink	70
Ethos	90

2. What percent of the voters polled chose Ethos in the poll?
   A) 20.0%
   B) 23.3%
   C) 26.7%
   D) 30.0%
   E) 33.3%

3. If the poll is indicative of how the 15,000 registered voters of Midtown will actually vote in the election, which of the following is the best estimate of the number of votes Dink will receive in the election?
   A) 3,000
   B) 3,500
   C) 4,000
   D) 4,500
   E) 5,000

4. In the poll above, what is the ratio of voters who chose Ethos to voters who chose Kim?
   A) 2:5
   B) 3:5
   C) 2:3
   D) 3:2
   E) 5:3

5. Kyung cut a length of rope 60 feet long into 2 pieces. The ratio of the lengths of the 2 pieces is 5:7. To the nearest foot, how much longer is the long piece than the short piece?
   A) 10
   B) 15
   C) 17
   D) 26
   E) 42

   25 35

6. A model rocket 50 meters above ground is falling at a constant rate of 4 meters per second while another model rocket is 20 meters above ground is rising at a constant rate of 8 meters per second. After how many seconds will the 2 model rockets be the same height above the ground?
   A) 1.5
   B) 2.0
   C) 2.5
   D) 3.0
   E) 4.0

   40 42

7. If there are 6×10^{10} helium atoms in a volume of 3×10^4 cubic centimeters, what is the average number of helium atoms per cubic centimeter?
   A) 5.0×10^{-7}
   B) 2.0×10^6
   C) 1.8×10^{14}
   D) 2.0×10^{14}
   E) 1.8×10^{15}

8. Kima plans to drive 1,200 miles to her vacation destination, driving an average of 50 miles per hour. How many more miles per hour must she average, while driving, to reduce her total driving time by 4 hours?
   A) 4
   B) 5
   C) 10
   D) 12
   E) 15

   24

9. To keep up with inflation, a hotel needs to raise the price of a $75.00 room by 15%. What will be the new rate?
   A) $11.25
   B) $63.75
   C) $75.15
   D) $86.25
   E) $90.00

10. In a bag of 250 jelly beans, 40% of the jelly beans are green, 100 are yellow, and the rest are blue. What percentage of the jelly beans are blue?
    A) 20%
    B) 25%
    C) 40%
    D) 50%
    E) 60%

11. Carlisle is getting a loan of $1,200. To pay back the loan, he needs to add 3% of the price of the loan. How much does Carlisle need to pay back in all?
    A) $36.00
    B) $360.00
    C) $1,164.00
    D) $1,236.00
    E) $1,560.00

12. John's salary increases from $42,000 to $48,000. Which of the following is closest to the percent increase in his salary?
    A) 11%
    B) 12%
    C) 14%
    D) 16%
    E) 18%

13. A baseball team has won 10 of its 18 games. If it has 12 more games to play and must win at least 70% of its games to qualify for the playoffs, how many more games must it win?
    A) 8
    B) 9
    C) 10
    D) 11
    E) 12

14. 15% of 23 is equivalent to 23% of what number?
    A) 1.50
    B) 7.94
    C) 15.00
    D) 22.94
    E) 79.35

15. For the past 3 months, Jason has lost 5 pounds per month. If he has lost 10% of his total weight, what is his weight at the end of the 3 months?

A) 135 pounds

B) 143.5 pounds

C) 150 pounds

D) 156.5 pounds

E) 165 pounds

15

1 50

ACT Math: Algebraic Operations

Operations on Polynomials

- Expressions with **like terms** have the same exact variables raised to the same powers:

  $5y^2$ and $-3y^2$, de and $\frac{1}{2}de$, and $6ab^2c$ and $-2ab^2c$ are all examples of pairs of like terms.

  $-23x^2$ and $7x^3$, $5jk$ and $6jk^2$, and $-8ab$ and $17abc$ are NOT examples of pairs of like terms.

- You can only add or subtract like terms when simplifying or solving equations and expressions:

$$\frac{1}{2}de + de = \frac{3}{2}de$$
$$5jk + 6jk^2 \text{ cannot be combined}$$

- To multiply terms, multiply coefficients, but add the exponents of like terms. You do not have to have like terms to multiply:

$$(4x^3y)(-2x^{-1}y) = -8x^2y^2$$

- To divide terms, divide coefficients, but subtract the exponents of like terms. You do not need like terms to divide:

$$\frac{12x^4y}{-6x^2y^3} = -\frac{2x^2}{y^2}$$

Distributive Property

- When a **coefficient** is outside a parentheses that has multiple terms inside, multiply each term inside the parentheses by the coefficient to simplify:

$$2x(x + 6) = 2x(x) + 2x(6) = 2x^2 + 12x$$

FOILing

- When multiplying two binomials, remember the mnemonic device **FOIL**: First, Outer, Inner, Last.
- To multiply $(5y - 3)(4y + 2)$, first multiply the first terms, then the outer terms, then the inner terms, then the last terms. Finally, simplify by combining like terms:

$$5y(4y) + 5y(2) + -3(4y) + -3(3) = 20y^2 - 2y - 6$$

Example 1

The expression $-8x^3(7x^6 - 3x^5)$ is equivalent to:

A) $-56x^9 + 24x^8$
B) $-56x^9 - 24x^8$
C) $-56x^{18} + 24x^{15}$
D) $-56x^{18} - 24x^{15}$
E) $-32x^4$

Let's start out by using our distributive property:

$-8x^3(7x^6 - 3x^5) = -8x^3(7x^6) - 8x^3(-3x^5) = -56x^9 + 24x^8$. Thus, our answer is **A**.

Substitution

- Substitution is the act of replacing variables in an expression with numerical values:

What is the value of $\frac{3xy}{x^2y^2}$ when $x = -3$ and $y = -2$?

Replace each variable with its numerical term and simplify:

$$\frac{3xy}{x^2y^2} = \frac{3(-3)(-2)}{(-3)^2(-2)^2} = \frac{18}{36} = \frac{1}{2}$$

Example 2

What is the value of $\left|\frac{xy+y^2}{x^0-y}\right|$ when $x = 2$ and $y = 5$?

A) $-\frac{35}{4}$
B) -7
C) $\frac{7}{2}$
D) 7
E) $\frac{35}{4}$

Again, replace each variable with its numerical term and simplify:

$\left|\frac{xy+y^2}{x^0-y}\right| = \left|\frac{(2)(5)+(5)^2}{(2)^0-(5)}\right| = \left|\frac{10+25}{1-5}\right| = \left|\frac{35}{-4}\right| = \frac{35}{4}$. Thus, the answer is **E**.

PRACTICE EXERCISE

1. If $a = 2$, $b = 3$, and $c = -4$, what does $(a + b - c)(c - b)$ equal?
   A) -63
   B) -7
   C) 3
   D) 7
   E) 63

2. The expression $(5x - 3y^2)(5x + 3y^2)$ is equivalent to:
   A) $25x^2 - 9y^2$
   B) $25x^2 - 9y^4$
   C) $10x^2 - 6y^2$
   D) $10x^2 - 6y^4$
   E) $25x^2 + 9y^4$

3. $(f - g + 3h) - (2f + 3g - 2h)$ is equivalent to:
   A) $-f - 4g + h$
   B) $-f - 4g - 5h$
   C) $-f - 4g + 5h$
   D) $-f - 4g - h$
   E) $f + 4g + 5h$

4. The expression $(3 - y)(2y - 4)$ is equivalent to:
   A) $6y^2 - 14y + 4$
   B) $2y^2 + 10y - 12$
   C) $2y^2 - 10y - 12$
   D) $-2y^2 + 10y - 12$
   E) $-2y^2 - 10y - 12$

5. $k^2 - 63k + 23 - 45k^2 + 32k$ is equivalent to:
   A) $-52k^2$
   B) $-52k^6$
   C) $-44k^4 - 31k^2 + 23$
   D) $-44k^2 - 31k + 23$
   E) $-45k^2 - 31k + 23$

6. The expression $(x + y - 2)(x - y)$ is equivalent to:
   A) $x^2 - y^2 - 2x + 2y$
   B) $x^2 - y^2 - 2x - 2y$
   C) $x^2 - y^2 + 2xy - 2x - 2y$
   D) $x^2 + y^2 - 2x + 2y$
   E) $x^2 + y^2 - 2x - 2y$

7. $(4u^4)^4$ is equivalent to:
   A) u
   B) $16u^8$
   C) $16u^{16}$
   D) $256u^8$
   E) $256u^{16}$

8. Which of the following is an equivalent simplified expression for $3(5p - 5) - 2(8p + 4)$?
   A) $-p - 23$
   B) $-p - 7$
   C) $p - 23$
   D) $p - 7$
   E) $31p - 23$

9. For all x, $(7 - 2x)^2 = ?$
   A) $49 + 4x^2$
   B) $49 - 4x^2$
   C) $49 + 28x + 4x^2$
   D) $49 - 28x - 4x^2$
   E) $49 - 28x + 4x^2$

10. For all positive integers x, what is the greatest common factor $165x$ and $150x^2$?
    A) 5
    B) 15
    C) $5x$
    D) $15x$
    E) $15x^2$

11. If $x = -2$, $y = -9$, and $z = 0$, what does $xy + xz - yz$ equal?
    A) -18
    B) -7
    C) 0
    D) 7
    E) 18

12. The expression $\frac{gf + dg}{dfg}$ is equivalent to:
    A) d
    B) g
    C) f
    D) $\frac{f + d}{dfg}$
    E) $\frac{f + d}{df}$

13. $(x + 1)^3$ is equivalent to:
   A) $x^3 + 1$
   B) $3x + 3$
   C) $x^3 + 2x^2 + 2x + 1$
   D) $x^3 + 3x^2 + 3x + 1$
   E) $x^3 + 3x^2 + 3x + 3$

14. The expression $(2y - 3)(2y + 3)$ is equivalent to what value when $y = 6$?
   A) 81
   B) 108
   C) 135
   D) 225
   E) 667

15. For all positive integers a, b and c, what is the greatest common factor of $6abc$ and $12a^2b^2c^2$, and $15bc^2$?
   A) $3bc$
   B) $60bc$
   C) $3bc^2$
   D) $3a^2b^2c^2$
   E) $60a^2b^2c^2$

ACT Math: Solving and Modeling Linear Equations

Solving Linear Equations

- When solving an equation, whatever you do to one side of the equation you must do to the other as well:

$$-2x = -6 \rightarrow -2x \div -2 = -6 \div -2 \rightarrow x = 3$$

- To solve an equation, you must first isolate the variable:

$$4x - 2 = 7 \rightarrow 4x - 2 + 2 = 7 + 2 \rightarrow 4x = 9 \rightarrow 4x \div 4 = 9 \div 4 \rightarrow x = \frac{9}{4}$$

- First, simplify both sides of the equation by using the distributive property, eliminating fractions, or combining like terms, as necessary:

$$-3(x + 6) = 9 \rightarrow -3x - 18 = 9 \rightarrow -3x = 27 \rightarrow x = -9$$

$$\frac{2}{5}x - 4 = 3 \rightarrow 5\left(\frac{2}{5}x - 4\right) = 5(3) \rightarrow 2x - 20 = 15 \rightarrow 2x = 35 \rightarrow x = \frac{35}{2}$$

$$12x - 5x = 18 + 3 \rightarrow 7x = 21 \rightarrow x = 3$$

- To solve a one-variable equation, add or subtract all of your variable terms to one side of the equation and all of your constant terms to the other side:

$$3x - 7 = 5x - 9 \rightarrow 9 - 7 = 5x - 3x \rightarrow 2 = 2x \rightarrow 1 = x$$

Example 1

If $7 + 3x = 22$, then $2x = ?$

A) 5
B) 10
C) 12
D) 14
E) $\frac{58}{3}$

First, let's isolate the variable:

$$7 + 3x = 22 \rightarrow 7 + 3x - 7 = 22 - 7 \rightarrow 3x = 15$$
$$3x \div 3 = 15 \div 3 \rightarrow x = 5$$

Note, however, that we're looking for the value of $2x$: $2x = 2(5) = 10$. The answer is **B**.

Modeling Linear Equations

- Word problems on the ACT often focus on real-world situations like people getting paid for doing a job or a relationship that exists in science or economics:

    Jaime earns $7.75 per hour at her restaurant job. If she currently has $52.00 saved, how many hours, h, must she work to save a total of $300.00?

- The ACT will usually tell you which quantity you are solving for and occasionally assign it a variable:

    Jaime earns $7.75 per hour at her restaurant job. If she currently has $52.00 saved, **how many hours, h, must she work to save a total of $300.00**?

    $$52.00 + 7.75h = 300.00 \rightarrow 7.75h = 248.00 \rightarrow h = 32$$

- The ACT will sometimes ask you to interpret the meaning of a part of an equation or to translate a situation into an equation:

    Jaime earns $7.75 per hour at her restaurant job. If she currently has $52.00 saved, which of the following expressions can be used to find the number of hours, h, that she must work to save a total of T?

    $$52.00 + 7.75h = T$$

- Always be aware of keywords for addition, subtraction, multiplication, division, and equality:

Algebraic Term	Key Words
+	more than, increased by, greater than, additional, exceeds, sum
−	less than, decreased by, fewer than, difference
×	of, each, product, per
÷	per, ratio of, for every
=	is, equals, is equivalent to

Example 2

The fixed costs of manufacturing basketballs in a factory are $1,400.00 per day. The variable costs are $5.25 per basketball. Which of the following expressions can be used to model the cost of manufacturing b basketballs in 1 day?

A) $1,405.25b$
B) $5.25b - \$1,400.00$
C) $1,400.00b + \$5.25$
D) $1,400.00 - \$5.25b$
E) $1,400.00 + \$5.25b$

Every day, the factory pays $1,400.00 as a fixed cost, no matter how many basketballs are produced. So, this cost does not need to be multiplied by a variable. However, it does cost $5.25 per basketball. So, in addition to the $1,400.00 fixed cost, we must add on $5.25b$. Thus, our answer is **E**.

PRACTICE EXERCISE

1. Which of the following mathematical expressions is equivalent to the verbal expression "Three more than twice a number, a, is 52"?
   A) $3a + 2a = 52$
   B) $3 + 2a = 52$
   C) $2a + 3 = 52$
   D) $2a - 3 = 52$
   E) $3a - 2 = 52$

$2a + 3 = 52$

2. If $3(x - 3) = -14$, then $x = ?$
   A) -14
   B) $-\frac{23}{3}$
   C) $-\frac{17}{3}$
   D) $-\frac{11}{3}$
   E) $-\frac{5}{3}$

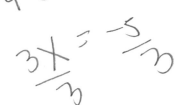

$3x - 9 = -14$

$\frac{3x}{3} = \frac{-5}{3}$

3. A plumber charges $30 for each hour he works on a job, plus a flat $100 fee. How many hours of work are included in a $270 bill?
   A) $\frac{12}{5}$
   B) $\frac{27}{10}$
   C) 4
   D) $\frac{17}{3}$
   E) 9

5.66

$30x + 100 = 270$

$30x = 170$

4. When $\frac{1}{2}x - \frac{1}{3}x = 1$, what is the value of x?
   A) -6
   B) -1
   C) 3
   D) 6
   E) 12

$-.17x = 1$

$.17$

5. Jamalia went to a clothing store to price winter clothing. All winter clothing was discounted 15% off the marked price. Jamalia wanted to program her calculator so she could input the marked price and the discounted price would be the output. Which of the following is an expression for the discounted price on a marked price of d dollars?
   A) $d - 15d$
   B) $d - 0.15d$
   C) $d - 0.15$
   D) $d - 15$
   E) $0.15d$

6. If $12x - 9 = 17$, then $3x = ?$

A) $\frac{2}{3}$

B) 2

C) $\frac{13}{6}$

D) $\frac{13}{2}$

E) 13

$2x = 26$

2.16

7. The cost of a taxi ride is \$2.50 for the first $\frac{1}{2}$ of a mile and 25 cents for each additional $\frac{1}{8}$ of a mile. How many miles long is a taxi ride that costs \$7.75?

A) $\frac{5}{8}$

B) $\frac{13}{8}$

C) $\frac{21}{8}$

D) $\frac{25}{8}$

E) $\frac{31}{8}$

2.50

3.00

1st mile

5.00

2nd mile

7.00

3rd mile

8. James has decided to begin building garages. In order to begin his business, he must invest \$3 million in startup costs. The cost to produce each garage is \$5,000, and the selling price of each garage will be \$12,000. Accounting for his startup costs, which of the following expressions represents the profit, in dollars, that James will make when x garages are produced and sold?

A) $7,000x - 3,000,000$

B) $12,000x - 2,995,000$

C) $17,000x - 3,000,000$

D) $7,000x$

E) $2,993,000x$

9. If $3\left(x - \frac{1}{2}\right) = 2(2 - x)$, then $x = ?$

A) $\frac{9}{10}$

B) $\frac{11}{10}$

C) $\frac{9}{8}$

D) $\frac{9}{2}$

E) $\frac{11}{2}$

$3x - 1.5 = 4 - 2x$

$\frac{-5.5}{.5} = \frac{-5x}{.5}$

$\frac{}{.5}$

10. When a number is increased by 19, the sum is equal to twice the number. Which of the following could be the number?
    A) −19
    B) −8.5
    C) 8.5
    D) 19
    E) 38

$x + 19 = 2x$

$19 = x$

11. Which of the following mathematical expressions is equivalent to the verbal expression "Six less than one-half of a number, b, is 13"?
    A) $\frac{1}{2}b - 6 = 13$
    B) $6 - \frac{1}{2}b = 13$
    C) $\frac{b-6}{2} = 13$
    D) $\frac{6-b}{2} = 13$
    E) $6 - b = 13 \times \frac{1}{2}$

$\frac{1}{S}b - 6 = 13$

12. If $2x - 5x = 3x + 6x$, then $x = ?$
    A) −3
    B) $-\frac{1}{3}$
    C) 0
    D) $\frac{1}{3}$
    E) 3

$-3x = 9x$
$-9x \quad -9x$
$-12x = 0$

13. If $\frac{3x-2}{6} = 3$, then $6x = ?$
    A) 5
    B) $\frac{20}{3}$
    C) 10
    D) 20
    E) 40

$3x - 2 = 18$
$3x = 20$

6.66

14. If $3x - 2 = 9$ and $4y - 2 = 11$, then what is the value of $x + y$?
    A) $\frac{13}{4}$
    B) $\frac{24}{7}$
    C) $\frac{11}{3}$
    D) $\frac{79}{12}$
    E) $\frac{83}{12}$

$3x = 11$

$x = 3.66$

crack Act .com

15. If $3x - 2 = 3(x - 4)$, what is the value of x?

A) −10

B) −2

C) 0

D) 10

E) No solution exists

$$3x - 2 = 3x - 12$$
$$+2 \qquad\qquad +2$$

$$3x = 3x - 10$$
$$-3x$$

Functions

- A **function** is a relationship between a set of **inputs** and a set of **outputs** – each input is related to exactly one output:

  The image below contains a function on the left. Each input in the left oval goes to exactly one output in the right oval. The image below also contains a relation that is not a function on the right. The relation is not a function because an input of 2 leads to two outputs: 6 or 9.

- The inputs, or x-values of the function, are known as the function's **domain**. The outputs, or y-values of the function, are known as its **range**:

  In the image of the function below, the numbers on the left, $3, -7, 2$, and 0, are the domain of the function, while the numbers on the right, $0, 11$, and -4, are the range of the function.

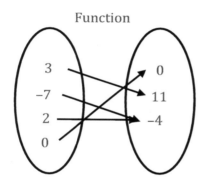
Function

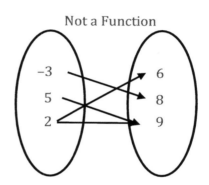
Not a Function

- In function notation, the input of the function is represented by x while the output of the function is represented as $f(x)$ or y. The ordered pair (x, y) is a solution to the function $f(x)$:

  $(3, 8)$ is a solution to the function $f(x) = 5x - 7$. Another way to write this is $f(3) = 8$.
  $$f(3) = 5(3) - 7 = 8$$

- Functions can be added, subtracted, multiplied or divided just like any other algebraic terms:

$$f(x) = 2 - x \quad g(x) = 3x + 5$$
$$f(x) + g(x) = 2 - x + 3x + 5 = 2x + 7$$
$$f(x) - g(x) = 2 - x - (3x + 5) = -4x - 3$$
$$f(x) \times g(x) = (2 - x)(3x + 5) = 10 + x - 3x^2$$
$$f(x) \div g(x) = \frac{2-x}{3x+5}$$

- **Composition** is the process by which one function becomes the input of another function:

$$f(x) = 2x^2 \qquad g(x) = 8 + x$$
$$f(g(x)) = 2(8 + x)^2 = 2(64 + 16x + x^2) = 2x^2 + 32x + 128$$
$$g(f(x)) = 8 + (2x^2) = 2x^2 + 8$$

Note that $f(g(x))$ is not necessarily equivalent to $g(f(x))$.

Example 1

A function $f(x)$ is defined as $f(x) = -8x^2$. What is $f(-3)$?

A) -72
B) 72
C) 192
D) -576
E) 576

To solve this, all we need to do is plug our x-value, -3, into $f(x)$:

$$f(-3) = -8(-3)^2 = -8(9) = -72$$

The answer is **A**.

Special Functions

- Some functions on the ACT won't necessarily use $f(x)$ notation. These usually mention the phrase "defined a new operation" and involve a symbol you've probably never seen in math before, like @, &, or ♡. These questions generally show a function and ask you to simply plug numbers in. However, the wording can be deceptive. Let's look at an example problem:

Example 2

Charles defined a new operation, ♦, on pairs of ordered pairs of integers as follows: $(a, b) ♦ (c, d) = \frac{ac+bd}{ab-cd}$. What is the value of $(2,1) ♦ (3, 4)$?

A) -2
B) -1
C) 2
D) 5
E) 10

All we have to do to solve this problem is plug in the values of $a, b, c,$ and d:

$$\frac{ac+bd}{ab-cd} = \frac{(2)(3)+(1)(4)}{(2)(1)-(3)(4)} = \frac{10}{-10} = -1.$$ The answer is **B**.

PRACTICE EXERCISE

1. A function is defined as $f(x) = \frac{x-3}{1-x}$ for all $x \neq 1$. What is the value of $f(5) - f(3)$?

    A) $-\frac{1}{2}$

    B) 0

    C) $\frac{1}{2}$

    D) $\frac{3}{2}$

    E) $\frac{5}{2}$

    $\frac{2}{-4} = \frac{1}{2} -$

2. A function $A(x)$ is defined as follows:

    For $x > 0, A(x) = x^3 - x^2 + x$

    For $x < 0, A(x) = -x^3 + x^2 - x$

    What is the value of $A(-3)$? $-27 - 9 + -3$

    A) -39

    B) -21

    C) 0

    D) 21

    E) 39

3. For the function defined as $g(x) = x^{\frac{1}{2}}$ for all $x > 0$, for what value of x is $g(x) = 0.6$?

    A) 0.30

    B) 0.36

    C) 0.60

    D) 0.77

    E) 1.20

4. In a science experiment, a cart was rolled at a constant rate along a straight line. Sara recorded in the chart below the cart's distance, x, in feet, from a reference point at the start of the experiment, $t = 0$, to $t = 6$ in seconds.

t	0	1	2	3	4	5	6
x	12	19	26	33	40	47	54

    Which of the following equations represents this data?

    A) $x = 7t$

    B) $x = 7t + 12$

    C) $x = 12t$

    D) $x = 12t + 7$

    E) $x = 19t$

5. Consider the function $f(x) = 3x - b$. If $f(5) = 12$ is a solution to the function, what is the value of b?
   A) -3
   B) 0
   C) 2
   D) 3
   E) 31

6. The function $f(x) = \frac{3+x}{2-x}$ is defined for every value of $x \neq a$. What is the value of a?
   A) -3
   B) -2
   C) 0
   D) 2
   E) 3

7. Given $f(x) = 3x + 2$ and $g(x) = 12 - x$, which of the following is an expression for $f(g(x))$?
   A) $38 - 3x$
   B) $36 - 3x$
   C) $34 - 3x$
   D) $14 - 3x$
   E) $10 - 3x$

8. Given $f(x) = x^2 - 3x$ and $g(x) = 2 - x^2$, which of the following is an expression for $g(x) - f(x)$?
   A) $-2x^2 + 3x - 2$
   B) $-2x^2 - 3x - 2$
   C) $-2x^2 - 3x + 2$
   D) $2x^2 + 3x - 2$
   E) $2x^2 - 3x - 2$

9. If $h(x) = (-3)^x$, then $h(3) = ?$
   A) -27
   B) -9
   C) -1
   D) 9
   E) 27

10. If $g(x-3) = x^2 + 2$, what is the value of $g(12)$?
    A) 79
    B) 83
    C) 146
    D) 223
    E) 227

$g(9) =$

11. A function is defined as $f(x) = x^{-1} + x^{-2}$ for all $x \neq 0$. What is the value of $f(4)$?
    A) -12
    B) $\frac{1}{20}$
    C) $\frac{1}{10}$
    D) $\frac{5}{16}$
    E) 20

12. A function $A(x)$ is defined by cubing the positive difference between x and 3. What is the value of the function when $x = -2$?
    A) -125
    B) -1
    C) 0
    D) 1
    E) 125

$-2 \qquad 3$

13. For the function defined as $g(x) = x^3 - x^2$, which of the following is largest?
    A) $g(-3)$
    B) $g(-1)$
    C) $g(0)$
    D) $g(1)$
    E) $g(3)$

$27 - 9 = 18$

$-27 - 9 =$

14. For the function defined as $g(x) = x^2 - x^3$, which of the following is largest?
    A) $g(-3)$
    B) $g(-1)$
    C) $g(0)$
    D) $g(1)$
    E) $g(3)$

$9 + 27$

$9 - 27$

15. Consider the function $y@x = -\frac{x+y}{3-x}$. What is the value of $(-3)@2$?
    A) -2
    B) -1
    C) 1
    D) 2
    E) 4

$2 + -3 = \frac{-1}{3-2=} \quad \frac{-1}{1} = -1$

ACT Math: Solving and Modeling Linear Inequalities and Absolute Value Equations

Solving and Modeling Linear Inequalities

- **Linear inequalities** should be solved just like linear equations:

$$2y - 6 > 14 \;\rightarrow\; 2y - 6 + 6 > 14 + 6 \;\rightarrow\; 2y > 20 \;\rightarrow\; y > 10$$

- Whenever you multiply or divide both sides of the inequality by a negative number, you MUST flip the inequality sign (so $<$ becomes $>$, or $\geq$ becomes $\leq$).
- Below are some of the most common key words for inequalities:

Algebraic Term	Key Words
$<$	less than, fewer than
$>$	more than, greater than
$\leq$	at most, no more than, no greater than
$\geq$	at least, no less than, no fewer than

Example 1

The inequality $6(x + 2) > 7(x - 5)$ is equivalent to which of the following inequalities?

A) $x < -23$
B) $x < 7$
C) $x < 17$
D) $x < 37$
E) $x < 47$

First, let's use the distributive property to simplify both sides of the inequality:

$$6(x + 2) > 7(x - 5) \;\rightarrow\; 6x + 12 > 7x - 35 \;\rightarrow\; -x > -47 \;\rightarrow\; x < 47$$

The answer is **E**.

Absolute Value Equations and Inequalities

- Occasionally, equations and inequalities involving **absolute value bars** show up on the ACT. Let's take a look at how we would solve one of these:
$$|x - 3| = 9$$

- We know there are two ways for the term inside a set of absolute value bars to end up equaling 9:
$$|9| = 9 \text{ or } |-9| = 9$$

- Since we know the term inside of the absolute value bars could be 9 or -9, let's set the term inside the absolute value bars equal to those two numbers and solve:

$$x - 3 = 9 \quad \text{or} \quad x - 3 = -9$$
$$x = 12 \quad \text{or} \quad x = -6$$

So, both -6 and 12 are answers to the equation above.

- Absolute value inequalities can be solved in much the same way. Notice how we changed the sign of one of the 9's in the example above? In the case of an inequality, flip the inequality symbol of the inequality in which we changed the sign of the 9:

$$|x - 3| > 9$$
$$x - 3 > 9 \quad \text{or} \quad x - 3 < -9$$
$$x > 12 \quad \text{or} \quad x < -6$$

Example 2

The diameter, d centimeters, of the metal poles Goodpole Manufacturing produces must satisfy the inequality $|d - 3| \leq 0.001$. What is the maximum diameter, in centimeters, such a metal pole may have?

A) 1.4995
B) 1.5005
C) 2.999
D) 3.000
E) 3.001

Since we want the largest possible diameter, let's start by plugging in the largest answer choice to see if it satisfies the inequality above.

$$|3.001 - 3| \leq 0.001$$
$$|0.001| \leq 0.001$$
$$0.001 \leq 0.001$$

Since this is true, our answer must be **E**.

PRACTICE EXERCISE

1. If $2^x = 24$, then which of the following must be true?
   A) $2 < x < 3$
   B) $3 < x < 4$
   C) $4 < x < 5$
   D) $6 < x < 8$
   E) $11 < x < 13$

2. Which of the following is equivalent to the inequality $5x - 3 \geq 7x + 9$?
   A) $x \leq -6$
   B) $x \geq -6$
   C) $x \geq -12$
   D) $x \leq 6$
   E) $x \geq 6$

$$X \leq -6$$

$$\begin{array}{cc} +3 & +3 \\ 5X \geq 7X + 12 \\ -7X & -7X \\ \hline -2X \geq 12 \end{array}$$

3. Jim makes \$12.25 per hour at his summer job at the library. If Jim needs to make at least \$350.00 to go on a vacation trip to a theme park, what is the least number of hours he can work and still afford to go?
   A) 27
   B) 28
   C) 29
   D) 30
   E) 31

$$12.25x \geq 350$$

4. The number line above is the graph of which of the following inequalities?
   A) $-2 \leq x$ and $5 \geq x$
   B) $-2 \leq x$ and $5 \leq x$
   C) $-2 \geq x$ or $5 \leq x$
   D) $-2 \leq x$ or $5 \geq x$
   E) $-2 < x < 5$

5. If $g(x) = -3x - 9$, for which values of x is $g(x) > 15$?
   A) $x < 8$
   B) $x < 2$
   C) $x > 2$
   D) $x < -2$
   E) $x < -8$

$$6 \cdot 9 = -3$$
$$-24$$
$$24 - 9 =$$

6. The temperature of a refrigerator must be kept within 1.5 degrees of 38°F. Which of the following inequalities expresses the possible temperatures, T, in degrees Fahrenheit, of the refrigerator?
   A) $|T + 1.5| \geq 38$
   B) $|T - 1.5| \leq 38$
   C) $|T + 38| \geq 1.5$
   D) $|T - 38| \geq 1.5$
   E) $|T - 38| \leq 1.5$

7. If $f(x) = 3x - 2$ and $g(x) = 9x - 18$, for which values of x is $f(x) > g(x)$?
   A) $x < \frac{8}{3}$
   B) $x > \frac{8}{3}$
   C) $x < -\frac{8}{3}$
   D) $x > -\frac{8}{3}$
   E) $x < -\frac{10}{3}$

8. If $3|a - 2| = 18$, which of the following lists all of the possible values of a?
   A) 8 only
   B) -4 only
   C) -8 only
   D) -8 and 4
   E) -4 and 8

   $3a - 6 = 18$
   $ +6 +6$
   $\dfrac{3a}{3} = \dfrac{24}{3}$

   $3 \quad a + 2$
   $3a + 6 = 18$
   $ -6 -6$

9. If $3(5 - 2x) > \frac{3x}{2}$, then which of the following lists all of the possible values of x?
   A) $x < -2$
   B) $x > -2$
   C) $x < 2$
   D) $x > 2$
   E) $x > \frac{30}{7}$

   $15 - 6x > \dfrac{3x}{2}$
   $30 - 12x > 3x$
   $ +12x +12x$

   $x < 2$
   $\dfrac{30}{15} > \dfrac{15x}{15}$

10. If $|c + 5| - 2 > 3$, which of the following lists all of the possible values of c?
    A) $c > 0$
    B) $c < -10$
    C) $-10 < c < 0$
    D) $c > 0$ or $c < -10$
    E) $c < 0$ or $c > 10$

    $c + 5$
    $c + 3 > 3$
    $ -3 -3$
    $c > 0$

11. If $-3(x - 2) < 0$, then which of the following must be true?

A) $x < -2$
B) $x > -2$
C) $x < 2$
D) $x > 2$
E) $x < 5$

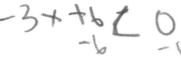

12. Which of the following is equivalent to the inequality $\frac{2x+5}{2} \geq \frac{-(x-1)}{3}$?

A) $x \geq -\frac{8}{13}$
B) $x \geq -\frac{13}{8}$
C) $x \leq -\frac{8}{13}$
D) $x \leq -\frac{13}{8}$
E) $x \geq \frac{13}{8}$

13. For which of the following values is $x^3 \geq x^4$?

A) -2
B) -1
C) 0
D) 2
E) None of the above

14. For which of the following values of x is $-2|x - 3| = 6$?

A) $x = 0$ and $x = 6$
B) $x = 0$ and $x = -6$
C) $x = 6$ and $x = -6$
D) $x = 6$ and $x = 3$
E) There are no solutions to the above equation

15. The number line above is the graph of which of the following inequalities?

A) $1 < x$ and $8 > x$
B) $1 \leq x$ and $8 \leq x$
C) $1 \geq x$ or $8 \leq x$
D) $1 \geq x$ or $8 \geq x$
E) $1 \leq x \leq 8$

ACT Math: Solving and Modeling Systems of Equations

Solving Systems of Equations

- There are three common ways to solve a system of equations: **Substitution**, **Elimination**, and **Graphing**.

- **Substitution** requires you to solve one of the two equations for a variable, then to plug that variable's value or expression into the second equation. This will yield a value for one of the variables. You can use the value in either equation to find the second variable's value. You will use substitution most often:

$$\begin{matrix} 5x - 2y = 12 \\ y - x = 3 \end{matrix} \rightarrow \begin{matrix} 5x - 2y = 12 \\ y = x + 3 \end{matrix} \rightarrow 5x - 2(x+3) = 12 \rightarrow 3x - 6 = 12 \rightarrow x = 6$$

$$y - (6) = 3 \rightarrow y = 9 \rightarrow \text{Solution: } (6, 9)$$

- **Elimination** requires you to multiply one of the two equations by a constant (if necessary), then to add the two equations together to eliminate a variable. Elimination is the fastest method when variables are easily eliminated:

$$\begin{matrix} 5x - 2y = 12 \\ y - x = 3 \end{matrix} \rightarrow \begin{matrix} 5x - 2y = 12 \\ 2y - 2x = 6 \end{matrix} \rightarrow 3x = 18 \rightarrow x = 6$$

$$y - (6) = 3 \rightarrow y = 9 \rightarrow \text{Solution: } (6, 9)$$

- **Graphing** requires you to graph each of the two equations then find the point of intersection of the two lines. Graphing is the most time consuming of the three methods, even with a calculator, and you should avoid using it if possible.

- Sometimes, two equations never intersect. In this situation, the system has no solution. These systems of equations occur when the two lines are parallel, as shown below:

$$3x - 4y = 7 \rightarrow 3x - 4y = 7$$
$$6x = 8y - 15 \rightarrow 3x - 4y = -\frac{15}{2}$$

(We can tell the two lines are parallel because the coefficients for x and y are in the same ratio for both equations, but the constants are different)

- Sometimes, two equations overlap each other. In this situation, the system has an infinite number of solutions. These systems of equations occur when both lines are the same line, as shown below:

$$3x - 2y = 7 \rightarrow 3x - 2y = 7$$
$$0 = 4y - 6x + 14 \rightarrow 3x - 2y = 7$$

(We can tell the two lines overlap because they can be manipulated by multiplication or division to be the exact same equation)

Example 1

At what point do the lines $y = 3x + 8$ and $y = -2x - 7$ intersect?

A) $(1, 3)$
B) $(1, -3)$
C) $(-1, -3)$
D) $(-3, -1)$
E) $(-3, -1)$

Since we're just looking for the point where these two lines intersect, let's try substitution:

$$y = 3x + 8$$
$$y = -2x - 7$$

$$3x + 8 = -2x - 7 \rightarrow 5x = -15 \rightarrow x = -3$$

Now we can substitute our x-value into either of the two equations and solve for y.
$y = -2(-3) - 7 \rightarrow y = -1$. The answer is **E**.

Example 2

The sum of the real numbers x and y is 11. Their difference is 5. What is the value of xy?

A) 3
B) 5
C) 8
D) 24
E) 55

Let's start by coming up with equations to model the situation above:

$$x + y = 11$$
$$x - y = 5$$

Since the y coefficients in both equations are opposites, we can use elimination to solve. First, add both equations together to cancel out the y-values:

$$2x = 16 \rightarrow x = 8$$

Since $x = 8$, y must be 3 ($8 - y = 3 \rightarrow y = 5$). Thus, $xy = (8)(3) = 24$, and our answer is **D**.

PRACTICE EXERCISE

1. The linear equations below are of a system in which $a, b,$ and c are integers greater than 1:
$$ax = by + c$$
$$ax = -by + c$$

   Which of the following describes the graph of at least 1 such system of equations in the standard (x, y) coordinate plane?
   I.   2 intersecting lines
   II. 2 perpendicular lines
   III. 2 parallel lines
   A) I only
   B) II only
   C) III only
   D) I or II only
   E) I, II, or III

2. A rectangle has an area of 30 square feet and a perimeter of 22 feet. What is the longest of the side lengths, in feet, of the rectangle?
   A) 3
   B) 5
   C) 6
   D) 10
   E) 11

3. At what point do the lines $3y = 2x - 4$ and $9y = 5x - 4$ intersect?
   A) $(1, -\frac{2}{3})$
   B) $(2, 0)$
   C) $(3, \frac{2}{3})$
   D) $(4, 8)$
   E) $(8, 4)$

4. If $2x - 3y = 12$ and $5x + 2y = 18$, then $7x - y = ?$
   A) -24
   B) 19
   C) 24
   D) 30
   E) 78

5. If $x = \frac{3-y}{3}$ and $y = 3 - x$, what is the value of x?

   A) -3

   B) 0

   C) 3

   D) 6

   E) 9

6. A food truck operator has two options for meals: hamburger plates for $\$x$ and hot dog plates for $\$y$. On Tuesday, she sold 53 hot dog plates and 27 hamburger plates to bring in $\$534$. On Wednesday, she sold 47 hot dog plates and 36 hamburger plates to bring in $\$570$. What is the price difference between a hamburger plate and a hot dog plate?

   A) $\$2$

   B) $\$4$

   C) $\$6$

   D) $\$8$

   E) $\$14$

7. A gym teacher must separate his 76 students into groups of 3 or 4 students each for exercise drills. If the teacher makes a total of 24 groups, how many of the groups will contain 3 students?

   A) 4

   B) 12

   C) 16

   D) 20

   E) 60

8. If $3(x - y) = -9$ and $2(x + y) = 4$, what is the value of x?

   A) $-\frac{5}{2}$

   B) -1

   C) $-\frac{1}{2}$

   D) $\frac{1}{2}$

   E) $\frac{5}{2}$

9. If the sum of two numbers is 12 and their difference is 7, what is the value of the larger number?

   A) 1

   B) $\frac{5}{2}$

   C) $\frac{7}{2}$

   D) 9

   E) $\frac{19}{2}$

10. Which of the following lines intersects $3x - 2y = 8$ at the point $(4, 2)$?
- A) $2x - 5y = 2$
- B) $3x - 4y = -4$
- C) $5x + y = 22$
- D) $3x - y = 9$
- E) $x + y = -6$

11. If $\frac{a}{2} = \frac{b}{3}$ and $\frac{a}{3} = b + 1$ what is the value of b?
- A) $-\frac{9}{7}$
- B) $-\frac{7}{9}$
- C) $\frac{7}{9}$
- D) $\frac{9}{7}$
- E) 9

12. If $x + 2y \leq 9$ and $x + y = 6$, what is a possible solution, (x, y), to the system?
- A) $(-1, 7)$
- B) $(0, 6)$
- C) $(1, 5)$
- D) $(2, 4)$
- E) $(3, 3)$

13. At what point do the lines $y = \frac{1}{2}x + 3$ and $y = \frac{2}{3}x - 4$ intersect?
- A) $(-42, 24)$
- B) $(-24, 42)$
- C) $(24, 42)$
- D) $(42, 24)$
- E) $(42, -24)$

14. If $3x + y = 2$ and $2x - 4y = 2$, then $-x - 5y = ?$
- A) -5
- B) -3
- C) 0
- D) 3
- E) 5

15. If $x = 6y$ and $2y = -3(2 - x)$, what is the value of $3x$?

A) $-\dfrac{27}{4}$

B) $-\dfrac{9}{4}$

C) $\dfrac{9}{4}$

D) $\dfrac{27}{8}$

E) $\dfrac{27}{4}$

ACT Math: Coordinate Plane Geometry

Graphing Linear Equations

- The general format of a **linear equation** is $y = mx + b$, where m is the slope of the line and b is its y-intercept.
- The **slope**, m, of an equation represents the rate at which the y-values of the equation change as the x-values change.
- A **positive** slope indicates that a line is moving up and to the right, as shown on the left below. A **negative** slope indicates that a line is moving down and to the right, as shown on the right below:

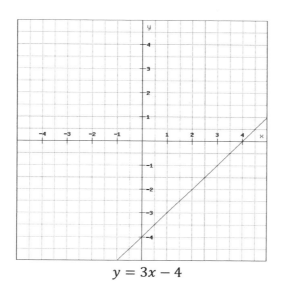

$$y = 3x - 4$$

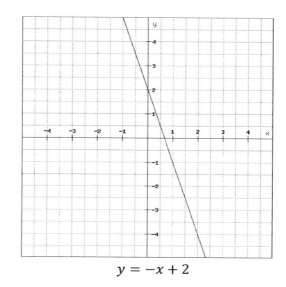

$$y = -x + 2$$

- Given two points, (x_1, y_1) and (x_2, y_2), of a linear equation, the slope, or change in rise divided by change in run, of the equation can be found by the equation $m = \frac{\text{rise}}{\text{run}} = \frac{y_2 - y_1}{x_2 - x_1}$.
- A **horizontal** line has a slope of 0. A **vertical** line has an undefined slope.
- If two lines have the same slope, they are **parallel**. For example, the lines $y = 4x - 2$ and $y = 4x + 5$ are parallel as they both have slopes of 4.
- If two lines have slopes that are negative reciprocals of each other, they are **perpendicular**. For example, the lines $y = 2x - 3$ and $y = -\frac{1}{2}x + 1$ are perpendicular as the slopes of 2 and $-\frac{1}{2}$ are negative reciprocals of each other.

- The **y-intercept**, b, of an equation represents the initial point of the equation: the value of y when x equals 0. The graph on the left above has a y-intercept of -4, while the graph on the right has a y-intercept of 2.
- You can obtain the equation of a linear graph when you have either two of the points that lie on that line or one of the points and the line's y-intercept.

- Use the equation $y = mx + b$, where m is the slope of the linear equation and b is its y-intercept, when you are given both the slope and the y-intercept of the line:

    The line with slope 3 and and y-intercept of 4 has the equation $y = 3x + 4$.

- Use the equation $y - y_1 = m(x - x_1)$ when you are given both the slope and a single point on the line:

    The line with slope 8 that passes through the point $(2, -1)$ has the equation:

    $$y - (-1) = 8(x - 2) \rightarrow y + 1 = 8x - 16 \rightarrow y = 8x - 17$$

Example 1

What is the slope of a line passing through $(-5, 2)$ and $(6, 7)$ in the standard (x, y) coordinate plane?

A) 9

B) 5

C) -5

D) $\dfrac{5}{11}$

E) $-\dfrac{5}{11}$

Since we're just looking for the slope between these two points, let's use the slope formula:

$$m = \frac{\text{rise}}{\text{run}} = \frac{y_2 - y_1}{x_2 - x_1} = \frac{7 - 2}{6 - (-5)} = \frac{5}{11}$$

The answer is **D**.

Midpoint and Distance Formulas

- The **midpoint** between two points, (x_1, y_1) and (x_2, y_2), can be found by using the midpoint formula $\left(\dfrac{x_1 + x_2}{2}, \dfrac{y_1 + y_2}{2}\right)$:

    The midpoint of $(3, 4)$ and $(2, 5)$ is $(2.5, 4.5)$

- The **distance** between two points, (x_1, y_1) and (x_2, y_2), can be found by using the distance formula $d = \sqrt{(x_2 - x_1)^2 + (y_2 - y_1)^2}$:

    The distance between $(3, 4)$ and $(2, 5)$ is $d = \sqrt{(3 - 2)^2 + (4 - 5)^2} = \sqrt{1 + 1} = \sqrt{2}$

Since we're given the midpoint and one of the two endpoints, we can use the midpoint formula to find the other endpoint:

$$x_{midpoint} = \frac{x_1 + x_2}{2} \rightarrow 5 = \frac{7 + x_2}{2} \rightarrow x_2 = 3$$

$$y_{midpoint} = \frac{y_1 + y_2}{2} \rightarrow 4 = \frac{3 + y_2}{2} \rightarrow y_2 = 5$$

So, the answer must be **D**.

Graphing Linear Inequalities

- Graphing linear inequalities is similar to graphing linear equations, except you must shade all areas of the graph that satisfy the given inequality.
- When graphing inequalities with a < or > sign, use a dashed line.
- When graphing inequalities with a ≤ or ≥ sign, use a solid line.
- The easiest way to check which part of the graph to shade involves picking a point that does not lie on the line of the inequality, then plugging that point into the inequality. If the point makes the inequality true, shade the portion of the graph that contains that point. If the point makes the inequality false, shade the other portion of the graph:

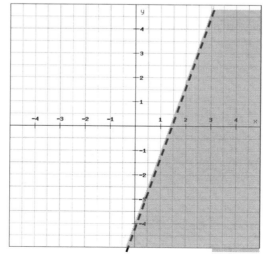

$y < 3x - 4$

Check point $(0, 0)$:
$$0 < 3(0) - 4$$
$$0 < -4 \rightarrow \text{false}$$
Shade the portion of the graph that does not contain $(0, 0)$.

Graphing Systems of Linear Equations or Inequalities

- To graph a system of linear equations, graph both lines. The point of intersection of the two graphs is the solution to the system of equations:

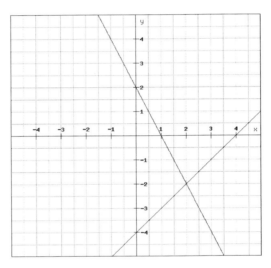

$$y = x - 4$$
$$y = -2x + 2$$

The solution to the system of equations above is $(2, -2)$.

- To graph a system of linear inequalities, graph both inequalities and determine which areas of the graph should be shaded for each inequality. The points in the area that is shaded by both inequalities (overlap) are all of the solutions to the system of linear inequalities.

PRACTICE EXERCISE

1. What are the quadrants of the standard (x, y) coordinate plane below that contains points on the graph of the equation $3x - 5y = 12$?

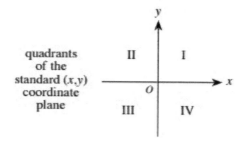

A) I and III only
B) I, II, and III only
C) I, II, and IV only
D) I, III, and IV only
E) II, III, and IV only

2. The coordinates of the endpoints of the line segment of XY, in the standard (x, y) coordinate plane, are $(3, 18)$ and $(10, -2)$. What is the y-coordinate of the midpoint of segment XY?
A) 6.5
B) 8
C) 10
D) 13
E) 16

3. What is the length of the line segment with endpoints $(5, 7)$ and $(2, 11)$?
A) 3
B) 4
C) 5
D) 6
E) 7

4. The line $y = -\frac{2}{7}x - 2$ intersects another line perpendicular to it in the (x, y) coordinate plane at the point $(5, 10)$. What is the y-intercept of the second line?
A) $-\frac{15}{2}$
B) 3
C) 5
D) $\frac{25}{3}$
E) $\frac{35}{3}$

5. Which of the following is the slope of a line parallel to the line $y = -\frac{2}{7}x - 2$ in the standard (x, y) coordinate plane?

A) $-\frac{7}{2}$

B) -2

C) $-\frac{2}{7}$

D) $\frac{2}{7}$

E) $\frac{7}{2}$

6. If point J has a non-zero x-coordinate and a non-zero y-coordinate and the coordinates have the same signs, then point J *must* be located in which of the 4 quadrants labeled below?

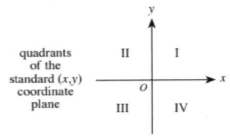

A) II only

B) III only

C) I or III only

D) II or III only

E) II or IV only

7. The slope of the line with equation $y = ax + b$ is less than the slope of the line with equation $y = cx + d$. Which of the following statements must be true about the relationship between a and c?

A) $a > c$

B) $a < c$

C) $a \geq c$

D) $a \leq c$

E) $a > 0 > c$

8. In the standard (x, y) coordinate plane, the midpoint of line segment CD is $(3, 7)$ and C is located at $(1, 5)$. If (a, b) are the coordinates of D, what is the value of ab?

A) -3

B) 5

C) 9

D) 15

E) 45

9. The point $(3, 4)$ exists in the standard (x, y) coordinate plane. Which of the following is another point on the line through the point $(3, 4)$ with a slope of $-\frac{1}{2}$?
   A) $(1, 8)$
   B) $(2, 6)$
   C) $(4, 3)$
   D) $(5, 3)$
   E) $(6, 7)$

10. Which of the following lines is perpendicular to $5x - 3y = 6$?
    A) $y = \frac{3}{5}x - 2$
    B) $y = -\frac{3}{5}x + 2$
    C) $y = \frac{5}{3}x - 2$
    D) $y = -\frac{5}{3}x + 2$
    E) $y = \frac{1}{3}x - 2$

11. What is the perimeter of the triangle in the coordinate plane formed by the points $(3, 4)$, $(9, 4)$, and $(6, 8)$?
    A) 10
    B) 12
    C) 14
    D) 16
    E) 18

12. What is the equation of the line that passes through the point $(3, 6)$ in the standard (x, y) coordinate plane and is parallel to the a with a slope of $\frac{3}{2}$?
    A) $y = -\frac{3}{2}x + \frac{21}{2}$
    B) $y = -\frac{2}{3}x + 8$
    C) $y = \frac{2}{3}x + 4$
    D) $y = \frac{3}{2}x + \frac{3}{2}$
    E) $y = \frac{3}{2}x - 6$

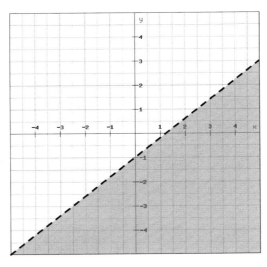

13. What is the equation of the inequality graphed in the coordinate plane above?

   A) $y > \frac{4}{5}x - 1$

   B) $y < \frac{4}{5}x - 1$

   C) $y > -\frac{4}{5}x - 1$

   D) $y > -\frac{4}{5}x - 1$

   E) $y > -\frac{4}{5}x + 1$

14. At how many points do the lines $y + 3x = -2$, $6x + 2y = 4$, and $3y + 9x = 5$ intersect?

   A) 0

   B) 1

   C) 2

   D) 3

   E) 4

15. What is the slope of the line that passes through the points $\left(-\frac{1}{2}, \frac{1}{2}\right)$ and $\left(\frac{1}{2}, \frac{1}{2}\right)$ in the standard (x, y) coordinate plane?

   A) -2

   B) -1

   C) 0

   D) 1

   E) The slope is undefined.

ACT Math: Quadratics and Polynomials

Quadratic Formula

- A **polynomial** is a **quadratic** if its highest-powered term is x^2.
- A quadratic expression, $ax^2 + bx + c = 0$, can be solved by using the quadratic formula $x = \frac{-b \pm \sqrt{b^2 - 4ac}}{2a}$:

$$2x^2 + 5x - 4 = 0$$
$$x = \frac{-5 \pm \sqrt{5^2 - 4(2)(-4)}}{2(2)}$$
$$x = \frac{-5 \pm \sqrt{25 + 32}}{4}$$
$$x = \frac{-5 \pm \sqrt{57}}{4}$$

- Some quadratic expressions can be solved by factoring, the opposite of FOILing, or by completing the square. Both of these methods are very situational and cannot be used on every problem. However, reviewing these methods will help you be successful when taking the ACT. However, every quadratic problem on the ACT can be solved with the quadratic formula above.

Example 1

What values of x are solutions for $x^2 + 2x = 8$?

A) -4 and 2
B) -2 and 0
C) -2 and 4
D) 0 and 2
E) 6 and 8

Let's use the quadratic formula to solve this question: $x = \frac{-b \pm \sqrt{b^2 - 4ac}}{2a}$

$$x^2 + 2x = 8 \rightarrow x^2 + 2x - 8 = 0$$

$$x = \frac{-2 \pm \sqrt{2^2 - 4(1)(-8)}}{2(1)}$$
$$x = \frac{-2 \pm \sqrt{4 + 32}}{2}$$
$$x = \frac{-2 \pm \sqrt{36}}{2}$$
$$x = \frac{-2 + 6}{2}, \frac{-2 - 6}{2}$$
$$x = 2, -4$$

The answer is **A**.

Solving Quadratic Expressions

- Solving quadratic expressions with the quadratic equation can be extremely time-consuming, even if it does always produce the correct answer. A quicker way to solve quadratics is by applying the opposite of FOILing – **factoring**. The goal of factoring is to turn a quadratic into the product of two binomials which can be easily solved. For example, $x^2 + 7x + 12 = 0$ can be factored as $(x + 3)(x + 4) = 0$.

- Given the quadratic $ax^2 + bx + c$, where $a = 1$, look for factors of c that add up to b:

$$x^2 + 5x + 6 = 0$$

First, list out all of the factor pairs that produce 6:

$$2 \times 3 = 6 \qquad 1 \times 6 = 6$$
$$-2 \times -3 = 6 \qquad -1 \times -6 = 6$$

Which pair adds up to 5? 2 and 3. So, we can turn $x^2 + 5x + 6 = 0$ into $(x + 2)(x + 3) = 0$.

- Now that we've turned our quadratic into the product of two binomials, it is much easier to solve:

$$(x + 2)(x + 3) = 0$$
$$x + 2 = 0 \qquad x + 3 = 0$$
$$x = -2 \qquad x = -3$$

- Let's look at Example 1 again and solve it by factoring:

Example 1

What values of x are solutions for $x^2 + 2x = 8$?

A) -4 and 2
B) -2 and 0
C) -2 and 4
D) 0 and 2
E) 6 and 8

First, we'll start by setting the quadratic equal to 0:

$$x^2 + 2x = 8 \rightarrow x^2 + 2x - 8 = 0$$

Now we want to find a factor pair of -8 that sums to 2. Let's list all of the factor pairs:

$$2 \times -4 = -8 \qquad -1 \times 8 = -8$$
$$-2 \times 4 = -8 \qquad 1 \times -8 = -8$$

Which pair adds up to 2? -2 and 4. So, we can turn $x^2 + 2x - 8 = 0$ into $(x - 2)(x + 4) = 0$. Let's solve:

$$(x - 2)(x + 4) = 0$$
$$x - 2 = 0 \qquad x + 4 = 0$$
$$x = 2 \qquad x = -4$$

The answer is still **A**.

Graphing Quadratic Equations

- The graphs of quadratic functions are known as **parabolas**. They are symmetric – they increase and then decrease, or decrease and then increase, as shown below:

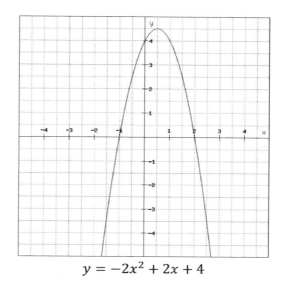

$$y = -2x^2 + 2x + 4$$

- The x-coordinate of the vertex of a quadratic with equation $y = ax^2 + bx + c$ is located at $x = -\frac{b}{2a}$. The y-coordinate can be found by plugging the value for x into the equation to find y. In the graph above, the vertex is at $(\frac{1}{2}, \frac{9}{2})$.

- The **zeros** or **roots** of a quadratic function are the places where the graph of the quadratic crosses the x-axis. Most quadratics will have 2 roots, while others will have 1 or 0. A quick way to determine the number of roots of a quadratic is to analyze $b^2 - 4ac$ (the part of the quadratic formula that is under the square root). If this value is positive, the quadratic will have 2 roots, if it is 0, the quadratic will have 1 root, and if it is negative, the quadratic will have 0 roots.

- The roots of the quadratic above are located at $(-1, 0)$ and $(2, 0)$. Notice also that the vertex of the quadratic is located halfway between the roots. This is always true.

Properties of the Graphs of Polynomials

- The **degree** of a polynomial refers to the exponent of its highest-powered term.
- The **leading coefficient** of a polynomial refers to the coefficient in front of its highest-powered term:

$$y = -7x^5 + 2x^2 - 6$$

The degree of the above polynomial is 5 while its leading coefficient is -7.

- To match the sketch of a graph to a polynomial, remember these key points:
    - The **domain** of a polynomial is all of the values of x that the polynomial can take on. For all polynomials, the domain will be all real numbers.
    - The **range** of a polynomial is all of the values of y that the polynomial can take on. For polynomials of odd degree, the range will be all real numbers. For polynomials of even degree, the range will have a maximum or minimum value as shown in the graphs below.
    - Every zero of a polynomial is a place where its graph crosses the x-axis. Polynomials can have a number of zeroes up to their degrees.

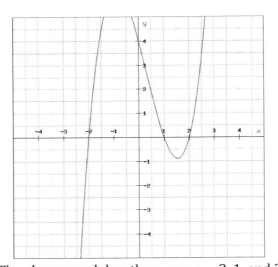

The above graph has three zeros: -2, 1, and 2

- Polynomials of even degree with a positive leading coefficient have increasing end behavior on both ends, while those of even degree with a negative leading coefficient have decreasing end behavior on both ends.

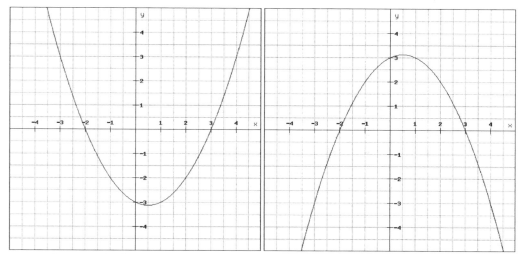

Polynomial of Even Degree and
Positive Leading Coefficient

Polynomial of Even Degree and
Negative Leading Coefficient

- Polynomials of odd degree and a positive leading coefficient have increasing end behavior as x increases (gets closer to ∞) and decreasing end behavior as x decreases (gets closer to $-\infty$).
- Polynomials of odd degree and a negative leading coefficient have decreasing end behavior as x increases (gets closer to ∞) and increasing end behavior as x decreases (gets closer to $-\infty$).

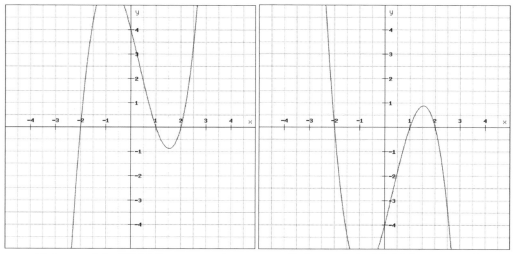

Polynomial of Odd Degree and
Positive Leading Coefficient

Polynomial of Odd Degree and
Negative Leading Coefficient

- The maximum (or minimum) of a polynomial's graph in a certain range is the highest (or lowest) y-value that is on that graph within that range.

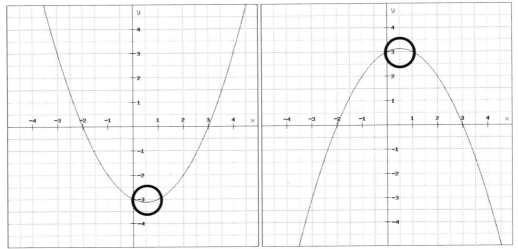

| Minimum Value | Maximum Value |

Special Factoring

- The following polynomial patterns occur frequently on the ACT. Memorizing these patterns will help you save time on the exam:

- $a^2 - b^2 = (a - b)(a + b)$:

$$4x^2 - 16 = (2x - 4)(2x + 4)$$

- $a^2 \pm 2ab + b^2 = (a \pm b)^2$:

$$9x^2 - 6x + 4 = (3x - 2)^2$$

- $a^3 - b^3 = (a - b)(a^2 + ab + b^2)$:

$$x^3 - 8 = (x - 2)(x^2 + 2x + 4)$$

- $a^3 + b^3 = (a + b)(a^2 - ab + b^2)$:

$$8x^3 + 27 = (2x + 3)(4x^2 - 6x + 9)$$

PRACTICE EXERCISE

1. Which of the following mathematical expressions is equivalent to the verbal expression "A number, x, squared is 12 more than the product of 6 and x"?
   A) $2x = 12 + 6x$
   B) $2x = 12x + 6x$
   C) $x^2 = 12 - 6x$
   D) $x^2 = 12 + x^6$
   E) $x^2 = 12 + 6x$

2. The graph of $y = -3x^2 + 6$ passes through $(-1, -c)$ in the standard (x, y) coordinate plane. What is the value of c?
   A) -4
   B) -3
   C) 0
   D) 3
   E) 4

3. In the equation $x^2 + bx + c = 0$, b and c are integers. The *only* possible value for x is -5. What is the value of b?
   A) -25
   B) -10
   C) 0
   D) 10
   E) 25

4. What values of x are solutions to the equation $4x^2 - 6x = 0$?
   A) $-\frac{3}{2}$ only
   B) 0 only
   C) $\frac{3}{2}$ only
   D) 0 and $-\frac{3}{2}$
   E) 0 and $\frac{3}{2}$

5. Which of the following is a factored form of the expression $6x^2 + 7x - 20$?
   A) $(3x - 10)(2x + 2)$
   B) $(3x - 2)(2x + 10)$
   C) $(3x - 5)(2x + 4)$
   D) $(3x - 4)(2x + 5)$
   E) $(6x - 4)(x + 5)$

6. When $y = -x^2$, which of the following expressions is always equivalent to $-y$?
   A) $(-x)^2$
   B) $-(-x)^2$
   C) $-x$
   D) x
   E) x^{-2}

7. Given the function $f(x) = 3x^2 - 8x$, for what value or values of x does $f(x) = -5$?
   A) 115 only
   B) $\frac{5}{3}$ only
   C) 1 or $\frac{5}{3}$
   D) 1 or $-\frac{5}{3}$
   E) -1 or $\frac{5}{3}$

8. If $2x^2 - 9 = -3x$, what are the possible values of x?
   A) -3 only
   B) $-\frac{3}{2}$ only
   C) $\frac{3}{2}$ only
   D) -3 or $\frac{3}{2}$
   E) -3 or $-\frac{3}{2}$

9. What is the y-coordinate of the vertex of the parabola represented by the equation $y = x^2 - 3x - 4$?
   A) $-\frac{25}{4}$
   B) $\frac{3}{2}$
   C) 0
   D) $\frac{3}{2}$
   E) $\frac{25}{4}$

10. Which of the following quadratics has no roots?
    A) $y = 5x^2 - 4x - 9$
    B) $y = 2x^2 - 4x + 2$
    C) $y = 4x^2 - 4x + 12$
    D) $y = 3x^2 - 4x - 9$
    E) $y = x^2 + 7x + 2$

11. What are the roots of the polynomial $y = x^3 - 1$?

    A) 1 only

    B) 0 and 1

    C) 0 and -1

    D) 1 and -1

    E) $-1, 0,$ and 1

12. What is the maximum value of the parabola $y = -\frac{1}{2}x^2 + 2$?

    A) -2

    B) $-\frac{1}{2}$

    C) 0

    D) 1

    E) 2

13. What is the positive difference between the degree and the leading coefficient of the polynomial $y = -\frac{1}{2}x^3 - 3x^2 - 4$?

    A) -2.5

    B) -1.5

    C) 1.5

    D) 2.5

    E) 3.5

14. At what points does the line $y = 2$ intersect $y = x^2 + 1$?

    A) $(5, 2)$ only

    B) $(2, 5)$ only

    C) $(1, 2)$ only

    D) $(-1, 2)$ and $(1, 2)$

    E) $(-2, 5)$ and $(2, 5)$

15. How many roots does the polynomial $y = (x^2 - 1)^2$ have?

    A) 0

    B) 1

    C) 2

    D) 3

    E) 4

ACT Math: Radical Expressions and Complex Numbers

Radical and Exponent Expressions

- Sometimes, you will have to solve an equation that contains radicals or exponents. As with solving any other equation, solving these types of equations requires doing the opposite of what is being done to the variable.
- So, if you need to get rid of an exponent, for example $x^3 + 4 = -23$, take the cube root of both sides after isolating the x^3:

$$x^3 + 4 = -23 \rightarrow x^3 = -27 \rightarrow \sqrt[3]{x^3} = \sqrt[3]{-27} \rightarrow x = -3$$

- If you need to get rid of a radical, raise both sides to that power after isolating the radical. So, when solving the equation $\sqrt{x-2} = \frac{1}{2}$, your first step would be to square both sides:

$$\sqrt{x-2} = \frac{1}{2} \rightarrow \left(\sqrt{x-2}\right)^2 = \left(\frac{1}{2}\right)^2 \rightarrow x - 2 = \frac{1}{4} \rightarrow x = \frac{9}{4}$$

- Whenever you obtain a final solution for an equation featuring radicals or exponents, always plug your answer back into the initial expression to make sure it works. If it does not check out, it is an **extraneous solution**.

Example 1

If $x + 3 = \sqrt{-x - 3}$, then $x = ?$

A) -4 only
B) -3 only
C) 4 only
D) -4 and -3
E) 4 and -3

Since one side of the equation has a square root, let's square both sides and then simplify:

$$x + 3 = \sqrt{-x - 3}$$
$$(x + 3)^2 = \left(\sqrt{-x - 3}\right)^2$$
$$x^2 + 6x + 9 = -x - 3$$
$$x^2 + 7x + 12 = 0$$

Now that we've turned our original equation into a quadratic, we must factor and solve:

$$x^2 + 7x + 12 = 0$$
$$(x + 4)(x + 3) = 0$$
$$x + 4 = 0 \quad x + 3 = 0$$
$$x = -4 \quad\quad x = -3$$

Be sure to plug both answers into the original equation to make sure they work:

$$x + 3 = \sqrt{-x - 3} \rightarrow -4 + 3 = \sqrt{-(-4) - 3} \rightarrow -1 = \sqrt{1} \rightarrow -1 = \pm 1$$
$$x + 3 = \sqrt{-x - 3} \rightarrow -3 + 3 = \sqrt{-(-3) - 3} \rightarrow 0 = \sqrt{0} \rightarrow 0 = 0$$

The answer is **D**.

Complex Numbers

- The **imaginary number**, i, is equivalent to $\sqrt{-1}$. Thus, $i^2 = -1$, $i^3 = -i$, and $i^4 = 1$.
- To quickly simplify an imaginary number raised to an integer power, use long division to divide the exponent by 4. The imaginary number's power can be reduced to the remainder that results from that long division. If the remainder is 0, the imaginary number's power should be reduced to $i^4 = 1$. For example, $i^{27} = i^3 = -i$ and $i^{16} = i^4 = 1$.
- A **complex number** is a number in the form $a + bi$; it contains both real (a) and imaginary numbers (bi).
- Adding and subtracting complex numbers is similar to adding and subtracting variables. You can only add (or subtract) i terms to other i terms. So, $(3 - 2i) - (2 + 8i) \rightarrow 1 - 10i$.
- Multiplying complex numbers is similar to multiplying variables, as well. However, be sure to simplify after you get your answer. So, $3i(9 - 2i) \rightarrow 27i - 6i^2 \rightarrow 27i - 6(-1) \rightarrow 27i + 6$.
- Sometimes, you will see a complex number divided by another complex number. To simplify these, you must multiply both the numerator and the denominator by the **conjugate** of the denominator.
- To find the conjugate of the denominator, change the sign of the bi term. So, the conjugate of $3 - 2i$ is $3 + 2i$. Then, multiply and simplify as you normally would.

Example 2

For $i^2 = -1$, $(4 + i)^2 = ?$

A) 15
B) 17
C) $15 + 4i$
D) $15 + 8i$
E) $16 + 4i$

First, we'll start off by FOILing our expression:

$$(4 + i)^2 = 16 + 8i + i^2$$

Since we know that $i^2 = -1$, we can substitute that into our FOILed expression:

$$16 + 8i + i^2 = 16 + 8i - 1 = 15 + 8i$$

The answer is **D**.

PRACTICE EXERCISE

1. If $x^5 - 7 = 25$ then $2x = ?$
   A) 1
   B) 2
   C) 4
   D) 12
   E) 24

2. If $i^2 = -1$, then i^{12} is equivalent to which of the following?
   A) $-i$
   B) i
   C) i^2
   D) i^3
   E) i^4

3. If $\sqrt{3x + 2} = 2$ then $\frac{3x}{2} = ?$
   A) 1
   B) $\frac{3}{2}$
   C) 2
   D) $\frac{5}{2}$
   E) 6

4. For $i^2 = -1$, $5 - (2i + 3) = ?$
   A) $2 + 2i$
   B) $2 - 2i$
   C) $8 + 2i$
   D) $8 - 2i$
   E) $-30i$

5. The square root of a number is 20 less than the number itself. Which of the following is a possible value of the number?
   A) 4
   B) 5
   C) 16
   D) 20
   E) 400

6. If $i^2 = -1$, which of the following expressions is always equivalent to $\frac{3}{i-5}$?

A) $\frac{3i-15}{-24}$

B) $\frac{3i+15}{-24}$

C) $\frac{3i+15}{-26}$

D) $\frac{3i-15}{-26}$

E) $\frac{3i-5}{-26}$

7. For what values of x does $\sqrt{x-5} = \sqrt{x+5}$?

A) -5 only

B) 0 only

C) 5 only

D) -5 or 5

E) There are no values of x that satisfy this equation.

8. If $16x^4 = 81$, what are the possible values of x?

A) $-\frac{3}{2}$ only

B) $-\frac{5}{4}$ only

C) $\frac{3}{2}$ only

D) $-\frac{3}{2}$ or $\frac{3}{2}$

E) $-\frac{5}{4}$ or $\frac{5}{4}$

9. For $i^2 = -1$, $(3 - 5i)(5 + 2i) = ?$

A) $5 - 19i$

B) $25 - 19i$

C) $19i - 5$

D) $19i - 25$

E) 25

10. If $x^2 - 5 > 20$, what are the possible values of x?

A) $x > 5$

B) $x < -5$

C) $-5 < x < 5$

D) $x > 5$ or $x > -5$

E) $x > 5$ or $x < -5$

11. If $x^3 = -27$ then $x^2 = ?$
   A) -9
   B) -3
   C) 3
   D) 9
   E) 729

12. If $i^2 = -1$, then i^{53} is equivalent to which of the following?
   A) $-i$
   B) i
   C) i^2
   D) i^3
   E) i^4

13. If $\sqrt{x-6} = x$ then $x = ?$
   A) -3
   B) -2
   C) 3
   D) -2 or 3
   E) No solutions exist.

14. For $i^2 = -1$, $(3i - 5) - (2i + 2) = ?$
   A) $-i - 7$
   B) $i - 7$
   C) $-i + 7$
   D) $i + 7$
   E) $i - 3$

15. The square root of a number is equal to the cube root of the same number. What are the possible values of the number?
   A) -1 only
   B) 0 only
   C) 1 only
   D) 0 or 1 only
   E) -1 or 0 only

ACT Math: Rational Expressions

Operations on Rational Expressions

- Multiplying rational expressions does not require a common denominator. Just multiply across the numerators and denominators. For all operations involving rational functions, factor out each term as much as possible before attempting to multiply (factors in the numerator and denominator may cancel):

$$\frac{x+2}{x} \times \frac{4x+12}{2x+4} \rightarrow \frac{x+2}{x} \times \frac{4(x+3)}{2(x+2)}$$

Here, we have a couple of places we can simplify. Since we have the same term, $x + 2$, in the numerator and the denominator, we can eliminate them. We can also divide the 4 by 2:

$$\frac{\cancel{x+2}}{x} \times \frac{4(x+3)}{2(\cancel{x+2})} \rightarrow \frac{4(x+3)}{2x} \rightarrow \frac{2(x+3)}{x} \rightarrow \frac{2x+6}{x}$$

- Dividing rational expressions requires the same process as dividing fractions does. We must change the division sign to a multiplication sign and take the reciprocal of the second rational expression. Then, follow the rules of multiplying rational expressions:

$$\frac{3x-1}{x+2} \div \frac{1-3x}{x+4} \rightarrow \frac{3x-1}{x+2} \times \frac{x+4}{1-3x} \rightarrow \frac{\cancel{3x-1}}{x+2} \times \frac{x+4}{-1(\cancel{3x-1})} \rightarrow \frac{x+4}{-x-2}$$

- Adding and subtracting rational expressions is similar to adding and subtracting fractions; you can only do so when you have a common denominator:

$$\frac{1}{x} + \frac{3}{x+1} \rightarrow \frac{1}{x}\left(\frac{x+1}{x+1}\right) + \frac{3}{x+1}\left(\frac{x}{x}\right) \rightarrow \frac{x+1}{x^2+x} + \frac{3x}{x^2+x} \rightarrow \frac{4x+1}{x^2+x}$$

Example 1

If $\dfrac{A}{30} + \dfrac{B}{105} = \dfrac{7A+2B}{x}$, and A, B, and x are integers greater than 1, then what must x equal?

A) 9
B) 135
C) 210
D) 630
E) 3,150

Since we are adding two rational functions, we need to find a common denominator:

$$\frac{A}{30} + \frac{B}{105} = \frac{7A+2B}{x} \rightarrow \frac{7A}{210} + \frac{2B}{210} = \frac{7A+2B}{x} \rightarrow \frac{7A+2B}{210} = \frac{7A+2B}{x}$$

At this point, we can see that $x = 210$. The answer must be **C**.

Solving Equations with Rational Expressions

- For polynomials and rational expressions represented as fractions, the domain sometimes does not consist of all real numbers.
- To find the values that do not exist in the domain of a rational function, set each of the terms in the denominators equal to 0, then solve. The values the variable yields cannot be included in the domain. Also, these excluded values can never be the solution to an equation with rational functions since such values result in denominators of 0.
- Solving equations with rational functions generally involves using the operations discussed above to simplify the expression. Let's look at a sample:

$$\frac{1}{x} + \frac{2}{x+1} = \frac{3}{x^2+x}$$

First, let's find the excluded values:

$$
\begin{array}{ccc}
x = 0 & x + 1 = 0 & x^2 + x = 0 \\
x = 0 & x = -1 & x(x + 1) = 0 \\
x = 0 & x + 1 = 0 & x = 0, -1
\end{array}
$$

Neither of these two values will be solutions to the original equation above. Next, we'll get a common denominator:

$$\frac{1}{x}\left(\frac{x+1}{x+1}\right) + \frac{2}{x+1} \times \left(\frac{x}{x}\right) = \frac{3}{x^2+x}$$

$$\frac{x+1}{x^2+x} + \frac{2x}{x^2+x} = \frac{3}{x^2+x}$$

$$\frac{3x+1}{x^2+x} = \frac{3}{x^2+x}$$

At this point, we can multiply each side of the equation by the denominator. Then we can solve:

$$\left(\frac{3x+1}{x^2+x}\right) \times (x^2+x) = \frac{3}{x^2+x} \times (x^2+x)$$

$$3x + 1 = 3$$

$$3x = 2$$

$$x = \frac{2}{3}$$

Always be sure that the solution(s) do not include your excluded values!

Example 2

For all x in the domain of the function $\frac{x+1}{x^3-x}$, this function is equivalent to:

A) $\frac{1}{x^2} - \frac{1}{x^3}$

B) $\frac{1}{x^3} - \frac{1}{x}$

C) $\frac{1}{x^2-1}$

D) $\frac{1}{x^2-x}$

E) $\frac{1}{x^3}$

Let's start off by finding the domain of the function above. Set the denominator equal to zero and solve:

$$x^3 - x = 0$$
$$x(x^2 - 1) = 0$$
$$x(x + 1)(x - 1) = 0$$
$$x = 0 \quad x + 1 = 0 \quad x - 1 = 0$$
$$x = 0, -1, 1$$

The two functions should be identical everywhere except these three points.
Next, we should simplify our initial rational function:

$$\frac{x+1}{x^3-x} \rightarrow \frac{\cancel{x+1}}{x(\cancel{x+1})(x-1)} \rightarrow \frac{1}{x(x-1)} \rightarrow \frac{1}{x^2-x}$$

You can graph both of these equations in your graphing calculator to verify that they are identical at all other points except those listed above. Since they are, the answer is **D**.

PRACTICE EXERCISE

1. For what value(s) of x does $\frac{3}{x^2-9} = 0$?

   A) -3

   B) 0

   C) 3

   D) -3 or 3

   E) No values of x satisfy the equation above.

2. What is the domain of the function $f(x) = \frac{x-3}{x^3-27}$?

   A) All real numbers except 3

   B) All real numbers except 3 and -3

   C) All real numbers except 3 and 27

   D) All real numbers except -3, 3, and 27

   E) All real numbers

3. For all x in the domain of the function $f(x) = \frac{x-2}{x-5} + \frac{x+5}{x+2}$, this function is equivalent to:

   A) -2

   B) $\frac{2x+3}{2x-3}$

   C) $\frac{31}{-3x-10}$

   D) $\frac{2x^2-29}{x^2-3x-10}$

   E) $\frac{2x^2+29}{x^2-3x-10}$

4. For what values of x is $\frac{1}{x} - \frac{1}{2x} = x$?

   A) $-\sqrt{2}$

   B) $-\frac{\sqrt{2}}{2}$

   C) $\frac{\sqrt{2}}{2}$

   D) $-\frac{\sqrt{2}}{2}$ or $\frac{\sqrt{2}}{2}$

   E) $-\sqrt{2}$ or $\sqrt{2}$

5. For all x in the domain of the function $f(x) = \frac{2-x}{x^2-9} \div \frac{x-2}{3-x}$, this function is equivalent to:

   A) $x - 3$

   B) $3 - x$

   C) $-\frac{1}{x+3}$

   D) $\frac{1}{x-3}$

   E) $\frac{1}{x+3}$

6. For what values of x does $x + 1 = \frac{30}{x}$?

   A) -6

   B) -5

   C) 5

   D) 5 or -6

   E) -5 or 6

7. What is the domain of the function $f(x) = \frac{3-x}{\sqrt{x-3}}$?

   A) All real numbers greater than -3

   B) All real numbers greater than 3

   C) All real numbers greater than or equal to -3

   D) All real numbers greater than or equal to 3

   E) All real numbers except 3

8. For what values of x does $\frac{3}{x} = \frac{2}{x+3}$?

   A) -9

   B) -3

   C) 0

   D) 3

   E) 9

9. For what values of x does $\frac{-5}{x^2} + \frac{6}{x} = 1$?

   A) -5

   B) 1

   C) 5

   D) -5 or 1

   E) 1 or 5

10. If $\frac{C}{15} + \frac{D}{75} = \frac{5C+D}{3x}$, and C, D, and x are integers greater than 1, then what must x equal?

    A) 5

    B) 15

    C) 25

    D) 225

    E) 375

11. For what values of x does $\frac{3}{2x} = \frac{1}{x-5}$?

    A) -5

    B) 10

    C) 15

    D) 30

    E) 45

12. What is the domain of the function $f(x) = \frac{x+5}{x^2+5x}$?

   A) All real numbers except 0
   B) All real numbers except 0 and -5
   C) All real numbers except 0 and 5
   D) All real numbers except 0, 5, and -5
   E) All real numbers

13. For all x in the domain of the function $f(x) = \frac{A}{x+1} + \frac{B}{x}$, this function is equivalent to:

   A) $\frac{Ax+Bx}{x^2+x}$
   B) $\frac{ABx+B}{x^2+x}$
   C) $\frac{ABx+AB}{x^2+x}$
   D) $\frac{Ax+Bx+B}{x^2+x}$
   E) $\frac{AB}{x^2+x}$

14. For what values of x is $\frac{1}{x} + \frac{1}{2x} = 0$?

   A) -2
   B) 0
   C) 2
   D) -2 or 2
   E) No values of x satisfy the equation above.

15. For all x in the domain of the function $f(x) = \frac{x^2-3x+2}{x+1} \div \frac{x-2}{x-1}$, this function is equivalent to:

   A) $x - 1$
   B) $x + 1$
   C) $\frac{(x-1)^2}{x+1}$
   D) $\frac{(x+1)^2}{x-1}$
   E) $\frac{(x-1)^2}{1-x}$

ACT Math: Exponential and Logarithmic Expressions

Exponential Functions

- **Exponential functions** usually model situations that involve continuous increases or decreases over time, such as a changing population or the amount of money in a bank account that is accruing interest.
- Exponential functions are typically of the form $f(x) = a \cdot b^x$, where b is a positive constant not equal to 1. The variable a refers to a starting amount, b refers to the rate of increase or decrease, and x refers to the amount of time elapsed:

    For example, the population, $P(x)$, of a species of turtle increases by a factor of 1.05 for every year that has passed since the year 2000. If the population of the turtle in the year 2000 as 150,000 animals, its population in 2010 would be: $P(x) = 150,000 \cdot (1.05)^{10}$

- If the value of b is greater than 1, then the exponential function is increasing. If b is between 0 and 1, the function is decreasing:

    In the turtle population example above, b is greater than 1 since the turtle population is increasing.

Example 1

A group of cells grows in number as described by the equation $y = 16(2)^t$, where t represents the number of days and y represents the number of cells. According to this formula, how many cells will be in the group at the end of the first 5 days?

A) 80
B) 160
C) 400
D) 512
E) 1,280

Since we know the value of t is 5, we can plug it into the equation and solve:

$$y = 16(2)^5 = 512$$

The answer is **D**.

Interest

- The ACT will generally give us one of the following formulas for any problem involving the value of a savings account or loan involving an interest rate: $A = P(1 + r)^t$ or $A = P\left(1 + \frac{r}{n}\right)^{nt}$. For both formulas, A is the ending amount, P is the principal, or starting amount, r is the interest rate (remember to convert the percentage to a decimal), n is the number of times interest is compounded per year, and t is the total number of years for which the interest is compounded.

- Most of these questions will give you all but one of these values, as well as the required formula. In these problems, you will be asked to solve the equation to find the remaining value.

Example 2

A formula used to compute the current value of a savings account is $A = P(1 + r)^n$, where A is the current value; P is the amount deposited; r is the rate of interest for 1 compounding period, expressed as a decimal; and n is the number of compounding periods. Which of the following is closest to the value of a savings account after 5 years if $10,000 is deposited at 4% annual interest compounded yearly?

A) $10,400
B) $12,167
C) $42,000
D) $52,000
E) $53,782

Let's start off by turning our annual interest rate into a decimal (4% = 0.04) and plugging the given values into the equation:

$$A = P(1 + r)^n$$
$$A = \$10,000(1 + 0.04)^5$$
$$A = \$12,166.53$$

The answer is **B**.

Solving Exponential Equations

- Sometimes, the ACT will give you equations to solve that involve exponentials. These equations will look like this:

$$27^{2x} = 9^{x+6}$$

- To solve these eequations, we need each term to have the same base. To do so, figure out the lowest value base that the original bases are powers of. On the ACT, most of these questions will involve bases of 2 or 3. In the example on the previous page, 27 and 9 are both powers of 3 ($3^2 = 9, 3^3 = 27$):

Make this conversion in your initial equation:

$$27^{2x} = 9^{x+6} \rightarrow (3^3)^{2x} = (3^2)^{x+6}$$

When a power is raised to a power, multiply the powers:

$$(3^3)^{2x} = (3^2)^{x+6} \rightarrow 3^{6x} = 3^{2x+12}$$

Since the bases are the same, set both powers equal to each other and solve:

$$3^{6x} = 3^{2x+12} \rightarrow 6x = 2x + 12 \rightarrow 4x = 12 \rightarrow x = 3$$

Check your answers to make sure they work:

$$27^{2(3)} = 27^6 = 387{,}420{,}489$$
$$9^{3+6} = 9^9 = 387{,}420{,}489$$

Example 3

What is the solution of the equation $8^{2x+1} = 4^{1-x}$?

A) $-\dfrac{1}{3}$

B) $-\dfrac{1}{4}$

C) $-\dfrac{1}{8}$

D) 0

E) $\dfrac{1}{7}$

Since 8 and 4 are both powers of 2, let's start there:

$$8^{2x+1} = 4^{1-x}$$
$$(2^3)^{2x+1} = (2^2)^{1-x}$$
$$2^{6x+3} = 2^{2-2x}$$
$$6x + 3 = 2 - 2x$$
$$8x = -1$$
$$x = -\frac{1}{8}$$

Let's check our answer:

$$8^{2x+1} = 8^{2\left(-\frac{1}{8}\right)+1} = 8^{\frac{3}{4}} = 4.75682846$$
$$4^{1-x} = 4^{1-\frac{1}{8}} = 4^{\frac{9}{8}} = 4.75682846$$

Our answer is **C**.

Logarithms

- **Logarithms** are the inverse, or opposite, of exponentials, just like addition is the inverse of subtraction and taking the square root of a number is the inverse of squaring a number.
- $y = a^x$ is equivalent to the expression $\log_a y = x$. For example, $81 = 3^4$ or $\log_3 81 = 4$
- A logarithm with base 10 is typically written without a base: $\log_{10} 1000 = \log 1000 = 3$
- The **natural logarithm**, which has a base of $e = 2.71828 \ldots$, is typically written as $\ln x$, though it is not commonly seen on the ACT.
- The **log change of base formula** is helpful to know: $\log_a y = \frac{\log y}{\log a}$. You can use this formula to double check problems involving logarithms in your calculator.

- $\log_b(mn) = \log_b m + \log_b n$:
$$\log_4(36) = \log_4 9 + \log_4 4$$

- $\log_b\left(\frac{m}{n}\right) = \log_b m - \log_b n$:
$$\log_2\left(\frac{1}{4}\right) = \log_2 1 - \log_2 4$$

- $\log_b(m^n) = n\log_b m$:
$$\log_3(3^9) = n = 9\log_3 3$$

- $\log_b(1) = 0$
- $\log_b(0) = $ undefined
- $\log_b(\text{negative number}) = $ undefined

Example 4

What is the value of $\log_2 8$?

A) 3
B) 4
C) 6
D) 10
E) 16

Remember, $\log_a y = x$ is equivalent to $y = a^x$:

$$\log_2 8 = x$$
$$8 = 2^x$$
$$x = 3$$

In this case, $x = 3$ and our answer is **A**.

PRACTICE EXERCISE

1. A formula for finding the value, A dollars, of P dollars invested at 5% interest compounded annually for n years is $A = P(1 + 0.05)^n$. Which of the following is an expression for P in terms of n and A?

    A) $A - 0.05^n$

    B) $A + 0.05^n$

    C) $\left(\frac{A}{1-0.05}\right)^n$

    D) $\frac{A}{(1+0.05)^n}$

    E) $\frac{A}{(1-0.05)^n}$

2. A population of wild horses decreases in number as described by the equation $P = 179(0.95)^t$, where t represents the number of months and P represents the number of horses. According to this formula, approximately how many horses will be in the group at the end of the 2 years?

    A) 52

    B) 85

    C) 162

    D) 198

    E) 340

3. A formula used to compute the current value of a savings account is $A = P(1 + r)^n$, where A is the current value; P is the amount deposited; r is the rate of interest for 1 compounding period, expressed as a decimal; and n is the number of compounding periods. Which of the following is closest to the value of a savings account after 3 years if $20,000 is deposited at 2.5% annual interest compounded yearly?

    A) $20,500

    B) $21,538

    C) $39,063

    D) $150,000

    E) $312,500

4. What is the solution to the equation $4^x = 2^{x+2}$?

    A) $\frac{1}{2}$

    B) 1

    C) 2

    D) 4

    E) 8

5. The cost of a hotel room has increased by 3% each year for the past 30 years. If the cost of the hotel room was $89.95 in 2011, what was its approximate cost in 2008?
   A) $40.94
   B) $79.92
   C) $82.31
   D) $98.56
   E) $101.24

6. What is the solution to the equation $16^{x-2} = 8^{3x}$?
   A) -4
   B) -2
   C) $-\dfrac{12}{5}$
   D) $-\dfrac{8}{5}$
   E) $-\dfrac{2}{5}$

7. A group of cells grows in number as described by the equation $P = 108(1.2)^t$, where t represents the number of hours and P represents the number of cells. According to this formula, how many cells, to the nearest cell, will be in the group at the end of the first day?
   A) 110
   B) 130
   C) 174
   D) 3,110
   E) 8,586

8. What is the value of $\log_2 16$?
   A) $\dfrac{1}{8}$
   B) $\dfrac{1}{4}$
   C) 2
   D) 4
   E) 8

9. What is the value of x in the equation $\log_3 36 - \log_3 4 = \log_6 x$?
   A) 3
   B) 12
   C) 36
   D) 64
   E) 72

10. If $\log_2 5 = 2.322$ and $\log_2 7 = 2.808$, what is the value of $\log_2 175$?
    A) 2.243
    B) 5.165
    C) 6.520
    D) 7.452
    E) 15.140

11. What is the value of $\log_{10} 0.0001$?
    A) -5
    B) -4
    C) -3
    D) -2
    E) -1

12. What is the solution to the equation $3^{x+2} = 9^{x-2}$?
    A) -6
    B) 2
    C) 4
    D) 6
    E) 12

13. A group of cells doubles in number every 3 days. How many hours will it take the cells to quadruple in population?
    A) 6
    B) 18
    C) 24
    D) 72
    E) 144

14. What is the value of $\log_2 -4$?
    A) -16
    B) -8
    C) -2
    D) 0
    E) Undefined

15. What is the value of x in the equation $\log_2 32 - \log_4 16 = x$?
    A) 0
    B) 1
    C) 2
    D) 3
    E) 5

Lines and Angles

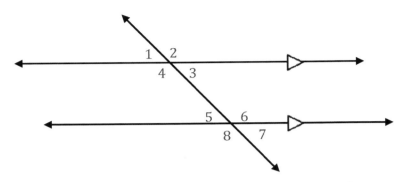

- Given two **parallel lines** (lines in the same plane that never intersect) cut by a **transversal** (a line that intersects a system of lines), certain angles formed are always **congruent** (have equal angle measures), and certain pairs of angles are always **supplementary** (their angle measures add up to 180°).
- In the image above, the odd-numbered angles (angles 1, 3, 5, and 7) are congruent to each other, and the even-numbered angles (angles 2, 4, 6, and 8) are congruent to each other.
- Likewise, each odd-numbered angle is supplementary to each even-numbered angle, and each even-numbered angle is supplementary to each odd-numbered angle.
- Two angles that are across from each other, such as Angles 1 and 3, are **vertical angles**. Vertical angles are always congruent.
- If an angle or line segment is **bisected**, it is cut into two equal parts.

Example 1

In the figure below, $AB \| CD$, AE bisects $\angle BAC$, and CE bisects $\angle ACD$. If the measure of $\angle BAC$ is 82°, what is the measure of $\angle AEC$?

A) 86°
B) 88°
C) 90°
D) 92°
E) Cannot be determined from the given information

We know ∠BAC and ∠ACD are supplementary since AB||CD. If m∠BAC = 82° and m∠BAC + m∠ACD = 180°, then m∠ACD = 98°.

We also know that AE bisects ∠BAC, so m∠EAC = 41°. Likewise, m∠ECA = 49°.

Since the sum of the angles of a triangle is 180°, the last angle of the triangle, ∠AEC, must measure 90°. The answer is **C**.

Triangles

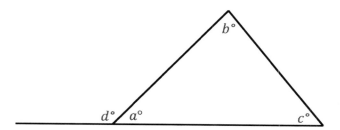

- The measures of the interior angles of a triangle sum to 180° ($a + b + c = 180$).
- The measure of an exterior angle of a triangle is equal to the sum of the two interior angles of the triangle that are not adjacent to that exterior angle ($d = b + c$).
- The longest side of a triangle is always opposite the largest interior angle of the triangle. Likewise, the shortest side of a triangle is always opposite the smallest interior angle of the triangle.
- If two of the interior angles of a triangle have equal measures, then the sides opposite those two angles have equal lengths as well.
- The lengths of any two sides of a triangle must add up to more than the third side of the triangle.
- A triangle with two equal sides and two equal angles is called an **isosceles triangle**.
- A triangle with three equal sides and three equal angles is called an **equilateral triangle**.
- If two triangles have at least two equal angles, then they are similar (their side lengths are proportional).
- Two triangles are congruent if they have exactly the same 3 side lengths and the same 3 angle measures. The following relationships between two triangles also prove that congruency:
    - **SSS** – Two triangles with all three side lengths equal
    - **SAS** – Two triangles with two side lengths and the angle between those side lengths equal
    - **ASA** – Two triangles with two angles and the side between those angles equal
    - **AAS** – Two triangles with two angles and a side adjacent to, but not between, those angles equal
    - **HL** – Two right triangles that have an equal pair of hypotenuses and an equal pair of legs
- The perimeter of a triangle is the sum of the lengths of its sides.

Example 2

Given the triangle shown below with exterior angles that measure $x°$, $y°$, and $z°$ as shown, what is the sum of x, y, and z?

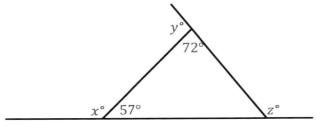

A) 180
B) 231
C) 309
D) 360
E) Cannot be determined from the given information

The first things that stand out are that the angles with measurements $x°$ and $57°$ are supplementary, thus they sum to $180°$. So, the value of x is 123.

Likewise, the angles with measurements $y°$ and $72°$ are supplementary, so $y = 108$.

Because the angle with measurement $z°$ is an exterior angle of the triangle, its measurement must be $57° + 72° = 129°$.

So, $x + y + z = 123 + 108 + 129 = 360$. The answer is **D**. In fact, the sum of the exterior angles of any polygon will always sum to $360°$!

Right Triangles

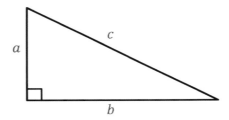

- For a right triangle with leg lengths a and b and hypotenuse of length c, the relation $a^2 + b^2 = c^2$ must hold true. This equation is known as the **Pythagorean Theorem**. For example, if a triangle has legs of length 6 and 8, the length of its hypotenuse must be:

$$a^2 + b^2 = c^2$$
$$6^2 + 8^2 = c^2$$
$$100 = c^2$$
$$10 = c$$

- The most common right triangle lengths on the ACT are in the ratio of $3:4:5$. The ratio $5:12:13$ is also common, as is the ratio $8:15:17$. Memorize these ratios to help save time on the exam!

- The area of a triangle can be found by the formula $A = \frac{1}{2}bh$, where b is the length of the base of the triangle and h is the height of the triangle. Remember, the base and height of the triangle must be perpendicular!

Example 3

For ΔFGH, shown below, which of the following is an expression for y in terms of x ?

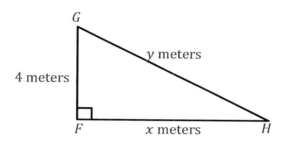

A) $x + 4$
B) $\sqrt{x^2 + 4}$
C) $\sqrt{x^2 + 8}$
D) $\sqrt{x^2 - 16}$
E) $\sqrt{x^2 + 16}$

Since we're given a right triangle with marked side lengths, let's start with the Pythagorean Theorem:

$$x^2 + 4^2 = y^2$$
$$x^2 + 16 = y^2$$

Now we need to solve for y. To get y by itself let's take the square root of each side:

$$\sqrt{x^2 + 16} = \sqrt{y^2}$$
$$\sqrt{x^2 + 16} = y$$

The answer is **E**.

Quadrilaterals

- The quadrilaterals the ACT presents are typically parallelograms, rectangles, squares, and trapezoids.
- A **parallelogram** is a quadrilateral in which opposite sides are both congruent and have equal lengths.
- Opposite angles of a parallelogram are congruent while adjacent angles are supplementary.
- The area of a parallelogram can be found by multiplying the lengths of the base and the height: $A = hl$. The height and base must be perpendicular.
- A **rectangle** is a special type of parallelogram in which each of its angles measures $90°$.
- The area of a rectangle can be found by multiplying the length and the width. $A = lw$
- A **square** is a rectangle in which each side is of equal length.
- The area of a square can be found by squaring the length of one of its sides. $A = s^2$
- A **trapezoid** consists of one pair of parallel sides and another pair of non-parallel sides.
- The area of a trapezoid can be found by multiplying one-half of the sum of the lengths of the two parallel bases, b_1 and b_2, by the height: $A = \frac{1}{2}(b_1 + b_2)h$

Example 4

In square $ABCE$ shown below, D is the midpoint of CE. Which of the following is the ratio of the area of $\triangle ADE$ to the area of $\triangle ADB$?

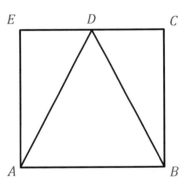

A) $1:1$
B) $1:2$
C) $1:3$
D) $1:4$
E) $1:8$

Both the bases and heights of square $ABCE$ and $\triangle ADB$ are identical. Since the area of the triangle is $\frac{1}{2}bh$ and the area of the square is bh, the ratio of the area of the triangle to the square must be:

$$\frac{\frac{1}{2}bh}{bh} = \frac{1}{2}$$

The answer is **B**.

Other Polygon-Related Formulas

Volume of a Cube: $V = s^3$

Surface Area of a Cube: $SA = 6s^2$

Volume of a Rectangular Prism: $V = lwh$

Surface Area of a Rectangular Prism: $SA = 2(lw + lh + wh)$

Sum of the Interior Angles of a Polygon: $180(n-2)$, where n is the number of sides of the polygon

Measure of Each Interior Angle of a Regular Polygon: $\frac{180(n-2)}{n}$, where n is the number of sides of the polygon

Sum of the Exterior Angles of a Polygon: 360, where n is the number of sides of the polygon

Measure of Each Exterior Angle of a Regular Polygon: $\frac{360}{n}$, where n is the number of sides of the polygon

PRACTICE EXERCISE

1. A computer company is designing a new computer tower for gaming PCs. The tower is a rectangular prism of length 20 centimeters, height 35 centimeters, and volume 35,000 cubic centimeters. What is the width, in centimeters, of the box?
    A) 20
    B) 35
    C) 50
    D) 75
    E) 100

Questions 2 and 3 use the following information.

In right triangle ΔXYZ below, VW is parallel to XZ, and VW is perpendicular to ZY at W. The length of XY is 20 feet, the length of VW is 12 feet, and the length of WY is 9 feet.

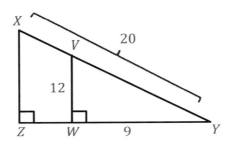

2. What is the length of ZW, in feet?
    A) 3
    B) 6
    C) 9
    D) 12
    E) 15

3. What is the length of XZ, in feet?
    A) 3
    B) 6
    C) 9
    D) 12
    E) 16

4. The sides of a square are 2 cm long. One vertex of the square is at $(1, 1)$ on a square coordinate grid marked in centimeter units. Which of the following points could also be a vertex of the square?

A) $(1, 2)$

B) $(-1, -1)$

C) $(-1, 0)$

D) $(3, 0)$

E) $(-2, 2)$

5. The perimeter of a rectangle is 6 times as long as its width. If the length of the rectangle is 10, what is the width of the rectangle?

A) 5

B) 6

C) 10

D) 12

E) 30

6. A right triangle has a hypotenuse of length 169 and a leg of length 156. What is the length of the other leg of the triangle?

A) 5

B) 13

C) 65

D) 230

E) 4,225

7. A cube has a surface area of 294 square inches. What is the volume of the cube in cubic inches?

A) 216

B) 343

C) 512

D) 1,728

E) 5,041

8. A triangle has side lengths of 7, 9, and x. Which of the following gives the range of possible values of x?

A) $2 \leq x \leq 16$

B) $2 < x < 16$

C) $2 \leq x \leq 9$

D) $2 < x < 9$

E) $7 < x < 9$

9. The measure of an interior angle of a regular 7-sided polygon is approximately how many more degrees than the measure of one of its exterior angles?

    A) 51.4
    B) 77.1
    C) 102.9
    D) 205.7
    E) 257.1

10. A trapezoid has a height of h, bases of length b_1 and b_2, and an area of A. What is the height of the trapezoid in terms of b_1, b_2, and A?

    A) $\dfrac{A}{2b_1+2b_2}$
    B) $\dfrac{A}{b_1+b_2}$
    C) $\dfrac{2A}{b_1+b_2}$
    D) $\dfrac{A(b_1+b_2)}{2}$
    E) $\dfrac{A(b_1-b_2)}{2}$

11. A fence is being put up around a rectangular garden with an area of 3600 square feet. What is the perimeter of the garden?

    A) 240
    B) 260
    C) 280
    D) 300
    E) It cannot be determined from the information provided.

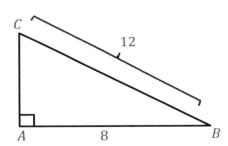

12. What is the length of AC, in units?

    A) 4
    B) $2\sqrt{5}$
    C) $4\sqrt{5}$
    D) 8
    E) $8\sqrt{5}$

13. The side length a cube is increased by 10%. By what percent does the surface area of the cube increase?
    A) 10%
    B) 11%
    C) 20%
    D) 21%
    E) 121%

14. The side length of a cube is decreased by 10%. By what percent does the volume of the cube decrease?
    A) 9.1%
    B) 10.2%
    C) 27.1%
    D) 30.3%
    E) 33.5%

15. A triangle has side lengths of 4 and 6. Which of the following is not a possible side length of the triangle?
    A) 3
    B) 4
    C) 6
    D) 9
    E) 10

Circles

- A circle measures $360°$.

- The **circumference** of a circle, or the distance around a circle, is $C = 2\pi r$ or $C = \pi d$:

  The circumference of a circle with a radius of 2 meters is $C = 2\pi r \rightarrow 2\pi(2) \rightarrow 4\pi$ meters.

- The **area** of a circle can be found by $A = \pi r^2$:

  The area of a circle with a diameter of 10 cm is $A = \pi r^2 \rightarrow \pi(5)^2 \rightarrow 25\pi$ cm.

- A **central angle** of a circle is one whose vertex is the center of a circle and whose sides are radii of the circle. The degree measure of the minor arc (shorter distance along the circle) between the intersections of the two radii is equal to the measure of the central angle. $\angle ADC$ and minor arc $\overarc{AC}$ in the image on the left below show this relationship.

- An **inscribed angle** is an angle made from points on a circle's circumference. The measure of a circle's inscribed angle is half the measure of the central angle that it encloses.

  $\angle ABC$ and minor arc $\overarc{AC}$ in the image on the right below show this relationship.

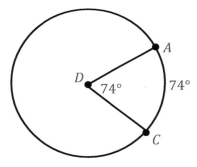 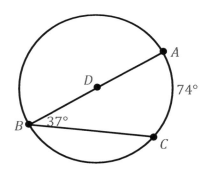

- The ratio of the **arc length** of a circle to the circumference of the circle is equal to the ratio of the central angle of the circle to $360°$ (or 2π):

$$\frac{arc\ length}{2\pi r} = \frac{central\ angle\ measure}{360°}$$

A circle has an arc length of 10π cm and a radius of 15 cm. What is the measure of the central angle measure of the circle?

$$\frac{10\pi}{2\pi(15)} = \frac{central\ angle\ measure}{360°}$$

$$\frac{1}{3} = \frac{central\ angle\ measure}{360°}$$

$$central\ angle\ measure = 120°$$

- The ratio of the **area of a sector** of a circle to the area of the circle is also equal to the ratio of the central angle of the circle to 360° (or 2π):

$$\frac{sector\ area}{\pi r^2} = \frac{central\ angle\ measure}{360°}$$

What is the area of a quarter circle with a radius of 10 in?

A quarter circle is 90°

$$\frac{sector\ area}{\pi(10)^2} = \frac{90°}{360°}$$

$$\frac{sector\ area}{100\pi} = \frac{1}{4°}$$

$$sector\ area = 25\pi$$

Example 1

In the circle shown below, chords TR and QS intersect at P, which is the center of the circle, and the measure of $\angle PST$ is 30°. What is the degree measure of minor arc $\widehat{RS}$?

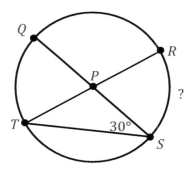

A) 30°
B) 45°
C) 60°
D) 90°
E) Cannot be determined from the given information

Let's start by figuring out the information we know:

PS and PT are both radii of the circle. Since all of the radii of a circle are the same length, we know that $\triangle PTS$ must be isosceles. So, $m\angle PTS$ is also 30°, and thus $m\angle TPS = 120°$.

Since $m\angle TPS = 120°$, $m\angle RPS = 60°$ (the two angles are supplementary).

Since the measure of a central angle is equivalent to the measure of its corresponding minor arc, the measure of minor arc $\overset{\frown}{RS}$ must also be 60°. The answer is **C**.

Other Circle-Related Formulas and Definitions

Chord: A line segment within a circle that touches 2 points on the circle. Every diameter is also a chord of the circle.

Tangent: A line perpendicular to the radius of a circle that touches only 1 point on the circle.

Volume of a Sphere: $V = \frac{4}{3}\pi r^3$

Surface Area of a Sphere: $SA = 4\pi r^2$

Volume of a Right Cylinder: $V = \pi r^2 h$

Surface Area of a Right Cylinder: $SA = 2\pi rh + 2\pi r^2$

Volume of a Cone: $V = \frac{1}{3}\pi r^2 h$

PRACTICE EXERCISE

1. Three points, W, X, and Y lie on a circle having a circumference of 20 units. W is 4 units clockwise from X. Y is 12 units counterclockwise from X. How many units apart, in the clockwise direction, are points W and Y?

   A) 4
   B) 6
   C) 8
   D) 12
   E) 16

Questions 2 and 3 use the following information.

The figure below consists of a square of side length 12 units and 2 semicircles, with dimensions shown.

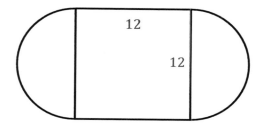

2. What is the outside perimeter of the figure above, in units?

   A) $12 + 12\pi$
   B) $24 + 12\pi$
   C) $12 + 24\pi$
   D) $24 + 24\pi$
   E) $48 + 24\pi$

3. What is the area of the figure above, in square units?

   A) $48 + 36\pi$
   B) $48 + 144\pi$
   C) $144 + 36\pi$
   D) $144 + 72\pi$
   E) $144 + 144\pi$

4. A right circular cylinder has a height of 10 in and a diameter of 10 cm. What is the total surface area of the cylinder, in square inches?

   A) 50π
   B) 90π
   C) 100π
   D) 150π
   E) 400π

5. In the circle shown below, A is the center and lies on CD and BE. Which of the following statements is NOT true?

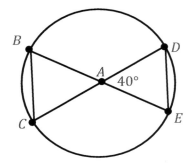

A) $\angle BCA$ measures 70°.
B) $\angle BAD$ measures 140°.
C) Minor arc $\widehat{CE}$ measures 70°.
D) BC is parallel to DE.
E) $\triangle BAC$ is an isosceles triangle.

6. A circle is inscribed inside of a square with side length 4. What is the area of the circle?
A) 2π
B) 4π
C) 8π
D) 16π
E) 32π

7. A square with side length 4 is inscribed in a circle. What is the area of the circle?
A) 2π
B) 4π
C) 8π
D) 16π
E) 32π

8. A circle has diameter CE. If point C is at $(3, 5)$ and the center of the circle is at $(5, 6)$, what are the coordinates of E in the coordinate plane?
A) $(1, 4)$
B) $(2, 3)$
C) $(4, 5.5)$
D) $(7, 4)$
E) $(7, 7)$

9. A circle has an area of $6\pi x$ square units and a circumference of $2\pi x$ units. What is the length of the diameter of the circle?

    A) 3
    B) 6
    C) 12
    D) 18
    E) 36

10. If the radius of a circle increases by 12%, then the area of the circle increases by:

    A) 12%
    B) 14.4%
    C) 25.4%
    D) 144%
    E) Cannot be determined from the given information.

11. In the circle shown below, A is the center and lies on CD. If BC and DE are parallel, what is the measure of minor arc $\overset{\frown}{CE}$?

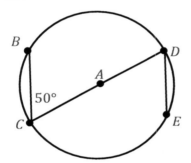

    A) 25°
    B) 50°
    C) 80°
    D) 100°
    E) 160°

12. A parallelogram is inscribed inside of a circle of diameter 15. The parallelogram has a base length of 12 and an area of 84. What is the height of the parallelogram?

    A) 7
    B) 14
    C) 21
    D) 42
    E) It cannot be determined from the given information.

13. A cylindrical swimming pool of diameter 30 meters and height 5 meters is half-filled with water. If water is added to the pool at a rate of 1 cubic meter per minute, approximately how long will it take until the pool is 95% full?
    A) 13.5 hours
    B) 26.5 hours
    C) 28 hours
    D) 56 hours
    E) 106 hours

14. A circle has diameter AB. If point A is at $(2, -5)$ and point B is at $(5, -9)$, what is the area of the circle?
    A) 2.5π
    B) 5π
    C) 6.25π
    D) 10π
    E) 25π

15. If the diameter of a circle increases from 12 to 15, by how much does its area increase?
    A) 2.5π
    B) 6.25π
    C) 9π
    D) 20.25π
    E) 81π

ACT Math: Conic Sections

Conic Sections

- A **conic section** is the intersection of a plane and a cone.
- The four conic sections are **parabolas**, **circles**, **ellipses**, and **hyperbolas**.
- Circles are by far the most common on the ACT. Ellipses show up rarely, and hyperbolas almost never appear on the ACT.
- If an ellipse or a hyperbola does show up on the ACT, you will be given its formula and asked to find a certain value based on other values and the equation.

Circles

- The equation of a circle in the coordinate plane is $(x - h)^2 + (y - k)^2 = r^2$.

- The center of the circle can be found at (h, k). The length of the radius of the circle is r:

  The circle $(x - 3)^2 + (y + 2)^2 = 9$ has its center at $(3, -2)$ and a radius of 3.

Example 1

A circle in the standard (x, y) coordinate plane has an equation of $(x - 5)^2 + y^2 = 38$. What are the radius of the circle and the coordinates of the center of the circle?

	Radius	Center
A)	$\sqrt{38}$	(5,0)
B)	19	(5,0)
C)	38	(5,0)
D)	$\sqrt{38}$	(−5,0)
E)	19	(−5,0)

From the information above, the center of the circle is $(5,0)$ and the length of the radius of the circle is $\sqrt{38}$. Thus, the answer must be **A**.

PRACTICE EXERCISE

1. What is the equation of a circle with a diameter of 10 and a center located at the point $(3, -1)$?
    A) $(x - 3)^2 + (y + 1)^2 = 5$
    B) $(x - 3)^2 + (y + 1)^2 = 10$
    C) $(x - 3)^2 + (y + 1)^2 = 25$
    D) $(x - 3)^2 + (y + 1)^2 = 50$
    E) $(x - 3)^2 + (y + 1)^2 = 100$

2. A circle with the equation $(x + 1)^2 + (y - 1)^2 = 25$ passes through the point $(3, b)$. What are the possible values of b?
    A) -4 only
    B) -2 only
    C) 4 only
    D) -2 or -4
    E) -2 or 4

3. Which of the following points is located on the circle in the coordinate plane with equation $(x - 2)^2 + y^2 = 9$?
    A) $(-2, 3)$
    B) $(-2, -3)$
    C) $(0, 5)$
    D) $(1, 8)$
    E) $(2, -3)$

4. A circle in the (x, y) coordinate plane is tangent to the y-axis at $(0, 2)$ and the x-axis. Which of the following is a possible equation of that circle?
    A) $(x - 2)^2 + (y - 2)^2 = 2$
    B) $(x + 2)^2 + (y - 2)^2 = 2$
    C) $x^2 + (y - 2)^2 = 2$
    D) $x^2 + (y - 2)^2 = 4$
    E) $(x + 2)^2 + (y - 2)^2 = 4$

5. At which of the following points does the line $y = 2x$ intersect the circle $x^2 + y^2 = 20$?
    A) $(1, 2)$
    B) $(2, -4)$
    C) $(-2, -4)$
    D) $(-3, 6)$
    E) $(3, -6)$

6. What is the area, in square units, of the circle represented by the equation
    $(x - 8)^2 + (y - 3)^2 = 16$?
    A) 4π
    B) 8π
    C) 16π
    D) 64π
    E) 256π

7. What is the circumference, in units, of the circle represented by the equation
    $(x - 8)^2 + (y - 3)^2 = 16$?
    A) 4π
    B) 8π
    C) 16π
    D) 32π
    E) 64π

8. A circle has diameter of 12 and the center of the circle is at point $(4, -3)$. Which of the
    following lines does not intersect the circle?
    A) $y = 2$
    B) $y = -6$
    C) $x = -3$
    D) $x = -1$
    E) $y = x$

9. What is the equation of a circle with an area of 36π and a center located at the point
    $(0, -5)$?
    A) $(x + 5)^2 + (y + 1)^2 = 36$
    B) $x^2 + (y - 5)^2 = 36$
    C) $x^2 + (y + 5)^2 = 36$
    D) $(x + 5)^2 + y^2 = 1296$
    E) $x^2 + (y + 5)^2 = 1296$

10. A circle has a circumference of 6π and a center located at $(0, -1)$. What is the equation of
    the circle?
    A) $x^2 + (y - 1)^2 = 36$
    B) $x^2 + (y - 1)^2 = 9$
    C) $x^2 + (y + 1)^2 = 36$
    D) $x^2 + (y + 1)^2 = 9$
    E) $(x + 1)^2 + y^2 = 9$

11. The minor axis of an ellipse has endpoints at $(3, 5)$ and $(9, 5)$, and the major axis of the ellipse has endpoints at $(6, 15)$ and $(6, -5)$. What is the length of the longer of the two axes?
    A) 5
    B) 6
    C) 10
    D) 12
    E) 20

12. What is the area, in square units, of the circle represented by the equation
    $(x - 2)^2 + (y + 4)^2 = \frac{9}{4}$?
    A) $\frac{3}{2}\pi$
    B) $\frac{9}{4}\pi$
    C) 3π
    D) 6π
    E) 12π

13. A circle with the equation $(x + 1)^2 + (y - 2)^2 = 2$ goes through which of the following points?
    A) $(-1, 3)$
    B) $(0, 1)$
    C) $(1, 1)$
    D) $(2, -1)$
    E) $(3, 2)$

14. A circle has a diameter of 3 and the center of the circle is at point $(1, 0)$. Which of the following is the equation of the circle?
    A) $(x - 1)^2 + y^2 = 9$
    B) $x^2 + (y - 1)^2 = 9$
    C) $(x + 1)^2 + y^2 = \frac{9}{4}$
    D) $x^2 + (y - 1)^2 = \frac{9}{4}$
    E) $(x - 1)^2 + y^2 = \frac{9}{4}$

15. The equation of which of the following circles has the greatest area?
    A) $(x + 2)^2 + (y + 3)^2 = 14$
    B) $(x - 4)^2 + (y - 2)^2 = 16$
    C) $(x + 1)^2 + \left(y + \frac{1}{2}\right)^2 = 18$
    D) $(x - 3)^2 + y^2 = 12$
    E) $(x - 1)^2 + \left(y - \frac{1}{2}\right)^2 = 16$

ACT Math: Sequences and Patterns

Arithmetic Sequences

- An **arithmetic sequence** is a sequence of numbers in which the difference between each consecutive term is constant:

  2, 4, 6, 8, 10 is an example of an arithmetic sequence. Here, the common difference is 2.

- Every arithmetic sequence can be defined by the formula $a_n = d(n-1) + a_1$, where a_1 is the first term in the sequence, a_n is the last term in the sequence, n is the number of terms in the sequence, and d is the common difference:

  Find the 10th term of an arithmetic sequence whose first term is 5 and whose common difference is -1:

$$a_n = d(n-1) + a_1 = -1(10-1) + 5 = -4$$

- We can find the sum of all of the terms in an arithmetic sequence of n terms by the formula $S_n = n\frac{(a_1 + a_n)}{2}$, where all the constants are defined above:

  Find the sum of the first 10 terms of an arithmetic sequence whose first term is 5 and whose common difference is -1.

  Since we already found the nth term using the equation above, let's plug everything in:

$$S_n = n\frac{(a_1 + a_n)}{2} = 10 \times \frac{(5 + -4)}{2} = 5$$

Example 1

What is the sum of the first 4 terms of the arithmetic sequence in which the 6th term is 8 and the 10th term is 13?

A) 10.5
B) 14.5
C) 18
D) 21.25
E) 39.5

One way we can figure the common difference is to line up all of the terms we know:

___, ___, ___, ___, ___, 8, ___, ___, ___, 13

To figure out the common difference, we must notice that we add the difference 4 times to get from 8 to 13: $\frac{13-8}{4} = \frac{5}{4}$ or 1.25

Now we should figure out the 1ˢᵗ term of the sequence (we'll use $n = 6$):

$$a_n = d(n-1) + a_1$$
$$8 = 1.25(6-1) + a_1$$
$$1.75 = a_1$$

Next, we need to figure out the 4ᵗʰ term of the sequence:

$$a_n = d(n-1) + a_1 = 1.25(4-1) + 1.75 = 5.5$$

Now that we know a_1, we can use the sum formula (here, $n = 4$):

$$S_n = n\frac{(a_1 + a_n)}{2} = 4 \times \frac{(1.75 + 5.5)}{2} = 14.5$$

The answer is **B**.

Geometric Sequences

- A **geometric sequence** is a sequence of numbers in which the ratio of any term to the previous term is constant:

  2, 4, 8, 16, 32 is an example of a geometric sequence. Here, the common ratio is 2.

- Every geometric sequence can be defined by the formula $a_n = a_1(r^{n-1})$, where a_1 is the first term in the sequence, a_n is the last term in the sequence, n is the number of terms in the sequence, and r is the common ratio:

  Find the 7ᵗʰ term of a geometric sequence whose first term is 4 and whose common ratio is -3:
  $$a_n = a_1(r^{n-1}) = 4((-3)^{7-1}) = 2916$$

- We can find the sum of all of the terms in a geometric sequence of n terms by the formula $S_n = \frac{a_1(1-r^n)}{1-r}$, where all the constants are defined above:

  Find the sum of the first 7 terms of a geometric sequence whose first term is 4 and whose common ratio is -3:
  $$S_n = \frac{a_1(1-r^n)}{1-r} = \frac{4(1-(-3)^7)}{1--3} = 2188$$

The sum of an infinite geometric series with first term a and common ratio $r < 1$ is given by $\frac{a}{1-r}$. The sum of a given infinite geometric series is 200, and the common ratio is 0.15. What is the second term of this series?

A) 25.5
B) 30
C) 169.85
D) 170
E) 199.85

Here, we're told about a series instead of a sequence. A **series** is another way to say the sum of the numbers in a sequence, usually an infinite sequence. Let's plug in our givens to find the first term:

$$200 = \frac{a}{1-0.15} \rightarrow a = 170$$

Now we can multiply our first term by our common ratio to find the second term. $170 \times 0.15 = 25.5$. The answer is **A**.

Other Patterns

- Other types of patterns can show up on the ACT. Some of these are based on numbers, but have patterns that extend beyond arithmetic or geometric sequences:

  1, 1, 2, 3, 5, 8, ... is a sequence known as the Fibonacci Sequence. To obtain each term in the sequence, add the two numbers before the term. The first two terms are always 1, 1.

- Other types of patterns may involve the alphabet or symbols. Use logic and your best judgement to figure out the patterns present in these questions.

Example 3

In a basketball passing drill, 5 basketball players stand evenly spaced around a circle. The player with the ball (the passer) passes it to another player (the receiver). The receiver cannot be the player to the passer's immediate right or left and cannot be the player who last passed the ball. A designated player begins the drill as the first passer. This player will be the receiver for the first time on which pass of the ball?

A) 4th
B) 5th
C) 6th
D) 10th
E) 24th

Many questions involving patterns will be easier if you draw a picture to help you out:

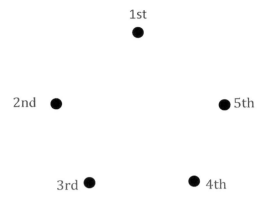

Each circle represents a person. We'll choose the top circle to be the 1st player.
Since the player can't pass it to any player next to him or herself, he must pass it to the 3rd or 4th player. Let's pass to the 3rd, though the result is the same if we pass to the 4th:

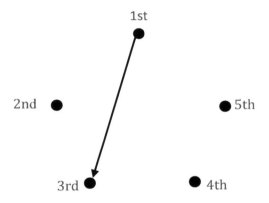

Now this player only has one option. He can't pass it back to 1st player, or to the 2nd or 4th player (since they're on his right and left). He must pass it to 5th player. Let's show the rest of the pattern:

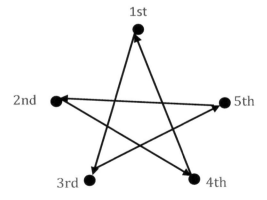

We see that it takes 5 passes to get back to 1st player. The answer is **B**.

PRACTICE EXERCISE

1. What is the 8th term in the arithmetic sequence 1, 4, 7, ... ?
   A) 16
   B) 19
   C) 22
   D) 25
   E) 28

2. The first term of a geometric sequence is −3 and the 4th term in the sequence is 24. What is the sum of the first 5 terms of the sequence?
   A) −37
   B) −33
   C) −30
   D) −26
   E) −21

3. The 9th term of an arithmetic sequence is 12, while the 10th term of the sequence is 9. What is the 1st term of the sequence?
   A) −21
   B) −18
   C) 33
   D) 36
   E) 39

4. What is the next term in the sequence 5, 6, 8, 11, 15, 20, ... ?
   A) 24
   B) 25
   C) 26
   D) 27
   E) 28

5. Which of the following best describes the sequence 32, −16, 8, −4, 2, 0?
   A) Arithmetic
   B) Geometric
   C) Both Arithmetic and Geometric
   D) Neither Arithmetic nor Geometric
   E) Cannot be determined from the information provided

6. What are the missing numbers in the geometric sequence 2, 3, ___, 6.75, ___?
   A) 4, 9
   B) 4, 9.5
   C) 4.5, 9.5
   D) 4.5, 10.125
   E) 5, 8.25

7. A geometric sequence has four terms. If the 3rd term is 10 and the common ratio is 2, what is the sum of the sequence?
   A) 34.0
   B) 35.0
   C) 36.0
   D) 37.5
   E) 75.0

8. The sum of an infinite geometric series with first term a and common ratio $r < 1$ is given by $\frac{a}{1-r}$. The sum of a given infinite geometric series is 150, and the common ratio is 0.20. What is the second term of this series?
   A) $\frac{1}{5}$
   B) 12
   C) 24
   D) 120
   E) 600

9. What is the next term in the sequence A, C, E, G, ... ?
   A) H
   B) I
   C) J
   D) K
   E) L

10. What are the missing terms in the sequence 2, 5, 10, 17, ___, 37, ___?
    A) 24, 50
    B) 26, 50
    C) 27, 47
    D) 28, 58
    E) 30, 32

11. What is the sum of the first 10 terms of the arithmetic sequence in which $a_1 = 56$ and $a_{10} = 11$?
    A) 264.5
    B) 268.0
    C) 301.5
    D) 335.0
    E) 372.0

12. The first term of a geometric sequence is 12 and the 7th term in the sequence is 0. What is the sum of the first 6 terms of the sequence?
    A) −42
    B) −12
    C) 0
    D) 12
    E) 42

13. The 5th term of an arithmetic sequence is 10, while the 7th term of the sequence is 16. What is the product of the first 3 terms of the sequence?
    A) −8
    B) −2
    C) 6
    D) 8
    E) 36

14. How many dots are in the next term in the sequence below?

| 1st | 2nd | 3rd |
| term | term | term |

    A) 4
    B) 8
    C) 9
    D) 10
    E) 12

15. The first term of an arithmetic sequence is 12, the last term is 20, and the sequence's sum is 144. How many terms does the sequence have?
    A) 8
    B) 9
    C) 10
    D) 11
    E) 12

ACT Math: Matrices

Matrix Operations

- The size of a **matrix** is based on the number of rows and columns it has:

  A 2 × 3 matrix has 2 rows and 3 columns

  $$\begin{bmatrix} 3 & 2 & 1 \\ -6 & -5 & 0.5 \end{bmatrix}$$

  A 3 × 1 matrix has 3 rows and 1 column

  $$\begin{bmatrix} 0 \\ 2 \\ -3 \end{bmatrix}$$

- Two matrices can only be equal if they have the same dimensions and the exact same entries in each corresponding position of the matrix.

- A matrix can be multiplied by a **scalar**, or regular number. To do so, multiply the scalar to every term in the matrix:

  If $A = \begin{bmatrix} 2 & 9 & 0 \\ 4 & 8 & 10 \\ 6 & -6 & 3 \end{bmatrix}$, what is $-\frac{1}{2}A$?

  $$-\frac{1}{2}\begin{bmatrix} 2 & 9 & 0 \\ 4 & 8 & 10 \\ 6 & -6 & 3 \end{bmatrix} = \begin{bmatrix} -1 & -\frac{9}{2} & 0 \\ -2 & -4 & -5 \\ -3 & 3 & -\frac{3}{2} \end{bmatrix}$$

- Matrices can be added or subtracted only if they have the same dimensions:

  $$\begin{bmatrix} 7 & -8 \\ 5 & -2 \\ 0 & 3 \end{bmatrix} + \begin{bmatrix} 3 & 3 \\ 5 & 2 \\ -6 & 10 \end{bmatrix} = \begin{bmatrix} 10 & -5 \\ 10 & 0 \\ -6 & 13 \end{bmatrix}$$

- To multiply two matrices, we must first determine if their product is defined. To do this, place the dimensions of the two matrices next to each other (with the left matrix being on the left): (2 × 3)(3 × 3). We can perform the multiplication if the two innermost numbers are the same. The dimensions of the product matrix will be the outermost numbers, in this case, (2 × 3):

  $$\begin{bmatrix} 3 & 4 & 5 \\ 1 & 2 & 0 \end{bmatrix} \times \begin{bmatrix} 1 & 2 & 3 \\ 2 & 3 & 4 \\ 4 & 5 & 6 \end{bmatrix} = \begin{bmatrix} ? & ? & ? \\ ? & ? & ? \end{bmatrix}$$

- Take the 1st entry of the 1st row of the matrix on the left and multiply it by the 1st entry of the 1st column of the matrix on the right. Then do the same with the 2nd entry of the 1st row of the matrix on the left and the 2nd entry of the 1st column of the matrix on the right and the 3rd entry of each. Sum these products up, and place it in its position:

$$3(1) + 4(2) + 5(4) = 31$$

$$\begin{bmatrix} 3 & 4 & 5 \\ 1 & 2 & 0 \end{bmatrix} \times \begin{bmatrix} 1 & 2 & 3 \\ 2 & 3 & 4 \\ 4 & 5 & 6 \end{bmatrix} = \begin{bmatrix} 31 & ? & ? \\ ? & ? & ? \end{bmatrix}$$

- The same process follows for each entry in our answer. For example, for the entry in the 1st row, 2nd column of the product, use the 1st row of the matrix on the left and the 2nd column of the matrix on the right:

$$\begin{bmatrix} 3 & 4 & 5 \\ 1 & 2 & 0 \end{bmatrix} \times \begin{bmatrix} 1 & 2 & 3 \\ 2 & 3 & 4 \\ 4 & 5 & 6 \end{bmatrix} = \begin{bmatrix} 31 & 43 & 55 \\ 5 & 8 & 11 \end{bmatrix}$$

Example 1

What is the product AB below?

$$A = \begin{bmatrix} -1 & -2 & 4 \end{bmatrix} \quad B = \begin{bmatrix} 5 \\ 8 \\ 2 \end{bmatrix}$$

A) $[-13]$

B) $[13]$

C) $\begin{bmatrix} -5 \\ -16 \\ 8 \end{bmatrix}$

D) $\begin{bmatrix} -5 & -10 & 20 \\ -8 & -16 & 32 \\ -2 & -4 & 8 \end{bmatrix}$

E) The product does not exist.

First, let's analyze the dimensions of the product: (1×3)(3×1)

The inner numbers are identical, so we can multiply. The outer numbers tell us we'll have a 1×1 matrix as the answer. So, the answer must be A or B.

Now, we can multiply: $-1(5) + -2(8) + 4(2) = -13$. The answer is **A**.

Other Uses for Matrices

- Matrices can be used to both represent systems of equations and as a means of storing data.

- When matrices are used to store data, each row and column is typically labeled, as shown in Example 2 below.

- A system of equations is sometimes represented as a matrix. These are usually more quickly solved as systems of equations:

$$\begin{bmatrix} 1 & 1 & 1 \\ 0 & 2 & 5 \\ 2 & 5 & -1 \end{bmatrix} \cdot \begin{bmatrix} x \\ y \\ z \end{bmatrix} = \begin{bmatrix} 6 \\ -4 \\ 27 \end{bmatrix}$$

Translates to the system of equations:

$$1x + 1y + 1z = 6$$
$$0x + 2y + 2z = -4$$
$$2x + 5y - 1z = 27$$

- Sometimes, other matrix operations will show up on the ACT. In cases like these, your knowledge of the information above will be all you need – the ACT will provide all other information relevant to answer these questions.

Example 2

Daisun owns 2 sportswear stores (X and Y). She stocks 3 brands of T-shirts (A, B, and C) in each store. The matrices below show the numbers of each type of T-shirt in each store and the cost for each type of T-shirt. The value of Daisun's T-shirt inventory is computed using the costs listed. What is the total value of the T-shirt inventory for Daisun's 2 stores?

$$\begin{array}{cc} & \begin{array}{ccc} A & B & C \end{array} \\ \begin{array}{c} X \\ Y \end{array} & \begin{bmatrix} 100 & 200 & 150 \\ 120 & 50 & 100 \end{bmatrix} \end{array} \qquad \begin{array}{cc} & \text{Cost} \\ \begin{array}{c} A \\ B \\ C \end{array} & \begin{bmatrix} \$ 5 \\ \$10 \\ \$15 \end{bmatrix} \end{array}$$

A) $2,200
B) $2,220
C) $4,965
D) $5,450
E) $7,350

Here, we have two different matrices used to store data. The matrix on the left tells us the number of T-shirts of each type present in each store, while the other tells us the price of each type. To figure out the total value of the inventory, we should multiply the matrices:

$$\begin{bmatrix} 100 & 200 & 150 \\ 120 & 50 & 100 \end{bmatrix} \times \begin{bmatrix} \$5 \\ \$10 \\ \$15 \end{bmatrix} = \begin{bmatrix} \$4,750 \\ \$2,600 \end{bmatrix}$$

So, we have a total of $7,350 of inventory in both stores. The answer is **E**.

PRACTICE EXERCISE

1. What is the value of $x + y$ in the matrix equation below?

$$\begin{bmatrix} 3 & 5 \\ 2x & 7 \end{bmatrix} = \begin{bmatrix} 3 & 10y \\ -4 & 7 \end{bmatrix}$$

A) $-\dfrac{5}{2}$

B) $-\dfrac{3}{2}$

C) $\dfrac{3}{2}$

D) 2

E) $\dfrac{5}{2}$

2. Which of the following matrices is equivalent to $2B - A$?

$$A = \begin{bmatrix} 7 & 1 \\ -2 & 0 \end{bmatrix} \quad B = \begin{bmatrix} 3 & 4 \\ 5 & 2 \end{bmatrix}$$

A) $\begin{bmatrix} 11 & -2 \\ -9 & -2 \end{bmatrix}$

B) $\begin{bmatrix} -1 & 7 \\ 12 & 4 \end{bmatrix}$

C) $\begin{bmatrix} -1 & 7 \\ 8 & 4 \end{bmatrix}$

D) $\begin{bmatrix} 1 & 7 \\ 8 & 4 \end{bmatrix}$

E) $\begin{bmatrix} 11 & -2 \\ 9 & 2 \end{bmatrix}$

3. The determinant of a matrix $\begin{bmatrix} a & b \\ c & d \end{bmatrix}$ equals $ad - bc$. What must be the value of x for the matrix $\begin{bmatrix} x & x \\ 4 & x \end{bmatrix}$ to have a determinant of -4?

A) -4

B) -2

C) 0

D) 2

E) 4

4. The determinant of a matrix $\begin{bmatrix} a & b \\ c & d \end{bmatrix}$ equals $ad - bc$. What is the determinant of the matrix $\begin{bmatrix} 3 & 2 \\ 1 & 0 \end{bmatrix}$?

A) -6

B) -2

C) 2

D) 3

E) 6

5. Which of the following matrices is the product $\begin{bmatrix} 2 & 1 & 2 \\ 3 & -5 & 1 \end{bmatrix} \cdot \begin{bmatrix} 0 \\ 0 \end{bmatrix}$?

   A) $\begin{bmatrix} 0 & 0 \end{bmatrix}$
   B) $\begin{bmatrix} 0 & 0 & 0 \end{bmatrix}$
   C) $\begin{bmatrix} 0 \\ 0 \end{bmatrix}$
   D) $\begin{bmatrix} 0 \\ 0 \\ 0 \end{bmatrix}$
   E) The product of the matrices cannot be calculated.

6. Which of the following coordinates, (x, y), is a solution to the system provided below?
$$\begin{bmatrix} 2 & 3 \\ 5 & 0 \end{bmatrix} \cdot \begin{bmatrix} x \\ y \end{bmatrix} = \begin{bmatrix} 7 \\ 10 \end{bmatrix}$$

   A) $(-2, -1)$
   B) $(-2, 1)$
   C) $(2, -1)$
   D) $(2, 1)$
   E) $(3, 1)$

7. What is the value of $2x$ in the matrix equation below?
$$\begin{bmatrix} x & z \\ 2x & 3x \end{bmatrix} = \begin{bmatrix} 2y & 3y \\ 4y & 12 \end{bmatrix}$$

   A) 3
   B) 6
   C) 8
   D) 12
   E) 24

8. What is the value of z in the matrix equation below?
$$\begin{bmatrix} x & z \\ 2x & 3x \end{bmatrix} = \begin{bmatrix} 2y & 3y \\ 4y & 12 \end{bmatrix}$$

   A) 3
   B) 6
   C) 8
   D) 12
   E) 24

9. What is the product BA below?

$$A = \begin{bmatrix} 1 & -3 & 1 \\ 2 & 2 & 0 \end{bmatrix} \quad B = \begin{bmatrix} 2 \\ 3 \\ 1 \end{bmatrix}$$

A) $\begin{bmatrix} -6 \\ 10 \end{bmatrix}$

B) $\begin{bmatrix} 6 \\ 10 \end{bmatrix}$

C) $\begin{bmatrix} 6 \\ -10 \end{bmatrix}$

D) $\begin{bmatrix} -6 \\ -10 \end{bmatrix}$

E) The product of the matrices cannot be calculated.

10. What is the product AB below?

$$A = \begin{bmatrix} 1 & -3 & 1 \\ 2 & 2 & 0 \end{bmatrix} \quad B = \begin{bmatrix} 2 \\ 3 \\ 1 \end{bmatrix}$$

A) $\begin{bmatrix} -6 \\ 10 \end{bmatrix}$

B) $\begin{bmatrix} 6 \\ 10 \end{bmatrix}$

C) $\begin{bmatrix} 6 \\ -10 \end{bmatrix}$

D) $\begin{bmatrix} -6 \\ -10 \end{bmatrix}$

E) The product of the matrices cannot be calculated.

11. What is the value of $x^2 - y$ in the matrix equation below?

$$\begin{bmatrix} 1 & 2 & y \\ 3 & x & 4 \end{bmatrix} = \begin{bmatrix} 0 & 2 & -2 \\ 3 & -2y & 4 \end{bmatrix}$$

A) 4
B) 8
C) 14
D) 16
E) 18

12. What is the product $-2A$ if $A = \begin{bmatrix} 0 & -\frac{3}{2} & 1 \\ 4 & \frac{1}{2} & \frac{5}{2} \end{bmatrix}$?

A) $\begin{bmatrix} 0 & 3 & 2 \\ -8 & 1 & -5 \end{bmatrix}$

B) $\begin{bmatrix} 0 & -3 & 2 \\ 8 & 1 & -5 \end{bmatrix}$

C) $\begin{bmatrix} 0 & 3 & 2 \\ -8 & -1 & -5 \end{bmatrix}$

D) $\begin{bmatrix} 0 & -3 & -2 \\ -8 & -1 & -5 \end{bmatrix}$

E) $\begin{bmatrix} 0 & 3 & -2 \\ 8 & 1 & 5 \end{bmatrix}$

13. The determinant of a matrix $\begin{bmatrix} a & b \\ c & d \end{bmatrix}$ equals $ad - bc$. What is the determinant of the matrix $\begin{bmatrix} -2 & 4 \\ 3 & 5 \end{bmatrix}$?

A) -22

B) -2

C) 2

D) 4

E) 22

14. Which of the following coordinates, (x, y), is a solution to the system provided below?
$$\begin{bmatrix} 1 & -1 \\ 3 & 2 \end{bmatrix} \cdot \begin{bmatrix} x \\ y \end{bmatrix} = \begin{bmatrix} 2 \\ 21 \end{bmatrix}$$

A) $(-5, 3)$

B) $(-3, 5)$

C) $(3, -5)$

D) $(5, -3)$

E) $(5, 3)$

15. Which of the following matrices is equivalent to $B + 3A$?

$$A = \begin{bmatrix} 1 & 3 \\ -2 & 2 \end{bmatrix} \quad B = \begin{bmatrix} x & y \\ y & x \end{bmatrix}$$

A) $\begin{bmatrix} x + 3 & y + 9 \\ y - 6 & x + 6 \end{bmatrix}$

B) $\begin{bmatrix} 3x & 9y \\ -6y & 6x \end{bmatrix}$

C) $\begin{bmatrix} x + 3 & y - 9 \\ y - 6 & x + 6 \end{bmatrix}$

D) $\begin{bmatrix} 3x & 9y \\ 6y & 6x \end{bmatrix}$

E) $\begin{bmatrix} 3x + 1 & 3y + 3 \\ 3y - 2 & 3x + 2 \end{bmatrix}$

ACT Math: Statistics and Probability

Basic Statistics

- The **mean** (or **average**) of a dataset can be found by adding up each point in the data set, then dividing that sum by the number of points in the data set:

  The mean of the dataset {3, 3, 6, 9, 15} is $\frac{3+3+6+9+15}{5} = \frac{36}{5} = 7.2$

- The **median** of a data set is the value in the middle. To find the median, first make sure all the data points are in ascending (increasing) order:

  The median of the dataset {2, 5, 5, 1, 3} is 3

- If there is an even number of points in the data set, the median is the mean of the two middle values:

  The mean of the dataset {1, 2, 3, 4, 6, 9} is $\frac{3+4}{2} = 3.5$

- The **mode** of a data set is the most frequent data point. If two or more data points are the most frequent, all of them are considered to be the mode. Note that for a data point to be the mode, there must be more than one instance of that point in the data set:

  The mode of the dataset {3, 3, 6, 7, 7, 7, 8, 9, 9, 9, 11} is both 7 and 9

- The **range** of a data set is the difference between the largest and smallest data points:

  The range of the dataset {1, 2, 4, 7, 8, 9, 11} is $11 - 1 = 10$

Example 1

Marlon is bowling in a tournament and has the highest average after 5 games, with scores of 210, 225, 254, 231, and 280. In order to maintain this exact average, what *must* be Marlon's score for his 6th game?

A) 200
B) 210
C) 231
D) 240
E) 245

First let's figure out what Marlon's current average is:

$$\frac{210+225+254+231+280}{5} = \frac{1200}{5} = 240$$

In order to keep the average the same, let's call his sixth score x and solve for the new average of six scores:

$$\frac{210+225+254+231+280+x}{6} = 240$$
$$1200 + x = 1440$$
$$x = 240$$

The answer is **D**.

Graph-Based Statistics

- The ACT tests your ability to understand information presented in graphs, tables, and charts.
- **Circle Graphs** are a common means of distributing data separated into different categories into percentages. Look below for an example of a circle graph:

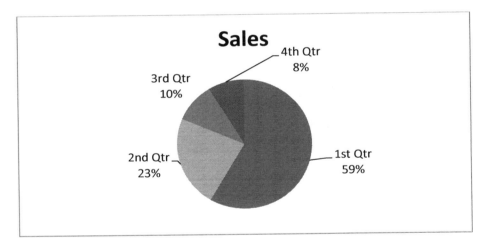

- Each wedge of the circle graph corresponds to a different category of sales, dependent upon the quarter in which the sales were completed.

- **Bar Graphs** show the relative size of different categories of data. Look below for an example of a bar graph:

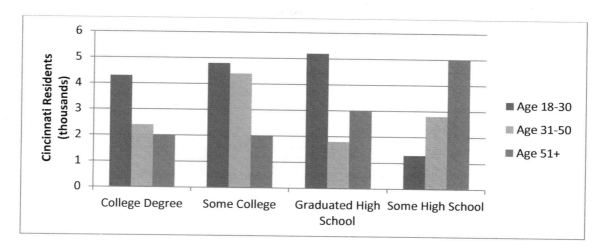

- The bar graph above breaks the residents of Cincinnati into age groups (represented by the differently shaded bars) and education level (represented on the y-axis).
- Other information on the ACT is presented in **Tables.** Tables generally express numerical data, separating the contents of the data into 2 or more different categories. Look below for an example of a table:

	% Iron	% Aluminum	% Carbon
Ore A	63.5	23.2	10.1
Ore B	48.3	36.2	13.9

- Each row of the table shows the percentage of various substances in an ore, while each column shows which substance the numbers are referring to.
- There are many other ways of organizing data on the ACT, but these are the most commonly used.

Example 2

The circle graph below shows the distribution of registered voters, by age, for a community. Registered voters are randomly selected from this distribution to be called for jury duty. What are the odds (in the age range: not in the age range) that the first person called for jury duty is in the range of 25-35 years?

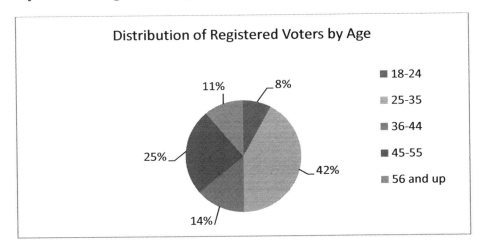

A) 1:3

B) 7:8

C) 7:43

D) 21:29

E) 42:25

Here, we're asked to compare two things: people in the 25-35 age range to people not in that range. 42% of the people are in the 25-35 range, while 58% of people are outside of it.

42%: 58% → 21: 29. The answer must be **D**.

Counting and Probability

- The **fundamental counting principle** is used to figure out the total number of ways that different events can occur. To do so, multiply the total number of options for each occurrence:

  A sandwich store has 3 meat options, 3 cheese options, and 5 bread options. How many possible options of sandwiches are there?

  $$3 \times 3 \times 5 = 45 \text{ sandwich options}$$

- The **probability** of something occurring is the ratio of the number of times it could occur to the total number of possible cases. The probability of all of the different occurrences of an event must add up to 1:

  A 6-sided die is rolled; what is the probability of rolling a prime number?

  We have 6 total options (1 to 6), but only 3 of them are prime (2, 3, 5). Thus, the probability is $\frac{3}{6} = \frac{1}{2}$

- When dealing with the probability of two different options (option A or option B), the probability of either one happening can be found by adding the two probabilities together (as long as the two options do not overlap):

  The probability of rain is 0.3, while the probability of cloudy skies with no rain is 0.5. What is the probability of neither?

  First, let's calculate the chance of it raining or having cloudy skies with no rain: $0.3 + 0.5 = 0.8$. However, we want the probability of neither happening. So, let's subtract this from 1: $1 - 0.8 = 0.2$.

- When dealing with the probability of two options both happening, the probability can be found by multiplying the two probabilities together:

  What is the probability of flipping a coin twice and obtaining Heads both times?

  The probability of flipping Heads is $\frac{1}{2}$. So, the probability of flipping Heads, AND flipping heads is: $\frac{1}{2} \times \frac{1}{2} = \frac{1}{4}$.

- **Permutations** are all of the possible arrangements of a collection of things, in which the order is important. You can calculate permutations using the **nPr function** in your graphing calculator, where n is the total number of things you have and r is the number of things you are choosing from n:

If 8 people are running a race, in how many possible ways can the gold, silver, and bronze medals be awarded?

Since order matters (gold and silver are different places), use a permutation:

$$nPr = 8P3 = 336.$$

- **Combinations** are all of the possible arrangements of a collection of things, in which the order is not important (combinations focus on the number of **unique** groups). You can calculate combinations using the **nCr function** in your graphing calculator, where n is the total number of things you have and r is the number of things you are choosing from n:

If 8 people are running a race, in how many possible ways can 3 people be picked for a random drug test?

Since order does not matter, use a combination:

$$nCr = 8C3 = 56.$$

Example 3

A bag contains 12 red marbles, 5 yellow marbles, and 15 green marbles. How many additional red marbles must be added to the 32 marbles already in the bag so that the probability of randomly drawing a red marble is $\frac{3}{5}$?

A) 13
B) 18
C) 28
D) 32
E) 40

Let's first figure out the probability of drawing a red marble: $\frac{12}{35}$. We want to increase this probability by only adding red marbles. Every red marble added affects both the top and bottom value of the ratio, so we can add r to both the numerator and the denominator of the ratio, set it equal to $\frac{3}{5}$, and solve for r:

$$\frac{12+r}{32+r} = \frac{3}{5}$$
$$5(12 + r) = 3(32 + r)$$
$$60 + 5r = 96 + 3r$$
$$2r = 36$$
$$r = 18$$

The answer is **B**.

PRACTICE EXERCISE

1. What is the probability of flipping 3 coins and obtaining 2 tails and 1 heads?
   A) $\frac{1}{4}$
   B) $\frac{3}{8}$
   C) $\frac{5}{8}$
   D) $\frac{2}{3}$
   E) $\frac{3}{4}$

2. What is the positive difference between the range and the median of the dataset below?
   $$\{1, 3, 3, 3, 5, 8, 8, 10, 10, 12\}$$

   A) 2
   B) 4.5
   C) 5.5
   D) 6.5
   E) 8

3. A man has a wardrobe that consists of 2 pairs of shoes, 4 pairs of pants, 3 jackets, 2 sweaters, and 6 shirts. If he must choose a pair of shoes and pants, a shirt, and either a jacket or a sweater to wear to work, how many options does he have?
   A) 17
   B) 32
   C) 120
   D) 240
   E) 288

4. A student obtained scores of 75, 82, 90, and 94 on her 4 science tests. What score must she get on her 5th test to finish with an average of at least 88 over her 5 tests?
   A) 91
   B) 95
   C) 97
   D) 98
   E) 99

5. A student council of 3 students is being formed from the 18 members of the honor society. How many unique student councils can be formed?
   A) 54
   B) 108
   C) 816
   D) 4,896
   E) 5,832

The circle graph below shows the distribution of vertebrates, by type, in a nature preserve.

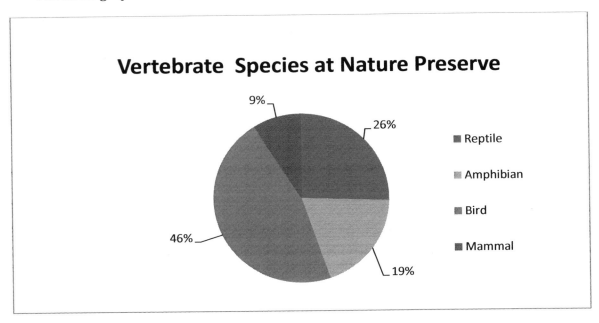

6. If 168 different species of vertebrates exist at the nature preserve, approximately how many of them are reptiles or amphibians?
   A) 35
   B) 45
   C) 57
   D) 76
   E) 83

7. To the nearest percent, the number of bird species at the nature preserve is what percent greater than the number of amphibian species?
   A) 42%
   B) 45%
   C) 142%
   D) 242%
   E) 245%

8. What is the ratio of reptile and mammal species in the nature preserve to other species?
   A) 7 : 20
   B) 9 : 20
   C) 7 : 13
   D) 9 : 11
   E) 7 : 11

The table below shows the number of runs scored in each of 68 baseball games in a tournament.

Total number of runs scored in a game	Number of games with this total
1	2
2	6
3	12
4	9
5	16
6	8
7	15

9. What is the average number of runs scored per game, to the nearest tenth?
   A) 3.0
   B) 3.3
   C) 4.0
   D) 4.7
   E) 5.0

10. What is the median number of runs scored per game?
   A) 3
   B) 3.5
   C) 4
   D) 4.5
   E) 5

11. Six boys are arranged in a circle, and each shakes hands with each other boy exactly once. How many handshakes are given?
   A) 6
   B) 12
   C) 15
   D) 30
   E) 36

12. Two 6-sided dice are rolled and their results are summed. What is the probability of rolling a 6, 7, or 8 on the two dice?
   A) $\frac{3}{11}$
   B) $\frac{1}{4}$
   C) $\frac{4}{9}$
   D) $\frac{2}{3}$
   E) $\frac{5}{6}$

13. An integer from 100 through 999, inclusive, is to be chosen at random. What is the probability that the number chosen will have 9 as at least 1 digit?

A) $\frac{152}{900}$

B) $\frac{171}{900}$

C) $\frac{252}{900}$

D) $\frac{171}{1000}$

E) $\frac{252}{1000}$

14. Seven people are standing in a group. If they get in line so that the tallest person is first, the shortest person is last, and the remaining people are between them in any order, how many ways are there to arrange the people?

A) 15

B) 21

C) 35

D) 120

E) 5,040

15. An integer from 1 through 50, inclusive, is to be chosen at random. What is the probability that the number chosen is even or a multiple of 5, but not both?

A) $\frac{19}{50}$

B) $\frac{2}{5}$

C) $\frac{1}{2}$

D) $\frac{3}{5}$

E) $\frac{31}{50}$

ACT Math: Trigonometry

Trigonometric Ratios

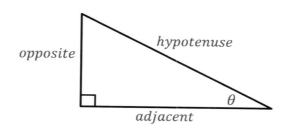

- Use trigonometric ratios to find missing side lengths or angle measurements of right triangles:

  SOH CAH TOA: $\sin\theta = \frac{opposite}{hypotenuse}$ $\qquad \cos\theta = \frac{adjacent}{hypotenuse} \qquad \tan\theta = \frac{opposite}{adjacent}$

- The inverse of the trigonometric ratios can be used to find an angle measurement when given two side lengths:

  $$\sin^{-1}\left(\frac{opposite}{hypotenuse}\right) = \theta \qquad \cos^{-1}\left(\frac{adjacent}{hypotenuse}\right) = \theta \qquad \tan^{-1}\left(\frac{opposite}{adjacent}\right) = \theta$$

Example 1

According to the measurements given in the figure below, which of the following expressions gives the distance, in miles, from the boat to the dock?

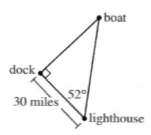

A) $30\tan 52°$

B) $30\cos 52°$

C) $30\sin 52°$

D) $\frac{30}{\cos 52°}$

E) $\frac{30}{\sin 52°}$

We are given the length of the leg adjacent to the angle and searching for the one opposite the angle given. So, we should use the tangent function:

$$\tan 52° = \frac{opposite}{30} \rightarrow opposite = 30 \tan 52°.$$ The answer must be **A**.

- Sine, cosine, and tangent have different values depending on where they are located at in the unit circle. Memorize the relationships shown in the image below:

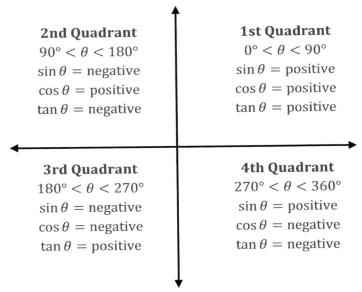

2nd Quadrant
$90° < \theta < 180°$
$\sin \theta = negative$
$\cos \theta = positive$
$\tan \theta = negative$

1st Quadrant
$0° < \theta < 90°$
$\sin \theta = positive$
$\cos \theta = positive$
$\tan \theta = positive$

3rd Quadrant
$180° < \theta < 270°$
$\sin \theta = negative$
$\cos \theta = negative$
$\tan \theta = positive$

4th Quadrant
$270° < \theta < 360°$
$\sin \theta = positive$
$\cos \theta = negative$
$\tan \theta = negative$

Trigonometric Relationships

- The ACT tests your ability to understand relationships between the different trigonometric functions. These equations will be given to you on the test, but being familiar with them will help you on test day:

$$\sin \theta = \cos(90° - \theta) \text{ and } \cos \theta = \sin(90° - \theta)$$

$$\frac{\sin \theta}{\cos \theta} = \tan \theta$$

The Law of Sines: For a triangle with side lengths a, b, and c opposite angles $\angle A$, $\angle B$, and $\angle C$, respectively, the Law of Sines states $\frac{\sin \angle A}{a} = \frac{\sin \angle B}{b} = \frac{\sin \angle C}{c}$.

The Law of Cosines: For a triangle with side lengths a, b, and c opposite angles $\angle A$, $\angle B$, and $\angle C$, respectively, the Law of Cosines states $c^2 = a^2 + b^2 - 2ab \cos \angle C$.

$$\csc \theta = \frac{1}{\sin \theta} = \frac{hypotenuse}{opposite} \qquad \sec \theta = \frac{1}{\cos \theta} = \frac{hypotenuse}{adjacent} \qquad \cot \theta = \frac{1}{\tan \theta} = \frac{adjacent}{opposite}$$

$$\sin^2 \theta + \cos^2 \theta = 1 \qquad \tan^2 \theta + 1 = \sec^2 \theta \qquad \cot^2 \theta + 1 = \csc^2 \theta$$

Example 2

Triangle $\triangle ABC$ is shown in the figure below. The measure of $\angle A$ is $40°$, $AB = 18$ cm, and $AC = 12$ cm. Which of the following is the length, in centimeters, of BC?

(Note: For a triangle with sides of length a, b, and c opposite angles $\angle A$, $\angle B$, and $\angle C$, respectively, the Law of Sines states $\frac{\sin \angle A}{a} = \frac{\sin \angle B}{b} = \frac{\sin \angle C}{c}$ and the Law of Cosines states $c^2 = a^2 + b^2 - 2ab \cos \angle C$.)

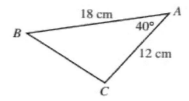

A) $12 \sin 40°$
B) $18 \sin 40°$
C) $\sqrt{18^2 - 12^2}$
D) $\sqrt{12^2 + 18^2}$
E) $\sqrt{12^2 + 18^2 - 2(12)(18) \cos 40°}$

We can rearrange the Law of Cosines to fit the variables given in our problem:

$$c^2 = a^2 + b^2 - 2ab \cos \angle C \rightarrow a^2 = b^2 + c^2 - 2bc \cos \angle A$$

Next, just plug in the given values and solve for a: $a^2 = 12^2 + 18^2 - 2(12)(18) \cos \angle 40°$.

Take the square root of each side to solve for a: $a = \sqrt{12^2 + 18^2 - 2(12)(18) \cos 40°}$

The answer is **E**.

Graphs of Trig Functions

- Occasionally, the ACT will test you on the graphs of trigonometric functions, usually the graphs of sine or cosine. You can always graph these functions in your graphing calculator, but make sure you keep the mode in Radians instead of Degrees ($180° = \pi$ radians).
- The graphs of $\sin x$ and $\cos x$ are shown below:

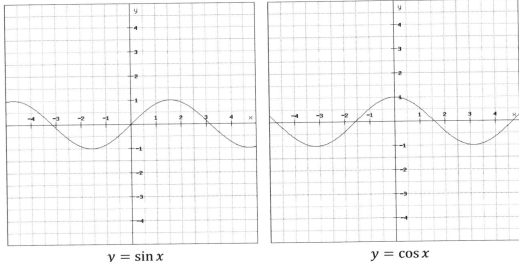

$$y = \sin x \qquad\qquad y = \cos x$$

- Trigonometric graphs can get more complicated through transformations. To account for these transformations, use the equation $y = a \sin(bx - c) + d$ or $y = a \cos(bx - c) + d$. There are four main parts of the graph that can be transformed:

- The **amplitude** of the function is represented by a. The amplitude of the graph is the maximum height the graph reaches from its center:

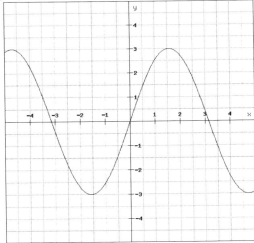

The graph above shows $y = 3 \sin x$. As you can see, its height is now 3 units from the midline instead of just 1 unit.

- The **period** of a graph is how long the graph takes to repeat itself and is represented by b. Normally, the graphs of sine and cosine functions repeat themselves every 2π radians (or $360°$). To find the period of a sine or cosine function, use $\frac{2\pi}{b}$:

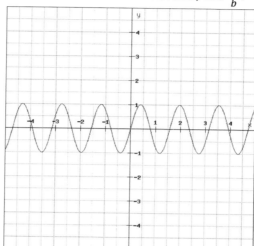

The graph above shows $y = \sin(4x)$. Thus, it repeats itself every $\frac{2\pi}{4} = \frac{\pi}{2}$ radians.

- The **phase shift** of a graph is how much the graph is shifted to the right or left of its usual starting point. If the value of c is positive, the shift is to the right $\frac{c}{b}$ units. If c is negative, the shift is to the left $\frac{c}{b}$ units:

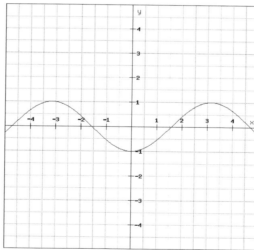

The graph above shows $y = \sin\left(x - \frac{\pi}{2}\right)$. Since c is positive (Remember, the equation is $y = a\sin(bx - c) + d$), the graph is shifted $\frac{\pi}{2}$ units to the right.

- The **vertical shift** of a graph is how much the graph is shifted up or down. If the value of d is positive, the graph is shifted up d units, while a negative d value shifts the graph down d units:

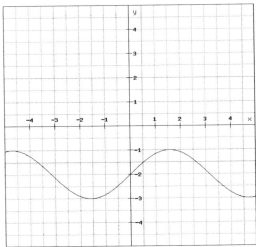

The graph above shows $y = \sin x - 2$. Since d is negative, the graph is shifted down 2 units.

- Sometimes, the value of a is negative. When this occurs, the entire graph is flipped over its center line.

Example 3

The graph of the trigonometric function $y = 2\cos\left(\frac{1}{2}x\right)$ is shown below.

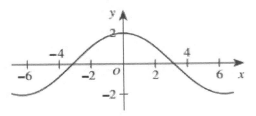

The function is:

A) even (that is $f(x) = f(-x)$ for all x).
B) odd (that is $f(-x) = -f(x)$ for all x).
C) Neither even nor odd.
D) The inverse of a cotangent function.
E) Undefined at $x = \pi$.

Since the graph above is symmetric over the y-axis, we know that $f(x) = f(-x)$. Thus, the answer must be **A**.

PRACTICE EXERCISE

1. The dimensions of the right triangle below are given in inches. What is tan θ?

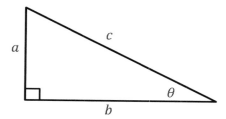

A) $\frac{a}{b}$

B) $\frac{a}{c}$

C) $\frac{b}{a}$

D) $\frac{b}{c}$

E) $\frac{c}{a}$

2. Which of the following is equivalent to sin 120°?

A) $\frac{1}{2}$

B) $\frac{\sqrt{3}}{2}$

C) 1

D) $\frac{-\sqrt{3}}{2}$

E) $\frac{-1}{2}$

3. The dimensions of the right triangle below are given in feet. What is cos θ?

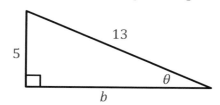

A) $\frac{5}{12}$

B) $\frac{5}{13}$

C) $\frac{12}{13}$

D) $\frac{13}{12}$

E) $\frac{12}{5}$

4. In $\triangle DEF$, shown below, G is on EF, the length of DF is 8 inches, and $\sin f = 0.6$. How many inches long is GF?

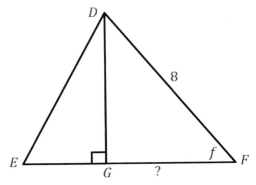

A) 4.8
B) 6.4
C) 6.9
D) 7.8
E) 13.3

5. If $\sin x = 0.75$, then $\cos(90 - x) = ?$
   A) 0.25
   B) 0.50
   C) 0.75
   D) 1.50
   E) Cannot be determined from the given information

6. If $\sin^2 A + \cos^2 A = 1$, then $2 - 2\sin^2 A = ?$
   A) $-2\cos^2 A$
   B) $-1\cos^2 A$
   C) $\cos^2 A$
   D) $2\cos^2 A$
   E) $4\cos^2 A$

7. What is the period of the function represented by $y = -3\cos(2x - 5) + 2$ in the coordinate plane?
   A) $\frac{\pi}{2}$
   B) π
   C) 2π
   D) 3π
   E) 5π

8. What is $\sin\theta - \cos\theta$ in the triangle below?

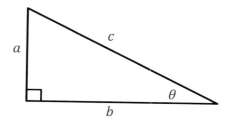

A) $\frac{a-b}{c}$

B) $\frac{b-a}{c}$

C) $\frac{a+b}{c}$

D) $\frac{b-c}{a}$

E) $\frac{c-b}{a}$

9. Joe places a ladder against a wall. The ladder makes an angle of 36° from the ground. If the ladder is 12 feet long, what is the expression for finding the distance the foot of the ladder is from the wall?
   A) $12\tan 36°$
   B) $12\cos 36°$
   C) $12\sin 36°$
   D) $\cos\frac{12}{36}$
   E) $\sin\frac{12}{36}$

10. If $\tan\theta = \frac{12}{5}$ and $180° < \theta < 270°$, what is $\cos\theta$?
    A) $-\frac{13}{12}$
    B) $-\frac{12}{13}$
    C) $-\frac{5}{13}$
    D) $\frac{5}{13}$
    E) $\frac{12}{13}$

11. A right triangle has leg lengths of 6 and 8. What is a possible angle measure of one of the acute angles of the triangle?
    A) 36.87°
    B) 41.41°
    C) 48.59°
    D) 55.78°
    E) 63.13°

12. A man is standing at ground level and looks up at a 23° angle to see the top of a building that is 250 feet tall. How far away is he standing from the base of the building, to the nearest foot?

A) 106
B) 230
C) 272
D) 589
E) 640

13. If $\sin \theta = -\frac{3}{5}$ and $90° < \theta < 180°$, what is $\tan \theta$?

A) $-\frac{4}{3}$
B) $-\frac{5}{4}$
C) $-\frac{3}{4}$
D) $\frac{3}{4}$
E) $\frac{4}{3}$

14. For θ such that $0 < \theta < 90°$, the expression $\frac{1-\sin^2 \theta}{\cos \theta} + \frac{1-\cos^2 \theta}{\sin \theta}$ is equivalent to:

A) 0
B) 1
C) 2
D) $\sin \theta + \cos \theta$
E) $\sin \theta \cos \theta$

15. What is the amplitude of the function represented by $y = -2 \sin(3x + \pi) + 1$ in the coordinate plane?

A) -2
B) -1
C) 1
D) 2
E) 3

Math Practice Exercises Answer Key

Pre-Algebra Review
1. D
2. E
3. B
4. C
5. B
6. C
7. D
8. A
9. C
10. C
11. D
12. E
13. D
14. C
15. D

Number Properties
1. C
2. C
3. E
4. C
5. C
6. B
7. B
8. C
9. E
10. D
11. D
12. C
13. A
14. B
15. B

Ratios, Rates, and Percent
1. C
2. D
3. B
4. D
5. A
6. C
7. B
8. C
9. D
10. A
11. D
12. C
13. D
14. C
15. A

Algebraic Operations
1. A
2. B
3. C
4. D
5. D
6. A
7. E
8. A
9. E
10. D
11. E
12. E
13. D
14. C
15. A

Solving and Modeling Linear Equations
1. C
2. E
3. D
4. D
5. B
6. D
7. D
8. A
9. B
10. D
11. A
12. C
13. E
14. E
15. E

Functions
1. A
2. E
3. B
4. B
5. D
6. D
7. A
8. C
9. A
10. E
11. D
12. E
13. E
14. A
15. C

Solving and Modeling Linear Inequalities and Absolute Value Equations

1. C
2. A
3. C
4. C
5. E
6. E
7. A
8. E
9. C
10. D
11. D
12. B
13. C
14. E
15. E

Solving and Modeling Systems of Equations

1. A
2. C
3. E
4. D
5. B
6. A
7. D
8. C
9. E
10. C
11. A
12. E
13. D
14. C
15. E

Coordinate Plane Geometry

1. D
2. B
3. C
4. A
5. C
6. C
7. B
8. E
9. D
10. B
11. D
12. D
13. B
14. A
15. C

Quadratics and Polynomials

1. E
2. B
3. D
4. E
5. D
6. A
7. C
8. D
9. A
10. C
11. A
12. E
13. E
14. D
15. C

Radical Expressions and Complex Numbers

1. C
2. E
3. A
4. B
5. C
6. C
7. E
8. D
9. B
10. E
11. D
12. B
13. E
14. B
15. D

Rational Expressions

1. E
2. A
3. D
4. D
5. E
6. D
7. B
8. A
9. E
10. C
11. C
12. B
13. D
14. E
15. C

**Exponential and
Logarithmic Expressions**

1. D
2. A
3. B
4. C
5. D
6. D
7. E
8. D
9. C
10. D
11. B
12. D
13. E
14. E
15. D

Lines, Angles, and Polygons

1. C
2. A
3. E
4. B
5. A
6. C
7. B
8. B
9. D
10. C
11. E
12. C
13. D
14. C
15. E

Circles

1. A
2. B
3. C
4. D
5. C
6. B
7. C
8. E
9. C
10. C
11. D
12. A
13. B
14. C
15. D

Conic Sections

1. C
2. E
3. E
4. E
5. C
6. C
7. B
8. C
9. C
10. D
11. E
12. B
13. B
14. E
15. C

Sequences and Patterns

1. C
2. B
3. D
4. C
5. D
6. D
7. D
8. C
9. B
10. B
11. D
12. D
13. A
14. D
15. B

Matrices

1. B
2. B
3. D
4. B
5. E
6. D
7. C
8. B
9. E
10. A
11. E
12. C
13. A
14. E
15. A

Statistics and Probability

1. B
2. B
3. D
4. E
5. C
6. D
7. D
8. C
9. D
10. E
11. C
12. C
13. C
14. D
15. C

Trigonometry

1. A
2. B
3. C
4. B
5. C
6. D
7. B
8. A
9. B
10. C
11. A
12. D
13. C
14. D
15. D

ACT Reading: Introduction

The ACT Reading Test is designed to assess your reading comprehension and analysis skills. This lesson will provide an overview of what you can expect from the ACT Reading Test.

Format of the ACT Reading Test

The Reading Test has four passages of approximately 750 total words each. The passages will either be a single long passage or two short paired passages. The passages are accompanied by a total of 40 questions.

Because you will have just 35 minutes to complete this section, the ability to read and analyze information quickly will be vital to success on the Reading Test.

The passages will be accompanied by line numbers that allow you to quickly reference certain parts of the passage. Some questions will reference these line numbers. Each passage will be followed by 10 questions of varying difficulty.

Content of the ACT Reading Passages

The four passages on the Reading Test will always fall into the same four categories and will appear in the same order: Literary Narrative, Social Science, Humanities, and Natural Science.

LITERARY NARRATIVE

This is the broadest of the passage categories because it includes both prose fiction and literary non-fiction such as memoirs and personal essays. In either case, the passage will be a narrative, which means it will tell a story of some sort. In addition to the plot of the passage, it is important to pay attention to character development, tone, style, and mood.

SOCIAL SCIENCE

This category includes subjects ranging from anthropology to politics to education. In essence, these passages deal with the ways in which societies and civilizations work. Many, though not all, will have a political context.

Because the subject of social science passages will often be heavily factual, it is helpful to underline key names, dates, and concepts and to pay close attention to cause-effect relationships and the chronology of events.

HUMANITIES

This category covers cultural matters, especially art and literature. In general, these passages are either analytical or informative. Unlike social science passages, which usually provide a political context, humanities passages generally focus on the cultural significance of the subject matter.

Like social science passages, humanities passages are often heavily factual, so it can be useful to underline key names, dates, and concepts.

NATURAL SCIENCE

This category of passages focuses on scientific topics. These passages may either be informative or persuasive. In either case, the passages are likely to rely on factual information. Pay particular attention to cause-effect relationships and comparisons.

Content of the ACT Reading Questions

The questions on the ACT Reading Test fall into two broad categories: explicit and implicit information. About half of the questions on the Reading Test will focus on what is explicitly stated in the passages while the other half will focus on implicit meanings of the passages.

In general, explicit information questions will ask you to accomplish tasks such as:

- Identifying main ideas
- Recalling specific details and facts
- Understanding sequence of events
- Comprehending cause-effect relationships
- Identifying character motivation

Implicit information questions will ask you to accomplish tasks such as:

- Defining words and phrases based on context
- Draw inferences based on information in the passage
- Make comparisons
- Draw generalizations
- Analyze the author's voice and method

General Strategies for the ACT Reading Test

Read often. Success on the Reading Test will rely on your ability to read quickly and efficiently. There is no quick trick to gaining reading comprehension and speed skills - the only effective method is to read frequently. The more often you read, the faster you will become.

Determine your personal order of difficulty. Neither the questions nor the passages appear in a specific order of difficulty, but most students find certain passage categories to be easier than others. If you enjoy literary narrative passages more than the other passage categories, start there. You will be able to answer the questions more quickly without worrying about time yet.

Read the entire passage first. By reading the passage first, you'll have a grasp of the plot, themes, or primary arguments of the passage before addressing the questions. You will also know where to locate the information referenced by various questions.

Mark the passage up. While you read, don't be afraid to scribble all over the booklet. Underline key words, phrases, or facts. Note the main ideas of different paragraphs. Note shifts in tone or argument. By doing this, you will make answering the questions easier. The more you practice for the ACT Reading Test, the better you will be at identifying information that is likely to be asked about, making your scribbles all the more useful.

ACT Reading: Explicit Information

Roughly half of all ACT Reading Test questions will focus on explicit information, meaning that the answers to these questions will be based on information in the passage without any interpretation required on your part.

Main Ideas

While some questions on the ACT Reading Test will focus on smaller details, many will ask you to identify main ideas or make generalizations about the passage. Such questions will often ask you to summarize the main argument of the passage, identify the author's purpose in writing it, or describe the tone of the passage as a whole. Other main idea questions may focus on only part of the passage by asking you to identify the main idea or primary argument presented in specific paragraphs.

There are typically one to two main idea questions per passage, so you can expect to see several of these types of questions scattered throughout the ACT Reading Test.

STRATEGIES FOR MAIN IDEAS

Since main idea questions will often ask about the main ideas of the passage as a whole, **consider saving them for last**. This will allow you to get a firmer grasp of the entire passage as you answer the other questions first.

Although there will rarely be a single line in the passage that you could point to as support for a main idea question, even these more generalized questions will be supported by evidence. You should be able to point to specific sentences within the passage to support the correct answer. **Eliminate any answer choices that you cannot support using evidence from the passage.**

For main idea questions that focus on the passage as a whole, focus your attention on the introduction and conclusion. **Author's will typically introduce their primary arguments in the introduction and/or reiterate those arguments in the conclusion.**

Details and Facts

Questions that focus on specific details and facts are both straightforward and common to the ACT Reading Test. You will likely see several of these questions with each passage. They are particularly common to Literary Narrative passages.

These questions will focus on specific lines, facts, or details in the passage rather than focusing on the passage as a whole or on entire chunks of the passage. One benefit of detail-oriented questions is that they will often (though not always) reference specific lines in the passage where the answer might be found. This can help you answer such questions quickly since you'll be able to focus directly on a single part of the passage instead of hunting for the correct answer. Be aware that many details questions will not reference a specific detail but will instead ask you to provide a certain detail. In such cases, your familiarity with the passage will be the key to finding the correct answer. Taking notes while you read, as we discussed in our first lesson, can also be very helpful in answering such questions.

A word of caution about detail-oriented questions: The answer choices will often include at least one tempting incorrect choice. For example, the test creators may include an answer choice that references a detail from elsewhere in the passage. Although such an answer might seem tempting since it could be supported by evidence from the passage, it is not directly related to the detail referenced in the question and is therefore incorrect.

STRATEGIES FOR DETAILS AND FACTS

Read the passage first. Even though these questions might reference a very specific part of the passage, it is difficult to interpret a detail or fact without adequate context. **The only way to understand the detail in context is to read the entire passage or at least the paragraph(s) containing the detail**. Other questions may not reference a specific part of the passage, in which case your familiarity with the passage as a whole will help you find the correct answer quickly and efficiently.

Then, read only the question. Don't even look at the answer choices. This will help you to avoid any tempting but incorrect answer choices. After carefully reading the question, look at the part of the passage being referenced and **answer the question in your own words**. Only then should you look at the answer choices. Look for an answer that is similar to the one you came up with. If no such answer exists, begin by eliminating answers that contradict the answer you came up with.

Always double check your answer. Questions focusing on details and facts will always have very clear and specific support from the passage. If you cannot locate specific support for your answer, check other answers.

Sequence of Events

Some questions will ask you to identify the sequence of events within a passage in order to determine how that sequence influences the content of the passage. There are several common organizational patterns that can help you to identify a passage's sequence of events.

In a narrative passage, including both literary narrative and prose fiction passages, the sequence of events often follows some sort of **chronological pattern**, discussing events in the order in which they occurred. This may also be the case in some of the other types of passages, such as a natural science passage that outlines the steps taken to achieve a particular discovery or a social science passage discussing historical events.

Events may also be discussed in a **cause-and-effect** sequence. This is the identification of a reason for a result. Usually, the reason will be discussed before the result, but some authors may discuss results before examining reasons.

Compare and contrast patterns of organization present one issue and then compare or contrast it to another issue.

Some passages may utilize more than one organizational structure. For example, a single paragraph or small group of paragraphs may present a cause-and-effect sequence within a passage that generally follows a chronological pattern. By noting shifts in organizational structure, you can set yourself up for success when dealing with sequence of events questions.

STRATEGIES FOR SEQUENCE OF EVENTS QUESTIONS

Take notes while you read. **Make note of the passage's overall organizational structure as well as shifts in organization from paragraph to paragraph.**

Pay attention to transitions and transitional phrases, both within and between paragraphs, because these transitions can help identify the sequence of events.

PRACTICE EXERCISE

Directions: Read the following passage and answer the accompanying questions.

A few days ago, a lady, crossing in one of the ferry boats that ply from this city, saw a young boy, poorly dressed, sitting with an infant in his
Line arms on one of the benches. She observed that the
(5) baby looked sickly and coughed. This, as the day was raw, made her anxious on its behalf, and she went to the boy and asked whether he was alone there with the baby, and if he did not think the cold breeze dangerous for it. He replied that he
(10) was sent out with the child to take care of it, and that his father said the fresh air from the water would do it good.

While he made this simple answer, a number of persons had collected around to listen, and one
(15) of them, a well-dressed woman, addressed the boy with a string of such questions and remarks as these:

"What is your name? Where do you live? Are you telling us the truth? It's a shame to have that
(20) baby out in such weather; you'll be the death of it. (To the bystanders:) I would go and see his mother and tell her about it, if I was sure he had told us the truth about where he lived. How do you expect to get back? Here, (in the rudest
(25) voice,) somebody says you have not told the truth about where you live."

The child, whose only offense consisted in taking care of the little one in public and answering when he was spoken to, began to shed
(30) tears at the accusations thus grossly preferred against him. The bystanders stared at both; but among them all there was not one with sufficiently clear notions of propriety and moral energy to say to this impudent questioner,
(35) "Woman, do you suppose, because you wear a handsome shawl, and that boy a patched jacket, that you have any right to speak to him at all, unless he wishes it - far less to prefer against him these rude accusations? Your vulgarity is
(40) unendurable; leave the place or alter your manner."

Many such instances have we seen of insolent rudeness, or more insolent affability, founded on no apparent grounds, except an
(45) apparent difference in pecuniary position. It was sad to see how the poor would endure -

mortifying to see how the purse-proud dared to offend, often with no intent to do so. An excellent man, who was, in his early years, a missionary to
(50) the poor, used to speak afterwards with great shame of the manner in which he had conducted himself toward them. "When I recollect," said he, "the freedom with which I entered their houses, inquired into all their affairs, commented on their
(55) conduct, and disputed their statements, I wonder I was never horsewhipped, and feel that I ought to have been; it would have done me good, for I needed as severe a lesson on the universal obligations of politeness in its only genuine form
(60) of respect for man as man, and delicate sympathy with each in his peculiar position."

To doubt the veracity of another is an insult which in most *civilized* communities must in the so-called higher classes be atoned for by blood,
(65) but, in those same communities, the same men will, with the utmost lightness, doubt the truth of one who wears a ragged coat, and thus do all they can to injure and degrade him by assailing his self-respect, and breaking the feeling of personal
(70) honor - a wound to which hurts a man as a wound to its bark does a tree.

Then how rudely are favors conferred, just as a bone is thrown to a dog! A gentleman, indeed, will not do that without accompanying signs of
(75) sympathy and regard. Just as this woman said, "If you have told the truth I will go and see your mother," are many acts performed on which the actors pride themselves as kind and charitable.

In Catholic countries there is more courtesy
(80) for charity is there a duty, and must be done for God's sake; there is less room for a man to give himself the pharisaical tone about it. A rich man is not so surprised to find himself in contact with a poor one; nor is the custom of kneeling on the
(85) open pavement, the silk robe close to the beggar's rags, without profit. The separation by pews, even on the day when all meet nearest, is as bad for the manners as the soul.

Blessed be he, or she, who has passed
(90) through this world, not only with an open purse and willingness to render the aid of mere outward benefits, but with an open eye and open heart,

ready to cheer the downcast, and enlighten the dull by words of comfort and looks of love. The (95) wayside charities are the most valuable both as to sustaining hope and diffusing knowledge, and none can render them who has not an expansive nature, a heart alive to affection, and some true notion, however imperfectly developed, of the (100) meaning of human brotherhood.

Such a one can never sauce the given meat with taunts, freeze the viand by a cold glance of doubt, or plunge the man, who asked for his hand, deeper back into the mud by any kind of rudeness.

(105) In the little instance with which we began, no help was asked, unless by the sight of the timid little boy's old jacket. But the license which this seemed to the well-clothed woman to give to rudeness, was so characteristic of a deep fault (110) now existing, that a volume of comments might follow and a host of anecdotes be drawn from almost any one's experience in exposition of it. These few words, perhaps, may awaken thought in those who have drawn tears from other's eyes (115) through an ignorance brutal, but not hopelessly so, if they are willing to rise above it.

1. According to the passage, the weather that day on the ferry was:

    A) cold and windy.
    B) clear but humid.
    C) damp and freezing.
    D) warm but windy.

2. Which of the following is an accusation leveled at the boy by the well-dressed woman?

    A) That the boy had no mother
    B) That the boy was trying to kill the baby
    C) That the boy was poorly dressed
    D) That the boy lied about where he lived

3. The boy began to cry because:

    A) he was cold and hungry.
    B) the woman spoke so rudely to him.
    C) he wanted to go home.
    D) the woman tried to take the baby.

4. Which of the following most accurately summarizes the main idea of the fifth paragraph (lines 42-61)?

    A) Many people regret the rudeness with which they treated the poor.
    B) Those who are better off often mistreat the poor without intending to offend.
    C) Missionaries routinely offend the people they intend to convert.
    D) The poor endure insults because they rely on charity.

5. The missionary referred to in the fifth paragraph was ashamed of his views toward the poor:

   A) in his early years, before becoming a missionary.
   B) in his later years, after being horsewhipped.
   C) during his visits, when he entered their houses.
   D) after his visits, upon reflection of his conduct.

6. According to the passage, which of the following is an insult that must "be atoned for by blood" (line 63) among the upper classes but that is frequently visited upon the poor?

   A) Insulting someone's ragged coat
   B) Cutting down someone's tree
   C) Accusing someone of lying
   D) Questioning one's civilization

7. According to the passage, people often engage in charitable acts in order to:

   A) feel good about their own generosity.
   B) show sympathy to others.
   C) encourage others to engage in similar acts.
   D) atone for their previous rudeness.

8. Catholics help others primarily because:

   A) they want others to see how generous they are.
   B) they feel duty-bound to do so.
   C) they are told that they must do so by their bishops.
   D) they are wealthy and can afford to do so.

9. According to the passage, those who engage in charity "with an open eye and open heart":

   A) are not rude, but comforting.
   B) are often rude.
   C) do so for selfish reasons.
   D) are generally condescending.

10. The main idea of the passage as a whole can most accurately be summarized as:

   A) rich people and poor people should avoid interacting with one another in order to prevent rudeness.
   B) the wealthy have a right to engage in rudeness toward the poor because they are charitable toward the poor.
   C) rudeness toward the poor is unfortunately common, but that should change.
   D) all charitable acts carry with them an element of rude condescension.

ACT Reading: Implicit Information

Roughly half of all ACT Reading Test questions will focus on implicit information, meaning that the answers to these questions will require that you go beyond what is specifically stated in the text in order to draw conclusions or make inferences. However, the answers to these questions will still be supported by evidence from the text.

Drawing Inferences

These questions ask you to draw conclusions based on information in the passage. The biggest trick to remember regarding inference questions is to always stick to the passage. It can be tempting to draw an inference that goes further than what the passage states.

For example, if someone were to say that their hair is wet, you might infer that that person had just gotten out of the shower. This seems reasonable, but there are other perfectly plausible explanations for wet hair. Perhaps the person took a bath, walked through the rain, got caught in the sprinklers, or just went swimming. Without additional context, you cannot infer a reason for the wet hair.

Inference questions will usually include words like *suggest*, *infer*, *conclude*, or *imply*. They will often, although not always, reference a specific part of the passage. Locating the right part of the passage is half the battle, which is where taking notes while you read comes in handy.

STRATEGIES FOR DRAWING INFERENCES

Look for context. The question will often reference something specific in the passage. Once you've located the relevant sentence(s), read the surrounding paragraphs to provide enough context.

Answer the question in your own words before looking at the answer choices. Since you're more likely to include only relevant information in your own answer, this can help you to avoid seemingly plausible answers.

Look for the answer that is most similar to your self-generated answer. Don't be tempted by answers that include extraneous or unrelated information that make them seem like they could be true.

Author's Voice and Method

You will encounter a handful of questions that ask about the author's attitude or tone. Such questions might ask you to identify the author's overall attitude or tone, or they might focus on inferring the author's attitude based on a specific part of the passage.

The author's voice and method indicate his attitude toward his subject matter. Vocabulary, syntax, character development, punctuation and other elements of the author's technique communicate the author's feelings about the topic of the text. By looking for clues in the author's style, you can determine how the author feels about the subject.

Voice questions often accompany literary narrative or prose fiction passages, but even the non-fiction passages may include voice questions. These questions may ask, for example, whether the author is opinionated or objective.

Your best barometer to determine the author's attitude is his vocabulary. Look for words and phrases that have positive or negative connotations. For example, one author might say of global climate change theory that "the globe's foremost scientists have overwhelmingly agreed that climate change is an immediate problem exacerbated by human activity," while another might say that "a group of irresponsible scientists have put forth a series of unsubstantiated studies that create an environment of fear that is simply not supported by scientific proof." In the first quote, the scientists are "the globe's foremost" scientists, suggesting a positive attitude toward the scientific community; in the second, the scientists are "irresponsible," suggesting a negative attitude toward the scientific community.

STRATEGIES FOR VOICE AND METHOD QUESTIONS

Underline or circle key words and phrases that reveal the author's attitude toward his subject matter. **Pay particular attention to phrases with positive or negative connotations.**

Based on your interpretation of the passage, determine whether the author's attitude is generally positive or negative. **Eliminate any answer choices that disagree with your general assessment.**

Carefully scrutinize any extreme answer choices. These answer choices are not often correct. For instance, an author who is skeptical of an idea wouldn't be accurately described as being "vehemently opposed" to an idea.

PRACTICE EXERCISE

Directions: Read the following passage and answer the accompanying questions.

With improvements in technology, you can buy a refrigerator that puts eggs on your grocery list when you are almost out, a safe that counts
Line money as it is being placed inside, or even a
(5) vehicle that lets you stream music from the Internet without having to use your phone.

While all of these so-called smart gadgets sound great, you may be shocked when you discover the threats that come with this level of
(10) connectivity. Two security investigators set out to reveal these dangers by remotely taking over a sports utility vehicle speeding along the highway. From the comfort of their couch, they were able to shut down its engine as an 18-wheeler barreled
(15) toward it. Even though this was just a stunt and no one was hurt, the fact remains that their combined skills could give them access to any Internet-connected vehicle produced by this particular car manufacturer in the same way as
(20) long as they had the car's I.P. address, its network address on the Internet.

Though the car manufacturer eventually recalled 1.4 million vehicles to remedy this weakness, the recall occurred a year after the
(25) issue was originally reported, and only after the manufacturer received a request from the government following the investigators' spectacular publicity stunt. Even though the company provided a software fix, they insisted
(30) that no defect had been discovered. If two people sitting on a couch stopping a speeding car's engine from miles away does not count as a defect in the eyes of this company, I cannot imagine that they are truly concerned with their
(35) customer's safety as you might otherwise believe.

Nevertheless, a hacked car is just one example of what can go wrong when objects are software equipped and digitally connected. While it may be said that these well-connected objects
(40) offer improved convenience and safety, the reality is that these objects are nothing more than a fast-motion train wreck in privacy and security. The problem is that Internet security was never meant to handle the three billion users of today. The goal
(45) of the early Internet was to connect small numbers of people in secure groups. As the

number of Internet users has increased rapidly, efforts to toughen security have been thwarted due to cost, shortsightedness, and competing
(50) interests. Thus, linking everyday objects to this vulnerable platform is reckless and potentially disastrous.

Highly publicized hacks draw the most attention, but the software defects that let them
(55) happen are pervasive. While intricate breaches can require genuine effort — the car hacker duo's stunt necessitated two years of research — simple errors in code can also result in substantial failure. Connecting everyday objects to this defective
(60) platform introduces new risks if glitches are taken advantage of on a mass scale. While the malfunction of thousands of smart refrigerators would likely be a hassle as opposed to a danger, thousands of hacked cars — two-ton metal
(65) objects — on our roadways is a completely different story. Most people would laugh at the prospect of this scenario, but those individuals might be surprised to learn that the contemporary automobile is composed of dozens of computers
(70) that most manufacturers link using an antiquated system that is vulnerable to hacking. Once hackers gain access, they have every component of the vehicle — engine, steering, transmission and brakes, the entertainment system—in the
(75) palm of their hands.

This is not new information. For years, security experts have cautioned about the hazards of coupling so many systems in vehicles. Anxious researchers have written academic papers, hacked
(80) cars, and plead with the industry to do something. In response, the industry has respectfully nodded and simply remedied the known flaws without truly altering the way they operate.

Honestly, no corporation, especially not in
(85) the automotive industry, wants to be the first to pay the price for an update to fix an issue of which most consumers would not otherwise be aware. In 1965, a documentary underscored the car manufacturers' opposition to spending money
(90) on safety features like seatbelts. After public deliberation and federal legislation, manufacturers were finally required to incorporate safety

technologies. This highlights the necessity of
federal safety regulations to push automakers to
(95) change, as a whole industry. In this case, we need
a new definition of car safety, and of the safety of
anything running software or connecting to the
Internet.

It may be difficult to permanently fix security
(100) on the Internet, but we cannot continue to build
on a defective foundation. Reacting to digital
threats by mending only exposed susceptibilities
is no better than only providing a very ill patient
with aspirin. Nevertheless, the cause is not lost.
(105) We can make programs more dependable and
data bases safer. But the required changes will
necessitate an initial investment to avert future
problems - the exact reverse of the present
corporate desire.

1. It can be most reasonably inferred from the
   first paragraph that:

   A) the most common smart-gadgets are
      vehicles.
   B) most smart-gadgets are household items.
   C) smart-gadgets are gadgets that think for
      themselves.
   D) smart-gadgets were not available in the
      past.

2. The second paragraph (lines 7-21) suggests
   that:

   A) only the cars made by one particular
      manufacturer are vulnerable to such
      hacks.
   B) the investigators hoped to cause an
      accident by hacking the vehicle.
   C) the investigators' goal was to become
      famous by hacking a vehicle.
   D) the investigators' goal was to prove the
      dangers of Internet-connected vehicles.

3. In the third paragraph, the author's tone
   suggests that the author:

   A) is sympathetic towards the car
      manufacturer's response.
   B) disapproves of the car manufacturer's
      response.
   C) is impressed by the car manufacturer's
      response.
   D) disapproves of the investigators' actions.

4. Based on information in the passage, it can
   most reasonably be concluded that the security
   issues inherent in Internet-connected devices:

   A) must be addressed by car manufacturers.
   B) can only be solved through federal
      regulation.
   C) cannot be solved without first addressing
      fundamental problems with the Internet.
   D) will never be solved because hackers will
      always find a hole in security measures.

5. The passage suggests that threats to Internet-connected devices:

   A) stem primarily from the concentrated efforts of skilled hackers.
   B) can result from intentional hacking or from simple error.
   C) come primarily from poorly written code.
   D) could be entirely prevented by simply avoiding the Internet.

6. The author's shift in tone in the second half of the passage reveals that the author:

   A) takes Internet-connected devices' threat to public safety seriously.
   B) considers many of the latest advances in smart technology to be a joke.
   C) believes that Internet-connected devices should be outlawed.
   D) advocates government regulation of the Internet.

7. It can be concluded from the fifth paragraph (lines 53-75) that:

   A) car hacking is an overblown fear.
   B) the potential for car hacking is not limited to a single manufacturer.
   C) car hacking is actually far more pervasive than most people believe.
   D) only certain components of vehicles are vulnerable to hacking.

8. The passage implies which of the following similarities between seat belts and updated computer systems in cars?

   A) Both address safety issues that the public is currently unaware of.
   B) Both are required by federal law to be built into vehicles.
   C) Both are safety features that are unlikely to be widely incorporated into cars until required by law.
   D) Both are proven to save lives.

9. The author's tone can best be described as:

   A) critical yet cautiously optimistic.
   B) amused and enthusiastic.
   C) condescending and passionate.
   D) angry yet exuberantly hopeful.

10. The author's overall attitude toward software-enabled technology can best be described as:

   A) skeptical and apprehensive.
   B) admiring but slightly concerned.
   C) passive, but pessimistic.
   D) complimentary but reserved.

ACT Reading: Words in Context

At least one or two questions for each passage will ask you to define a word or phrase based on its context.

Words in Context

These questions are among the easiest to spot on the ACT Reading Test because they are almost always phrased in the same way:

As it is used in *line XX, this word/phrase* most nearly means...

The fact that such questions are easy to locate does not mean that they are easy to answer. Keep in mind that the words or phrases in question will usually have more than one correct definition. This means that you cannot simply look at the answer choices without referencing the passage because more than one answer choice is likely to offer an accurate definition of the word. Instead, you must consider what the word means as it is used in the passage.

For example, the word "read" has several possible meanings. If asked what the word "read" means, you could correctly answer that it means "to learn from print," "to observe," or "to predict," depending on the use of the word:

I like to **read** about combustion engines.

Scientists were able to **read** the growth rings using a microscope.

The gypsy used to **read** palms at the fair.

Always look to the passage to determine a word or phrase's meaning before answering the question!

STRATEGIES FOR DEFINITIONS IN CONTEXT

Before looking at the answer choices, locate the word or phrase as it is used in the passage. **Come up with a definition based on its usage using your own words.**

Eliminate answer choices that clearly don't fit based on your chosen definition. Don't be fooled by answer choices that could be true if you squint and look at them the right way - the ACT seeks correct answers, not plausible answers.

Choose the answer choice that best matches your assessment of the word's meaning. **Plug the answer choice into the sentence in the passage to be sure that it suits the context.**

PRACTICE EXERCISE

Directions: Read the following passage and answer the accompanying questions.

While every new technology has its benefits, each also comes with its own set of horrors. For instance, the experience of waking up at 30,000
Line feet resting on the shoulder of a complete stranger
(5) who is drenched in your drool did not exist until we developed commercial air flight and sleeping aids.

Thus, one minor email "feature" with which we are addicted has forced the majority of those
(10) who have ever texted or emailed to face a moment of sheer dread. I am referring to auto-fill.

Although you may not be familiar with the terminology, you are most definitely familiar with auto-fill if you use a computer. Auto-fill is what
(15) automatically puts in email addresses as you type the first few letters into the recipient field. Auto-fill provides a dropdown menu when you are using the Internet to search for information, fill out a form, or type in an address to get directions.
(20) This simple marvel of modern technology is so incredibly commonplace in our lives that most people do not even notice it exists.

Why is auto-fill problematic? Especially in emails, this function can result in not only
(25) misinterpretations in wording, but the transmission of sensitive information to the wrong people. Secrets can be revealed without thought. No one is safe.

The mayor of New York learned this lesson
(30) the hard way. Recently, he wrote an email to a few staff members in which he was grumbling that taking one of those I'm-a-man-of-the-people subway trips to an event had caused him to be late. Unfortunately, a newspaper reporter for a
(35) major publication was one of the recipients of this cantankerous email due to the mayor's use of the auto-fill function. What happened? The reporter published an article about the mayor's chronic lateness.

(40) Just ponder how often people send emails to precisely the individual who should never ever get them. Contemplate what would happen if you unintentionally included your boss in an email that you sent out to friends to tell them you need a
(45) new job. You might also consider the cautionary experience of a prestigious book editor. The editor had paid seven figures for a celebrity memoir, but the celebrity's manager was constantly meddling with the revisions of the
(50) memoir. Exasperated, he sent an email to his coworkers with the title *A Few Wise Words from a Brain-Dead Manager.* One of his coworkers and the manager shared the same unusual last name. I don't need to tell you what happened
(55) next.

Even if we are more vigilant when sending our daily emails, we occasionally forget how auto-fill works in other programs we use. Social media websites can access your contacts, sending
(60) out invites to people which you may have been trying to avoid or including the wrong people in a private message chain. If your computer is used by more than one person, you could inadvertently sign them up for emails or other services.
(65) Moreover, you could end up filling in an old address when trying to have an important package delivered. The unfavorable effects of auto-fill are endless.

So what can be done by people who have
(70) committed a colossal auto-fill blunder? First, some email programs will let you can take back your email within the first 30 seconds of sending. This is a function you may have to enable, so be sure to check that this feature is turned on.

(75) What if you recognize your error after the 30-second window has expired? These are the moments of slow-motion horror, where I instantaneously recognize my gaffe, smash my keyboard, and begin concocting the most credible
(80) lie, all while hyperventilating at my desk. When this happens, there is nothing left to do, but apologize. When I say apologize, I mean you need to do something more than just email an apology or explanation. The bigger the flub, the
(85) more dramatic the gesture of remorse must be.

At this point, you might be wondering if it is possible to disable auto-fill all together. It is possible, but tedious. It may be better to practice caution than to stop using the function. Plus, you
(90) never know what might result from an auto-fill gaffe. It may be the push you need to say something that needs to be said to a friend, your

boss, or your parents. Nevertheless, it is important that we be aware that this risk is the price we pay
(95) for living in our advanced technological world.

1. As it is used in line 8, *minor* most nearly means:

   A) immature.
   B) trivial.
   C) younger.
   D) significant.

2. As it is used in line 11, *sheer* most nearly means:

   A) steep.
   B) outright.
   C) translucent.
   D) precipitous.

3. As it is used in line 20, *marvel* most nearly means:

   A) to stare.
   B) genius.
   C) wonder.
   D) to be amazed.

4. As it is used in line 26, *transmission* most nearly means:

   A) communication.
   B) program.
   C) gears.
   D) signal.

5. As it is used in line 36, *cantankerous* most nearly means:

   A) elderly.
   B) cheerful.
   C) snobbish.
   D) cranky.

6. As it is used in line 42, *contemplate* most nearly means:

   A) consider.
   B) plan.
   C) notice.
   D) study.

7. As it is used in line 56, *vigilant* most nearly means:

   A) unaware.
   B) wakeful.
   C) anxious.
   D) attentive.

8. As it is used in line 63, *inadvertently* most nearly means:

   A) rashly.
   B) carelessly.
   C) unintentionally.
   D) forcefully.

9. As it is used in line 70, *colossal* most nearly means:

   A) monument.
   B) minute.
   C) gigantic.
   D) vast.

10. As it is used in line 73, *enable* most nearly means to:

    A) support.
    B) facilitate.
    C) turn on.
    D) refuse.

11. As it is used in line 74, *feature* most nearly means:

    A) emphasize.
    B) column.
    C) main item.
    D) aspect.

12. As it is used in line 88, *tedious* most nearly means:

    A) boring.
    B) annoying.
    C) repetitive.
    D) impossible.

ACT Reading: Literary Narrative

The literary narrative passage includes both narrative nonfiction (like memoirs) and prose fiction (like short stories). In either case, the passage is likely to be a narrative, meaning that it will tell some sort of story. You should read these passages carefully, as you would a passage for literature class.

Likely Question Types

Literary narrative passages lend themselves to certain types of questions. By knowing what types of questions you are likely to face on the literary narrative passage, you can be sure to look for certain aspects of the passage as you read. These questions include:

Details and facts: These are very common to literary narrative passages. In fact, up to three or four of the ten questions might focus on specific details and facts. The key to succeeding on these questions is to read the passage carefully before addressing the questions.

Draw inferences: These are generally less straightforward than details and facts questions because they require that you use information from the passage to draw conclusions or make generalizations, but these questions are just as common as details and facts questions. As with details and facts questions, the most important part of correctly answering an inferences question is to read the passage carefully.

Character generalization: These types of questions are limited to literary narrative passages since characters generally appear only in stories. Such questions will generally expect you to take all of the details you are given about a particular character and boil them down into a simple statement about that character. For example, if a character gives candy to children, adopts stray animals, and hugs everyone she meets, we might describe her as soft-hearted and generous.

Narrator's point of view: These questions are also typically unique to literary narrative passages. You will often see at least one question asking you to identify the narrator's point of view. As long as you pay close attention while reading the passage, these questions should be fairly simple to answer.

Sequence of events: Since these passages typically tell a story, there will often be a clear sequence of events in the passage. It is likely that you will encounter at least one question asking about the sequence of events. Remember that this can include not only questions that ask about the order in which events occurred but also questions that ask about cause and effect.

Attitude and tone: In the case of literary narratives, you may be asked about the attitude or tone of both the author and the characters. It is important to pay attention to word choice in the passage overall and in any thoughts or dialogue spoken by the characters.

LITERARY NARRATIVE READING STRATEGIES

Look carefully for a **main theme** in the narrative. This can often be inferred based on the events within the story and the tone of the overall passage.

Note both the overall tone of the passage and any shifts in tone. **Shifts in tone may help to reveal the attitudes of individual characters.**

Underline any adjectives or phrases that reveal information about the characters. This may help you to answer character generalization questions and questions about the relationships between characters.

Circle or underline transitions that reveal the **sequence of events** or how events are related to one another.

Note any specific words, phrases, or sentences that reveal the narrator's **point of view or attitude.**

After reading the passage, jot down a very brief summary of the events in the passage.

PRACTICE EXERCISE

Directions: Read the following passage and answer the accompanying questions.

Shortly after six in the evening on May 31, 2013, the 55-year-old, scholarly, and handsome storm chaser briefly stares, mouth agape, at the video camera that the driver of the white
(5) Chevrolet Cobalt points at him. He then looks back out the window towards the wheat fields that rim the outskirts of El Reno, Oklahoma. The fields are awash with a creepy glow and are whipped around by vicious winds. Not far from
(10) the car, maybe two miles away, twin funnel clouds coil down from the endless black sky. What we can observe from the man's voice on the video is not exactly horror, but his words are not as analytically factual as one might expect from
(15) the scientist he happens to be.

"Oh, my God. This is gonna be a huge one," he says.

This man is Tim Samaras, the man who has spent the majority of his adult life in the company
(20) of dangerous tornadoes. His obsession with them has led his wife, Kathy, to laughingly say that her husband "had an affair with Mother Nature."

Samaras kissed Kathy goodbye on the morning of May 18, making sure that his lucky
(25) token – an actual McDonald's cheeseburger, albeit a moldy one – was sitting in its special spot on the dashboard of his Cobalt. He and two crew members – a 45-year-old meteorologist named Carl Young and Samaras' 24-year-old son, Paul –
(30) zipped eastward towards the Midwestern plains known as Tornado Alley.

The tornado that hit Rozel, Kansas that very evening had been beautiful, glowing orange set against the sun, with its long twisting funnel
(35) swerving and dancing. Luckily, it had left Rozel mostly unharmed during its dance. Samaras' team, known as TWISTEX, would come across at least a dozen tornadoes over the next four days, recording thousands of miles of storm chasing
(40) through Kansas, Oklahoma, and Texas. They rested for four nights back home in Colorado before returning to the chase.

Samaras sits in his Cobalt in the May 31 video, a storm chaser on yet another chase – a
(45) man in ebullient pursuit of his passion. Yet it is heavily apparent that there is something different about this particular video, possibly because the audience is aware of something that Samaras is not.

(50) This tornado is the product of numerous thunderstorms that had matured along a cold front over central Oklahoma that afternoon. It shook trees as if they were possessed by the devil as it rotated counterclockwise across plains. Unlike the
(55) magnificently geometric tornado in Rozel, El Reno's tornado is a dark, black wedge of no certain structure.

"OK, I'm gonna stop," says Young as he filmed the storm while driving. "We'll get a great
(60) view of it. This good?"

The Cobalt comes to a stop and both of the Samaras and Young jump out. Paul is filming on a different camera, viewing the storm from a different lens. As the three men line up along the
(65) edge of a gravel path and peer through rain with squinted eyes, a third funnel drops out of the sky.

"Three vortices!" Young exclaims.

"Yep," says Samaras. When he faces the camera again, his awe is apparent. His expression
(70) is one of marvel as he witnesses the might of the storm. "Wow. This is gonna be a gigantic wedge."

A few minutes later, they return to the car. The windshield wipers flap helplessly as they
(75) silently drive eastward with the tornado flanking their south. Lightening smatters the bleak sky, power lines dance and flick madly in the wind. The wedge of darkness grows and grows, diminishing any trace of sunlight, casting
(80) darkness over the three men in their car.

None of the men can tell just how big the beast beneath the dark rain cloud really is. They can't see the tornado uprooting telephone poles and pulverizing brick homes. They only see the
(85) dark, blurry suggestion of violence.

When he at last sees the storm, what he witnesses is something that Tim Samaras has never seen before and will never see again. The tornado shifts to the left, ordinarily a sign of a
(90) dissipating vortex. But this tornado doesn't shrink. It swells grotesquely to nearly three miles in diameter, larger than any other tornado on record.

And the tornado's new path brings it straight for the TWISTEX team.

(95)   "Let's keep going," Samaras says. "This is a very bad spot."

The tape clicks off at 6:20 p.m. Three minutes later, the storm and its chasers meet.

In all, the storm killed 22 people, including (100) the TWISTEX chasers. In the wake of Tim Samaras's death, chasers wondered: If it had happened to Tim, a man known for his caution, couldn't it happen to any of them? Every one of them knew the answer, yet not a single one vowed (105) to give up the chase. Nor, in truth, would have Tim Samaras.

1. Which of the following can be most reasonably inferred about the marriage of Tim and Kathy Samaras?

   A) Kathy has not been very accepting of Tim's frequent absences.
   B) Kathy has often accompanied Tim on his tornado chases.
   C) Kathy has accepted Tim's frequent absences with good nature.
   D) Kathy does not allow Tim to leave to chase storms very often.

2. Tim Samaras believes that which of the following brings him good luck?

   A) His wife
   B) His son
   C) His Chevy Cobalt
   D) A moldy cheeseburger

3. The passage suggests that storm chasers frequent the Midwestern plains because:

   A) the plains make it easier to see tornadoes.
   B) most tornado chasers live near the Midwest.
   C) many tornadoes occur there.
   D) tornadoes never occur elsewhere.

4. Which of the following best identifies the purpose of the sentence "Yet it is…Samaras is not." (lines 45 through 49)?

   A) To illustrate Samaras's ignorance about tornadoes
   B) To foreshadow a coming event in the story
   C) To show that knowledge of tornadoes has greatly increased since Samaras's time
   D) To show that few tornado chasers videotaped their chases

5. As it is used in line 70, *might* most nearly means:

   A) possibility.
   B) potential.
   C) power.
   D) authority.

6. It can be inferred from the passage that Samaras:

   A) should have been able to predict what the storm would do.
   B) could not have predicted what the storm would do.
   C) was known to be reckless when chasing storms.
   D) was not paying attention on May 31.

7. The narrator's point of view is that of:

   A) a detached observer.
   B) a member of the TWISTEX team.
   C) a fellow storm chaser.
   D) a meteorologist studying tornadoes.

8. All of the following are differences between the tornado in Rozel and the tornado in El Reno EXCEPT:

   A) the Rozel tornado did not occur on the plains.
   B) there was greater visibility during the Rozel tornado.
   C) the Rozel tornado caused less damage.
   D) the sun was shining during the Rozel tornado.

9. The narrator would most likely agree with which of the following characterizations of Tim Samaras?

   A) He should have shown greater dedication to his family.
   B) He was engaged in a pointless and harmful career.
   C) He was needlessly reckless but brave.
   D) He was an experienced, dedicated, and courageous.

10. The author's overall tone can best be described as:

   A) didactic and, at times, academic.
   B) condescending and, at times, mocking.
   C) accusatory and, at times, bitter.
   D) admiring and, at times, poetic.

ACT Reading: Social Studies

The social studies passage will likely resemble your idea of a generic nonfiction passage. It is the most versatile of the passages on the ACT Reading Test because it can include all question types and covers a wide range of possible topics.

Likely Question Types

Social studies passages can include any type of question, but certain passages may lend themselves more to certain question types.

INFORMATIVE PASSAGES

Many social studies passages are informative, particularly those that discuss history or anthropology. Passages that are primarily intended to inform have the following types of questions:

Facts and details: Since informative passages will deal almost exclusively with fact rather than opinion, you will likely see several facts and details questions along with any informative social studies passage. Since these questions will ask you to identify a specific fact or detail, careful reading of the passage is vital.

Sequence of events: When dealing with a straightforward history passage, you will likely see at least one or two questions that ask you about the order in which events occurred. Other social studies passages may lend themselves more to questions about cause and effect. By paying close attention to the passage's organizational structure, you can set yourself up for success with sequence of events questions.

PERSUASIVE PASSAGES

Other social studies passages are more persuasive in nature. Given that these passages tend to involve arguments and opinions, there are certain question types that are likely to appear along with persuasive passages:

Main idea or argument: These are very common question types, particularly with persuasive passages. Main idea or argument questions will ask you to identify the main idea or primary argument of the passage as a whole or of a specific part of the passage. By noting the main ideas and arguments of each paragraph as you read, you can answer such questions more efficiently.

Author's attitude: Persuasive passages will commonly reveal a bias or opinion on the part of the author. Look for specific instances of word choice and for specific arguments that reveal the author's attitude toward his subject matter.

Both informative and persuasive passages have the following types of questions:

Drawing inferences: Like literary narrative passages, social studies passages will likely feature several inference questions. As with all inference questions, the correct answer will always be supported by specific evidence from the passage.

Compare or contrast: These questions will require that you compare or contrast different viewpoints or data. These questions can be challenging because they require you to identify two pieces of information and then analyze the similarities and differences between the two. As with inference questions, part of the challenge will be to locate the appropriate parts of the passage. A thorough reading of the passage can help you to answer such questions more effectively.

SOCIAL STUDIES PASSAGE READING STRATEGIES

While reading, note the **main idea or argument** of each paragraph in the passage.

After reading, write a very brief summary of the main idea or argument of the passage as a whole.

Underline any important facts or pieces of data.

Underline or circle particular words or phrases that reveal the **author's attitude** toward the subject matter.

Underline or circle transitional words or phrases that reveal the passage's **overall organizational structure.**

PRACTICE EXERCISE

Directions: Read the following passage and answer the accompanying questions.

It's just after nightfall on a hot evening in August of 1945. Workers hurry home through dark streets, weaving between the scattered and burnt rubble of the spring fire-bomb raids. Suddenly, the night turns to day by a blinding flash. A column of fire rises angrily up into the sky. Glass shatters into millions of pieces. Great winds whip through the city as floored onlookers gaze upwards from the streets, buildings, and the Imperial Palace. There are only a few injuries and even fewer deaths. The next day, U.S. radio broadcasts to the Japanese people confirm the existence of a new deadly weapon – the atomic bomb. It was set off at a high altitude, off shore, to demonstrate the mighty power of the new weapon but also spare Japan the devastating effects. They are told to surrender within a week or the new bomb would be dropped on one of Japan's cities. After six days of deadlock by the Cabinet, the Emperor himself declares that Japan must submit.

It is one of man's greatest tragedies that this story is untrue. The grim and inextensible facts are very different. Over a half-century later, the question still haunts the world today: Was the bombing of Hiroshima – and Nagasaki – unavoidable?

The ironic nature of history and wishful thinking has complicated this question. The original intent for the bomb was as a counter measure to the threat of Hitler's Nazi Germany building the bomb first. However, the bomb was not completed until after Germany's surrender.

The Japanese Empire was already in decline by the spring of 1945. They were subjected to a blockade, bombarded daily by air, and were scraping by on dwindling stores of food and fuel. Nonetheless, the Japanese stood firm and refused to surrender, which made an invasion the last possible move. Over a million American casualties as well as millions of Japanese casualties were estimated if an invasion were to take place. On the other hand, a single bomb that had yet to reveal its 3-year, $2 billion potential, could quickly meliorate the situation.

The Interim Committee, a group given the task of advising the President on atomic energy and the bomb, met for a two-day session at the end of May. The committee pushed for the use of the bomb in a surprise attack on Japan immediately; but the committee itself was not fully satisfied with the thought of bombing a city and asked its scientific panel to contemplate other options. Although the panel ultimately supported the committee's decision, many others did not. The Franck Report - devised by physicists James Franck and Leo Szilard and chemist Eugene Rabinowitch – suggested that the implementation of the atomic bomb could set off a nuclear arms race that would be impossible to physically and mentally overcome; the consequent distrust between all nations would not be worth what small leverage the U.S. could gain.

The Franck Report sparked the start of a swell of disapproval throughout the scientific community, atomic laboratories, and government executives. Some of the disapproving urged for a warning to the enemy but were met with objections that Allied prisoners could be relocated to the target area. Others suggested an exhibition of the bomb in action in front of an international inspection group; physicist Edward Teller may have even offhandedly proposed an extremely visible blast in Tokyo Bay – right on the steps of the Emperor's porch.

Could that exhibition have worked? The back-to-back bombings on Hiroshima and Nagasaki definitely pushed the Japanese war party into an unsustainable position, created a useful excuse for the Emperor to intervene on the crisis, and made it seem like America had bombs to spare. The initial bombing of Hiroshima was unfortunately untimely: 400 miles from Tokyo and out of the peripheral vision of the people who made national war policy. The Supreme War Council of Japan was only just receiving detailed reports of the damage in Hiroshima when the second bomb was dropped on Nagasaki.

In retrospect, Teller's idea of displaying the might of the bomb over Tokyo Bay, or even a military raid on a nearby establishment, could have had the same impact on the decision makers without the large scale loss of life. With many different factors contributing to the Japanese *(95)* surrender, a more creative form of diplomacy may have been produced if there was not such a heavy reliance on the bomb and its consequences.

1. Within the context of the passage as a whole, which of the following best identifies the purpose of the first paragraph?

    A) To illustrate a hypothetical series of events based on a suggestion that was not acted upon
    B) To share a fictional version of events based on the Interim Committee's recommendation
    C) To explore a commonly accepted historical theory
    D) To surprise the reader with a shockingly untrue statement of fact

2. Which of the following best describes the author's attitude toward the bombings of Hiroshima and Nagasaki?

    A) The bombings were tragic and possibly unnecessary.
    B) The bombings were an unfortunately necessary evil.
    C) The bombings were the tragic result of hasty decision making.
    D) The bombings were a justifiable response to the situation in Japan.

3. The atomic bomb was completed:

    A) before the Franck Report was released.
    B) after a failed invasion of Japan.
    C) after the war with Germany was over.
    D) just before Germany's surrender.

4. The primary purpose of the fourth paragraph (lines 34-45) is to:

    A) argue in favor of invading Japan.
    B) describe the situation in Japan when the decision of whether or not to bomb was being considered.
    C) argue against bombing Japan.
    D) describe why the Japanese did not yet have an atomic bomb.

5. It can be inferred from the passage that:

    A) the Interim Committee was made up of physicists and chemists.
    B) the Interim Committee unanimously and definitively recommended bombing Japan.
    C) the Interim Committee had reservations about the decision to bomb Japan.
    D) the Interim Committee was strongly concerned about the possibility of an arms race.

6. The Franck Report expressed which of the following concerns?

    A) Since the bomb was untested, no one could understand the possible ramifications of bombing Japan.
    B) Bombing Japan would be met with international disapproval.
    C) Bombing Japan would spark a devastating arms race with serious diplomatic implications.
    D) Bombing Japan could potentially kill millions of Allied prisoners.

7. The Americans chose not to warn Japan of the incoming bomb because:

A) a warning would have resulted in calls for an international exhibition.
B) the element of surprise was vital to the successful outcome of the bombing.
C) a warning would reduce the damage done by the bomb.
D) of fears that the Japanese would place Allied prisoners in the path of the bomb.

8. The passage suggests which of the following about the bombing of Nagasaki?

A) It was significantly more deadly than the bombing of Hiroshima because it was much closer to the Supreme War Council of Japan.
B) It may have been unnecessary since Nagasaki was bombed before the Japanese had time to assess the damage of Hiroshima.
C) It was too far from Tokyo to gain the attention of Japanese policy-makers.
D) It was flagrantly wasteful since the U.S. did not have many atomic bombs.

9. As it is used in line 95, the word *form* most nearly means:

A) regulation.
B) condition.
C) shape.
D) style.

10. Which of the following best summarizes the main argument of the passage as a whole?

A) The Japanese bombings were likely avoidable.
B) The Franck Report should have become national policy.
C) The Americans should have limited their bombing to Hiroshima.
D) The bombings of Japan resulted in a lengthy international arms race.

ACT Reading: Humanities

The humanities passage will discuss some aspect of culture or the arts. Aside from its more narrow scope, the humanities passage is otherwise very similar to the social studies passage.

Likely Question Types

Like the social studies passage, the humanities passage is likely to be either informative (objective) or persuasive (subjective). The question types for humanities passages will be exactly the same as for social studies passages.

INFORMATIVE PASSAGES

Informative humanities passages will generally present an objective overview of a particular cultural event, issue, person, or artifact. Like informative social studies passages, informative humanities passages have the following question types:

> **Facts and details:** Be careful to avoid using any outside knowledge - you may be knowledgeable about the subject matter, but the answers must be supported solely by information from the passage. Since these questions will ask you to identify a specific fact or detail, careful reading of the passage is vital.

> **Sequence of events:** Though somewhat less common on informative humanities passages than on informative social studies passages, you may be asked about the passage's sequence of events or organizational structure. Be sure to look for clues to the passage's organizational structure while reading.

PERSUASIVE PASSAGES

Other humanities passages will be more persuasive in nature. Such passages will generally present the author's opinion regarding a cultural event or icon. As with persuasive social studies passage, persuasive humanities passages have certain question types:

> **Main idea or argument:** By using the same strategy as with social studies passages, noting the main ideas or arguments of each paragraph, you can answer these questions on humanities passages effectively.

> **Author's attitude:** Persuasive passages will almost always reveal a bias or opinion on the part of the author. Look for specific instances of word choice and for specific arguments that reveal the author's attitude toward his subject matter.

OTHER QUESTION TYPES

Both informative and persuasive passages have the following types of questions:

> **Drawing inferences:** Like other passages, humanities passages will likely feature several inference questions. As with all inference questions, the correct answer will always be supported by specific evidence from the passage.

> **Compare or contrast:** As with inference questions, part of the challenge will be to locate the appropriate parts of the passage. Thorough reading of the passage can help you answer such questions more efficiently.

HUMANITIES PASSAGE READING STRATEGIES

While reading, note the **main idea or argument** of each paragraph in the passage.

After reading, **write a very brief summary** of the main idea or argument of the passage as a whole.

Underline any important facts or pieces of data.

Underline or circle particular words or phrases that reveal the **author's attitude** toward the subject matter.

Underline or circle transitional words or phrases that reveal the passage's **overall organizational structure.**

PRACTICE EXERCISE

Directions: Read the following passage and answer the accompanying questions.

Like other pleasurable experiences, there are two components to enjoying music: the anticipation of hearing your favorite song, and
Line then actually getting to listen to it. The brain
(5) signaling the chemical dopamine, which is linked to reward, is involved in both components. For years, neuroscientists have wondered whether there was more to it – what gives music its power to induce euphoria?

(10) The brain's naturally-occurring opioids could be the key. An experiment carried out by Daniel Levitin's team at McGill University in Montreal, Canada, showed that when opioid signals in the brain are blocked via the drug Naltrexone, the
(15) amount of pleasure subjects report getting from their favorite song sharply diminished. Oddly, they still enjoyed the anticipation of hearing the song just as much. Although dopamine must have been involved, the point when the opioids kicked
(20) in was the point when music really started to affect subjects' minds.

The sudden appearance of opioids in the brain helps explain music's effect on our body. Listening to music raises people's pain thresholds,
(25) so much that occasionally it can be used to reduce the need for painkillers.

Robin Dunbar of the University of Oxford thinks Levitin's results, which were presented at the Society for Music Perception and Cognition's
(30) conference, help confirm opioids as the mediator of music's power. His research shows that actively engaging with the music strengthens the effect even more – singing, dancing, or drumming along with the music is even more helpful in reducing
(35) pain than just listening to music.

Tom Fritz of the Max Planck Institute for Human Cognitive and Brain Sciences in Leipzig, Germany, and Daniel Bowling of the University of Vienna in Austria are trying to harness this
(40) effect. They are working with a "jymmin" machine, a special type of exercise apparatus that allows music to be paired with weight training. The sounds change as the user pushes harder, and the music's rhythm matches that of their workout.
(45) "It makes the music really pleasurable -- you have the perception that you're being really extremely

musically expressive," says Fritz.

They have shown that after 6 minutes of using the machine, the amount of effort people
(50) perceive they are making falls by half. Exercising with machines also seems to raise a person's pain threshold more than a standard, music-accompanied workout, they told conference delegates.

(55) Their experiments are further support that opioids are involved. "It's another piece of the puzzle," says Bowling. "You don't need a neuroscientist to tell you that music can be invigorating, intensely pleasurable or sad, but this
(60) is an exciting time for research on music's biological foundations."

Fritz is working on software that can provide similar "musical feedback" to users, which he says might help relieve pain for people recovering
(65) from strokes or drug addiction. Some hospitals already use music to relieve anxiety before surgery and pain after. But Sven Bringman of the Karolinska Institute in Sweden says it could be used more. "Music is not used as much as it
(70) should be because it takes more of a nurse's time than just giving a sedative."

While music has yet to be fully exploited clinically, Levitin says we routinely take advantage of its effects on our brain. "Many
(75) people use music to regulate their mood throughout the day. We use music to create a soundtrack to our lives," he says.

The beneficial effects of music aren't just related to how we deal with pain; some people
(80) use music to control their mood as much as they use alcohol or caffeine, says Daniel Levitin of McGill University.

"We reach for a certain kind of music when we want to get going in the morning, and a
(85) different kind of music after we've had a fight with somebody and we want to calm down," he says. Music also seems to have an impact on our immune system, affecting immune molecules such as leukocytes, cytokines and
(90) immunoglobulins.

And here's one that we can all relate to: music can trigger memories - a feature that even seems to be preserved in some people with Alzheimer's disease. Researchers at the University (95) of California, Davis, have found that while music-evoked memories tend to be less vivid than those triggered by other means, our recollections tend to be happy ones – just another reason to make music the soundtrack of your life.

1. According to the passage, which of the following are the components of enjoying a pleasurable experience?

    I. Being told about the experience
    II. Anticipating the experience
    III. Participating in the experience

A) I only
B) II only
C) III only
D) II and III only

2. According to the passage, which of the following causes us to feel pleasure from music?

A) Opioids
B) Exercise
C) Singing
D) Recalling songs

3. Which of the following can best be inferred from the passage about opioids?

A) They cause people to feel less pain.
B) They cause people to experience positive memories.
C) They put people to sleep.
D) They increase the effects of exercise.

4. As it is used in line 32, the word *engaging* most nearly means:

A) attacking.
B) employing.
C) connecting.
D) committing.

5. According to the passage, what does a "jymmin" machine do?

A) It teaches listeners to react to rhythms.
B) It learns a listener's music preferences.
C) It reads the mind to make music selections.
D) It matches music to working out.

6. It can be inferred from the passage that the results of the experiment with the "jymmin" machine were caused by:

A) the strengthened effect of opioids that comes with actively engaging with music.
B) the kinds of exercise done with exercise equipment versus without exercise equipment.
C) the pleasure caused by anticipating a favorite song.
D) the pleasure caused by anticipating a good workout.

7. Which of the following best summarizes the main idea of the paragraph in lines 55 through 61?

   A) Understanding the biological reasons for music's emotional effects could have practical applications in medicine.
   B) Scientists are beginning to understand the biological reasons for music's emotional effects.
   C) People have long understood the emotional effects of music.
   D) Scientists have proven that opioids brought on by music explain the emotional effects of music.

8. The passage suggests that music is not utilized to its full potential in the field of medicine primarily because:

   A) conventional medicine does not recognize music's pain management effects.
   B) the mechanisms of music's effects on pain are not fully understood.
   C) it requires greater effort from medical staff than does administering traditional medications.
   D) music preferences are too individualized to be applied on a broad scale.

9. According to the passage, music has all of the following effects EXCEPT:

   A) raising pain thresholds.
   B) lessening anxiety.
   C) increasing the effects of exercise.
   D) regulating mood.

10. The author's attitude toward music can best be described as:

    A) passionate and knowledgeable.
    B) interested and supportive.
    C) uninterested and disapproving.
    D) reverent and in awe.

ACT Reading: Natural Science

The natural science passage will discuss some area of science such as biology, technology, medicine, or physics. By their very nature, these passages are exceptionally heavy on data, facts, and studies.

Likely Question Types

Natural science passages are more likely to be informative than persuasive. As a result, they will generally focus less on the author's opinions. In order from most to least common, the likely question types on natural science passages include:

Facts and details: These passages will be very dense with data, facts, and study results. Therefore, facts and details questions appear more frequently for these passage types than any other. While reading, pay attention to numbers, studies, and quotes from experts. One common facts and details question will ask you to match certain opinions to certain scientists or studies. As such, you should also pay close attention to names.

Drawing inferences: Like other passages, natural science passages will feature several inference questions. As with all inference questions, the correct answer will always be supported by specific evidence from the passage.

Organizational structure: Natural science passages often focus on questions that examine the organizational structure of the passage or paragraph. Though some science passages may focus on the sequence of events questions that are common to other passage types, most will utilize one of the following structures:

Cause and effect: Science passages often discuss cause and effect relationships. For example, almost every scientific study will determine whether a cause leads to a predicted effect. Pay particular attention to these types of relationships.

Point-counterpoint: Natural science passages will frequently give an overview of a scientific debate about a particular idea. Such passages will often begin with the point of view of one side and then offer the opinions of disagreeing scientists or groups. Take care to note the differing opinions of each scientist as this is likely to provide fodder for questions.

Compare or contrast: Since passages that contain a lot of factual information tend to lend themselves to comparison or contrast questions, you will likely see at least one compare or contrast question with each science passage. As with inference questions, part of the challenge will be to locate the appropriate parts of the passage. A thorough reading of the passage can help you to answer such questions more efficiently.

Main idea: Since these questions are more likely to accompany persuasive passages and since science passages are more often informative than persuasive, you may or may not see main idea questions on the science passage. If you do, the same strategies apply to science passages as to other non-fiction passages.

NATURAL SCIENCE PASSAGE READING STRATEGIES

Map the passage by noting the **main idea** of each paragraph. This will help you locate the relevant parts of the passage when addressing facts and details, inferences, and compare or contrast questions.

Read the passage in small pieces. Natural science passages tend to be significantly more dense than other passages, so they are often not as reader-friendly. By breaking them down into smaller chunks, you can read natural science passages more quickly and efficiently.

Underline data, numbers, and specific studies. These are likely to be addressed in facts and details or inference questions.

PRACTICE EXERCISE

Directions: Read the following passage and answer the accompanying questions.

There are many phenomena in science that cause deep intrigue and scientific interest – the creation of the universe and its potential demise, the complexities of the human brain and functions, and the way dogs look at humans. The faces and looks dogs make can be translated as loving, disappointed, sad, happy, inquisitive, understanding, and sometimes just silly. These looks cause dog lovers' hearts to melt, cat lovers' eyes to roll, and researchers in animal cognition to put sausage into containers to see how dogs and wolves will react to it.

Repetitive trials have clarified a lot of things. Dogs tend to look at humans at much higher rates than wolves do. While the wolves tend to go immediately at the sausage in the Tupperware and keep at it, the dogs look at the humans giving them food while they eat. This finding has led to the (unsurprising) conclusion that dogs are more socially attuned with humans while wolves are more self-reliant.

But beyond this basic conclusion, scientific agreement is somewhat more elusive.

In order to assess the most recent research, published in Biology Letters by Monique Udell at Oregon State University, some context can be drawn from earlier research that garnered a lot of attention over a decade ago.

In 2003, Adam Miklosi, current director of the Family Dog Project, published a paper at Eotvos Lorand University in Budapest describing research on dogs and wolves that were raised by humans. The dogs and wolves were both conditioned to learn how to open containers to get food. Later on, they were given the same containers with food, which were altered so that they could not be opened. The wolves would keep trying to open the impossible contraption while the dogs would just look back at the nearby humans.

Many dog lovers might think that the dogs are geniuses, essentially saying to the humans, "Can I get some help here? You closed it; you open it." But that's not what Dr. Miklosi is saying; he concluded that dogs are just genetically predisposed to look at humans, which could essentially be the basis for the strong but often flawed communications between dogs and humans.

Dr. Udell modified Dr. Miklosi's experiment by giving the wolves and dogs tasks that they could solve, if they tried. The difference, she stated, was that "the animals could get it open – they just had to exert themselves." Similar to the first experiment, the wolves persisted and were able to get the food out of the container. The dogs, in both groups, would quickly look back at the humans. Her interpretation of these results are that the findings of Dr. Miklosi's experiment are "not evidence of advanced cognitive ability," that the different approaches to problem solving are, in fact, completely unrelated to cognitive ability.

Dr. Miklosi retorted in an email that Dr. Udell had made a "huge straw man" and that he had never drawn any such conclusions about cognitive ability. "There is not much about cognition in my test."

In a separate email, Brian Hare, an evolutionary anthropologist and specialist in canine cognition at Duke University, stated that Dr. Udell's research essentially reestablished a common and known phenomenon of dogs looking to humans. He also highlighted the fact that intelligence is not something that can qualitatively be analyzed between different species. This statement simplifies the matter: Dogs are more likely to look at humans, wolves are more likely to tend to their own affairs, and neither behavior is related to intelligence.

But there is still the lingering question of what exactly explains this difference in behavior.

Dr. Mikloski maintains that dogs are genetically predisposed to look at humans.

Clive D. L. Wynne, Dr. Udell's former Ph.D adviser and frequent collaborator, agreed that there is a genetic contribution but that a brief note in Dr. Udell's recent paper intrigued him: An 8-week-old puppy was able to open the puzzle box, which Dr. Udell noted as proof that the dogs were physically capable of opening the container. But Dr. Udell went further, hypothesizing that perhaps the older dogs had learned, through a combination of owner training and sheer habit, not to try to solve problems.

(95) "Dogs around people learn that they should not help themselves," Dr. Wynne said, pointing out that dog owners certainly have incentive to teach their dogs not to open sealed food containers. "I will go so far as to say that we teach (100) our dogs to be stupid."

Further research involving feral dogs may well shine some light on the role of social conditioning in such tests. In the meantime, it would seem that we still have many questions (105) about the relationships between dogs and their humans.

1. The passage suggests that:

   A) the reasons for why dogs look at humans are of equal scientific importance as the complexities of the human brain.
   B) the reasons for why dogs look at humans have long been the subject of scientific research.
   C) wolves are generally smarter than domestic dogs.
   D) dog lovers often underestimate the intelligence of their dogs.

2. According to the passage, which of the following is a conclusion that has widespread scientific agreement?

   A) Dogs are more cognitively advanced than wolves.
   B) Wolves are more self-reliant while dogs are attuned to humans.
   C) Wolves are more cognitively advanced than dogs.
   D) People have made dogs less intelligent than wolves.

3. Following his 2003 experiment, Dr. Miklosi concluded that:

   A) wolves are genetically predisposed to look at humans.
   B) dogs are genetically predisposed to look at humans.
   C) dogs are more cognitively advanced than are wolves.
   D) communication between dogs and humans is imperfect.

4. As it is used in line 47, *strong* most nearly means:

   A) powerful.
   B) sharp.
   C) aggressive.
   D) vigorous.

5. Dr. Udell's experiment and Dr. Miklosi's experiment differed in that:

   A) Dr. Udell's experiment did not examine cognition while Dr. Miklosi's experiment did.
   B) Dr. Udell's experiment definitively proved that wolves are cognitively more advanced than are dogs while Dr. Miklosi's experiment did not.
   C) Dr. Udell's experiment involved a container that was challenging to open while Dr. Miklosi's experiment involved a container that was impossible to open.
   D) Dr. Udell's research definitively disproved Dr. Miklosi's conclusion that dogs are genetically predisposed to look at humans.

6. According to the passage, Miklosi, Udell, and Hare have all made statements that agree that:

   A) dogs' tendency to look at humans is not a reflection of cognition.
   B) dogs are more cognitively advanced than wolves are.
   C) wolves are more cognitively advanced than dogs are.
   D) intelligence of different species cannot be accurately compared.

7. According to Dr. Wynne, the grown dogs were likely unable to open the containers because:

   A) humans have taught them not to solve problems.
   B) only puppies have problem solving skills.
   C) the container was physically impossible to open.
   D) the container could only be opened by puppies.

8. It can be reasonably inferred from the passage that:

   A) the experiments discussed should have used feral dogs instead of wolves.
   B) feral dogs likely lack the same genetic preconditioning that domesticated dogs have.
   C) feral dogs likely have the same genetic preconditioning as domesticated dogs.
   D) similar studies on feral dogs may show whether Wynne's theories are correct.

9. With which statement would the author most likely agree?

   A) Learning about the interactions between dogs and humans is just as important as studying the complexities of the human brain.
   B) Dogs are genetically predisposed to look at humans because it has been evolutionarily beneficial to them.
   C) The reasons for humans' relationships with their dogs are scientifically interesting.
   D) Domesticated dogs are likely much smarter than are either wolves or feral dogs.

10. The main point of the passage is to:

   A) show the flaws in a variety of scientific experiments onto canine behavior.
   B) argue that recent research into canine behavior is more accurate than prior research.
   C) explain why people keep dogs as pets.
   D) explore theories of why dogs look at people.

ACT Reading: Paired Passages

The most recent addition to the ACT Reading Test is the introduction of paired passages. These paired passages consist of two short passages that will total roughly the same word count as the other passages. Sometimes, these passages will present opposing points of view on the same issue; other times, the passages will discuss related topics.

Paired Passage Question Breakdown

The paired passages will be accompanied by ten questions, just as the other passages are. Roughly 3-4 questions will focus solely on the first passage, roughly 3-4 will focus solely on the second passage, and the remaining questions will require that you synthesize information from both passages.

This means that approximately 3 questions per paired passage will focus on the synthesized information.

Answering Paired Passage Questions

Paired passage questions will almost always ask you to compare or contrast the two passages, so you will need to note similarities and differences between the passages while you read.

When you address the questions that focus on both passages, your best strategy will be to utilize the process of elimination. Remember that the correct answer must accurately reflect the information in *both* passages. First, eliminate answer choices that do not accurately reflect the first passage; then eliminate answer choices that do not accurately reflect the second passage. This should significantly narrow down your options.

Of the remaining answer choices, choose the one that most closely reflects both passages.

PAIRED PASSAGE STRATEGIES

While reading, **annotate the paired passages** as you would any other ACT Reading passage: **Note main ideas and arguments; underline or circle word choices** that reveal tone or attitude; and **underline or circle transitions** that reveal organizational structure.

After reading the passages, **briefly summarize** the main ideas and the authors' tones or attitudes in each passage.

Save the paired passage questions for last. These questions tend to be more complex and time consuming than other reading questions. Since there are only about 3 of these questions, it is a good time management strategy to focus your energies on the other questions first.

PRACTICE EXERCISE

Directions: Read the following passage and answer the accompanying questions.

Passage A

Media in the 21ˢᵗ century has given the public
the idea that work should be fun: images of video
games, catered meals, and at-work massages at tech
Line companies make people think of vacation more
(5) than work. Every once in a while, though, the
media exposes us to the tough work environments
of other companies who make people work under
less than Disney-esque conditions.

Work is not supposed to be fun - it's not play.
(10) In the best case scenario, it's rewarding, maybe
financially, maybe psychologically, but it's not a
family trip to Disneyland. Everybody is not
supposed to win. Unlike today's youth baseball or
softball leagues, playing the game isn't enough to
(15) get a trophy. People get paid to go to work, not to
have fun.

A simple anecdote can prove just about
anything you want in an organization with
thousands of employees. Want to prove that
(20) working somewhere is miserable? Find disgruntled
employees. Want to prove that it's all sunshine and
daisies? Find ecstatic employees. There's also self-
selection: The most disgruntled and the most
contented employees are the most likely to share
(25) their experiences.

Every company has jobs that are less fun or
even miserable - the "dirty jobs" as a noted
television star might say. But without such jobs,
there would be little incentive to study and work
(30) hard to advance yourself and your kids. My
grandparents didn't enjoy driving taxis and cleaning
homes, so they pushed their kids, and their kids, in
turn, pushed me.

If these employees are that miserable at work,
(35) they can go elsewhere. There is slavery and
oppression in the world, even in the United States,
but working at Amazon isn't slavery. If people are
miserable, they can try to change the organization,
or they can leave.

(40) Let me tell you a story. I once asked a longtime
Apple employee why he stayed at Apple after it
was possible to make big bucks elsewhere, and it
had become a large, bureaucratic organization with
controls, pressure, and politics. His answer stunned
(45) me: "Because I can do the best work of my career

there."

The bottom line is that if you want to be happy
at your job, find one that is psychologically
rewarding with adequate compensation - in short,
(50) one that enables, encourages and even requires
good work. But good work is hard. When you need
a break from that work and want to have fun,
however, well then you can go to Disneyland.

Passage B

Not only can companies do well by doing right
(55) by their employees – their long-term success and
competitiveness depend on it.

Misery at work largely leads to one thing: high
turnover. High turnover, in turn, leads to high costs.
Ongoing research estimates that turnover costs
(60) employers 20 percent of the departing worker's
salary – significantly more than the cost of
preventing that turnover with benefits such as paid
sick days. By accounting for and investing in the
well-being of employees, companies can greatly
(65) increase retention and, in the long run, save money.

Certain companies have been taking proactive
steps, such as offering paid fertility
treatments and unlimited vacation, to reducing
employee turnover. But these apply only to a fairly
(70) elite group of companies. Some businesses have
announced that they are raising pay levels beyond
the minimum wage, helping workers even more.
Still, others, like Amazon, remain unapologetic for
a cut-throat culture.

(75) On the whole, American businesses are
confusing perks and policies as measures of a good
job. If a company caters three meals a day to its
workers, does that mean the worker has to be at
work long enough to sit through three meals?
(80) People still need time to rejuvenate, even with
benefits.

This disconnect was a theme we heard
repeatedly over the course of a campaign we funded
in the lead up to Labor Day, which traveled the
(85) country asking Americans what makes a job a good
job. Based on the definitions we've heard, it won't
take major financial investments or novel perks to
turn the tide. For many workers, a "good job" is as
basic as knowing their schedule in advance or being

(90) able to take time off for a sick relative. They want flexibility, stability, opportunity, and to take pride in their work.

This is true for workers at all levels and industries, whether they work for a tech giant or *(95)* behind the counter at a fast-food chain. So while we should feel optimistic about recent progress at some companies, we cannot stop there if we want to build a more inclusive economy. And rather than pit employer versus employee, focus on one privileged *(100)* section of the economy, or idealize company perks over substantive benefits, we need to engage around the basics of a good job for all.

1. A rhetorical device used by the author of the first passage is:

    A) asking questions, then immediately answering them.
    B) quotes from authority to reinforce his points.
    C) withholding details to force readers to think for themselves.
    D) statistics and data to emphasize his point of view.

2. The main purpose of the third paragraph of Passage A (lines 17 – 25) is to:

    A) prove that employees work only as hard as they must to avoid being fired.
    B) show how difficult it is to use circumstantial evidence to provide legitimate information about a work environment.
    C) highlight the major differences between disgruntled and happy employees of a company.
    D) prove that self-selection can be an unbiased means of gathering information about the psychology of a company's employees.

3. The author of Passage A seems to criticize all of the following ideas EXCEPT:

    A) participation trophies in youth sports.
    B) popular vacation resorts.
    C) modern-day media outlets.
    D) refusing to work without proper benefits.

4. The author of Passage A posits that one of the benefits of horrible working conditions is that they:

    A) provide better pay than similar jobs.
    B) drive employee turnover.
    C) are at least better than slavery.
    D) incentivize people to advance themselves.

5. With which of the following statements would the author of Passage B most likely agree with?

    A) Delicious, catered meals are more than enough to keep employees happy.
    B) Reducing turnover should be one of the top priorities for businesses wishing to save money.
    C) Every top job in America should have a number of perks and benefits.
    D) Increasing the minimum wage is of utmost importance in helping workers.

6. According to the study done by the author of Passage B, which of the following characteristics do Americans least associate with a "good job"?

   A) Steadiness
   B) The prospect of advancement
   C) Flexibility
   D) Plenty of vacation time

7. As it is used in line 98, the word *pit* most nearly means:

   A) indent.
   B) sink in.
   C) set against.
   D) dig deep.

8. The tone of the author of Passage B can best be described as:

   A) forceful and objective.
   B) casual and subjective.
   C) consoling and reverent.
   D) condemnatory, but sympathetic.

9. Which of the following best describes the author of Passage A's opinion on Amazon versus the author of Passage B's opinion on Amazon?

   A) Reasonable versus ruthless
   B) Callous versus judicious
   C) Servile versus oppressive
   D) Rewarding versus callous

10. How would the author of Passage A most likely react to the author of Passage B's statement that "Misery at work largely leads to one thing: high turnover"?

   A) These jobs need to provide more vacation days for their employees to help reduce turnover.
   B) If people are miserable at work and unable to change the company's culture, then they should leave.
   C) Employees should talk to psychologists or psychiatrists to find the root of their misery.
   D) In a company with thousands of employees, some amount of turnover is inevitable.

ACT Reading: Overview

In this final ACT Reading Test lesson we will examine two unique question types that we have not yet discussed and review key strategies that will help with all passage and question types.

Special Question Types

The ACT Reading Test includes two unique question formats that require special strategies.

I/II/III QUESTIONS

These questions are easy to spot because they will provide you with Roman numerated answer choices. For example:

> The passage suggests that:
>
> I. This happened.
> II. That happened.
> III. Everyone was happy that happened.
>
> A) I only
> B) II only
> C) I and II only
> D) I, II, and III

These questions will often fall under the category of facts and details, relying on explicitly stated information. They may, however, also involve inferences or, in the case of literary narrative passages, character generalizations.

The process of elimination is the best method to approach such questions. Begin by examining the Roman numeral choices. Eliminate any that are definitely false. Based on this elimination, you can then eliminate any answer choices that include that Roman numeral.

NOT/EXCEPT QUESTIONS

Almost any type of question can be phrased as a NOT/EXCEPT question. These questions will include the word "not" or "except" as part of the question, and the exclusionary word will be capitalized. These questions pose a challenge because they require that you look for a false answer rather than a true answer. If you don't carefully read the question, you can easily fall into the trap of choosing one of the true answers - which would be wrong!

As with many other questions, process of elimination is the best strategy to use. In this case, rather than eliminating untrue answer choices, you will eliminate answers that are true.

Strategy Review

Throughout this book, we have repeated several strategies that apply to all types of passages and questions.

ACTIVE READING

Regardless of passage type, it is a good idea to engage in active reading by taking notes and marking up the passage as you read.

Main ideas: Briefly note the main idea of each paragraph. This will not only help you answer main idea and argument questions, but will also provide you with a sort of map to help you locate specific areas of the passage.

Word choice: Underline or circle specific words, phrases, and sentences that suggest a strong positive or negative connotation that might reveal the author's tone or attitude.

Transitions: Underline or circle transitions that can help you to determine the overall organizational structure of the passage. This can help you answer questions about sequence of events or cause and effect more effectively.

Data: Particularly when addressing natural science passages or somewhat scientific social studies passages, take note of data, numbers, and studies. This may help you answer facts and details questions.

Shifts in tone or argument: Note any significant changes in tone or argument as these areas often provide fodder for questions.

PROCESS OF ELIMINATION

With the exception of questions that you are able to quickly and easily answer, your best strategy will be to utilize the process of elimination. Remember to do the following:

Eliminate clearly wrong answers: You should be able to eliminate at least one or two answers immediately because they will be clearly wrong based on the passage.

Eliminate answers that are disproved by the passage: Look at the passage to determine whether any answer choices are negated.

Be wary of extreme answers: While it is not impossible for more extreme answers to be correct, it is rare. If you are debating between two answers and one is extreme, the extreme one can usually be eliminated.

Look for what *is* true, not what *could be* true: After eliminating as many answer choices as possible, if you still have more than one answer choice remaining, don't be tricked into choosing a plausible answer over a correct answer. You are not seeking answers that might be true; you are seeking answers that are proven to be true based on information in the passage.

PRACTICE EXERCISE 1

Directions: Read the following passage and then answer the accompanying questions.

Caroline, having been conveyed home by Robert, had no wish to pass what remained of the evening with her uncle. The room in which he sat
Line
(5) was very sacred ground to her; she seldom intruded on it; and to-night she kept aloof till the bell rang for prayers. Part of the evening church service was the form of worship observed in Mr. Helstone's household. He read it in his usual nasal voice, clear, loud, and monotonous. The rite over,
(10) his niece, according to her wont, stepped up to him.

"Good-night, uncle."

"Hey! You've been gadding abroad all day— visiting, dining out, and what not!"

(15) "Only at the cottage."

"And have you learned your lessons?"

"Yes."

"And made a shirt?"

"Only part of one."

(20) "Well, that will do. Stick to the needle, learn shirt-making and gown-making and piecrust-making, and you'll be a clever woman someday. Go to bed now. I'm busy with a pamphlet here."

Presently the niece was enclosed in her small
(25) bedroom, the door bolted, her white dressing-gown assumed, her long hair loosened and falling thick, soft, and wavy to her waist; and as, resting from the task of combing it out, she leaned her cheek on her hand and fixed her eyes on the
(30) carpet, before her rose, and close around her drew, the visions we see at eighteen years.

Her thoughts were speaking with her, speaking pleasantly, as it seemed, for she smiled as she listened. She looked pretty meditating thus;
(35) but a brighter thing than she was in that apartment—the spirit of youthful Hope. According to this flattering prophet, she was to know disappointment, to feel chill no more; she had entered on the dawn of a summer day—no
(40) false dawn, but the true spring of morning—and her sun would quickly rise. Impossible for her now to suspect that she was the sport of delusion; her expectations seemed warranted, the foundation on which they rested appeared solid.

(45) "When people love, the next step is they marry," was her argument. "Now, I love Robert, and I feel sure that Robert loves me. I have thought so many a time before; to-day I felt it. When I looked up at him after repeating Chénier's
(50) poem, his eyes (what handsome eyes he has!) sent the truth through my heart. Sometimes I am afraid to speak to him, lest I should be too frank, lest I should seem forward—for I have more than once regretted bitterly overflowing, superfluous words,
(55) and feared I had said more than he expected me to say, and that he would disapprove what he might deem my indiscretion; now, to-night I could have ventured to express any thought, he was so indulgent. How kind he was as we walked up the
(60) lane! He does not flatter or say foolish things; his love (friendship, I mean; of course I don't yet account him my lover, but I hope he will be so some day) is not like what we read of in books,— it is far better—original, quiet, manly, sincere. I
(65) do like him; I would be an excellent wife to him if he did marry me; I would tell him of his faults (for he has a few faults), but I would study his comfort, and cherish him, and do my best to make him happy. Now, I am sure he will not be cold to-
(70) morrow. I feel almost certain that to-morrow evening he will either come here, or ask me to go there."

She recommended combing her hair, long as a mermaid's. Turning her head as she arranged it
(75) she saw her own face and form in the glass. Such reflections are soberizing to plain people: their own eyes are not enchanted with the image; they are confident then that the eyes of others can see in it no fascination. But the fair must naturally
(80) draw other conclusions: the picture is charming, and must charm. Caroline saw a shape, a head, that, daguerreotyped in that attitude and with that expression, would have been lovely. She could not choose but derive from the spectacle
(85) confirmation to her hopes. It was then in undiminished gladness she sought her couch.

And in undiminished gladness she rose the next day. As she entered her uncle's breakfast-room, and with soft cheerfulness wished him
(90) good-morning, even that little man of bronze himself thought, for an instant, his niece was growing "a fine girl." Generally she was quiet and

timid with him—very docile, but not communicative; this morning, however, she found
(95) many things to say. Slight topics alone might be discussed between them; for with a woman—a girl—Mr. Helstone would touch on no other. She had taken an early walk in the garden, and she told him what flowers were beginning to spring
(100) there; she inquired when the gardener was to come and trim the borders; she informed him that certain starlings were beginning to build their nests in the church-tower (Briarfield church was close to Briarfield rectory); she wondered the
(105) tolling of the bells in the belfry did not scare them.

1. Mr. Helstone would most likely think a clever woman to be one who:

   A) can engage in lively and spirited conversation.
   B) has read much classic and edifying literature.
   C) is familiar with home-making skills.
   D) does not fill her head with dreams of impossible fancy.

2. The relationship between Caroline and Mr. Helstone can best be described as which of the following?

   A) A warm and loving connection that sustains them both
   B) A rigid and instructional relationship without much warmth
   C) A hateful mutual dislike
   D) One characterized by a great respect from both sides

3. As it is used in line 13, *gadding* most nearly means:

   A) kidding.
   B) playing.
   C) roaming.
   D) eating.

4. The point of view of the author can best be described as a:

   A) relative of Caroline's.
   B) psychoanalyst speaking about Caroline's mental state.
   C) impassive observer of Caroline's fate.
   D) sympathetic teller of Caroline's tale.

5. Caroline's mood as she goes to bed is most likely a result of:

   A) the approval of her uncle.
   B) her conversation with Robert.
   C) her contentment with her appearance in the mirror.
   D) Robert's proposal of marriage.

6. It can be inferred from the passage that Caroline is often:

   A) excessively talkative.
   B) given to shunning romances for herself.
   C) unimpressed with her appearance.
   D) late to evening prayers with her uncle.

7. When the narrator mentions that "the spirit of youthful Hope' is in Caroline's apartment, this suggests that:

   A) a mysterious spirit has visited Caroline in her room.
   B) Caroline is praying to a prophet.
   C) Caroline is filled with optimism about her future and prospects with Robert.
   D) Caroline is having dreams above her station.

8. Caroline would characterize Robert as which of the following?

   A) A perfect specimen of manhood
   B) Someone madly in love with her
   C) A better friend than a lover
   D) A quiet, sure man who has only a few flaws

9. Which of the following does the author imply about mirrors?

   A) The attitude of one looking into a mirror determines what impressions one gets from it.
   B) They are always injurious to the confidence of plain people.
   C) Sober people see the truth in them more often than those who are not.
   D) They should be avoided at all costs.

10. The author's overall tone can best be described as:

   A) respectful and sympathetic.
   B) sarcastic and cynical.
   C) overtly religious.
   D) entirely objective.

PRACTICE EXERCISE 2

Directions: Read the following passage and answer the accompanying questions.

In 1790, New York City was the capital of the United States. The first Congress passed the Bill of Rights, which affirmed our basic liberties as a free people: "Congress shall make no law abridging the freedom of speech, or of the press; or the right of the people peaceably to assemble."

In theory, this idea is simple. Unfortunately, the reality is a little more complicated: there hasn't been an unlimited right to assemble in New York City for 130 years.

The current controversy about where protestors can demonstrate during the upcoming Republican National Convention is the latest expression of a problem that has been dividing the city for the last 130 years. In most urban areas, finding places to parade or protest without interfering with the rights and needs of other residents is extremely difficult. In New York City, where traffic, crowds, and commerce are particularly intense, it is next to impossible to hold any sort of public assembly. Citizens demand to have their say anywhere, and at any time, on any subject, but they also want to be able to shop, walk, work, travel, and eat without disruption.

After the Civil War, New York began to require permits for individuals and groups seeking to use streets and parks for public assembly or marches. The 1863 Draft Riots, which left more than 100 people dead and turned the city into chaos, and the 1871 Irish Orange Riots, which left more than 40 dead, taught the city some bitter lessons. New York decided it would allow public assembly only in controlled circumstances.

The sources for that control lay not in the courts but with the city's municipal authorities, representing a broad class, ethnic, and religious spectrum. Their purpose was to keep order in the city, allowing it to function without economic disruption and preventing violence and loss of life.

The timing of the decision to require permits in the early 1870's was no accident. Socialists, trade unionists, and unemployed workers sought to redress economic and political grievances on city streets, and looked across the ocean to the model set by Londoners, who had seized Trafalgar Square and Hyde Park as the seats of the public.

The New York solution was reached largely by compromise. It allowed some parks to be used, but changed that decision after excessive wear and tear. After the 1874 "Blood or Bread" melee in Tompkins Square Park, the city closed down the square as a possible site of protest for decades.

In 1896, a neighborhood association complained about the noise and disruption from Italian street parades, but the police turned a deaf ear—the parade organizers had legal permits, after all. City authorities concluded that if they could control circumstances by setting clear conditions for meeting times and places through the permit, then disturbances to public peace, injury to individuals, and interruptions to traffic and commerce could be avoided, while still allowing free assembly. Each permit request was individually determined, but no place and no time frame was ever absolute or guaranteed for public assembly. The public during this period in the late 1800's had little legal recourse if denied a permit. Instead, many decided to take to the streets and face arrest to make their points known.

The 1920's and 1930's saw an increase of demonstrations and marches and much more discussion about public assembly. In 1941, Robert Moses, New York City Parks Commissioner at the time, banned a protest in Union Square Park, which prompted the New York Civil Liberties Committee to incorrectly charge that he was changing city policy about demonstrations. Citing a Supreme Court decision, Mr. Moses responded that the right to use a park was not absolute, especially if there was a likelihood of riot or fatalities. It was an old policy, he reminded the committee, and the city had usually managed to accommodate requests for public meetings.

More recently, a persistent fear of terrorism has added a new wrinkle to the long conflict between freedom and order in great cities. But we must remember that democracy is messy. Free speech is meaningless if we can only shout at 500 empty acres. We must accept the likelihood that some people will be late for work, some people will miss their lunch breaks, some public parks (95) will be overrun, and some people will sit in bumper-to-bumper traffic. The founders of our republic knew that freedom and convenience did not go hand in hand, and they knew the consequences of limiting the right of assembly.

1. The author of the passage asserts that the primary reason there is no right to assemble in New York City is largely the result of:

   A) the unjustness of democracy.
   B) the difficulty in not disrupting such a busy city.
   C) a fear of terroristic threats.
   D) a Supreme Court decision.

2. According to the passage, violent protests occurred in New York City in all of the following years EXCEPT:

   A) 1863.
   B) 1871.
   C) 1874.
   D) 1896.

3. The correlation between the increased presence of socialist influence in New York City and the requirement for permits to protest was:

   A) coincidental.
   B) intentional.
   C) unexpected.
   D) paradoxical.

4. The purpose of the passage as a whole is to:

   A) give reasons as to why an apparent contradiction exists.
   B) draw attention to one particular event in history.
   C) argue against the legitimacy of a form of government.
   D) provide a history of a string of protests in New York City.

5. Which of the following is a point of view most likely espoused by the author of the passage?

   A) The government has the right to change its laws when it suits them.
   B) Certain freedoms are more important than the public's convenience.
   C) Keeping socialists out of the government is more important than the right to publically demonstrate.
   D) Peaceful protests aren't always as effective as violent outbursts.

6. New York City's policy about public demonstration was heavily influenced by that of:

   A) London.
   B) Washington D.C.
   C) Ireland.
   D) Italy.

7. The main purpose of the ninth paragraph (lines 73-86) is to:

   A) describe the reasons for an increase in public demonstrations.
   B) give reasons as to why riots are bad for New York City.
   C) criticize the policy decisions of Robert Moses.
   D) describe a time in which there was renewed interest in public demonstration policy in New York City.

8. The quote "Free speech is meaningless if we can only shout at 500 empty acres." in lines 90-92 best serves to:

A) show the pointlessness in public demonstration if no one is around to hear it.
B) persuade protestors to move from rural to urban areas.
C) excuse the behavior of lawmakers who made protest difficult.
D) apologize to those arrested for public demonstrations.

9. The author of the passage feels most strongly about which of the following topics?

A) The power of socialism in helping the working class
B) The power of protest to affect change
C) The power of the government to control its populace
D) The power of cities to keep their citizens from disruption

10. According to Robert Moses, what was more important than the right to use a public park for protest?

A) Public safety
B) Public assembly
C) A lack of traffic in the city
D) Commerce continuing as usual

PRACTICE EXERCISE 3

Directions: Read the following passage and answer the accompanying questions.

Diana Martínez makes her way down the busy streets of an urban Buenos Aires sidewalk with difficulty. She walks slowly, leaning on the crutches she must use after contracting polio (5) before the age of one.

Coming off the elevator of an old Parisian-style building, she enters the lavish apartment of Argentine ballet legend María Fux. Diana leaves her crutches against the wall of the studio, (10) removes the leather and steel brace that allows her to stand upright, lies down on the floor, and prepares to dance.

"Dance for me was something prohibited until I discovered Fux six years ago," says Diana, (15) 53. "Thanks to her I've been able to recover my femininity. Imagine, having had a rigid body for so long, to discover I could dance, it helped me overcome social prejudices and my own prejudices regarding what I could do."

(20) Born in 1922, dance therapist Fux has spent the best part of her life giving people like Diana the gift of dance. Before that, Fux had a more traditional career in dance serving as prima ballerina for the Cólon opera house in Buenos (25) Aires. But in the 1960s, Fux turned her attention from her own stardom to helping the physically challenged do something they never could do: dance.

Ever since, her studio has been attended by (30) people who were barely able to live normal lives, let alone dance. Blind students, deaf students, teenagers with Down syndrome, persons dealing with psychological stress, all were made to dance by Fux.

(35) It is a work of infinite patience, replicated today by devoted followers outside of Argentina who have opened dance therapy schools to teach the "Fux method." The majority of these schools have opened in Italy, where the method has been (40) followed since the 1990s to great success.

"Her method is being taught in various countries in Europe, especially in Italy where there's a school in Milan and another in Florence," says Italian film director Ivan (45) Gergolet, who was in Buenos Aires this week for screenings in Argentina of his feature-length documentary *Dancing With Maria.*

Gergolet's 75-minute portrait of Fux and her miraculous work is a beautiful, emotional (50) rollercoaster of a film that took the prestigious "Nastrid'Argento" documentary award last month in Italy. Screened for the first time at the Venice Film Festival last year, where it took another award, it has been playing to packed, tear-filled (55) audiences in the documentary circuit across Europe since.

The film was born from the admiration of Gergolet's wife, the Italian dancer Martina Serban, for Fux. "I met Fux in Italy in 2006. She (60) has a charisma, a power, she transmits love. We are used to the idea that if someone has a limit, you have to help them. But she helps in a different way, by letting the student come up against their own limit and saying 'I trust you can (65) do it' to them."

Although she denies she has a method per se, Fux says that testing the limits of the human body is part of it. "I'm interested in limits, my limits and the limits of other people. I give that limit (70) that says, "No, I can't," the chance of saying "Yes, I can." It involves creativity. One and one is not always two, sometimes it is five, sometimes three, sometimes nothing."

It is a life lesson that for over five decades (75) she has imparted to various generations of Argentines, many of whom are crowding the current screenings of *Dancing With Maria* in Buenos Aires.

"Maybe it's not so surprising nowadays, but (80) a few decades ago when I attended her studio it was completely shocking and unheard of to have physically and mentally challenged students at a dance class," said a former student of Fux's at a screening Sunday night. As the credits rolled, the (85) film received a standing ovation.

Fux keeps her thoughts turned to the mystery of movement and the testing of limits through dance and music. "Music is like a string," she says. "Sometimes it breaks, sometimes it (90) continues. That's all. It's not a note, C or A. It's a movement in space that creates drawings. That's something you can understand, that I can understand, that everyone understands. It's about becoming a better person. That's what's most *(95)* important."

1. The majority of the new dance therapy schools have opened in:

   A) Argentina.
   B) Italy.
   C) the United States.
   D) other European countries.

2. The purpose of the passage as a whole is to:

   A) discuss one woman's efforts to use dance as a means of therapy.
   B) question the relevancy of dance therapy schools.
   C) praise a woman's innovative dance style.
   D) commend the effectiveness of alternative medical treatments.

3. The passage is best described as being told from the point of view of:

   A) an unbiased observer.
   B) an impartial journalist.
   C) a cynical columnist.
   D) a devoted fan.

4. The main purpose of lines 79-85 is to:

   A) describe how Fux's studio works.
   B) express the passion it takes to teach disabled students.
   C) show how Fux personally affected someone's life.
   D) acclaim the movie written about Fux.

5. According to the passage, one can infer that Fux gave up dancing herself because of:

   A) her sustaining of an injury.
   B) a desire to help others.
   C) the chance of a more lucrative career.
   D) a lack of interest in the art form.

6. The director of the full-length documentary about Fux was:

   A) Ivan Gergolet.
   B) Martina Serban.
   C) Diana Martinez.
   D) MaríaFux.

7. The author of the passage implies that one thing necessary to work with Fux's students is:

   A) fame.
   B) persistence.
   C) a realistic point of view.
   D) a feminine nature.

8. In the context of the last paragraph (lines 86-95), Fux is described as:

   A) philosophical, yet positive.
   B) theoretical and rational.
   C) moral, yet pessimistic.
   D) highly ethical.

9. According to Fux, one way to surpass one's own limits is through:

   A) epiphany.
   B) persistence.
   C) perseverance.
   D) innovation.

10. As it is used in line 16, the word *rigid* most nearly means:

   A) strict.
   B) inflexible.
   C) unvarying.
   D) uncompromising.

PRACTICE EXERCISE 4

Directions: Read the following passage and answer the accompanying questions.

Last week, I learned about the early human relative discovery deep within a cave in South Africa. Of course I had many questions; a fellow
Line primate had been found, but what kind?
(5)   They named this incredible find *Homo naledi* which has not only been celebrated for the quantity of fossils, but also the completeness of the fossils. Its feet and teeth correspond with the characteristics of the genus Homo, but it has
(10) australopithecine-like hips and a brain similar in size to an ape.

These mixed features found on these prehistoric remains contradict the human origin story, in which bipedalism brought along
(15) technology, dietary change, and high intelligence. This find has been called a mosaic species because different parts of its physique fall behind or ahead of the generalized evolutionary time lines.
(20)   We like to generalize and place every fossil along the preexisting timeline that has already been determined by current science. Chris Stringer, a British paleoanthropologist who did not take part in this particular study, said to BBC
(25) News: "What we are seeing is more and more species of creatures that suggests that nature was experimenting with how to evolve humans, thus giving rise to several different types of humanlike creatures originating in parallel in different parts
(30) of Africa."

This is a surprising explanation, as if natural selection is purposefully trying to force certain outcomes. But this is not the case, any more so than a river trying to reach the ocean.
(35)   The way news reports spoke of a "new ancestor," going so far as saying a "new human species" creates the idea of lateral movement in our ancestry. In actuality, there are no straight ladders – just a tangle of branches. There is no
(40) solid evidence dictating that *Homo naledi* belongs on the same branch that humans evolved from, but that does not make this find any less intriguing.

Every hominoid species reveals something
(45) about humans because hominoids – which consist of humans, apes, and everything in between – are

very closely linked genetically. Hominoids have had a lot less time to develop and evolve unlike other animal families such as equids and canids.
(50)   Generically the story of human evolution starts with apes that evolved into australopithecines. From that point, the australopithecines became more intelligent and eventually evolved into the modern day human.
(55) However, there is a theory that these two stages became genetically interbred – that some of the evolved returned to the original apes to mate in similar fashion to today's grizzlies and polar bears occasionally mating. Another theory
(60) disregards the idea of interbreeding and focuses on the thought that incomplete or divergent evolution created different branches of hominoids.

The main issue is the assumption that there is
(65) a specific point in time where we just became humans, that there was just a miraculous mental breakthrough that made humans vastly different from their predecessors. Fifty years of research on chimpanzees and other intelligent animals proves
(70) that this assumption is full of holes.

The only claim of human uniqueness that has endured longer than a decade is language capacity. All other claims such as tool use, tool making, culture, food sharing, planning,
(75) emotions, reasoning, and logic have all been observed in primates in the wild and in carefully controlled experiments. For example, apes are known to plan ahead, travelling with tools to implement when scavenging food in the wild as
(80) well as creating tools for prospective future use in lab settings. Animals think without words, as humans do most of the time.

The team researching *Homo naledi* was not deterred by its small brain and pursued the idea of
(85) its humanity – the bodies were discovered buried in a cave, implanting the idea that they mourned their dead. However, this distinction is not uncommon amongst hominids. Apes seem to be extremely affected by the death of a companion to
(90) the point of not eating, becoming completely silent, and showing distressed emotions. They even show a level of denial by trying to groom or

revive their dead. Due to the nomadic nature of apes, eventually, they move on.

(95)　　　There is no need to cover or bury their dead because they will not be affected for long periods of time. However, if they were established in a cave or specific area, they may notice that a corpse attracts scavengers, some of which could (100) be predators. In this case, they may have had the mental awareness to remove, hide, or bury the corpses. Some scholars believe that burial requires speculation of an afterlife – but this thought cannot be proved as there is no way to (105) determine if *Homo naledi* ceremoniously buried their dead or simply dropped the bodies into a hole to remove it.

　　　This discovery is a major paleontological breakthrough, but also gives us a chance to (110) recognize that hominoids are a very genetically, anatomically, and mentally diverse family.

1.　According to information presented in the passage, *Homo naledi* was discovered in a:

　　A)　laboratory.
　　B)　field.
　　C)　cave.
　　D)　forest.

2.　The purpose of the passage as a whole is to:

　　A)　discuss how a human relative was discovered.
　　B)　explain the differences between several different species of hominid.
　　C)　show how a discovery changed a previous method of thinking.
　　D)　question the validity of a recent discovery.

3.　According to the author of the passage, humans are unique because of their ability to:

　　A)　think to themselves.
　　B)　use language.
　　C)　form a culture.
　　D)　make tools.

4.　The main purpose of the first two paragraphs (lines 1-11) is to:

　　A)　disparage a specific group.
　　B)　express doubt about a discovery.
　　C)　describe a discovery in detail.
　　D)　introduce a line of questioning by scientists.

5.　According to the author, the best way to describe an evolutionary tree is as a:

　　A)　straight ladder.
　　B)　deep cave.
　　C)　field of grass.
　　D)　tangle of branches.

6.　According to the information provided in the passage, the most logical reason that *Homo naledi* buried its dead was:

　　A)　to prepare the dead for the afterlife.
　　B)　to prevent predators and scavengers from finding the dead.
　　C)　to participate in religious ceremonies.
　　D)　to help fertilize their crops.

7. Apes are affected by death in all of the following ways EXCEPT:

A) expressing themselves with language.
B) showing intense emotion.
C) prolonged silence.
D) avoiding food.

8. According to the author, when compared to other animals, hominids:

A) have had less time to evolve.
B) have had more time to evolve.
C) have evolved more efficiently.
D) have evolved less efficiently.

9. You can infer from the passage that the author believes that *Homo naledi* is:

A) a human ancestor.
B) a human relative.
C) a human descendent.
D) not related to humans.

10. According to the author, a "mosaic species" is one which:

A) eats a variety of foods.
B) embodies characteristics of many different species.
C) has been subjected to experiments during its evolution.
D) is extremely intelligent.

PRACTICE EXERCISE 5

Directions: Read the following passage and answer the accompanying questions.

Passage A

Anyone who has shopped for vegetables has experienced the inevitable choice: Organic or regular?

Line
(5) This seemingly simple question leads to so many other questions. However, the most significant question for most consumers is whether it is worth the extra money.

As most shoppers know, organic produce is usually more costly than the alternatives. In fact,
(10) a recent investigation found that the prices of organic foods were 47% higher on average than their conventional counterparts. Nevertheless, the higher price is not necessarily a result of the added cost of organic farming methods; the
(15) simple fact is that people will pay more for the label—even if they do not know what it means. "Organic" has basically become a synonym for "luxury."

While synthetic pesticides and fertilizers can
(20) have adverse effects on the environment, from possibly jeopardizing pollinators to contaminating natural waterways, most organic farmers, particularly the large ones, are still using pesticides and fertilizers; they simply utilize
(25) natural choices, which can come with their own risks. In 2010, a study determined that certain organic pesticides could actually have a more detrimental impact on the environment than common pesticides. Plus, another recent study
(30) discovered that the mass production of organic vegetables by large corporations caused the release of more greenhouse gases into the atmosphere than standard farming methods given that there was a lower yield of crops for the same
(35) amount of time utilizing heavy machinery.

You might expect that organic fruits and vegetables are better for you. However, the research available so far indicates that any added nutritional benefits from organic produce are
(40) minimal. In 2009, a meta-analysis found that there was no nutrient difference between organic and conventional produce. Subsequently, two larger meta-analyses revealed minor differences, but ones that are likely too slight to truly matter.
(45) A 2012 study found marginally higher phosphorous levels in organic produce, and a 2014 study found that organic foods had higher levels of valuable antioxidants and lower levels of cadmium, a toxic heavy metal.

(50) What is the solution? If you want to get quality fruits and vegetables, purchase them at the local farmers market, organic or not. The prices are often reasonable, and the in-season produce is fresher than those transported long distances. As a
(55) bonus, any questions you have can be answered on the spot. However, if you cannot get to the farmers market, don't throw away your money on a fancy label.

Passage B

For years, scientists have struggled to
(60) determine whether organic foods vary significantly from those grown conventionally. Research is starting to support the fact that organic foods can be better — and not only for the people who eat it.

(65) There is no question that pests and weeds can decimate crops. Just like conventional farmers, organic farmers use pesticides and weed killers to ensure successful yields. The difference is that they have fewer options from which they can
(70) choose because they can only use the pesticides that are not artificially produced.

In addition to pesticides and herbicides, there is another group of farm chemicals utilized by farmers: fertilizers. To grow properly, plants
(75) require nutrients, particularly nitrogen and phosphorus, which fertilizers offer. As is the case with pesticides and weed killers, organic farmers cannot use fertilizers that come from synthetic sources, such as ammonia salts. Instead, the
(80) farmers must find natural fertilizers. For example, they alternate planting beans in their fields because beans naturally increase the soil's nitrogen levels. With naturally more fertile soil, farmers are finding fewer pesticides or fertilizers
(85) are necessary. Since they do not need to utilize as many of these chemicals, naturally fertilized soils can cut the level of pollution associated with the repeated overuse of nitrogen and phosphorus.

Many people purchase organic food because

(90) they believe it's better for their health. In the scientific community, this fact is up for debate. A 2012 study found no significant nutritional difference between organic and conventional food. More recently, a group of experts in *(95)* England made the reverse conclusion. They studied all of the available research on this question and selected 343 studies to examine. They found that organic crops have an average of 17 percent more antioxidants than non-organic *(100)* crops. These antioxidants are the compounds found in fruits and vegetables that have been proven to lower an individual's risk of diseases such as stroke and cancer.

How should this impact your decisions at the *(105)* grocery store? Organically grown food can be beneficial for the environment and for the people who grow them, not to mention the potential returns to the people eating them. For families with the means to afford them, organic foods are *(110)* worth the additional price. For those with a tight wallet, purchasing targeted organic foods might be a better idea. This might mean eating an organic apple because the skin of that fruit will get eaten, while a conventionally grown avocado *(115)* might be preferential to the organic version given its skin will not be eaten.

Organic or not, no one should be discouraged from buying fruits or vegetables. An apple is always the better choice than chips — no matter *(120)* how the apple was grown.

1. Passage A suggests which of the following about why people buy organic foods?

   A) Many believe that organic foods are better because they cost more.
   B) Many believe that organic foods are better because they are better for the environment.
   C) Many purchase organic food due to the lower price of organic food.
   D) Many purchase organic food since organic food has more antioxidants than conventional food.

2. According to Passage A, organic vegetables may be worse for the environment than other vegetables because:

   A) most organic farmers use the same chemical pesticides and fertilizers as conventional farmers.
   B) organic farming methods jeopardize pollinators.
   C) air pollution from machine use is the same even though fewer vegetables are produced.
   D) organic fertilizers cause more water contamination than synthetic fertilizers do.

3. Passage A notes all of the following nutritional benefits of organic vegetables EXCEPT:

A) higher phosphorous levels.
B) higher antioxidant levels.
C) lower cadmium levels.
D) fewer chemicals.

4. As it is used in line 71, the word *artificially* most nearly means:

A) imitation.
B) falsely.
C) theatrically.
D) synthetically.

5. According to Passage B, plants cannot grow without:

A) pesticides and herbicides.
B) nitrogen and phosphorus.
C) ammonia salts.
D) beans.

6. According to Passage B, organic farmers often plant beans in unused fields because:

A) beans increase the phosphorus levels in the soil, thereby eliminating the need for synthetic fertilizers.
B) beans do not require fertilizers, pesticides, or herbicides.
C) beans naturally add nitrogen to the soil, thereby reducing the need for additional fertilizers.
D) beans are among the highest selling of all organically grown vegetables.

7. The author of Passage B would most likely agree with which of the following?

A) People should eat more produce regardless of whether it is organically grown.
B) Organically grown produce is worth the extra money because it has been definitively proven to be healthier.
C) Conventionally grown produce is often mislabeled as organic.
D) Organically grown produce is significantly better for the environment but has no nutritional benefits.

8. How would the author of Passage A most likely respond to the information in lines 98-103?

A) This increase in antioxidants is too slight to be considered significant.
B) Other research indicates that there is no difference in antioxidant levels.
C) Antioxidants have not been proven to be nutritionally beneficial.
D) Higher antioxidant levels don't offset organic produce's higher cadmium levels.

9. Which of the following most accurately summarizes the consumer advice of both authors?

A) The author of Passage A recommends buying conventionally grown produce while the author of Passage B advocates buying only organic produce.
B) The author of Passage A advises consumers to purchase locally grown produce while the author of Passage B suggests that consumers purchase targeted organic foods.
C) Both authors strongly recommend purchasing locally grown produce regardless of whether or not it is organically grown.
D) Neither author advocates spending additional money to purchase organically grown vegetables.

10. The authors of both passages would agree with all of the following EXCEPT:

A) the nutritional benefits of organically grown produce are debatable.
B) organically grown produce provides higher levels of antioxidants.
C) organically grown produce uses just as many chemicals as conventionally grown produce.
D) many purchase organic produce in the belief that it is nutritionally superior.

PRACTICE EXERCISE 6

Directions: Read the following passage and answer the accompanying questions.

Occasionally, my parents visit Jorge and Pocha on the weekends. These visits become an adventure for Martin and me as soon as we step
Line out of the car. Jorge and Pocha's apartment is on
(5) a cobblestone street and sits across from a quiet gray church. There is a metal booth - some kind of box that has to do with electricity or water utilities - on the church side of the street that Jorge tells us is a dwarf's house. Jorge knows a
(10) bunch of different and strange characters and takes us on searches for them without fear. During one such expedition, Martin and I went to the hiding spot of Noitila the witch, who lives deep in the pine woods of Rincon del Indio,
(15) creeping along the purplish hue of trees and floating like a shadow over the needle covered ground.

But the idea of adventures through haunted woods is not necessary to bribe us young kids into
(20) visiting Jorge and Pocha. Their apartment is full of mysteries and haunted corners: from the apartment building's lobby floor eerily decked in checkered black and white tiles, to a voluptuous statue of Eve with a sinister serpent wrapped
(25) around her thighs, to Jorge's upper-floor studio where he pens his books and sometimes let Martin make hits at a giant punching bag with red boxing gloves that we gave to Jorge as a birthday gift.
(30) Jorge and Pocha have a collection of many, many books around dark wood, leather armchairs. Paintings adorn every wall, framing reds, blues, yellows, ships, fishes, and bottles. A frightening black metal bull and two starfish packed with
(35) spikes and small teeth sit atop a ginormous chest of drawers, which probably has a large collection of strange things within. During one visit, I could not resist asking Jorge for the smallest starfish, and he gave it to me even though Mom and Dad
(40) did not approve – Martin and I are not allowed to ask people for gifts, particularly Jorge and Pocha.

However, the little starfish did not hold the magical prowess in my nightstand drawer as it did on Jorge's chest of drawers. It now lives among
(45) my small collection of treasures, next to coins and

trinkets and baubles. Without its big starfish companion, my small starfish is lonely and no longer tells tales of waves, sands, tides, and the sun. In fact, it just looks deader than ever.
(50) Jorge and Pocha have grown-up children who no longer stay with them – except Plato. Plato is old, has a mean temper, and hates kids; he is always growling at us and our efforts at making friends with him. So we vengefully chant back at
(55) him our cutting refrain: "Plato, the grumpy dog!"

Mom and Dad talk with Jorge and Pocha for what seems an eternity. I hate being excluded from any conversation, so I would always get an angry earful from them when I interrupt. Many
(60) times they speak of people I do not yet know, but will eventually come across years later when I start my classes at the University. At the University, Jorge is no longer just Jorge, but the great author of the twenty-four volume *Treatise*
(65) *on Uruguayan Civil Law*, his lifetime work and great accomplishment. Every law student has to not only read his work, but also understand it to pass the exam on the subject that Jorge facetiously calls "Our Lady of Obligations." From
(70) this point on, I will see Jorge in his own light, independent and separate from Pocha; but I will never be able to think of Pocha without Jorge.

The adults talk and smoke and drink; Jorge's whisky tumbler is in his hand and he speaks of a
(75) man called Dante. By the way Jorge talks about him with affection in his voice, I think that Dante is a member of the group of friends whose names always come up in conversations, like Vanni and Blanca. However, Jorge explains to me that Dante
(80) was an Italian who traversed through Hell with his friend and saw all of the horrible demons – demons who scared but did not hurt him.

Within the apartment on Masini Street, I compose some of my earliest work. Always
(85) eavesdropping on the grown-up conversations for details (you can't afford to miss anything at Jorge and Pocha's), I meticulously penned the stiff letters that try to emulate the font in my books, the only one I know.

1. The narrator's point of view is that of:

   A) a biased observer.
   B) a detached observer.
   C) a young child.
   D) an old woman reminiscing about childhood.

2. The author mentions all of the following outside of Jorge and Pocha's apartment EXCEPT for a:

   A) church.
   B) cobblestone street.
   C) large pine tree.
   D) utility box.

3. It can be inferred that, as a child, the narrator enjoyed spending time with Jorge because:

   A) he gave the narrator a starfish.
   B) he has a dog.
   C) he is knowledgeable.
   D) of his active imagination.

4. The passage suggests that the narrator views Jorge and Pocha's home with:

   A) awe and mystery.
   B) terror and fear.
   C) caution and nervousness.
   D) boredom and resignation.

5. As it is used in line 52, the word *temper* most nearly means:

   A) disposition.
   B) angriness.
   C) composure.
   D) atmosphere.

6. The narrator's view of Jorge changed when she:

   A) received the starfish.
   B) attended University.
   C) taught at University.
   D) learned about Dante.

7. Which of the following can be inferred about the starfish mentioned in the third and fourth paragraphs?

   A) Jorge found the starfish on the beach.
   B) The narrator found the starfish on the beach.
   C) The starfish died in the narrator's nightstand drawer.
   D) The starfish's appeal came largely from its setting.

8. The narrator's parents did not want her to have the starfish because:

   A) the narrator had misbehaved during the visit.
   B) they believe that asking for gifts is bad behavior.
   C) the narrator already had several starfish at home.
   D) they do not want the additional mess at home.

9. It can be most clearly inferred from the passage that:

   A) the narrator had poor penmanship.
   B) the narrator learned to write from Jorge.
   C) the narrator became a famous author.
   D) the narrator first began writing at Jorge and Pocha's apartment.

10. The narrator would most likely characterize Jorge as:

   A) a dedicated academic with a dry personality.
   B) a flighty but fun playmate.
   C) a brilliant academic with a generous heart.
   D) a short-tempered adult who tries to avoid spending time with children.

PRACTICE EXERCISE 7

Directions: Read the following passage and answer the accompanying questions.

Anger — a primal and destructive emotion, disrupting rational discourse and inflaming illogical passions. But can anything positive come
Line out of anger? Expressing anger has been known to
(5) be a useful tool in negotiations, as just one example. Over the past few years, researchers have been learning more about how anger can be used creatively and effectively.

Researchers in psychiatric fields have been
(10) testing the effectiveness of expressing anger in three types of negotiations: chiefly cooperative (jointly starting a team or group), chiefly competitive (dissolving a team or group), and those that are somewhere between the two.
(15) During two different experiments, negotiators were more willing to work with their partners who expressed anger — but only in balanced situations. When cooperating or competing, anger only seemed to make matters worse. But in those
(20) situations between the two, anger appeared to send a strategically useful signal.

What does that signal communicate? According to the researchers, anger allows us to express that we feel undervalued. Showing anger
(25) signals to others people that if we don't get what we deserve, we'll exert harm or withhold benefits. The researchers found that two groups — strong men and attractive women — were most prone to anger, perhaps because these two groups,
(30) historically, have had the most leverage in threatening harm or giving out benefits.

Studies show that when people prepare to enter a confrontational negotiation, as opposed to a cooperative one, they take steps to induce anger
(35) in themselves. For example, they may choose to listen to aggressive music instead of the happy music they're used to. We all seem to implicitly understand the value of anger in extracting better treatment from others.
(40) Additionally, the studies show that people induce anger in themselves only when there are actual benefits at stake in the negotiation. This qualification was essential in proving that it was the strategic benefit of being angry, and not just a
(45) reflex that we have when entering any confrontation, that prompted people to induce

anger in themselves. After all, who wants to be angry?

Whether planned or natural, anger must
(50) ultimately be genuine in order to be useful in provoking concessions. Faking anger, compared with playing it cool, leads a negotiation partner to see you as less trustworthy, and actually increases his demands on you.

(55) There are other important caveats. While expressions of anger can elicit compromises, they can also lead to covert retaliation. In two experiments, negotiators overtly made concessions when opponents expressed anger but,
(60) evidently feeling mistreated, covertly sabotaged their opponents afterward. In the real world, and not just the laboratory, this dynamic might take the form of acquiescing to an angry colleague's demands, only to spread gossip about him around
(65) the office.

Additionally, anger had a tendency to work better in negotiations when it was directed at the offer itself rather than at the person making the offer. Many of the same researchers also reported
(70) that expressing anger when you're in a position of low power merely irritates your opponent and leads to a backlash. When you have less power than your opponent, the researchers discovered that showing disappointment was a better strategy
(75) than expressing anger. It turns out that inducing feelings of guilt in your opponent can be just as powerful as inducing fear.

Expressing anger can sometimes benefit all the parties involved, not just one of them, by
(80) clarifying boundaries, needs, and concerns. Think of the loved one who doesn't realize how strongly you feel about the relationship until you express feelings of frustration with it. Another study found that anger is more likely to lead to such
(85) mutually positive outcomes when it is low in intensity; expressed verbally rather than physically; and takes place in an organization that considers it appropriate (like a labor union or a university athletic department).
(90) Finally, anger can also motivate large-scale political progress. Researchers reported in the Journal of Conflict Resolution in 2011 that among

Israeli Jews, inducing anger at Palestinians increased their desire to make necessary
(95) compromises in upcoming peace talks — as long as the attitudes of the Israelis toward Palestinians were not hateful. This finding suggested that while some angry people may try to remedy a frustrating situation with aggression, others —
(100) even those who are just as angry — may funnel their anger into less antagonistic solutions.

We tend to associate anger with the loss of control, but anger has clear applications and obeys distinct rules. It may be blunt, but it has its
(110) own particular logic. And used judiciously, it can get us better deals, galvanize coalitions, and ultimately improve our lives.

1. In which of the following situations might anger be helpful?

   A) Instructing a child
   B) Purchasing a piece of property
   C) Opening a business with a friend
   D) Telling your workers what to do

2. Which of the following is a step people often take to induce anger in themselves?

   A) Listening to calming music
   B) Listening to forceful music
   C) Spreading gossip about others
   D) Listening to gossip spread about oneself

3. Which of the following is a method of retaliation for anger referenced in the passage?

   A) Acquiescing to demands
   B) An unwillingness to negotiate
   C) Spreading gossip
   D) Dissolving teams or groups

4. The author's tone can best be described as:

   A) subjective.
   B) objective.
   C) unquestionable.
   D) flippant.

5. As it is used in line 37, the word *implicitly* most nearly means:

   A) indirectly.
   B) blatantly.
   C) questionably.
   D) undoubtedly.

6. While in a negotiation, faking anger to further your own cause may result in your partner:

   A) calling you out.
   B) getting back at you.
   C) allowing you to walk all over him.
   D) distrusting you.

7. The negotiations between the Israelis and Palestinians helped prove the idea that anger must not be:

   A) intolerable.
   B) hateful.
   C) undeserved.
   D) direct.

8. During studies, which of the following groups were found to be the most quick to anger?

    I.   Strong men
    II. Strong women
    III. Attractive men
    IV. Attractive women

    A) I and II only
    B) I and III only
    C) II and III only
    D) I and IV only

9. The author stresses the fact that to be successful in a negotiation, one must be angry at:

    A) your negotiation partner.
    B) yourself.
    C) the offer itself.
    D) an abstract idea apart from the negotiation.

10. The main purpose of the passage is to:

    A) discuss why people get angry.
    B) discuss when anger may not be appropriate.
    C) discuss ways in which anger may be helpful.
    D) discuss why anger causes a loss of control.

PRACTICE EXERCISE 8

Directions: Read the following passage and answer the accompanying questions.

With the rise of street art, a question of growing importance in today's art market is beginning to make itself known: Does intellectual *Line* property law protect unsanctioned graffiti art?
(5) Street art embraces metropolitan walls and streets, gifting the public with innovative imagery that becomes a part of the city as much as the wall it rests on. But does someone *own* that art?

Street art breaks boundaries and defies law; it
(10) is made both without consent and illegally. While this form of artwork was once condemned as a social nuisance and even vandalism, graffiti work has become not only a respectable form of art, but also a hot commodity among art collectors and
(15) connoisseurs. Communities are even beginning to embrace and value street art in their neighborhoods. Naturally, when something becomes popular, people want to profit from it. Street art is beginning to be ripped from its
(20) creators, copied and reprinted on merchandise, and even exhibited and sold at auction and in galleries without the artist's consent. As graffiti art becomes the next big art market, the question arises: Do street artists have intellectual property
(25) protection for unsanctioned artwork, and should they be able to prevent the unauthorized copying, sale, and destruction of their work?

To the dismay of many street artists, it is unclear whether current U.S. intellectual property
(30) law protects unsanctioned street art from unauthorized copying, removal, sale, and, perhaps most importantly, destruction. Many street artists attempt to assert copyright or moral rights to safeguard their works, but scholars have
(35) consistently questioned the validity of copyrights obtained for these works and have carved out moral rights protection for street art that is created illegally. The reality is that illegal graffiti art is inherently at conflict with the law. While many
(40) graffiti artists have their own identifying tags or a particular style that is easily identifiable as theirs, street artists generally remain anonymous.

Why the obscurity? Because graffiti art encompasses a bit of danger. An integral aspect of
(45) the art is to mark highly visible public spaces with the artist's imagery. In most circumstances, it

would prove nearly impossible to secure the property owner's permission beforehand. The reality is that street artists must consistently mask
(50) their identities to avoid conflicts with the law. As illegality and anonymity are integral components of graffiti, the majority of street art fits into the category of unsanctioned art difficult to be handled by intellectual property law as we know
(55) it.

Under current copyright law in the United States, a work immediately receives protection if it is an "original work of authorship fixed in any tangible medium of expression." Along with this
(60) protection, an artist has a bundle of exclusive rights to reproduce the work, prepare derivative works, distribute copies, and display the work publicly. These rights were traditionally understood as belonging exclusively to the artist,
(65) but this view has evolved with respect to unsanctioned street art. Some argue that the illegality of unsanctioned graffiti art bars copyrightability, while others argue that copyright entitlements must instead be split where the work
(70) was illegally created. While various cases have been filed by street artists to attempt to gain copyright protection for their work, most of the cases have been settled or dropped. Without going to litigation, it is nearly impossible to better
(75) define the rights of graffiti artists under the law.

As previously mentioned, street artists have very few options for protecting their works under U.S. Intellectual property law. Artists of illegal or unsanctioned works face even more limiting
(80) exclusions, leaving their works with little or no protection. In this respect, street art stands among industries such as fashion and stand-up comedy that embody and represent thriving creative industries but rest in intellectual property's
(85) "negative space."

While revising the copyright scheme seems desirable, does traditional intellectual property protection of street art truly fulfill intellectual property law's purpose of promoting creativity?
(90) Would it incentivize the creation of more street art? It seems unlikely. In fact, street art has flourished during the past 10 years despite public

resistance and the little protection afforded to artists under current law. This alone demonstrates
(95) that the lack of stringent intellectual property entitlements does not destroy the prevalence of street art. Street artists should continue to attempt to exercise U.S. copyright entitlements and depend on the current laws to protect their works
(100) from unauthorized copying, removal, sale, and destruction. However, it seems unlikely that the nature of street art will ever necessitate a robust dependence on traditional intellectual property entitlements.

1. According to the author, one of the primary purposes of street art is:

   A) infuse public spaces with the visions of the artist.
   B) expose the public to the danger inherent in graffiti.
   C) incentivize the creation of more street art.
   D) provide a source of income for the artist.

2. The purpose of the passage as a whole is to:

   A) discuss the political and cultural ramifications of illegal art in public places.
   B) highlight the intrinsic unfairness of United States copyright laws.
   C) question whether street art is able to be ruled by United States copyright laws.
   D) condemn the vagrancy of street artists who destroy public places.

3. The passage notes that each artist is known by his or her own:

   A) unique style.
   B) political agenda.
   C) level of obscurity.
   D) dependence on entitlements.

4. The author's attitude towards street art is largely:

   A) adverse.
   B) appreciative.
   C) irrefutable.
   D) deniable.

5. According to the author, what effect would the intellectual protection of street art have on the genre?

   A) Promote greater creativity among artists
   B) Encourage the creation of more street art
   C) Increase the dependence of street artists on the government
   D) None of the above

6. Based on the passage above, the "negative space" of copyright most likely refers to:

   A) genres of art that are too harmful to the public to be encouraged.
   B) creative works that are too generic to be worth copyrighting.
   C) works of art that are difficult or impossible to copyright.
   D) types of art that should be embraced by the public for their difficulty to perform.

7. According to the author, all of the following are detrimental to street art EXCEPT:

   A) its unauthorized copying.
   B) its unauthorized sale.
   C) the ease of destruction of street art.
   D) the offensive imagery it embodies.

8. Which of the following best espouses the author's feelings about copyright laws with respect to street art?

A) As street art is illegal, it is already in conflict with the law, making copyrighting difficult.
B) Copyright settlements should be split between the owner of the property and the artist.
C) The artist's moral rights are more important than the copyright laws associated with street art.
D) The prevalence of previous litigation against street artists hints that street art should be copyrightable.

9. According to information found in the passage, which of the following locations is the least likely for street art?

A) Public parks
B) Exteriors of corporate offices
C) Rural landscapes
D) Public transportation

10. In which of the following ways does the street artist most differ from the traditional artist?

A) The subject matter of the art
B) The creativity of the artist
C) The location of the art
D) The popularity of the art

PRACTICE EXERCISE 9

Directions: Read the following passage and answer the accompanying questions.

Many expecting parents are concerned with the sleeping habits of their newborn children. A small amber light bulb, called Sleepy Baby, may
Line be able to soothe their worries. This special bulb
(5) creates a soothing atmosphere for babies to naturally sleep to.

While this example may be specific to babies' sleep patterns, it is only a small part of a technological revolution that is infiltrating homes,
(10) offices, schools, and hotels and is designed to offset the harm of artificial lighting – both overhead and on screen. These lights can regulate sleep, bolster awareness and productivity, and even alter people's moods.

(15) "Lighting is really not about a fixture in the ceiling anymore," said Mariana Figueiro, who leads light and health research at the Lighting Research Center of Rensselaer Polytechnic Institute. "It's about delivering individualized
(20) light treatments to people."

For years, scientists have revealed the many effects of different colors and levels of light on our biological systems. But these lighting alternatives have always been in the form of
(25) expensive bulbs that could cost as much as $300,000. With the increase of sophistication and lower costs of production, new lighting technology, such as LEDs, are allowing companies to develop biological lighting for
(30) everyday consumers.

The creator of Sleepy Baby – the Lighting Science Group – is among the group of companies that focus on the biological effects of lighting, with bulbs like Good Night and Awake
(35) and Alert.

General Electric announced a color changing LED that would automate lighting in accordance with the natural sleep cycle. Philips branded the Hue, connecting the bulb to WiFi, and offered
(40) "light recipes" that encouraged waking up or resting. Digital Lumens has created lights for a study at Brown University that is testing levels and hues of colors that promote learning. Lumifi has an app that controls and adjusts lighting in not
(45) only homes but commercial areas such as hotels. The app provides settings such as Rest, Energize,

and Focus.

"With these kinds of bulbs that are coming to the market, you can suddenly now put better
(50) lighting controls systems, very affordable, into the hands of everyone," said Beatrice Witzgall, an architect and lighting designer who founded LumiFi. "It's a big revolution."

Milos Todorovic, bioelectronics research
(55) leader at Lux Research, stated that companies are concentrating on the health applications and implications for different lightings. They research the effects of light on mood, mentality, emotions, and even actual physical processes in the body
(60) such as healing wounds with enhanced collagen regeneration.

Essentially, the goal is to reverse or prevent the damage of regular lighting on the body's organic rhythms. For example, newly designed
(65) bulbs are intended to adjust and balance the body's need to rest and wake up by triggering receptors in the eyes that notify the brain when it is time to wake up or go to bed.

White artificial lights, especially LEDs used
(70) in every day consumer products such as phones, TVs, and illuminated screens, have high instances of blue short-wavelength light. These wavelengths suppress the release of the hormone melatonin which induces sleep. Therefore, being
(75) exposed to these types of lights at night makes people more alert and less likely to fall asleep.

Statistics show that within the last 50 years the amount of artificial light used per capita has had a tenfold increase. The world is becoming
(80) increasingly brighter at night every year, pushing people's internal clocks back by three to five hours and causing sleep disorders and other physical ailments.

While researchers continue studying how the
(85) brain is affected by spectrum and intensity of light, they have determined that the use of longer wavelength light does not obstruct the production of hormones and functions of neurons as much as shorter wavelength lights.

(90) Other research settings have produced ideas that red light can stimulate energy and activity without hindering the production of melatonin

and energy levels can be altered by light intensity regardless of hue. Brown University researchers
(95) are now studying both spectrum and intensity of lights to create a system that helps young students stay attentive in school.

The advances made in LED technology, engineering, and WiFi create a possibility for
(100) lighting systems to be developed and distributed at reasonable prices to everyday consumers. Purchasing several bulbs or bulb sets - such as the starter pack of the Hue that comes with three bulbs and a WiFi connected hub - can range in
(105) cost from $25-$200. However, what consumers will find reasonable depends solely on their individual priorities.

1. According to the passage, one of the main problems white lights have on the human body is:

   A) encouraging people to wake up by connecting to WiFi.
   B) causing sleep disorders by pushing back internal clocks.
   C) inhibiting sleep by suppressing the body's release of melatonin.
   D) obstructing learning because of a lack of different hues.

2. For many years, one of the limiting factors of new light bulb technology has been:

   A) a lack of development for adults.
   B) getting approval from government agencies.
   C) its great expense.
   D) a lack of commercial interest.

3. According to the passage, lighting can affect all of the following EXCEPT:

   A) learning.
   B) sleeping.
   C) health.
   D) creativity.

4. The main purpose of the second paragraph (lines 7-14) is to transition from:

   A) discussing how a product affects one specific group of people to discussing how that product affects people in general.
   B) discussing how a product affects people in general to discussing how that product affects one specific group of people.
   C) discussing a specific product to discussing uses for that product.
   D) discussing general uses of a product to discussing more specific uses of that product.

5. The main purpose of the last paragraph (lines 98-107) is to:

   A) give prices on several types of light bulbs.
   B) show how technological advances are making special light bulbs cheaper.
   C) describe how light bulbs can be connected to WiFi for home use.
   D) discuss the proper way to balance your home light budget.

6. The tone of the passage can best be described as:

A) favorable, but fact-based.
B) positive, yet ironic.
C) objective, but negative.
D) serious, yet comedic.

7. Light bulbs can influence the brain to sleep or wake up by:

A) artificially adjusting people's moods.
B) sending signals via WiFi-enabled devices.
C) making noises played via computer speakers.
D) triggering receptors located in the eyes.

8. In the context of the passage, the sixth paragraph (lines 36-47) primarily serves to:

A) list several different lighting companies.
B) describe some of the innovations different companies are making in lighting.
C) expand on the technological differences between several different light bulbs.
D) describe in detail how one company is revolutionizing the lighting industry.

9. As it is used in line 87, the word *obstruct* most nearly means:

A) hinder.
B) choke.
C) make difficult.
D) stop.

10. Mariana Figueiro would most likely make which of the following statements?

A) Many of the new lighting advances are superficial at best.
B) New advances in lighting are moving too fast for the public to keep up with.
C) Lighting is about more than just letting people see in the dark.
D) The installation of new light bulbs is now commercially viable in hotels and malls.

PRACTICE EXERCISE 10

Directions: Read the following passage and answer the accompanying questions.

Passage A

A historian of American higher education, Frederick Rudolph, once remarked that few universities forestalled the growth of fraternal *Line* organizations in the early 1800s. Rudolph (5) explained that presidents of these institutions had to deal with these student groups "that they had neither invited nor encouraged."

Nearly 200 years later, this assertion is still accurate. The latest attempt to rein in these groups (10) involves compelling fraternities and sororities to become coed. The theory is that this "sororternity" would still offer chances to bond while decreasing certain undesirable behaviors that plague the Greek system.

(15) Unfortunately, this will not work.

There has been a great debate for many years in the educational world regarding the advantages and disadvantages of homogeneous versus heterogeneous groups. Despite concerns of (20) inequality and discrimination, it is hard to deny that gender-based groups have their purposes. In higher education, research indicates that female students reap a number of benefits from attending women's colleges. Women who attend these (25) colleges are generally more satisfied and have higher self-esteem than their counterparts in coed colleges. To be frank, the move for a coed Greek organization centers on the fraternities, so it seems wrong to punish women for the conduct of (30) men.

Moreover, the law affords students the freedom of association. If students prefer a single-gender Greek experience, that is their right. If a college chooses to force campus Greeks to ignore (35) their bylaws and become coed organizations, the national organizations will withdraw, placing the complete responsibility of the local groups into the hand of the institution. Furthermore, there is nothing that inhibits the previous groups from (40) existing off campus as unrecognized groups. This would simply make the issues worse, particularly without the national headquarters of the Greek organizations to help address problems.

While there is a resounding dissatisfaction in (45) academia as a result of the sluggish change in Greek life, forcing coed Greeks is not the answer. This supposed solution will only serve to create a significantly greater problem.

Passage B

The time has come to assimilate college (50) Greek organizations, so that they are no longer split by gender. While I appreciate the deep relationships that happen in fraternities and sororities, it is no longer acceptable to rationalize the detrimental impact that segregation by sex (55) inflicts on young people's progress in both personal and career domains.

As a neuroscientist, my job is to investigate the impact of gender development on the wiring of our brains and behaviors. From a scientific (60) perspective, when young people spend a significant amount of time in homogenous groups, their development unsurprisingly shows a greater predisposition toward gender stereotyping. These findings have been corroborated through (65) studies on siblings, juvenile peers, and young adults. Being in the company of same gender peers most of the time alters a person's vocal pitch, interpersonal interactions, academic and extracurricular interests, and career selection in (70) ways that undoubtedly inhibit their complete development as humans.

Despite their technically coed configuration, most college campuses continue to be acutely gender segregated. Academic majors that are (75) traditionally dominated by one gender, such as engineering, computer science, and education, enroll less than 21 percent of the minority gender. The cause is the gender labels that are indirectly connected to almost every academic and career (80) choice. Undergraduates all too often opt to follow a career path based on gender conformity, which results in a considerable number of these students failing.

Gender segregation also influences (85) relationships, which is the driving force behind the effort to integrate Greek life at some colleges and universities. If the pledging candidates are comprised of both males and females, the odds are better that these students will not be

(90) objectified and mistreated by each other. Mixed gender groups lessen the chances of the questionable activities that colleges and universities have long fought to prevent in Greek life.

(95) Another important factor to note is that the U.S. military, which has traditionally been an extreme example of gender segregation, is already ahead of colleges in terms of gender integration. As part of the end of the combat exclusion for *(100)* women in 2016, all branches of the military have prepared with accelerated integrated training. Furthermore, they are confronting issues of gender discrimination and sexual harassment more blatantly than universities.

(105) While Greek organizations have customarily been given autonomy on college campuses, it is time for these institutions that promote gender inequality to change their ways. In the long run, integration is not only good for these students, but *(110)* good for society as a whole.

1. As it is used in line 10, the word *compelling* most nearly means:

   A) irresistible.
   B) constraining.
   C) interesting.
   D) forcing.

2. According to Passage A, female students:

   A) advocate making the Greek system coed.
   B) have higher self-esteem than their male counterparts.
   C) gain significant benefits from single-gender education.
   D) perform best at coed universities.

3. Passage A suggests that male students in the Greek system:

   A) should be punished for their conduct.
   B) would benefit from integration more than female students would.
   C) would simply move their fraternities off campus if forced integration were to occur.
   D) formed fraternities that were against the rules of their colleges.

4. Which of the following best summarizes the main argument of the paragraph in lines 31 through 43?

   A) Colleges would be violating their own codes and rules by forcing the integration of the Greek system.
   B) Students would protest forced integration of the Greek system.
   C) The Greek system must voluntarily integrate.
   D) Forced integration of the Greek system would be legally and logically impractical.

5. The second paragraph of Passage B (lines 57-71) primarily argues that:

A) students who participate in same gender groups choose careers that are traditionally dominated by one gender.
B) male students in homogenous groups exhibit sexist behaviors as adults.
C) gender homogeneity has lasting negative impacts on students' development.
D) the author's experience as a neuroscientist lends him greater credibility.

6. Passage B identifies all of the following as single-gender dominated majors EXCEPT:

A) engineering.
B) medicine.
C) computer science.
D) education.

7. The author of Passage B likely included the fifth paragraph (lines 95-104) in order to suggest that:

A) if an organization as segregated as the military can handle the issues inherent in gender integration, colleges should certainly be able to do the same.
B) the military experiences fewer gender discrimination and sexual harassment problems than do colleges.
C) colleges should provide accelerated integration training similar to that provided by the military.
D) like the Greek system, the military should have integrated long ago.

8. Which of the following most accurately contrasts the points of view of the authors of Passages A and B?

A) The author of Passage A opposes forced gender integration of the Greek system while the author of Passage B supports it.
B) The author of Passage A supports voluntary gender integration of the Greek system while the author of Passage B advocates forced gender integration.
C) The author of Passage A supports gender integration of the Greek system while the author of Passage B opposes it.
D) The author of Passage A believes that fraternities cause problems on campuses while the author of Passage B believes sororities cause problems.

9. Which of the following identifies a similarity in the evidence used by both authors?

A) Both cite statistics regarding gender integration.
B) Both cite research into single-gender education.
C) Neither cites statistics regarding gender integration.
D) Both use the military as an example.

10. How would the author of Passage A most likely respond to the assertion made in lines 90 through 94?

A) By pointing out that research suggests that gender integrated groups have historically failed to address problems associated with single gender groups.
B) By arguing that forced integration of the Greek system violates students' right to freedom of association.
C) By pointing out that only male students would alter their behavior under forced integration.
D) By arguing that these "questionable activities" would very likely simply move off-campus where there is even less oversight.

Reading Practice Exercises Answer Key

Explicit Information
1. A
2. D
3. B
4. B
5. D
6. C
7. A
8. B
9. A
10. C

Literary Narrative
1. C
2. D
3. C
4. B
5. C
6. B
7. A
8. A
9. D
10. D

Natural Science
1. B
2. B
3. B
4. A
5. C
6. A
7. A
8. D
9. C
10. D

Implicit Information
1. D
2. D
3. B
4. C
5. B
6. A
7. B
8. C
9. A
10. A

Social Studies
1. A
2. A
3. C
4. B
5. C
6. C
7. D
8. B
9. D
10. A

Paired Passages
1. A
2. B
3. B
4. D
5. B
6. D
7. C
8. B
9. A
10. B

Words in Context
1. B
2. B
3. C
4. A
5. D
6. A
7. D
8. C
9. C
10. C
11. D
12. B

Humanities
1. D
2. A
3. A
4. CC
5. D
6. A
7. B
8. C
9. C
10. B

Practice Exercise 1
1. C
2. B
3. C
4. D
5. B
6. A
7. C
8. D
9. A
10. A

Practice Exercise 2

1. B
2. D
3. B
4. A
5. B
6. A
7. D
8. A
9. B
10. A

Practice Exercise 3

1. B
2. A
3. B
4. C
5. B
6. A
7. B
8. A
9. D
10. B

Practice Exercise 4

1. C
2. C
3. B
4. C
5. D
6. B
7. A
8. A
9. B
10. B

Practice Exercise 5

1. A
2. C
3. D
4. D
5. B
6. C
7. A
8. A
9. B
10. C

Practice Exercise 6

1. C
2. C
3. D
4. A
5. A
6. B
7. D
8. B
9. D
10. C

Practice Exercise 7

1. B
2. B
3. C
4. B
5. A
6. D
7. B
8. D
9. C
10. C

Practice Exercise 8

1. A
2. C
3. A
4. B
5. D
6. C
7. D
8. A
9. C
10. C

Practice Exercise 9

1. C
2. C
3. D
4. A
5. B
6. A
7. D
8. B
9. A
10. C

Practice Exercise 10

1. D
2. C
3. B
4. D
5. C
6. B
7. A
8. A
9. B
10. D

ACT Science: Introduction

Introduction to the ACT Science Test

- The ACT Science Test focuses more on your ability to evaluate charts, graphs, information, and scientific experiments than your knowledge of scientific facts.
- As such, preparing for the ACT Science Test should focus mainly on increasing your ability to understand the information provided by, and the trends apparent in, this scientific data.
- The ACT Science Test is made up of 7 passages. Each passage has 5-7 questions for a total of 40 questions.
- You are given only 35 minutes to complete the exam, which works out to 5 minutes per passage. Being able to work quickly and effectively will be extremely important on the test – you will be exposed to a lot of information at once, and you have to be able to understand it. So, the more practice you can get deciphering information that is presented in the way the ACT does, the better you will do.

Types of Passages on the ACT Science Test

- There are 3 types of passages on the ACT Science Test: **Data Representation**, **Research Summaries**, and **Conflicting Viewpoints**.
- The exam features 3 **Data Representation** passages. Each of these passages contains 5 questions and features basic graphs or charts. These are the most straightforward of the 3 passage types.
- The exam also features 3 **Research Summaries** passages. Each contains 6 questions about a scientific experiment, and you will use information provided in the experiment to predict potential results of the experiment.
- Each exam has 1 **Conflicting Viewpoints** passage. This passage features 2 or more written arguments about a controversial scientific topic, and you will be asked 7 questions based on the information you read.

Types of Questions on the ACT Science Test

- The questions on the ACT can be distilled into 3 basic types: **Understanding**, **Analysis**, and **Generalization**.
- **Understanding** questions test your ability to identify facts from the information given in the passage.
- **Analysis** questions require you to analyze trends or draw conclusion from the information given in the passage.
- **Generalization** questions require you to understand the trends present in the passage enough to apply them to experiments or real-life scenarios not mentioned in the passage.

General ACT Science Strategies

- Typically, most of the relevant information for answering the questions will be found in the charts and graphs, not the introductory material. As such, stick to only skimming through the introductory material at first. You can always go back and read it later if you don't understand something mentioned in the charts, graphs, or questions.

- You will see many scientific terms and ideas that you've never been exposed to on the ACT Science Test, but don't worry. Most of these will be defined in the passage, and if not, they are probably not very relevant to answering the questions.

- Don't worry if you don't know the scientific reasoning behind the information in a passage: very few questions on the exam require any outside information, and when they do, it will be basic information that you would be expected to learn in high school, if not middle school.

- You're not allowed to use a calculator on this portion of the ACT, but this shouldn't slow you down. You should always be able to estimate any answer that requires math, so don't bother doing any calculation by hand. The answer choices should be far enough apart that estimation will be sufficient.

- When in doubt, skip a question. You get less than a minute per question, and that includes reading the passages. So, if you don't understand what's going on in a question, skip it and move on to the next question. If you have time at the end, go back and try again. Otherwise, guess! There is no penalty for guessing on the ACT, so you should answer every question.

PRACTICE EXERCISE

Passage 1

To study the effect of water temperature on the swimming speed of guppies, scientists set up an experiment in which they raised populations of guppies in 3 different aquariums.

Population 1 was raised at 10°C, Population 2 was raised at 20°C, and Population 3 was raised at 30°C. The results of the experiment are shown in the graph below.

Swimming Speeds of Two Guppy Populations

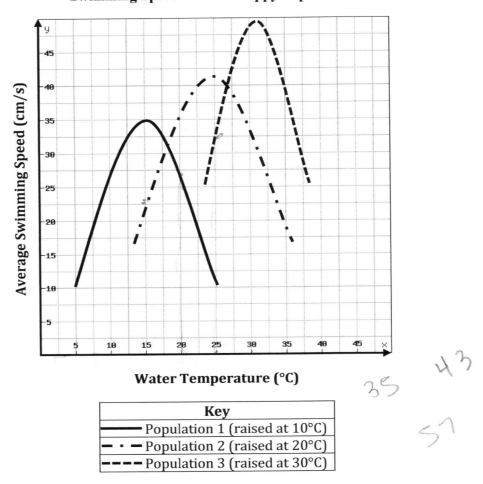

Key
—— Population 1 (raised at 10°C)
— · — Population 2 (raised at 20°C)
— — — Population 3 (raised at 30°C)

1. The lowest average swimming speed, in cm/s, of a guppy raised in 20°C, is approximately:
   A) 10 cm/s
   B) 17 cm/s
   C) 25 cm/s
   D) 41 cm/s

2. The range of temperatures a guppy can be expected to survive in is represented by its average swimming speeds on the graph. If a speed does not exist at a certain temperature, then the guppy cannot survive in that temperature water. As a rule, for temperatures a guppy can survive at, as the temperature a guppy is raised at increases, its average swimming speed:
   A) increases only.
   B) decreases only.
   C) increases, then decreases.
   D) decreases, then increases.

3. At 25°C, which of the following puts the populations in ascending order of average swimming speed?
   A) 1, 3, 2
   B) 1, 2, 3
   C) 2, 1, 3
   D) 3, 2, 1

4. A 4th population of guppies is raised at a temperature of 15°C. What is the expected maximum average swimming speed of this population of guppies?
   A) 36°C
   B) 38°C
   C) 42°C
   D) 46°C

5. Based on the results of the experiment above, a guppy typically swims fastest:
   A) at the temperature at which it was raised.
   B) at temperatures below at which it was raised.
   C) at temperatures much higher than which it was raised.
   D) at temperatures slightly higher than which it was raised.

Passage 2

Some students tested their hypothesis that different floor materials would alter the *roll time* (the time it took a ball to roll, without slipping, down an incline between 2 fixed points).

Identical steel balls, each weighing 3 kg, were used in the first two experiments. The angle of inclination of the incline was 2.5° in all 3 experiments.

Experiment 1

The students set up 3 identical inclines and covered each with a particular surface – linoleum, carpet, and sandpaper. They rolled the steel ball down each incline 3 times and averaged the time it took each ball to travel down the incline. The results are shown in Table 1.

Table 1				
Surface	Roll Time (seconds)			Three trial average
	Trial 1	Trial 2	Trial 3	
Linoleum	1.2	1.1	1.0	1.1
Carpet	2.1	2.2	2.1	2.1
Sandpaper	1.6	1.5	1.7	1.6

Experiment 2

The students repeated Experiment 1, but this time they doubled the length between the two fixed points. The results are shown in Table 2.

Table 2				
Surface	Roll Time (seconds)			Three trial average
	Trial 1	Trial 2	Trial 3	
Linoleum	2.1	2.0	2.1	2.1
Carpet	3.8	3.6	3.7	3.6
Sandpaper	2.4	2.6	2.4	2.5

Experiment 3

The students repeated Experiment 1, but this time they used a different ball with double the mass but the same size. The results are shown in Table 3.

Table 3				
Surface	Roll Time (seconds)			Three trial average
	Trial 1	Trial 2	Trial 3	
Linoleum	1.3	1.0	1.2	1.2
Carpet	2.0	2.1	2.1	2.1
Sandpaper	1.5	1.7	1.7	1.6

1. Based on the results of Experiments 1 and 3, one can conclude that:
   A) Mass and the time it takes to travel down the incline are directly related.
   B) Mass and the time it takes to travel down the incline are inversely related.
   C) Mass and the time it takes to travel down the incline are not related.
   D) Mass does not affect the time it takes to travel down the incline.

2. Friction is a force which slows the movement of objects along a path. The greater the force of friction, the more slowly the object moves. According to the data obtained during Experiment 1, which type of surface exerted the largest force of friction on the ball?
   A) Linoleum
   B) Carpet
   C) Sandpaper
   D) All of the surfaces exerted equal amounts of friction.

3. Based on the results of Experiment 2, one can conclude that doubling the length of the incline affected the time it took to travel the incline in which of the following ways?
   A) The times for each surface did not change.
   B) The times for each surface nearly doubled.
   C) The times for each surface exactly doubled.
   D) The times for each surface more than doubled.

4. If the length of the incline in Experiment 1 were tripled, which of the following would be the most likely time for the ball to travel down the sandpaper course?
   A) 3.0 seconds
   B) 3.5 seconds
   C) 4.5 seconds
   D) 6.0 seconds

5. Experiment 3 is repeated, but the length of the track is doubled. What is the expected time for the ball to travel down the carpeted incline?
   A) 2.1 seconds
   B) 2.5 seconds
   C) 3.0 seconds
   D) 3.6 seconds

6. Which of the following was a control of both Experiments 1 and 2?
   A) The type of surface covering the incline.
   B) The length of the incline.
   C) The mass of the ball.
   D) All 3 of the above were controls of Experiment 2.

Passage 3

Every year, approximately 26 million animals are used in the United States for scientific and commercial testing. These animals are used to develop medical treatments, to determine the safety of medications and products designed for human use, and for many other commercial and medical procedures. Below, two students list the pros and cons of using animals in scientific and commercial testing.

Student 1

Without animal testing, many of the medical breakthroughs discovered in the last 100 years would not have been discovered. While many of these procedures do cause pain, and even death, in these animals, it is better to harm or kill animals than people. As an example, experiments in which dogs had their pancreases removed lead to the discovery of insulin, which is crucial to the treating of diabetes. The polio vaccine was also tested heavily on animals, and today, polio is nearly wiped out.

Today, we have no adequate alternative ways to test on a living system. Even the most powerful supercomputers are not yet able to accurately simulate the workings of complex organs and organ systems. Thus, we must use animals to test. Animals are ideal research subjects because they are similar to human beings in many ways. Chimpanzees share 99% of their DNA with humans; mice share 98%. All mammals are descended from a common organism, so their organ systems and functions of those systems are nearly identical. Additionally, animals are susceptible to many of the same conditions and illnesses that humans are, including heart disease, cancer, and diabetes.

Student 2

Animals used in scientific experiments are commonly subjected to gruesome conditions, including overeating, the forced inhalation of dangerous chemicals, physical restraint, and the infliction of injuries to study the healing process. Many of these animals are not even given anesthesia for relief, adding to the horror of the experiments done.

Many alternative testing methods exist that can replace the need for animals. In vitro testing studies result in cell cultures and can produce better results than animal testing because human cells can be used. Microdosing is another valid method of testing in which small doses of a medication, too small for harmful effects to occur, are used. The blood is then analyzed to determine the efficacy of the medication.

Even though the DNA of many mammals is very similar, animals make poor models for human beings. Most notably, the size of a rat does not match up with the size of a human – how many 75 kg rats have you seen? A sleeping pill was tested on animals prior to its release to the public. The pill caused no adverse effects in these animals, but babies born to pregnant mothers on these pills had severe deformities.

We must improve our ability to use technology to model human organ systems, for both the betterment of science and medicine and the safety of animals. Neither is more important than the other.

1. With which of the following statements would both students agree?
   A) Many medical techniques are unable to be tested on animals.
   B) Without animal testing, the polio vaccine never would have been discovered.
   C) The DNA of some species of mammals is very similar.
   D) Microdosing is an effective method of testing new medicines on animals.

2. With which of the following statements would Student 2 disagree?
   A) Protecting human lives is more important than protecting animals from harm.
   B) Attempts to electronically model human organ systems should be ignored.
   C) Inflicting pain on animals without providing anesthesia is unethical.
   D) The organ systems of humans are not always mirrored perfectly by those of other mammals.

3. How would Student 2 respond to Student 1's claim that "animals are susceptible to many of the same conditions and illnesses that humans are, including heart disease, cancer, and diabetes"?
   A) Animals are too small to be affected by diseases that affect humans.
   B) While animals are affected by many of the same diseases as humans, their organ systems react to the diseases in different ways.
   C) Animal testing can just as easily find cures for diseases in animals as it finds cures for diseases in humans.
   D) The healing processes of animals with diseases is a valuable source of information in the study of those diseases.

4. Which of the following is an accurate description of "microdosing"?
   A) The use of a medication on an animal much smaller than a human to test its harmfulness.
   B) The use of a chemical on an animal much smaller than a human to test its harmfulness.
   C) The use of a small dose of a chemical or medicine on an animal to test its harmfulness.
   D) The use of a small dose of a chemical or medicine on a human to test its harmfulness.

5. A new species of primate is discovered that matches 99.8% of human DNA. Student 1's reaction would most likely be:
   A) We now have an even better subject to test medicines on, as it must be even more closely related to humans than chimpanzees are.
   B) We should abandon all of our testing on other animals and focus solely on this new primate.
   C) It is even more unethical to test on an animal that is this closely related to humans.
   D) Since this animal is so closely related to humans, the ethics of testing on it mirror that of testing on other humans.

6. Which student is most likely to use an argument involving the phrase "animals themselves benefit from the results of animal testing"?
   A) Student 1
   B) Student 2
   C) Both students
   D) Neither student

7. A new strain of the flu virus has developed that is able to be spread from humans to animals. This information invalidates which student's point of view?
   A) Student 1
   B) Student 2
   C) Both students
   D) Neither student

ACT Science: Understanding Charts and Graphs

Tables

- **Tables** are among the easiest ways that the ACT presents information:

Table 1			
		Roll Time (in secs)	
Trial	Liquid	Before Shaking	After Shaking
1	tap water	1.75	1.75
2	soapy water	1.97	2.15
3	flat-tasting beverage	1.75	1.96

- We can see from the table above that the information has been distilled into 3 different trials, each of which consists of a different liquid. The "roll time" of each liquid is measured, both before and after shaking.
- Always pay attention to the units of any information presented! Here, all of our roll times are measured in seconds.

Bar Graphs

- **Bar graphs** are another common way of presenting data on the ACT:

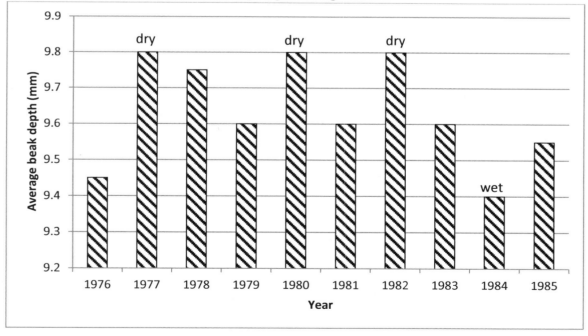

- Always pay attention to what is measured on each axis. Here, the x-axis represents the year, while the y-axis represents the average beak depth, in mm. Again, always pay attention to the units present for each axis!
- Occasionally, other information is added to the bar graph. Here, the words "dry" and "wet" are added above certain years. If this information doesn't immediately make sense, the passage will tell us what the information means. Here we can assume that these years are drier or wetter than normal.
- Always be aware of trends present in the data. Here, we can see that average beak depths usually alternate between high and low values. Also notice that beak depth is always highest on years with "dry" above them and lowest on years with "wet" above them.

Example 1

Based on the information above, how much larger was the average beak depth, in mm, in 1985 when compared to 1976?

A) 0.1 mm
B) 0.2 mm
C) 1.0 mm
D) 2.0 mm

All we need to do is find the values for the average beak depth in 1985 and 1976, then subtract. In 1985, the value was 9.55 mm, while in 1976 the value was 9.45 mm. The difference between the two is 0.1 mm, so the answer is **A**.

Line Graphs and Scatterplots

- **Line graphs** are another useful way of displaying information on the ACT:

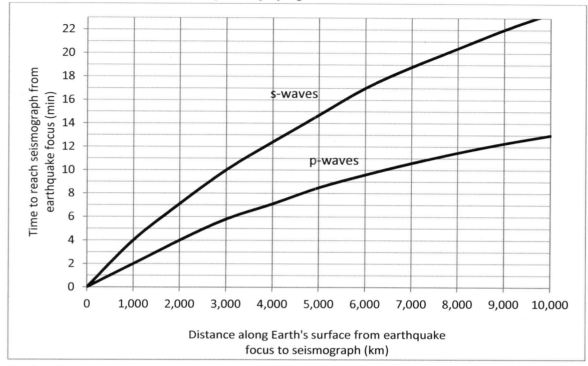

- Again, always pay attention to what is measured on each axis. Here, the x-axis represents a distance, in km, while the y-axis represents a time, in min. Always pay attention to the units present for each axis!
- With **line graphs**, it is much easier to **interpolate** and **extrapolate**.
- **Interpolation** is the act of looking between data points to find information. For example, we can estimate that a seismograph 3,500 km from an earthquake's focus can experience p-waves in approximately 6.5 minutes.
- **Extrapolation** is the act of looking beyond data points to find information. Although distances stop at 10,000 km in this chart, we could approximate the time at a distance of 12,000 km by following the general path of the curve.
- **Scatterplots** are similar to line graphs, but the data points presented are not generally connected by a line. It will usually be helpful to add a **trend line** (a line that indicates the general course of the data) to the data yourself before analyzing the information provided.

Use extrapolation to determine the time values at each point. For p-waves at 10,500 km, the time will be approximately 13.5 minutes, while for s-waves the time will be at least 24 minutes. The difference between the two would have to be greater than 10.5 minutes, so our answer is **D**.

Other Types of Data

- Scientific data can be presented in many different ways, so you are likely to see many other types of charts, graphs, and figures on the ACT than the ones presented above. Let's look at another sample graph:

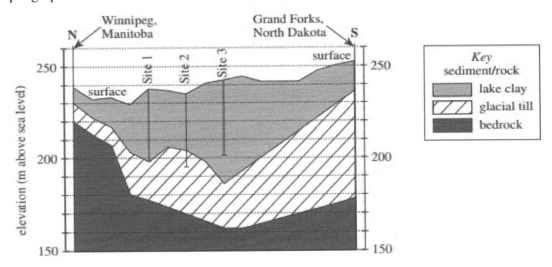

- This graph has a clearly marked y-axis, but nothing marked on the x-axis. We can tell that the y-axis measures the elevation of several points, in meters.
- With a little examination, we can figure out that the left-hand side of the x-axis is marked N and shows Winnipeg, Manitoba, while the right-hand side of the x-axis is marked S and shows Grand Forks, North Dakota. We can assume that the x-axis approximates the distance between the two cities, with N representing North and S representing South.
- We also see 3 sites listed between the two cities.
- The **key** shows us the types of sediment/rock present throughout the region at different elevations. With this information, we can see that Site 1 is located on the boundary of lake clay

and glacial till, Site 2 is located firmly in the glacial till region, and Site 3 is located in the lake clay region.

Example 3

According to the figure above, as the thickness of the lake clay deposits increases from Grand Forks to Site 3, the thickness of the glacial till beneath it:

A) increases.
B) remains the same.
C) first increases and then decreases.
D) decreases.

Watch out for trick questions! Most graphs ask you to read them from left to right, but this one asks you to go from right to left. As we travel from Grand Forks (glacial till thickness = 60 m) to Site 3 (glacial till thickness = 30 m), the thickness decreases. The answer is **D**.

- As you can see, the majority of these questions have just asked us to find information from the chart. Practicing the process of analyzing and understanding these graphs is the key to doing well on the ACT.

PRACTICE EXERCISE

Passage 1

A *food web* is the graphical representation of the natural interconnection of food chains in a particular ecological community. Food webs are also known as consumer-resource systems and are generally composed of two categories: *autotrophs* (organisms that create food from their surroundings using energy from light or chemical reactions) and *heterotrophs* (organisms which consume other organisms). Figure 1 shows an example of an ocean food web.

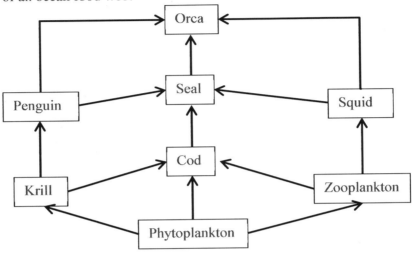

Figure 1

Although food webs are representations of real ecosystems, they don't necessarily contain all of the information necessary to determine the number of members of a species in a certain ecosystem. A *trophic pyramid* shows the *biomass*, or amount of living matter present in an organism, at each *trophic level* of a given ecosystem. A trophic level describes the position an organism or organisms occupy in a food chain. Typically, food chains start at level 1 on the bottom with primary producers and end at level 4 or 5 with apex predators. Only about 10% of the energy in a given trophic level is able to be used by the next level up, so each level of the trophic pyramid contains approximately 10 times the biomass of the level above it. Figure 2 below shows a trophic pyramid.

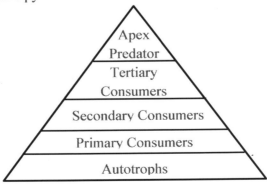

Figure 2

1. Which of the following organisms presented in the food web in Figure 1 most likely fits into the Apex Predator category of the trophic pyramid presented in Figure 2?
   A) Phytoplankton
   B) Zooplankton
   C) Seal
   D) Orca

2. Which of the following organisms in Figure 1 is not a heterotroph?
   A) Phytoplankton
   B) Zooplankton
   C) Krill
   D) Cod

3. A particular ecosystem in the Pacific Ocean contains approximately 10 million kilograms of Tertiary Consumers. Approximately how many kilograms of Autotrophs would be needed to sustain this much biomass of Tertiary Consumers?
   A) 10 billion kilograms
   B) 1 billion kilograms
   C) 100 thousand kilograms
   D) 10 thousand kilograms

4. According to information provided in Figure 1, a reduction in the number of Orcas in an ecosystem would most likely result in:
   A) a reduction in the number of Seals present.
   B) a reduction in the number of Penguins present.
   C) an increase in the number of Penguins present.
   D) an increase in the number of Decomposers present.

5. A species of seagull is introduced to the ecosystem presented in Figure 1. This seagull eats squid and cod and has no predators. It would most likely fill the same portion of the trophic pyramid as the:
   A) orca.
   B) seal.
   C) penguin.
   D) krill.

Passage 2

From a source, sound travels in all directions in a pattern similar to a sphere. The intensity of a sound is dependent on the power produced by the source and the size of the sphere at a certain distance away. Table 1 below shows several example sounds, their sound levels, and their intensities. All examples are from a distance of 1 meter unless otherwise noted. Figure 1 below shows the relationship between the relative intensity of a sound and the distance, in meters, the listener is from the source of that sound.

Table 1		
Sound Level (dB)	Intensity (W/m²)	Example
0	1×10^{-12}	Threshold of human hearing
10	1×10^{-11}	Rustling leaves
20	1×10^{-10}	Whisper
30	1×10^{-9}	Quiet rural area
40	1×10^{-8}	Bird call
50	1×10^{-7}	Normal conversation
60	1×10^{-6}	Background music
70	1×10^{-5}	Vacuum cleaner
80	1×10^{-4}	Garbage disposal
90	1×10^{-3}	Motorcycle (at 10 m)
100	1×10^{-2}	Garbage Truck
110	1×10^{-1}	Live rock music
120	1×10^{0}	Chain saw
140	1×10^{2}	Aircraft carrier deck
160	1×10^{4}	So loud that eardrums burst

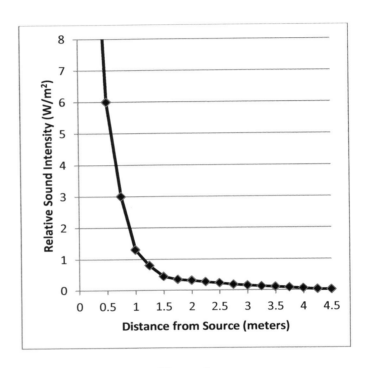

Figure 1

1. Based on the information provided in Figure 1, one can tell that as a person gets closer to the source of a sound, the intensity of the sound experienced by the person:
   A) increases.
   B) decreases.
   C) remains constant.
   D) fluctuates.

2. Based on the information in the passage, one can tell that the intensity experienced when 1 meter away from a motorcycle is approximately:
   A) 1×10^{-2} W/m^2.
   B) 1×10^{-3} W/m^2.
   C) 1×10^{-4} W/m^2.
   D) 1×10^{-5} W/m^2.

3. Which of the following objects best describes the source of the sound provided in Figure 1?
   A) Something barely audible to the human ear
   B) Rustling leaves
   C) A chain saw
   D) An aircraft carrier deck

4. A sound, from a distance of 1 meter away, has an intensity of 5×10^{-5} W/m^2. What is the approximate sound level, in dB, of the sound?
   A) 65
   B) 75
   C) 85
   D) 400

5. Based on the information presented above, would what be the intensity, in W/m^2, from 1 meter away, of a sound that measures 27 dB?
   A) Between 1×10^{-11} and 1×10^{-10}
   B) Between 1×10^{-10} and 1×10^{-9}
   C) Between 1×10^{-9} and 1×10^{-8}
   D) Between 1×10^{-8} and 1×10^{-7}

Passage 3

A group of research scientists is performing a set of experiments to test the fuel efficiency of 3 new pickup trucks. For the experiments, fuel efficiency is defined as the average miles traveled per gallon of gasoline used, or mi/gal.

Experiment 1

In order to simulate real-life driving conditions, the scientists attempted to find the fuel efficiency of the truck at several different speeds. For each of the speeds below (measured in miles per hour, mph), each of the trucks was kept within 2 miles per hour of the tested speed, so the gasoline required to accelerate to that speed, and decelerate to stop, was ignored in the calculation. The fuel efficiencies are listed in Table 1 below.

Table 1			
Speed (mph)	Truck A Fuel Efficiency (mi/gal)	Truck B Fuel Efficiency (mi/gal)	Truck C Fuel Efficiency (mi/gal)
35	16.5	17.2	16.8
55	21.2	23.4	22.9
75	18.3	21.5	20.8

Experiment 2

Vehicles become less fuel efficient when exposed to *drag*, the aerodynamic forces that oppose the motion of the object. To test the effect of drag on the 3 pickup trucks, the trucks are driven at 55 miles per hour in 3 conditions: tailgate up, tailgate halfway up, and tailgate down. The results of the experiment are shown below in Table 2.

Table 2			
Tailgate Position	Truck A Fuel Efficiency (mi/gal)	Truck B Fuel Efficiency (mi/gal)	Truck C Fuel Efficiency (mi/gal)
Tailgate Up	21.2	23.4	22.9
Tailgate Halfway Up	20.9	23.0	22.5
Tailgate Down	20.3	22.4	22.0

1. Based on the results of Experiment 1, as the speed of a vehicle increases, its fuel efficiency:
   A) increases only.
   B) decreases only.
   C) increases, then decreases.
   D) decreases, then increases.

2. The EPA (Environmental Protection Agency) derives its estimates from driving simulations done in a laboratory. The highway simulation covers 10.3 miles at an average speed of 48.3 mph with about half the time spent at 55-60 mph. Based on this information, the EPA's highway fuel efficiency for Truck B would be closest to:
   A) 15 mi/gal.
   B) 20 mi/gal.
   C) 25 mi/gal.
   D) 30 mi/gal.

3. Based on the information obtained in Experiment 2, which tailgate position exposes the truck to the most drag?
   A) Tailgate Up
   B) Tailgate Halfway Up
   C) Tailgate Down
   D) It is impossible to tell.

4. Truck C is driven with its windows down, but its tailgate up. At 55 mph, the truck's fuel efficiency was 22.3 mi/gal. Based on this information, one can tell that:
   A) open windows create more drag than the tailgate up, but less drag than the tailgate only halfway up.
   B) open windows create less drag than the tailgate up, but less drag than the tailgate only halfway up.
   C) open windows create more drag than the tailgate halfway up, but less drag than the tailgate down.
   D) open windows create less drag than the tailgate halfway up, but less drag than the tailgate down.

5. At an average speed of 35 mph with its tailgate down, the expected fuel efficiency of Truck A would be closest to:
   A) 13.2 mi/gal.
   B) 15.4 mi/gal.
   C) 16.5 mi/gal.
   D) 17.8 mi/gal.

6. A customer is interested in purchasing one of the 3 trucks for personal use. Which of the following situations is the most price-effective from a fuel economy point of view?
   A) Truck A with its tailgate down
   B) Truck B with its tailgate up
   C) Truck B with its tailgate down
   D) Truck C with its tailgate up.

Passage 4

A student designed an experiment to test how plants grow in different solutions. The student obtained 45 seedlings for each of 3 different species, A, B, and C, split them into 3 groups, and performed the following experiments:

Experiment 1

The student took 15 plants of each of the 3 different species, divided the plants into groups of 5, and grew them in 3 different solutions of water and sucrose ($C_{12}H_{22}O_{11}$). The student measured the height of each plant at the beginning of the experiment and 3 weeks later at the end of the experiment. The student kept all other factors constant. The recorded information can be found in Table 1. If a plant dies, its final height is counted as 0 cm.

Table 1			
Plant Species	Percent Sugar Solution	Average Initial Height (cm)	Average Final Height (cm)
A	0	2	25
A	5	3	15
A	10	2	5
B	0	2	30
B	5	4	14
B	10	3	0
C	0	2	15
C	5	3	12
C	10	2	9

Experiment 2

The student took 15 new plants of each of the 3 different species, divided the plants into groups of 5, and grew them in 3 different solutions of water and table salt (NaCl). The student measured the height of each plant at the beginning of the experiment and 3 weeks later at the end of the experiment. The student kept all other factors constant. The recorded information can be found in Table 2. If a plant dies, its final height is counted as 0 cm.

Table 2			
Plant Species	Percent Salt Solution	Average Initial Height (cm)	Average Final Height (cm)
A	0	3	27
A	5	2	14
A	10	3	9
B	0	3	29
B	5	2	38
B	10	3	33
C	0	3	16
C	5	2	6
C	10	4	0

Experiment 3

The student took 15 new plants of each of the 3 different species and repeated Experiment 2. The student reduced the amount of sunlight each plant received by 50%. The student kept all other factors constant. The recorded information can be found in Table 3. If a plant dies, its final height is counted as 0 cm.

		Table 3	
Plant Species	Percent Salt Solution	Average Initial Height (cm)	Average Final Height (cm)
A	0	3	23
A	5	2	12
A	10	3	0
B	0	4	26
B	5	4	32
B	10	3	26
C	0	3	7
C	5	2	0
C	10	3	0

1. In Experiment 1, a plant of Species B exposed to a 2.5% sugar solution would be expected to be how tall after 3 weeks?
   A) 8 cm
   B) 12 cm
   C) 20 cm
   D) 28 cm

2. Based on the results of Experiment 2, place the plant species in order of their ability to thrive in a 5% salt solution, from least able to survive to most able to survive.
   A) A, B, C
   B) B, A, C
   C) B, C, A
   D) C, A, B

3. Plant species B is a type of seagrass that is only found on beach shores in the Middle Atlantic Ocean. Provided that the salinity of the world's oceans is approximately 3.5%, what would be the expected height of Species B at Experiment 2 when grown in a 3.5% salt solution?
   A) Below 29 cm
   B) Between 29 and 33 cm
   C) Between 33 and 38 cm
   D) Above 38 cm

4. Suppose the student finds a misplaced plant that is definitely plant A, B, or C. Performing which of the following experiments on the seed would most likely determine its species?
   A) Experiment 1 at 5% solution
   B) Experiment 2 at 5% solution
   C) Experiment 2 at 10% solution
   D) Experiment 3 at 10% solution

5. What evidence from the passage supports Species C's ability to thrive in a densely-forested environment?
   A) Species C would not thrive in a densely-forested environment, as many forest plants produce sucrose via photosynthesis, and Species C was unable to survive as the amount of sucrose present in solution increased in Experiment 1.
   B) Species C would thrive in a densely-forested environment, as many forest plants produce sucrose via photosynthesis, and Species C increased in height as the amount of sucrose present in solution increased in Experiment 1.
   C) Species C would not thrive in a densely-forested environment, as Species C decreased in height as the amount of sunlight present decreased from Experiment 2 to Experiment 3.
   D) Species C would thrive in a densely-forested environment, as Species C increased in height as the amount of sunlight present decreased from Experiment 2 to Experiment 3.

6. Which of the following statements best characterizes the reaction of Plant A to the lower light levels present in Experiment 3?
   A) At salt solution levels less than or equal to 5%, the lack of light slightly diminished the plants' ability to survive, while at salt solution levels above 5%, the lack of light severely diminished the plants' ability to survive.
   B) At salt solution levels less than or equal to 5%, the lack of light severely diminished the plants' ability to survive, while at salt solution levels above 5%, the lack of light slightly diminished the plants' ability to survive.
   C) At all salt solution levels, the lack of light slightly diminished the plants' ability to survive.
   D) At all salt solution levels, the lack of light severely diminished the plants' ability to survive.

Understanding Questions

- **Understanding Questions** involves understanding the basic features of, and concepts related to, information provided in the passage.
- This information may be in the forms of charts, tables, and graphs. It is often information presented in the passages given in the Conflicting Viewpoints Passage, and can sometimes be found in the introductory material found at the beginning of each passage.
- These questions do not require you to make any assumptions about the given information or to analyze trends or predict future results.
- Let's look at some example questions dealing with Understanding Questions:

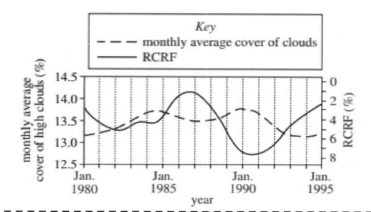

Example 1

The percent of Earth's surface covered by high clouds in January 1987 was closest to which of the following?

A) 13.0%
B) 13.5%
C) 14.0%
D) 14.5%

The presence of two lines makes the graph a little confusing, so look at the key. The dashed line shows our monthly cloud cover, and we should focus on the information on the axis to the left. In January 1987, 13.5% of Earth's surface was covered by high clouds. The answer is **B**.

Reading Passages

- Understanding Questions also show up in reading passages. These questions test your ability to comprehend what you read.

- As such, you should make it a point to read actively. When presented with reading material on the ACT, always circle important pieces of information, underline parts of the passage that reinforce those pieces of information, and take notes to the side of the passage as you feel necessary.
- Doing this will reduce the amount of time you spend looking back to the passage to find information. There is a strict time limit on the ACT, so you only have time to read the passage once!
- Practice reading actively on the passage excerpt below, then answer Example 2:

An astronomy class is given the following facts about stellar evolution.

1. A star's evolution can be divided into 3 stages: pre-main sequence (pre-MS), main sequence (MS), and post-main sequence (post-MS).

2. Gravity causes part of a cloud of gas and dust to collapse and heat up, creating a pre-MS star. The star's hot dust and gas emit its energy.

3. A pre-MS star becomes an MS star when the star produces the majority of its energy by fusing hydrogen nuclei (protons) at its center to make helium nuclei.

4. An MS star becomes a post-MS star when the star expands in volume and produces the majority of its energy by fusing hydrogen to make helium in a shell surrounding its center.

5. The more massive a star, the more rapidly the star passes through each of the 3 stages of its evolution.

Two students discuss the evolution of the Algol system—Algol A, a 3.6-solar-mass MS star; Algol B, a 0.8-solar-mass post-MS star; and Algol C, a 1.7-solar-mass MS star. (One solar mass = the Sun's mass.) The 3 stars orbit a mutual center of mass, with Algol A and Algol B much closer to each other and to the center of mass than to Algol C.

Student 2

Algol B was not part of the original Algol system (Algol A and Algol C). Algol B and the original Algol system formed in different clouds of gas and dust at different times and moved in 2 different but intersecting orbits around the center of the galaxy. During a particular orbit, Algol B encountered the original Algol system at the intersection of the 2 orbits and became part of the Algol system.

Algol B became a post-MS star while Algol A and Algol C remained MS stars. Algol B never lost mass to Algol A. Algol B was always less massive than Algol A.

Example 2

Based on Fact 5, would Student 2 agree that by the time Algol A stops being an MS star, Algol A will have spent as much time being an MS star as Algol B spent being an MS star?

A) Yes, because according to Student 2, Algol A has always been more massive than Algol B.
B) Yes, because according to Student 2, Algol A has always been less massive than Algol B.
C) No, because according to Student 2, Algol A has always been more massive than Algol B.
D) No, because according to Student 2, Algol A has always been less massive than Algol B.

First, let's look at Fact 5 again: "The more massive a star, the more rapidly the star passes through each of the 3 stages of its evolution."

So, we need to focus on comments that Student 2 makes about the mass of Algol A and B. Look at the last sentence of the Student 2's statement: "Algol B was always less massive than Algol A."

If Algol B has always been less massive than Algol A, then it will move more slowly through the 3 stages of its evolution according to Fact 5. Since Algol A moves more quickly through its evolution, it will be an MS star for less time than Algol B did. So, Student 2 will disagree with the statement in the question. Thus, **C** is our answer.

PRACTICE EXERCISE

Passage 1

The Earth's atmosphere contains several different layers that can be defined according to air temperature, shown in Figure 1 below. The first layer is called the *troposphere*, and it is where most of the Earth's weather occurs. Nearly 80% of the atmosphere's mass is located in the troposphere. Next comes the *stratosphere*, which contains most of the rest of the atmosphere's mass (19.9%). This region of the atmosphere experiences some weather, such as the tops of thunderstorms, and is occasionally influenced by the polar and subtropical jet streams. The higher temperature located here occurs because of the higher concentration of ozone molecules. The *mesosphere* contains the coldest temperatures of the Earth's atmosphere, while the *thermosphere* contains the highest temperatures, which can reach up to 1200°C.

While Figure 1 shows the atmosphere's properties in a tropical zone close to the equator, conditions elsewhere are much different. As an example, the average depth of the troposphere decreases as we approach the polar regions, to a minimum depth of approximately 8 km.

Additionally, Figure 1 shows the atmospheric pressure (in atm) and concentration of water vapor (in g/m^3) at certain altitudes.

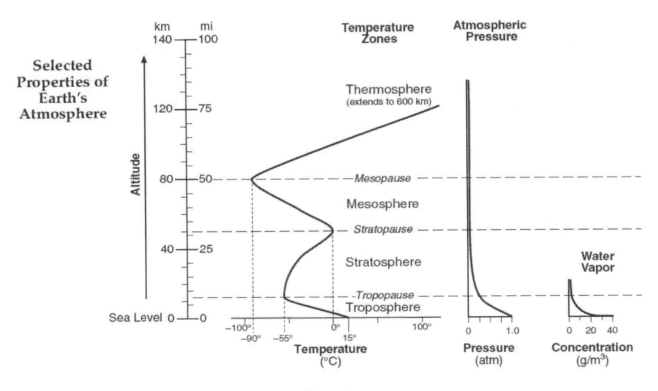

Figure 1

1. As the altitude from the tropopause to the mesopause increases, the temperature:
    A) increases only.
    B) decreases only.
    C) increases, then decreases.
    D) decreases, then increases.

2. Which of the following encompasses the range of atmospheric pressures present in the stratosphere?
    A) 0.0 to 0.25 atm
    B) 0.25 to 0.5 atm
    C) 0.5 to 0.75 atm
    D) 0.75 to 1.0 atm

3. A weather satellite is currently stationed at an area with a temperature of $-70°F$. Which of the following regions of the atmosphere is this satellite most likely located in?
    A) The troposphere or stratosphere only
    B) The stratosphere or mesosphere only
    C) The mesosphere or thermosphere only
    D) The mesosphere only

4. Mountaineers refer to altitudes above 8 km as the "death zone" – here, it is thought that human bodies cannot acclimatize to the change in pressure. What is the approximate pressure, in atm, at this altitude?
    A) 0 atm
    B) 0.2 atm
    C) 0.5 atm
    D) 0.8 atm

5. What is the approximate water vapor concentration at sea level on Earth?
    A) 50 g/m^3
    B) 40 g/m^3
    C) 20 g/m^3
    D) 0 g/m^3

Passage 2

A *calorimeter* is used to measure the heat released when a substance is burned in the presence of oxygen. The heat, measured in kilojoules (kJ), is calculated from the change in temperature of the water in the calorimeter. Table 1 shows the amounts of heat released when different amounts of sucrose (table sugar) were burned. Table 2 shows the amounts of heat released when different foods were burned. Table 3 shows the amounts of heat released when various alcohols were burned.

Table 1	
Amount of Sucrose (g)	Heat released (kJ)
0.1	1.6
0.5	8.0
1.0	16.0
2.5	40.0
5.0	80.0

Table 2		
Food	Change in water temperature (°C)	Heat released (kJ)
1 g of Rice	7.8	9.4
1 g of Chicken	9.3	11.2
1 g of Cabbage	3.4	4.1
1 g of Corn	4.5	5.4
1 g of Beef	12.3	14.8

Table 3			
Alcohol	Molecular Formula	Mass (g)	Heat released (kJ)
Methanol	CH_3OH	2.0	39.9
Ethanol	C_2H_5OH	2.0	57.7
Propanol	C_3H_7OH	2.0	61.0
Butanol	C_4H_9OH	2.0	66.2

1. Based on the information presented in Tables 1 and 2, approximately how much heat would be released by the burning of 200 g of rice and 50 g of beef?
   A) 26 kJ
   B) 260 kJ
   C) 2,600 kJ
   D) 26,000 kJ

2. Based on the information presented in Table 2, one can tell that as the water temperature increases in the calorimeter, the amount of heat released:
   A) decreases.
   B) increases.
   C) decreases, then stabilizes.
   D) increases, then stabilizes.

3. Based on the information presented in Table 1, one can conclude that when the mass of sucrose is doubled, the amount of heat released when it is burned in a calorimeter will:
   A) decrease by one-fourth.
   B) decrease by one-half.
   C) double.
   D) quadruple.

4. Based on the information presented in Table 1, one can conclude that the relationship between the number of C atoms in an alcohol and the heat released when that alcohol is burned is:
   A) direct.
   B) varying.
   C) inverse.
   D) direct, then inverse.

5. Based on the information presented in Tables 2 and 3, approximately how much more heat is released from the burning of 1.0 g of methanol than 1.0 g of beef?
   A) 5.0 kJ
   B) 10.0 kJ
   C) 15.0 kJ
   D) 25.0 kJ

Passage 3

The erosion of estuaries, tidal mouths of large rivers, has become a serious problem in recent years. Researchers predicted that this erosion would result in a decrease in both animal populations and plant biomass on estuary shorelines. They did several studies to test this prediction.

Study 1

The researchers monitored the plant biomass of fifteen 10 m × 10 m plots that had recently been shoreline, but were now completely covered by ocean or river waters for at least 12 hours of the day. Figure 1 shows the average change per plot in plant biomass (in hundreds of kilograms per year) based on how far the plot was from the mouth of the river (in km).

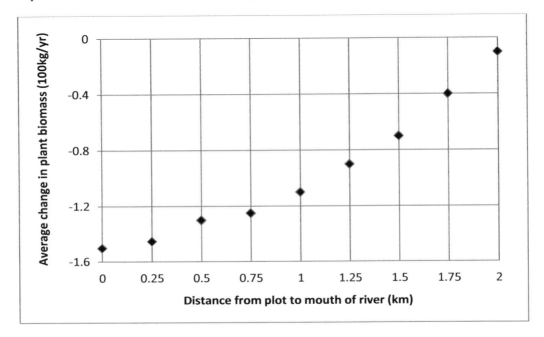

Figure 1

Study 2

Fifteen 10 × 10 plots were monitored as in Study 1. The center of each of these plots was at least 3 km from the mouth of the river. The average change in plant biomass was 0 kg per year.

Study 3

Researchers monitored fifteen different 10 m × 10 m shoreline plots, each of which was located no more than 0.25 km from the mouth of the river. The plant biomass was monitored yearly, and the average cumulative percent change in plant biomass was recorded in Figure 2.

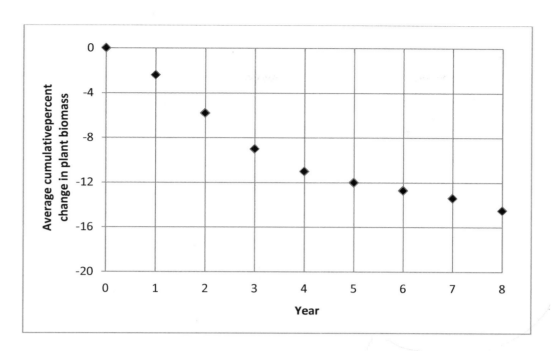

Figure 2

Study 4

Researchers trapped and released birds, fish, and crustaceans in 10 plots adjacent to areas studied in Study 3. Figure 3 shows the number of captures per 1,000 hours of trapping.

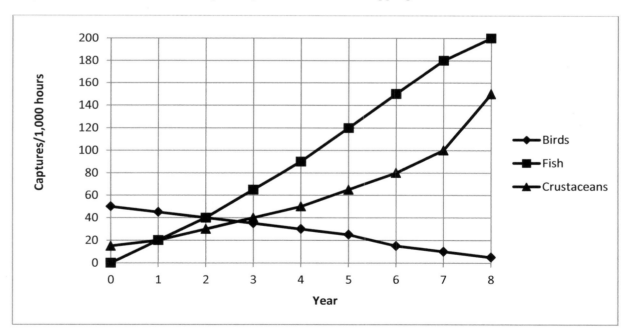

Figure 3

1. In Study 4, as time increased from Year 0 to Year 8, the captures/1,000 hours of crustaceans:
   A) decreased only.
   B) increased only.
   C) decreased, then increased.
   D) remained constant.

2. Which was the most likely reason for the 0 change in average plant biomass noted in Study 2?
   A) There was initially no plant life in each of the studied plots.
   B) Each plot was far enough from the mouth of the river that little erosion occurred.
   C) Each plant that died had at least 2 of its seeds sprout before its death.
   D) Each plot was close enough to the mouth of the river that its plant life received more than enough nutrients to survive.

3. In Study 1, as the distance from the mouth of the river increased, the average change in plant biomass of each plot:
   A) decreased only.
   B) increased only.
   C) decreased, then increased.
   D) increased, then decreased.

4. In Study 4, the researchers trapped fish for 5,000 hours per year. Approximately how many fish were trapped in Year 7?
   A) 100
   B) 500
   C) 900
   D) 1,000

5. In Study 3, which of the following was held constant?
   A) The distance from the mouth of the river
   B) Time
   C) Change in biomass
   D) All of the above were held constant

6. If Study 4 were extended to Year 9, what would be the expected number of birds caught per 1,000 hours?
   A) Less than 10 birds
   B) Between 10 and 150 birds
   C) Between 150 and 200 birds
   D) More than 200 birds

Passage 4

Temperatures on the Earth have risen by approximately 1.4°F since the early 20th century. During this time period, levels of greenhouse gases in the atmosphere, including carbon dioxide (CO_2) and methane (CH_4), have increased notably. Both sides in the global warming debate acknowledge both of these points. However, the two sides disagree on whether or not human activity is responsible for global climate change.

Scientist 1

Over the past 650,000 years, atmospheric CO_2 levels have not risen above 300 ppm (parts per million) – that is, until the mid-20th century. In 1958, atmospheric levels of CO_2 were measured at 317 ppm, but by 2013, those levels reached 400 ppm. Those levels are expected to reach 450 ppm by 2040 – the speed at which CO_2 concentrations are increasing has never seen before. Climate models using this information predict that an additional 5°F to 10°F of warming will occur based on CO_2 levels in the atmosphere alone.

Additionally, it can be proven that these rising CO_2 levels are caused by human activity. The CO_2 produced by the burning of fossil fuels like oil and coal can be differentiated in the atmosphere by its specific isotopic ratio. In this case ^{12}C is the most common, while ^{13}C is about 1% of the total, and ^{14}C is significantly less than 1%. The CO_2 emissions produced by other, natural processes, such as volcanic activity, ocean outgassing, and release from carbon sinks favor the lighter ^{12}C even more and thus produce even less ^{13}C and ^{14}C. Differentiating between the two is quite easy for modern scientists.

Finally, some blame global temperature fluctuations on natural changes in the sun's activity. However, recent studies show that solar activity can account for, at most, 10% of the observed global warming over the 20th century. Measurements in the upper atmosphere from 1979-2009 show the Sun's energy has gone up and down in cycles, with no net increase, while the temperature of the Earth has steadily increased. Humans are largely to blame for our changing climate.

Scientist 2

Although Earth has warmed since the 20th century began, it has always been in a constant state of warming and cooling. Over the past 3,000 years, the temperature of the Earth has fluctuated by approximately 5°F. In fact, studies show that the 20th century is probably not the warmest, or even a particularly unique, climactic period over the last millennium.

Human-produced CO_2 is re-absorbed by oceans, forests, and artificial carbon sinks like landfills, helping to negate climate change. In fact, at least 50% of the CO_2 produced by the burning of fossil fuels has already been reabsorbed. Even the oceans help out here, absorbing 26% of human-caused CO_2 emissions.

As atmospheric CO_2 levels rise, the amount of additional warming caused by its increased concentration becomes less pronounced. Since there is already so much CO_2 in the atmosphere, there is relatively little infrared radiation that is not already blocked. As such, humans can do little additional damage to the temperatures of Earth.

Much of global warming and cooling is caused by the Sun's heat, not human activity. Over the past 10,000 years, reduced sunspot activity has been synonymous with sharp climate changes. Between 1900 and 2000, solar irradiance increased by 0.19%, and this correlated with a rise in US surface temperatures. Thus, variations in solar activity, and not the burning of fossil fuels, are the direct cause of the fluctuations in the Earth's temperature.

1. Upon which of the following topics do the two scientists disagree?
   A) Earth's temperature has been rising for much of the 20th century.
   B) The Sun is responsible for some of the temperature changes which have occurred in the past few decades.
   C) As the amount of CO_2 in the atmosphere increases, Earth's temperature will increase at an exponential rate.
   D) Humans are responsible for releasing CO_2 into the atmosphere.

2. How would Scientist 2 react to Scientist 1's claim that "solar activity can account for, at most, 10% of the observed global warming over the 20th century"?
   A) This ignores sunspot activity completely.
   B) There is a correlation between solar irradiance and rising temperatures over the entire 20th century.
   C) It is impossible to measure how much of Earth's warming that solar activity can account for.
   D) The study ignored the cooling also caused by fluctuations in the Sun's activity.

3. In CO_2 released by man-made activities, the amount of ^{12}C is:
   A) higher than the amount in CO_2 produced by natural activities.
   B) lower than the amount in CO_2 produced by natural activities.
   C) equal to the amount in CO_2 produced by natural activities.
   D) too difficult to determine to be of any use to climate scientists.

4. According to Scientist 2, man-made CO_2 is absorbed by all of the following except:
   A) oceans.
   B) the Sun.
   C) vegetation.
   D) landfills

5. How would Scientist 2 respond to Scientist 1's claims of distinguishing between CO_2 released by man-made and natural processes?
   A) "At least 50% of CO_2 is reabsorbed either way, so telling them apart does not harm my argument."
   B) "At least 50% of man-made CO_2 is reabsorbed, so this will heavily affect the calculations obtained."
   C) "At least 26% of CO_2 is reabsorbed either way, so telling them apart does not harm my argument."
   D) "At least 26% of man-made CO_2 is reabsorbed, so this might affect the calculations obtained."

6. In 2015, it was discovered that CO_2 levels in Earth's atmosphere remained at 400 ppm. What affect does this have on Scientist 1's argument?
   A) A positive effect – it confirms that CO_2 levels are still increasing.
   B) A positive effect – it contradicts the claim that CO_2 levels are increasing.
   C) No effect – there are expected to be some fluctuations in CO_2 levels over any given time period.
   D) A negative effect – it proves that sunspot activity is affecting CO_2 levels.

7. It is discovered that there is a no correlation between sunspot activity and temperatures on Earth. This discovery affects the argument of which scientist most?
   A) Scientist 1
   B) Scientist 2
   C) Both scientists
   D) Neither scientist

Analysis Questions

- **Analysis Questions** require us to be able to examine critically the relationship between the information provided and the conclusions drawn or hypotheses developed.
- This information may be in the forms of charts, tables, and graphs. It is often information presented in the passages given in the Conflicting Viewpoints Passage, and can sometimes be found in the introductory material found at the beginning of each passage.
- These questions require you to analyze the information given, figure out trends, and even predict future results.
- You may have to come up with a conclusion or hypothesis that ties some, or all, of the data together.
- Let's look at some example questions dealing with Analysis Questions:

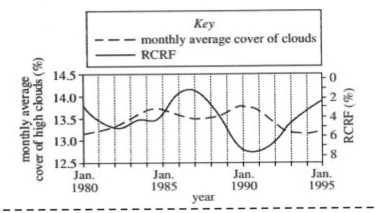

Example 1

The relative cosmic ray flux, RCRF, in January 1996 was most likely what?

A) 1.5%
B) 5.0%
C) 7.0%
D) 13.5%

We looked at this graph last chapter, but now we're asked about the RCRF instead of the monthly cloud cover. This time we need to look at the solid line and the axis on the right hand side of the graph. Additionally, our work is a little more difficult, as the years we have data for stop in 1995. However, look at the trends of the RCRF line: it has been decreasing (note that the scale is upside down and small numbers are on top) for the last 5 years or so. If we follow that trend, we can expect RCRF to decrease to 1.5% or so.

Reading Passages

- Analysis Questions also show up in reading passages. These questions simply test your ability to draw conclusions and compare statements given in the passage.
- Again, keep reading actively. It may be helpful to draw lines connecting parts of the passage that support or contradict each other, as these are common Analysis Questions.
- Try a new question on the passage from the previous lesson. This time, we'll add information given by another student as well.

An astronomy class is given the following facts about stellar evolution.

1. A star's evolution can be divided into 3 stages: pre-main sequence (pre-MS), main sequence (MS), and post-main sequence (post-MS).

2. Gravity causes part of a cloud of gas and dust to collapse and heat up, creating a pre-MS star. The star's hot dust and gas emit its energy.

3. A pre-MS star becomes an MS star when the star produces the majority of its energy by fusing hydrogen nuclei (protons) at its center to make helium nuclei.

4. An MS star becomes a post-MS star when the star expands in volume and produces the majority of its energy by fusing hydrogen to make helium in a shell surrounding its center.

5. The more massive a star, the more rapidly the star passes through each of the 3 stages of its evolution.

Two students discuss the evolution of the Algol system—Algol A, a 3.6-solar-mass MS star; Algol B, a 0.8-solar-mass post-MS star; and Algol C, a 1.7-solar-mass MS star. (One solar mass = the Sun's mass.) The 3 stars orbit a mutual center of mass, with Algol A and Algol B much closer to each other and to the center of mass than to Algol C.

Student 1

The 3 stars of the Algol system formed at the same time from the same cloud of gas and dust. Algol B, originally the most massive of the 3 stars, became a post-MS star and expanded in volume while Algol A remained an MS star. Because the matter in the outer parts of Algol B was more strongly attracted to Algol A than to the matter in the inner parts of Algol B, this matter flowed from Algol B to Algol A, and, over time, Algol A became more massive than Algol B.

Student 2

Algol B was not part of the original Algol system (Algol A and Algol C). Algol B and the original Algol system formed in different clouds of gas and dust at different times and moved in 2 different but intersecting orbits around the center of the galaxy. During a particular orbit, Algol B encountered the original Algol system at the intersection of the 2 orbits and became part of the Algol system.

Algol B became a post-MS star while Algol A and Algol C remained MS stars. Algol B never lost mass to Algol A. Algol B was always less massive than Algol A.

Example 2

If the mass of the Sun is 2.0×10^{30} kg, what is the mass of Algol C?

A) 1.6×10^{30} kg
B) 2.0×10^{30} kg
C) 3.4×10^{30} kg
D) 7.2×10^{30} kg

From the passage, we see "Algol C, a 1.7-solar-mass MS star (one solar mass = the Sun's mass). However, knowing this information isn't enough. We have to apply it to what we know. 2.0×10^{30} times 1.7 is 3.4×10^{30} kg, so the answer is **C**.

Let's try another one:

Example 3

Based on Student 1's discussion and Fact 4, while matter flowed between Algol A and Algol B, Algol B produced the majority of its energy by fusing:

A) hydrogen nuclei to make helium nuclei at its center.
B) hydrogen nuclei to make helium nuclei in a shell surrounding its center.
C) helium nuclei to make hydrogen nuclei at its center.
D) helium nuclei to make hydrogen nuclei in a shell surrounding its center.

Student 1 describes Algol B as expanding in volume while becoming a post-MS star. Fact 4 tells us why: "An MS star becomes a post-MS star when the star expands in volume and produces the majority of its energy by fusing hydrogen to make helium in a shell surrounding its center." A careful analysis of Fact 4, as well as the process of hydrogen fusing into helium, will allow us to answer this question. Thus, the correct answer is **B**.

PRACTICE EXERCISE

Passage 1

Density is defined as the mass of a substance divided by its volume. Table 1 lists the phases and densities, in grams per cubic centimeters (g/cm³), of various pure substances at 25°C and 1 atmosphere (atm) of pressure.

Table 1		
Substance	Phase	Density (g/cm³)
Aluminum	Solid	2.64
Copper	Solid	8.68
Lead	Solid	11.34
Rubber	Solid	1.52
Methanol	Liquid	0.79
Benzene	Liquid	0.88
Bromine	Liquid	3.12
Glycerin	Liquid	1.26
Butane	Gas	0.0025
Carbon Dioxide	Gas	0.0018
Argon	Gas	0.0015
Oxygen	Gas	0.0013

Figure 1 shows how the density of liquid and solid water changes with temperature.

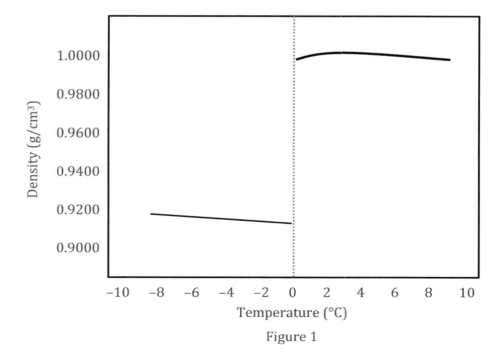

Figure 1

1. According to Figure 1, as the temperature of solid water increases from –8°C to 0°C, its density:
   A) increases.
   B) decreases.
   C) increases, then decreases.
   D) decreases, then increases.

2. A student claims that if the masses of 1 cm^3 of any solid and 1 cm^3 of any liquid are compared, the mass of the liquid will be smaller. Does the data in Table 1 support this claim?
   A) Yes, methanol has a lower density than any of the solids listed.
   B) Yes, bromine has a smaller density than some of the solids listed.
   C) No, methanol has a lower density than any of the solids listed.
   D) No, bromine has a higher density than some of the solids listed.

3. According to the data presented in Figure 1, 1 kg of water at 4°C would exactly fill a container having which of the following volumes? (1 kg = 1000 g)
   A) 1 cm^3
   B) 10 cm^3
   C) 100 cm^3
   D) 1,000 cm^3

4. Equal amounts of water (density = 0.9971 g/cm^3), benzene, and glycerin are poured into a single beaker. Three distinct layers of liquid form in the beaker. Based on the data in Table 1, which of the following presents the order, from bottom to top, of the liquids in the beaker?
   A) glycerin, water, benzene
   B) benzene, water, glycerin
   C) glycerin, benzene, water
   D) benzene, glycerin, water

5. Which of the following lists all of the solids from Table 1 which will float in a vat of liquid bromine?
   A) Copper and lead
   B) Copper, lead, and aluminum
   C) Copper, aluminum, and rubber
   D) Rubber and aluminum

Passage 2

To determine the effects of diet on the body weight of rats, a series of experiments was designed.

Experiment 1

A group of 100 adolescent rats, 50 male and 50 female, were each fed a diet of normal rat chow consisting of a mixture of plant materials which provide all of the protein, fat, carbohydrates, and vitamins rats need to survive. Figure 1 shows the average body weight, in grams (g), for these rats as they were fed this diet for 7 weeks.

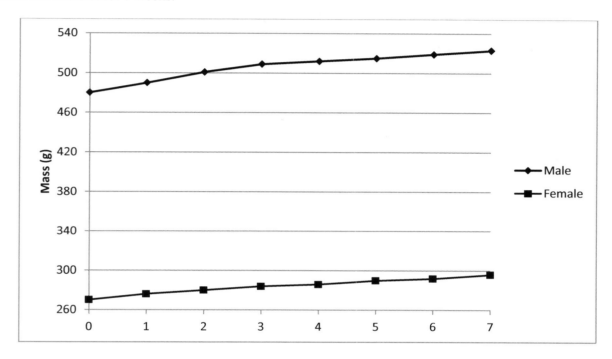

Figure 1

Experiment 2

Three groups of 50 adolescent rats, all male, were given new diets. Group A was given chocolate in addition to the standard rat chow, Group B was given crackers in addition to the rat chow, and Group C was given both in addition to the rat chow. The results of the study are shown in Figure 2.

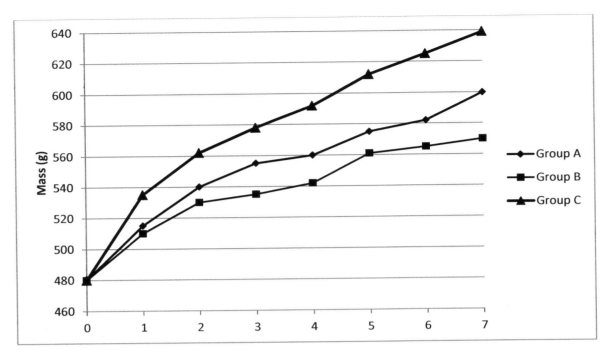

Figure 2

Experiment 3

Experiment 2 was repeated with female rats instead of males. The results of the study are shown in Figure 3.

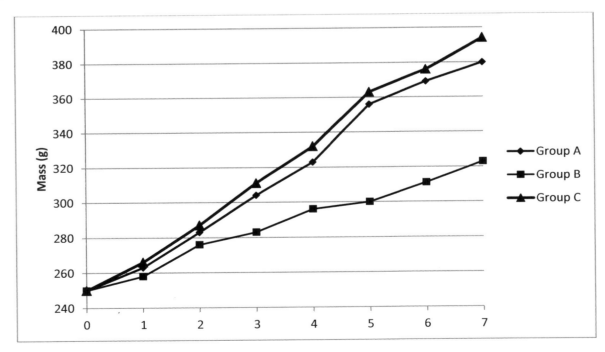

Figure 3

1. Based on the results of all 3 experiments, what was the average difference between the body weights of the male and female rats before starting the diets?
   A) 100 g
   B) 200 g
   C) 300 g
   D) 400 g

2. Based on the information provided in Experiments 2 and 3, which of the following is true?
   A) Male rats who were fed both chocolate and crackers in addition to chow gained slightly more weight than male rats who were fed just chocolate in addition to chow.
   B) Female rats who were fed both chocolate and crackers in addition to chow gained slightly more weight than female rats who were fed just chocolate in addition to chow.
   C) Male rats who were fed both chocolate and crackers in addition to chow gained slightly more weight than male rats who were fed just crackers in addition to chow.
   D) Female rats who were fed both chocolate and crackers in addition to chow gained slightly more weight than female rats who were fed just crackers in addition to chow.

3. The male rats who were fed both chocolate and crackers in addition to chow gained the most weight between which of the following weeks?
   A) 0 and 1
   B) 1 and 2
   C) 4 and 5
   D) 6 and 7

4. A group of scientists wants to examine the effects of a high-carbohydrate, high-sugar diet on teenage human girls. Which experiment or experiments would best simulate this activity?
   A) Experiment 1
   B) Experiment 2
   C) Experiment 3
   D) Experiments 2 and 3

5. It has been determined that, when only eating chow, rats stop gaining body mass at 9 weeks. What is the expected average mass of a male rat at 9 weeks?
   A) 650 g
   B) 550 g
   C) 400 g
   D) 250 g

6. A number of studies have shown that increasing food variety, regardless of caloric content, increases the amount of weight gained. Do the experiments performed backup the results of these studies?

A) No, both rat populations that ate one extra food type gained unequal amounts of weight.

B) No, both rat populations that ate two extra foods types gained just as much weight as the rat populations that ate one extra food type.

C) Yes, the rat populations that ate two extra food types gained more weight than the rat populations who only ate one extra food type, who in turn gained more weight than the rat populations who only ate one food type.

D) Yes, all of the rat populations gained weight during the experiment.

Passage 3

A group of physics students conducted experiments to test the amount of force necessary to undo various types of hook-and-loop fasteners.

Experiment 1

A student nailed the hook piece of a hook-and-loop fastener to a board. Next, the student attached clamps and a spring scale to the loop piece. The two pieces were pressed together tightly.

Another student then pulled the spring scale until the loop piece came undone. A second student recorded the force on the spring scale when the two pieces came apart.

The procedure was repeated for 3 different brands of hook-and-loop fastener, each of which came in different widths. The results are shown in Table 1.

Table 1					
Brand	Width (cm)	Force (N) to remove hook-and-loop fastener:			
		Trial 1	Trial 2	Trial 3	Average
A	1.0	36.0	38.0	35.0	36.3
	2.0	62.0	65.0	68.0	65.0
	3.0	90.0	92.0	88.0	90.0
B	1.0	23.0	18.0	19.0	20.0
	2.0	41.0	45.0	42.0	42.7
	3.0	82.5	81.0	83.0	82.2
C	2.0	36.0	38.0	34.0	36.0
	3.0	75.0	82.0	80.0	79.0
	4.0	180.0	170.0	172.0	174.0

Experiment 2

The students performed an experiment similar to Experiment 1, but soaked the hook-and-loop fastener in water immediately before nailing it to the board. The results are shown in Table 2.

Table 2					
Brand	Width (cm)	Force (N) to remove wet hook-and-loop fastener:			
		Trial 1	Trial 2	Trial 3	Average
A	1.0	12.0	15.0	13.0	13.3
	2.0	21.0	18.0	19.5	19.5
	3.0	30.0	31.0	29.0	30.0
B	1.0	6.5	8.0	9.5	8.0
	2.0	11.0	10.0	12.0	11.0
	3.0	15.5	16.5	17.0	16.3
C	2.0	8.0	10.0	7.0	8.3
	3.0	12.0	14.0	18.0	14.7
	4.0	30.5	31.0	33.0	31.5

1. The results of both experiments support the conclusion that, for a given brand of hook-and-loop fastener, as the width of the fastener decreases, the force required to detach the fasteners:
   A) increases only.
   B) decreases only.
   C) remains constant.
   D) cannot be predicted.

2. In Experiment 1, had Brand A been tested with a width of 4.0 cm, the force required detach the fasteners would have been closest to:
   A) 40 N
   B) 100 N
   C) 120 N
   D) 175 N

3. For a width of 3.0 cm, which brand required the most amount of force to detach in Experiment 1?
   A) Brand A
   B) Brand B
   C) Brand C
   D) It cannot be determined.

4. The group of students plans to take a particular brand and width of the hook-and-loop fasteners on their kayaking trip. Which brand and width would best allow them to keep their gear attached to their kayaks while traveling down rapids?
   A) Brand B, 1.0 cm
   B) Brand B, 3.0 cm
   C) Brand C, 2.0 cm
   D) Brand C, 4.0 cm

5. The students were given a piece of fastener 2.5 cm wide and asked to figure out the brand. The students tested the piece and acquired forces of 60.0 N dry and 12.0 N wet. Which of the following brands would most likely have produced these results?
   A) Brand A
   B) Brand B
   C) Brand C
   D) Brand B or Brand C

6. A wet fastener of Brand C and width 3.5 cm would be expected to require what force to detach?
   A) 35.0 N
   B) 30.0 N
   C) 25.0 N
   D) 15.0 N

Passage 4

For years, the scientific community has known about the presence of water on Mars in the form of polar ice caps. Recently, however, NASA scientists have discovered liquid water on Mars. This water flows down canyons and crater walls over Mars's summer months before drying up as the surface temperature drops in fall. As of right now, scientists are still unsure as to where the water comes from. Some believe it rises from underground ice or salty aquifers, while others believe that it condenses out of the Martian atmosphere.

While some scientists believe that these findings increase our probability of finding life on Mars, others conclude that even with the presence of liquid water, Mars is inhospitable. The arguments of two scientists are presented below.

Scientist 1

When searching for life, astrobiologists agree that the presence of water is of the utmost importance. All forms of life on Earth require water to survive. Even though the water recently discovered on Mars is full of chlorate and perchlorate salts, rendering this flowing water even saltier than the Dead Sea – the saltiest water on Earth – these salts are necessary for water to flow at Mars's low temperatures. These salts lower the freezing point of water to –23°C, allowing water to flow throughout enough of the Martian year to support life.

Many point to Mars's thin atmosphere, which allows radiation from the sun to irradiate the surface of the planet, as a huge deterrent to the presence of life on Mars. However, the water on the surface of Mars has to come from somewhere, and underground aquifers discharging water to the surface is the most likely scenario. The idea that water is present underground would certainly help life thrive underground, away from the bombardment of harmful radiation.

Ultimately, even though life on Earth requires water, it is possible that life could evolve without its presence. It is much easier for humans to search for conditions we know are optimal for life, rather than we suppose could be possible, of course, but this doesn't mean we should limit our search for life on Mars to the areas where we know flowing water exists. Life on Earth takes on myriad forms, and we have no reason to believe life on Mars is not even more fantastic.

Scientist 2

While humans have not yet found life that can survive without water, the presence of water on Mars does not necessarily mean life can survive. There are many reasons to believe that life does not, and has never, lived on Mars:

1. We have never found the presence of organic molecules, except for methane, on Mars. All life as we know it is made of organic compounds, so the lack of these on Mars is telling.

2. Too much carbon monoxide currently exists in the Martian atmosphere. In the presence of life, something would find a way to harvest this carbon monoxide as a food source.

3. Nitrogen is a structural element that holds proteins together. Life takes nitrogen from the air and puts it into the soil to form nitrates. After numerous studies of Martian soil, we have not yet found any evidence of nitrates.

4. We have no reason to believe that Mars has always been as warm as it currently is. Even now, only a small portion of the surface of Mars is warm enough to allow even highly-concentrated salt water to flow, and then only for part of the year. Favorable climate conditions are too short-lived and far between to ever support the evolution of life.

Together, all of these factors prove that it is highly unlikely that life has ever lived on Mars.

1. With which of the following statements would both scientists agree?
   A) Life on Earth requires water to survive.
   B) There are high levels of carbon monoxide in the Martian atmosphere.
   C) Water found on Mars originated from underground aquifers.
   D) The temperature on Mars is too low to support life that is currently found on Earth.

2. How would Scientist 1 most likely respond to Point 3 of Scientist 2?
   A) Water is the only requirement for life to exist, so the presence of nitrates in the soil does not mean that life does not exist.
   B) The thin atmosphere of Mars results in the irradiation of nitrates in the soil, preventing their detection.
   C) It is entirely possible that life on Mars has evolved in such a way that it does not produce nitrates in the soil.
   D) Water on the surface of Mars most likely washed nitrates out of the soil.

3. Why is water able to flow on Mars at temperatures below the freezing point of water?
   A) Water has a lower freezing point in underground aquifers.
   B) The presence of nitrates in the soil lowers the freezing point of surface water.
   C) Carbon monoxide in the atmosphere lowers the freezing point of liquids on Mars's surface.
   D) Dissolved salt particles in water lower its freezing point.

4. How would Scientist 2 least likely respond to Scientist 1's claim that life may be found under the surface of Mars?
   A) The lack of nitrates in the soil makes it unlikely that life has ever lived on Mars.
   B) Too much carbon monoxide exists in the atmosphere of Mars for life to exist.
   C) Because of Mars's thin atmosphere, radiation may affect organisms that live underground.
   D) Other than methane, no organic molecules have been found in Martian soil that would lead us to believe that life ever existed there.

5. One can tell from reading the passage that Scientist 2 believes that:
   A) A stable climate is necessary for the evolution of life.
   B) Certain types of radiation are not harmful to organisms.
   C) The presence of carbon monoxide in the atmosphere is the most telling sign that life on Mars has never existed.
   D) It is possible that life can evolve to be nitrogen-based instead of carbon-based.

6. Recently, it has been discovered that underground aquifers do exist on Mars. This discovery most strengthens the argument of:
   A) Scientist 1.
   B) Scientist 2.
   C) both scientists.
   D) neither scientist.

7. New data has shown that the surface of Mars can reach temperatures of up to 20°C. This discovery most strengthens the argument of:
   A) Scientist 1.
   B) Scientist 2.
   C) both scientists.
   D) neither scientist.

ACT Science: Generalization Questions

Generalization Questions

- **Generalization Questions** require us to be able to gain new information, draw conclusions, or make predictions based on the information and data presented in the passage.
- These questions involve more critical thinking than other questions in the Science portion of the ACT, and as such are among the most difficult, and the least common, on the ACT.
- These questions may extend application of the data to real-world situations, so some scientific knowledge may be helpful when solving these questions.
- Let's look at some example questions dealing with Generalization Questions:

Cloud cover is the percent of Earth's surface covered by clouds. Cloud cover may increase because of an increase in the cosmic ray flux (number of high-energy particles from space reaching Earth per m^2 per hour). Table 1 shows how Earth's cover of low clouds (0 km to 3.2 km altitude) varies with the cosmic ray flux. Figures 1–3 show the relative cosmic ray flux, RCRF (the percent below the flux measured on October 1, 1965), and the monthly average cover of high clouds (6.0 km to 16.0 km altitude), middle clouds (3.2 km to 6.0 km altitude), and low clouds, respectively, from January 1980 to January 1995.

Example 1

High clouds are composed primarily of ice crystals, whereas low clouds are composed primarily of water droplets. This difference is most likely because the average air temperature at altitudes from:

A) 0 km to 3.2 km is at or below 0°C, whereas the average air temperature at altitudes from 3.2 km to 6.0 km is above 0°C.

B) 0 km to 3.2 km is at or below 0°C, whereas the average air temperature at altitudes from 6.0 km to 16.0 km is above 0°C.

C) 0 km to 3.2 km is above 0°C, whereas the average air temperature at altitudes from 3.2 km to 6.0 km is at or below 0°C.

D) 0 km to 3.2 km is above 0°C, whereas the average air temperature at altitudes from 6.0 km to 16.0 km is at or below 0°C.

Here, we have to use a little science knowledge to help us draw a conclusion about the contents of the passage. Water turns into ice at temperatures below 0°C, thus the high clouds should be at temperatures less than 0°C, while the low clouds should be at temperatures above that. Since low clouds appear from 0 km to 3.2 km, and high clouds appear from 6.0 km to 16.0 km, the answer must be **D**.

Reading Passages

- Generalization Questions also show up in reading passages. These questions test your ability to extend the knowledge you obtained from reading the passage to situations outside the contents of the passage.
- Don't forget to read actively to reduce the amount of time necessary to answer these questions!
- Let's try one more question based on the passage from the last two chapters:

An astronomy class is given the following facts about stellar evolution.

1. A star's evolution can be divided into 3 stages: premain sequence (pre-MS), main sequence (MS), and post-main sequence (post-MS).

2. Gravity causes part of a cloud of gas and dust to collapse and heat up, creating a pre-MS star. The star's hot dust and gas emit its energy.

3. A pre-MS star becomes an MS star when the star produces the majority of its energy by fusing hydrogen nuclei (protons) at its center to make helium nuclei.

4. An MS star becomes a post-MS star when the star expands in volume and produces the majority of its energy by fusing hydrogen to make helium in a shell surrounding its center.

5. The more massive a star, the more rapidly the star passes through each of the 3 stages of its evolution.

Two students discuss the evolution of the Algol system—Algol A, a 3.6-solar-mass MS star; Algol B, a 0.8-solar-mass post-MS star; and Algol C, a 1.7-solar-mass MS star. (One solar mass = the Sun's mass.) The 3 stars orbit a mutual center of mass, with Algol A and Algol B much closer to each other and to the center of mass than to Algol C.

Student 1

The 3 stars of the Algol system formed at the same time from the same cloud of gas and dust. Algol B, originally the most massive of the 3 stars, became a post-MS star and expanded in volume while Algol A remained an MS star. Because the matter in the outer parts of Algol B was more strongly attracted to Algol A than to the matter in the inner parts of Algol B, this matter flowed from Algol B to Algol A, and, over time, Algol A became more massive than Algol B.

Student 2

Algol B was not part of the original Algol system (Algol A and Algol C). Algol B and the original Algol system formed in different clouds of gas and dust at different times and moved in 2 different but intersecting orbits around the center of the galaxy. During a particular orbit, Algol B encountered the original Algol system at the intersection of the 2 orbits and became part of the Algol system.

Algol B became a post-MS star while Algol A and Algol C remained MS stars. Algol B never lost mass to Algol A. Algol B was always less massive than Algol A.

Example 2

Which of the following statements best explains why the reaction described in Fact 3 requires a high temperature and pressure?

A) All protons are positively charged, and like charges attract each other.
B) All protons are positively charged, and like charges repel each other.
C) All electrons are negatively charged, and like charges attract each other.
D) All electrons are negatively charged, and like charges repel each other.

Again, we need to use a little bit of outside knowledge. We already know that the first part of each answer choice is true, so let's examine the second part. Like charges repel each other, so the answer must be **B** or **D**. Which one is true? Let's revisit Fact 3:

"A pre-MS star becomes an MS star when the star produces the majority of its energy by fusing hydrogen nuclei (protons) at its center to make helium nuclei."

Since we are discussing protons here, it makes sense that the answer must be **B** – at a high pressure and temperature, the protons would be moving around more quickly in a smaller space, and thus, interact with each other more often.

PRACTICE EXERCISE

Passage 1

Researchers conducted an experiment to determine the factors that affect heat flow. In each trial, a block of a particular material and width was placed between two walls at constant temperatures T_1 and T_2. Heat was transferred from the hotter wall to the cooler wall. This heat flow is measured in Table 1 and is shown in joules per second (J/sec). The surface area touching the walls of each block is equivalent for all trials.

		Table 1			
Trial	Block Material	Block Width (m)	T_1 (°C)	T_2 (°C)	Heat flow (J/sec)
1	Glass wool	0.1	60	30	0.025
2	Glass wool	0.5	60	30	0.005
3	Glass wool	1.0	60	30	0.0025
4	Glass wool	2.0	60	30	0.00125
5	Glass wool	0.5	100	40	0.01
6	Glass wool	1.0	30	0	0.0025
7	Steel	1.0	60	30	2.7
8	Steel	1.0	60	20	3.6
9	Steel	1.0	10	60	4.5
10	Silver	1.0	60	30	26.8
11	Zinc	1.0	60	30	7.25
12	Quartz	1.0	60	30	0.19
13	Iron	1.0	60	30	5.0
14	Glass	1.0	60	30	0.066

1. According to the information provided, heat flowed from the wall at temperature T_2 to the wall at temperature T_1 in which trial?
   A) Trial 5
   B) Trial 7
   C) Trial 9
   D) Trial 11

2. An insulator is a material that does not conduct heat well. According to Trials 10 through 14, a wall of a given thickness built of which of the following materials would provide the best insulation between a room and the outdoors?
   A) Silver
   B) Zinc
   C) Quartz
   D) Glass

3. The results of Trials 7 through 9 indicate that the temperature difference between two objects and the heat flow between them are:
   A) directly related.
   B) inversely related.
   C) not related.
   D) directly related between Trials 7 and 8, but inversely related between Trials 8 and 9.

4. The results of Trials 1 through 4 indicate that the width of the block between two objects and the heat flow between them are:
   A) directly related.
   B) inversely related.
   C) not related.
   D) both directly and inversely related.

5. After Trial 5, a new trial was conducted identical to Trial 5 but with a block width of 0.25 m. What is the expected heat flow of the new trial, in J/sec?
   A) 0.04
   B) 0.02
   C) 0.01
   D) 0.005

Passage 2

Astronomers are able to arrange stars into different groups depending on many different traits. A star's *luminosity* measures the total amount of energy emitted by the star per unit of time when compared to the Sun and is measured in watts. The surface temperature of a star is measured in Kelvin and also helps determine the star's color. The size of stars is also measured and typically helps determine what stage the star is in. Stars start, and spend most of their lifetimes, in the Main Sequence, or early stage, move on to become giants or super giants, and finally collapse into white dwarfs the size of Earth. Figure 1 below classifies several stars based on these characteristics.

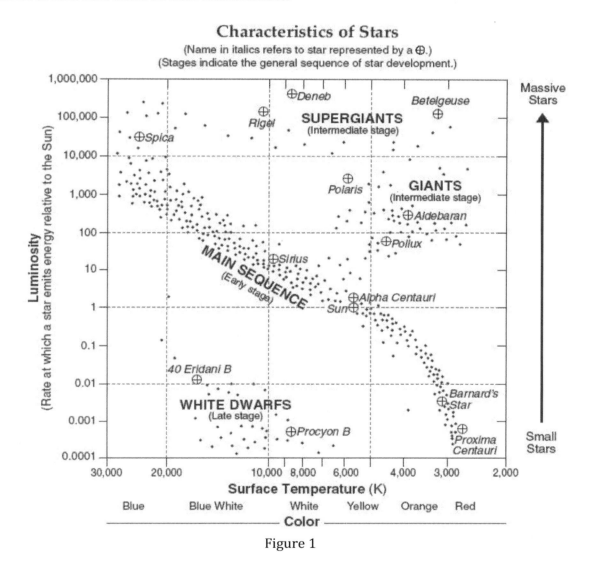

Figure 1

1. Which of the following stars is smaller than the Sun?
   A) Polaris
   B) Alpha Centauri
   C) Procyon B
   D) Spica

2. The star Sirius is how many times brighter than the Sun?
   A) 1 to 10 times brighter
   B) 10 to 50 times brighter
   C) 50 to 100 times brighter
   D) 100 to 1,000 times brighter

3. Which group of stars has the largest range of luminosities?
   A) White dwarfs
   B) Main sequence
   C) Giants
   D) Supergiants

4. Based on the information provided in Figure 1, the biggest difference between giants and supergiants is:
   A) their sizes only.
   B) their luminosities only.
   C) their sizes and colors only.
   D) their sizes and luminosities only.

5. The star Rigel is approximately how many times more luminous than Sirius?
   A) 100
   B) 1,000
   C) 10,000
   D) 100,000

Passage 3

When many electronic devices are exposed to certain high-stress conditions, many of their components, especially those components made of aluminum, began to corrode and eventually fail. A series of experiments was designed to test the *Time to Failure* of one of these electronic devices under certain conditions.

Experiment 1

Several copies of the electronic device were tested under different percentages of relative humidity, while held to a constant temperature of 125°C and a voltage of 6 V. The time to failure of each device, in hours, was recorded in Table 1.

Table 1			
Relative Humidity (%)	Voltage (V)	Temperature (°C)	Time to Failure (hours)
80	6	125	0.65
80	6	125	2.47
80	6	125	3.30
85	6	125	0.73
85	6	125	0.73
85	6	125	1.98
90	6	125	0.78
90	6	125	1.60
90	6	125	9.04

Experiment 2

Experiment 2 was performed under conditions identical to Experiment 1, except the voltage was increased to 7 V. Additionally, the temperature under which the experiment was conducted was dropped to 75°C. The time to failure of each device, in hours, was recorded in Table 2.

Table 2			
Relative Humidity (%)	Voltage (V)	Temperature (°C)	Time to Failure (hours)
80	7	75	21.68
80	7	75	89.06
80	7	75	108.00
85	7	75	13.63
85	7	75	16.60
85	7	75	38.45
90	7	75	24.82
90	7	75	37.63
90	7	75	39.61

Experiment 3

Experiment 3 was performed under conditions identical to Experiment 2, except the voltage was increased to 78 V. The time to failure of each device, in hours, was recorded in Table 3.

Table 3			
Relative Humidity (%)	Voltage (V)	Temperature (°C)	Time to Failure (hours)
80	8	75	20.91
80	8	75	23.12
80	8	75	64.78
85	8	75	6.60
85	8	75	17.43
85	8	75	75.64
90	8	75	12.33
90	8	75	16.14
90	8	75	33.70

1. Under which conditions did the electronic devices appear to fail the most often?
    A) Low temperatures
    B) High temperatures
    C) Low relative humidity
    D) High relative humidity

2. Under which of the following conditions did the electronic device have the longest average time to failure?
    A) 85% relative humidity, 6 V, 125°C
    B) 80% relative humidity, 7 V, 75°C
    C) 85% relative humidity, 7 V, 75°C
    D) 90% relative humidity, 8 V, 75°C

3. The relative humidity of a device at 7 V and 75°C is dropped to 75%. What is the expected result?
    A) The time to failure increases.
    B) The time to failure decreases.
    C) The time to failure stays approximately the same.
    D) It is impossible to tell.

4. The electronic device is set to be taken on an expedition to explore undersea volcanoes. While being used inside the probe, the device is expected to reach temperatures of 150°C for at least 2 hours. Should the device be used on the expedition?

A) Yes, if 3 of the devices tested at 125°C lasted at least 2 hours, they would be expected to last longer at 150°C.

B) Yes, the probe is underwater so the humidity should remain above 90%.

C) No, only 3 of the devices tested at 125°C lasted at least 2 hours, they would be expected to do worse at higher temperatures.

D) No, the probe is underwater so the humidity should remain above 90%.

5. Which of the following were controls of Experiment 3?

A) The temperature only

B) The relative humidity only

C) The voltage only

D) The temperature and voltage only

6. The time to failure for each indicated temperature, relative humidity, and voltage occasionally showed a wide range of values. Which would be the most likely way of obtaining 1 accurate, average reading at each set of conditions?

A) Perform the test under each set of conditions only once.

B) Average the time to failure of each of the 3 iterations of the test at each set of conditions.

C) Perform the test under each set of conditions many more times, then take the average of the time to failure for each set of conditions.

D) Perform the test under each set of conditions many more times, then choose the lowest time to failure for each set of conditions.

Passage 4

Two different camps exist in paleontology about what killed the dinosaurs and other organisms at the K-Pg boundary, the transition between the Cretaceous and Paleogene periods of geologic time, which occurred approximately 66 million years ago. The following facts are generally agreed upon by both sides of the argument:

1. Global climatic change occurred at the K-Pg boundary.
2. Additionally, less lasting changes occurred at the end of the Cretaceous period, possibly the result of a massive terrestrial disturbance which caused soot to enter the atmosphere. This, in turn, caused short term acid rain, poisonous gases, and a cooling period similar to a nuclear winter.
3. Many organisms, both marine and terrestrial, went extinct at this time. Climate change is the most likely cause for this extinction.
4. A thin layer of clay containing large amounts of iridium occurs at or near the K-Pg boundary in many places globally. This may be evidence of the dust cloud mentioned in Fact 2.

Intrinsic Gradualist Hypothesis

The cause of the K-Pg extinction was of an Earthly nature and took some time to occur, at least several million years. Two main hypotheses exist here:

1. There was increased volcanic activity at the end of the Cretaceous period. Over several million years, this activity could have created enough dust and soot to block out sunlight, ultimately causing climate change. Huge volcanic eruptions occurred in India during the Late Cretaceous, spewing forth large amounts of lava, which can be seen today at the K-Pg boundary. The chemical composition of the lava rocks shows that they originated in the Earth's mantle, which is much richer in iridium than the Earth's crust.
2. Continental drift, changing of the position of continental plates, occurred at the K-Pg boundary. The oceans, especially near North America, were receding from land. This would have caused a less mild climate to occur, and would have taken much longer.

Both hypotheses are tied together – volcanism cannot occur without plate tectonics, and vice versa. If the extinction was intrinsic and gradual, both processes must have occurred.

Extrinsic Catastrophe Hypothesis

The cause of the K-Pg extinction was of an extraterrestrial nature and happened both quickly and suddenly. A large extraterrestrial object collided with the Earth, its impact throwing up enough dust to cause climate change. Since asteroids and other extraterrestrial bodies are richer in iridium than the Earth's crust, the iridium layer must be composed of the dust from the vaporized meteor.

No crater has been found, but it is assumed that one existed that was about 65 million years old and 100 km in diameter. There is, however, evidence of a possible crater on the Yucatan peninsula in Mexico. The presence of shocked quartz (caused when an extremely powerful shockwave rearranged the crystal structure of quartz), glassy spheres (possibly caused by molten rock that cooled), and a soot layer found in many areas (most likely caused by widespread forest fires) all help prove an asteroid collision.

1. According to supporters of the Intrinsic Gradualist Hypothesis, what is the most likely source of the iridium found at the K-Pg boundary?
   A) Soot caused by shifting of the tectonic plates
   B) Oceans receding from the North American boundary
   C) The bombardment of the Earth by asteroids
   D) Volcanic lava that originated in the Earth's mantle

2. It has been discovered that some animals, some of which were smaller than dinosaurs, managed to survive the K-Pg extinction event. Which hypothesis does this help validate?
   A) The Intrinsic Gradualist Hypothesis only
   B) The Extrinsic Catastrophe Hypothesis only
   C) Both hypotheses
   D) Neither hypothesis

3. It has recently been discovered that every 26 million years, the Oort Cloud of comets crosses the path of the solar system. Supporters of the Extrinsic Catastrophe Hypothesis would most likely predict which of the following occurrences?
   A) A heavy instance of volcanic activity every 26 million years
   B) A mass extinction event caused by impacts every 26 million years
   C) An abundance of impact craters covering the Yucatan Peninsula
   D) An increased occurrence of forest fires globally

4. New research has shown that all of the marine organisms that were originally thought to go extinct at the K-Pg boundary instead went extinct 10 million years before the boundary. Which hypothesis or hypotheses would this affect?
   A) It would support the Intrinsic Gradualist Hypothesis only.
   B) It would invalidate the Extrinsic Catastrophe Hypothesis only.
   C) It would support both hypotheses.
   D) It would at least partially invalidate both hypotheses.

5. The supporters of both hypotheses agree on all of the following statements except:
   A) The earth's crust has lower levels of iridium than clay found at the K-Pg boundary.
   B) Climate change is the most likely cause of the mass extinction near the K-Pg boundary.
   C) Clay found at the K-Pg boundary is similar to material found in the Earth's mantle.
   D) The presence of materials in the atmosphere can bring about climate change.

6. Supporters of both hypotheses would agree that:
    A) climate change is the most likely cause of the mass extinction event at the K-Pg boundary.
    B) only a cloud of soot would be able to cause enough climate change to cause a mass extinction.
    C) iridium is among the metals found in extraterrestrial bodies.
    D) the chemical composition of extraterrestrial bodies is similar to that of the Earth's mantle.

7. Iridium-containing clay found near the K-Pg boundary can most likely be found in which of the following locations:
    A) Mexico.
    B) India.
    C) both Mexico and India.
    D) neither Mexico nor India.

ACT Science: Data Representation Passages

Data Representation Passages

- **Data Representation Passages** always contain exactly 5 questions.
- These are the most straightforward of the 3 passage types on the ACT Science Test, and as such, you should always attempt to tackle them first to save time. Overall, it is best to answer the easy questions and guess on the harder ones if you feel like you will run out of time.
- Each Data Representation Passage will contain some introductory material, which you should skim through, and at least 1 graph, table, or schematic diagram.
- While reading the passage, focus most of your effort on understanding the data, not the introductory material! Only look back to the introductory material if something in the data does not make sense.
- Let's look at an example Data Representation Passage and some typical questions:

Three experiments were done using CO_2, krypton (Kr), or O_2. For each gas:

1. A 3 L steel vessel was fitted with a cap that contained a gas inlet valve and a pressure and temperature sensor.
2. Air was pumped out of the vessel until the pressure measured 0.00 torr.
3. The vessel was placed on a balance, and the balance was reset to 0.000 g.
4. Some of the gas was added to the vessel.
5. When the gas in the vessel reached room temperature (22°C), mass and pressure were recorded.
6. Steps 4 and 5 were repeated several times.

The experiments were then repeated, except that a 6 L vessel was used (see Figures 1 and 2).

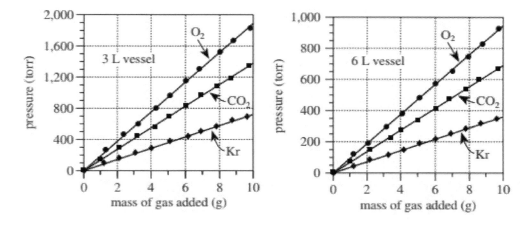

Figure 1   Figure 2

Example 1

Based on Figure 2, if 13 g of Kr had been added to the 6 L vessel, the pressure would have been:

A) less than 200 torr.
B) between 200 torr and 400 torr.
C) between 400 torr and 600 torr.
D) greater than 600 torr.

We know from the question that we need to look at Kr in Figure 2. Next, look at the slope of the Kr line: for every 2 g of Kr added, the pressure goes up by approximately 80 torr. At 10 g of Kr, the pressure is approximately 350 torr. Adding 120 torr gives us 470 torr, so our answer must be **C**.

Example 2

Which of the following best explains why equal masses of O_2 and CO_2 at the same temperature and in the same-size vessel had different pressures? The pressure exerted by the O_2 was:

A) less, because there were fewer O_2 molecules per gram than there were CO_2 molecules per gram.
B) less, because there were more O_2 molecules per gram than there were CO_2 molecules per gram.
C) greater, because there were fewer O_2 molecules per gram than there were CO_2 molecules per gram.
D) greater, because there were more O_2 molecules per gram than there were CO_2 molecules per gram.

Let's first compare the pressures of O_2 and CO_2: In both graphs, the pressure of O_2 is consistently higher than the pressure of CO_2. Thus, we know the answer must be **C** or **D**.

Next, let's visualize how the number of molecules would affect the pressure. If there are more molecules in a container, then the molecules will bump against the wall of the container more often. This extra force on the wall of the container is directly responsible for the increase in pressure. So, the answer must be **D**.

PRACTICE EXERCISE

Passage 1

Enzymes are large protein molecules that increase the rate of chemical reactions in living organisms. The *substrate* is the substance that interacts with the enzyme in a reaction. The *acceleration factor* is the factor by which the enzyme increases the rate of a reaction. Figures 1–3 show the effects that changes in temperature, pH, and substrate concentration have on the rate of reaction of a substrate when Enzymes A and B are present. Figure 4 shows the effects that changes in the concentrations of Enzymes A and B have on the rates of reaction in substrate solutions of the same concentration.

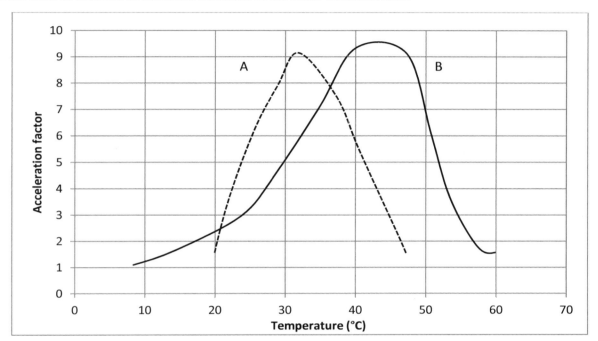

Figure 1

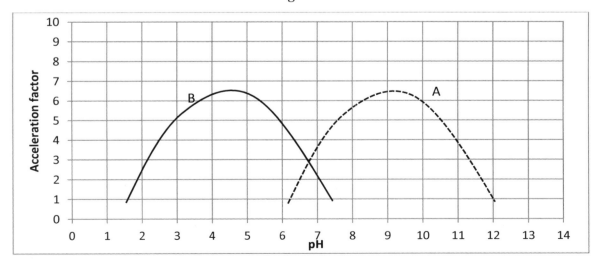

Figure 2

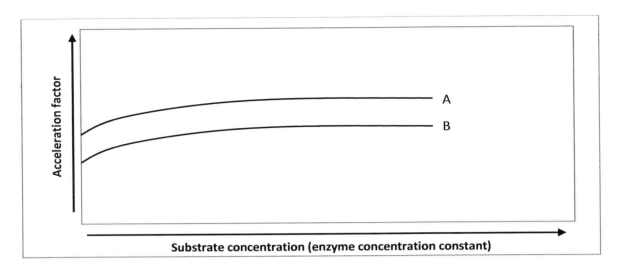

Figure 3

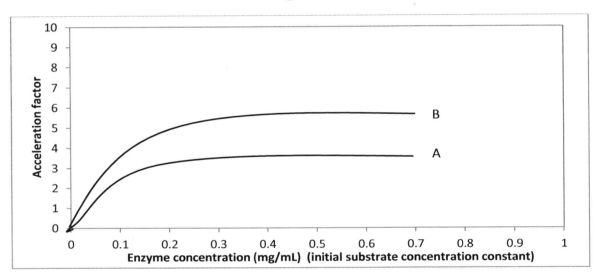

Figure 4

1. According to the Figure 1, Enzyme B has the fastest rate of reaction at a temperature closest to:
   A) 20°C.
   B) 30°C.
   C) 45°C.
   D) 60°C.

2. Based on the data in Figure 2, at which of the following pHs, if any, do Enzymes A and B have the same acceleration factor?
   A) At pH 1.7 only
   B) At pH 6.2 only
   C) At pH 6.7 only
   D) At pH 9.2 only

3. At a pH of 7, which enzyme has the lowest rate of reaction?
   A) Enzyme A
   B) Enzyme B
   C) Both enzymes have equivalent rates of reaction
   D) It is impossible to tell.

4. For both enzymes, as the substrate concentration increases, the acceleration factor:
   A) increases only.
   B) decreases only.
   C) increases, then levels off.
   D) decreases, then levels off.

5. For Enzyme A, an enzyme concentration of 0.8 mg/mL would equate to an acceleration factor of approximately:
   A) 2.
   B) 3.
   C) 4.
   D) 5 .

Passage 2

A *solubility curve* tells us what mass of a *solute* (a substance dissolved in a solution) will dissolve in 100 g of water over a range of temperatures. Figure 1 below shows the solubility curves for several different compounds.

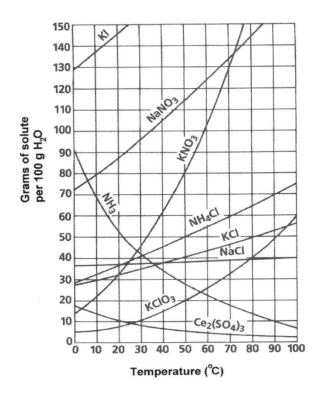

Figure 1

The lines in Figure 1 above show the concentration of a *saturated solution* – the maximum amount of solute that will dissolve at that specific temperature. An *unsaturated solution* is a solution in which more solute can be dissolved at a given temperature.

A *supersaturated solution* contains more of the dissolved material than could be dissolved by the solvent under normal conditions. One way of obtaining a supersaturated solution is to lower the temperature of an already saturated solution – for example, if a solution of NaCl contains 40 g of NaCl at 100°C, but then the temperature is lowered to 50°C, where NaCl can only contain a maximum of 38 g of NaCl, the remaining 2 g of NaCl would remain dissolved in the solution. On the other hand, pouring 40 g of NaCl into 100 g of H_2O at 50°C would result in 38 g of the NaCl being dissolved and the last 2 g of NaCl remaining undissolved at the bottom of the container.

1. Rank the 3 compounds NaCl, KCl, and NH_3 in order of increasing solubility at 30°C.
   A) NH_3, NaCl, KCl
   B) NH_3, KCl, NaCl
   C) KCl, NaCl, NH_3
   D) KCl, NH_3, NaCl

2. A container of 100 g of H$_2$O at 25°C has 60 g of NH$_4$Cl added to it, then is heated to 60°C. Upon reaching that temperature, the solution is:
   A) unsaturated.
   B) saturated.
   C) supersaturated.
   D) none of the above.

3. Which of the following techniques would result in a supersaturated solution (Assume each solution starts with 100 g of H$_2$O at 50°C)?
   A) Add 30 g of KClO$_3$, then increase the temperature of the solution to 70°C.
   B) Add 20 g of KClO$_3$, then increase the temperature of the solution to 70°C.
   C) Add 20 g of KClO$_3$, then decrease the temperature of the solution to 40°C.
   D) Add 30 g of Ce$_2$(SO$_4$)$_3$, then decrease the temperature of the solution to 40°C.

4. What is the approximate maximum amount of KI that can be added to 100 g of H$_2$O at 30°C?
   A) 135 g
   B) 145 g
   C) 155 g
   D) 165 g

5. At which of the following temperatures is the maximum amount of NH$_3$ and KNO$_3$ able to be dissolved in 100 g of H$_2$O the same?
   A) 0°C
   B) 14°C
   C) 28°C
   D) 36°C

Passage 3

Igneous rock is one of the 3 main rock types formed through the cooling and solidification of magma or lava. Two main types of igneous rocks exist – *extrusive*, formed on the surface, and *intrusive*, formed beneath the surface. Types of igneous rocks can be identified by their crystal size, texture, color, density, and mineral composition, all of which are shown in Figure 1 below.

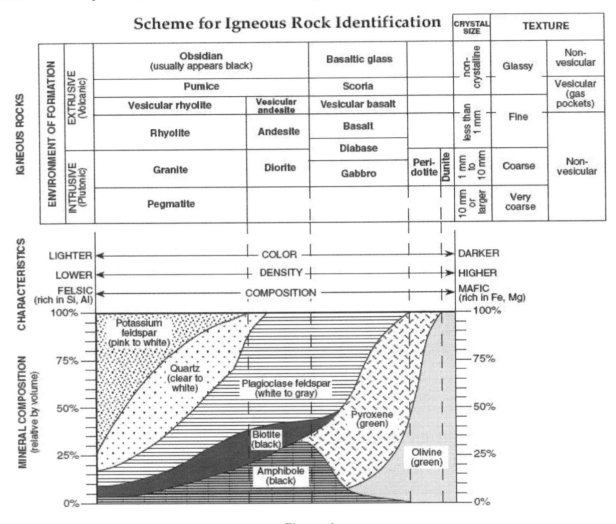

Figure 1

1. Vesicular rocks are noted for their pitted appearance caused by gas bubbles formed inside of magma. Based on the information provided in Figure 1, a pitted, glassy, dark-colored igneous rock is most likely:
   A) vesicular basalt.
   B) vesicular rhyolite.
   C) pumice.
   D) scoria.

2. By volume, a piece of biotite is what percent felsic?
   A) 5 to 45%
   B) 15 to 60%
   C) 40 to 75%
   D) 55 to 95%

3. Which of the following rocks is coarsest?
   A) Gabbro
   B) Diabase
   C) Andesite
   D) Pumice

4. Which of the following rocks has a crystal size less than 1 mm?
   A) Andesite
   B) Diorite
   C) Granite
   D) Pegmatite

5. Dunite is a type of peridotite composed of more than 90% olivine and has a Mg/Fe ratio of approximately 9:1. The expected color of dunite is:
   A) white.
   B) gray.
   C) green.
   D) black.

Passage 4

As the velocity of a stream increases, so too does the size of the particles that it can transport. Figure 1 below shows the particle diameters, in cm, of several different types of particles and the velocity, in cm/s, required to transport those particles once they've already begun moving.

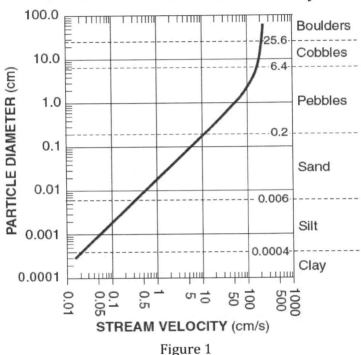

Figure 1

Figure 2 below shows how velocity of a stream changes at different areas of a stream based on both the distance from the center of the stream (for a stream of width 12 m) and the fraction of the total depth of the stream at the centerline.

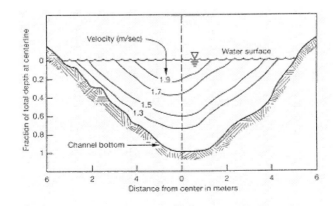

Figure 2

1. How fast must a stream be moving to carry a particle with a diameter of 1.0 cm?
   A) 25 cm/s
   B) 50 cm/s
   C) 75 cm/s
   D) 100 cm/s

2. What is the diameter of the largest particle that can be carried by a stream moving at 0.5 cm/s?
   A) 0.001 cm
   B) 0.01 cm
   C) 0.1 cm
   D) 1.0 cm

3. One can tell from the information provided in Figure 2 that:
   A) particles are easier to move near the bottom of a stream than the surface of a stream.
   B) particles are more difficult to move near the bottom of a stream than the surface of a stream.
   C) particles are easier to move near the center of a stream than the bottom of a stream.
   D) particles are easier to move near the outer edge of a stream than the surface of a stream.

4. Which of the following represents the range of velocities required to transport sand given by the information in Figure 1?
   A) 0.006 cm/s to 0.2 cm/s
   B) 0.006 cm/s to 0.35 cm/s
   C) 0.2 cm/s to 10 cm/s
   D) 0.35 cm/s to 11 cm/s

5. A particle of silt of diameter 0.005 cm is moving downstream at a velocity of 0.5 cm/s in the center of a stream of width 12 m. As it travels, a fork in the stream diverts its course and the particle of silt ends up moving just 1 m from the edge of the second stream, which is also 12 meters wide. Assuming no change in the depth of the particle or the stream, will the silt particle still be travelling?
   A) No, moving closer to the edge of the stream will significantly increase the velocity of the particle.
   B) No, moving closer to the edge of the stream will significantly decrease the velocity of the particle.
   C) Yes, moving closer to the edge of the stream will not significantly increase the velocity of the particle.
   D) Yes, moving closer to the edge of the stream will not significantly decrease the velocity of the particle.

ACT Science: Research Summaries Passages

Research Summaries Passages

- **Research Summaries Passages** always contain exactly 6 questions.
- Research Summaries Passages are generally more complicated than Data Representation Passages: they always involve at least 2, if not 3 different experiments, each with its own set of data to look at. Thus, they take a little bit more time to work through than the Data Representation Passages.
- Each Research Summaries Passage will contain some introductory material (which you should skim through), and then an experiment based on that material. Following this will be 1-3 more experiments, each changing the previous experiment in a small way.
- Pay close attention to what is changed in each successive experiment: this will be the focus of many of the questions in the passage!
- Let's look at an example Research Summaries Passage and some typical questions:

Acid-base titration is a technique in which precise volumes of a titrant (an acid or base solution) are added incrementally to a known volume of a *sample solution* (a base or acid solution, respectively). This process can be monitored by adding an *acid-base indicator* (a substance that changes color over a certain pH range) to the sample solution or by measuring the sample solution's *conductivity*. Conductivity (measured in kilosiemens per centimeter, kS/cm) is a measure of a substance's ability to conduct electricity.

Two titration experiments were done at 25°C using a 0.10 M sodium hydroxide (NaOH) solution and either a 0.0010 M hydrochloric acid (HCl) solution or a 0.0010 M acetic acid solution (where M is moles of acid or base per liter of solution). All solutions were aqueous. An acid-base indicator solution of *nitrazine yellow* was also used. Nitrazine yellow is yellow if the pH is less than 6.0 or blue if the pH is greater than 7.0.

Experiment 1

A drop of nitrazine yellow solution was added to a flask containing 100.0 mL of the HCl solution. A probe that measures conductivity was placed in the solution. The NaOH solution was slowly added to the HCl solution in small increments. After each addition, the HCl solution was stirred and then the solution's color and conductivity were recorded (see Figure 1).

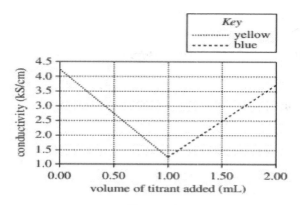

Figure 1

Experiment 2

Experiment 1 was repeated, except that the acetic acid solution was used instead of the HCl solution (see Figure 2).

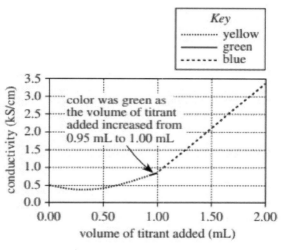

Figure 2

Example 1

In Experiments 1 and 2, the probe that was placed in the sample solution most likely did which of the following?

A) Cooled the solution to its freezing point
B) Heated the solution to its boiling point
C) Detected the concentration of nitrazine yellow in the solution
D) Passed an electrical current through a portion of the solution

---

In the introductory material for Experiment 1, the probe is mentioned: "A probe that measures conductivity was placed in the solution." Since conductivity is the degree to which a substance conducts electricity, **D** is the most likely answer. It would be hard to measure how the substance conducts electricity without exposing it to electricity, after all.

Example 2

A chemist claimed that in Experiment 2, the pH of the sample solution was greater at a value of 0.2 mL of titrant added than at a value of 1.8 mL of titrant added. Do the results of Experiment 2 support this claim?

A) No; at a value of 0.2 mL of titrant added, the sample solution was yellow, and at a value of 1.8 mL of titrant added, the sample solution was blue.

B) No; at a value of 0.2 mL of titrant added, the sample solution was blue, and at a value of 1.8 mL of titrant added, the sample solution was yellow.

C) Yes; at a value of 0.2 mL of titrant added, the sample solution was yellow, and at a value of 1.8 mL of titrant added, the sample solution was blue.

D) Yes; at a value of 0.2 mL of titrant added, the sample solution was blue, and at a value of 1.8 mL of titrant added, the sample solution was yellow.

From the introductory material, we know that the nitrazine yellow only changes to yellow if the pH is less than 6.0; at pHs above 7.0, the solution is blue. At 0.2 mL, the substance is yellow, while at 1.8 mL the substance is blue. Since the solution has a lower pH when the indicator is yellow, the answer must be **A**.

PRACTICE EXERCISE

Passage 1

In order to determine the influence of the flow of rivers of the Pantanal, the world's largest tropical wetland savanna, on the natural habitats supporting wild mammals in Brazil, a group of scientists established 5 tracts of land, each of which varied in width and crossed many different habitats. Each tract was surveyed heavily by a variety of methods, including GPS and human surveying by car, horse-back, boat, and foot.

Experiment 1

Over an 11-month period (with the exception of July), the scientists surveyed each of the 5 tracts of land at various times during the day and night, tallying each instance of a mammal seen. The results are located in Table 1 below. Each animal that was seen at least 30 times was recorded in Table 1.

Table 1												
Species	April 2003	May 2003	June 2003	Aug 2003	Sept 2003	Oct 2003	Nov 2003	Dec 2003	Jan 2003	Feb 2004	Mar 2004	Total
Marsh deer	5	3	4	9	6	5	8	4	2	5	0	51
Crab-eating fox	5	1	2	3	5	7	4	5	8	10	16	66
Capybara	8	1	6	15	17	11	5	6	2	6	4	81
Gray brocket	7	4	6	2	3	5	2	4	6	3	4	46
Pampas deer	1	0	2	1	2	6	4	3	9	1	1	30
Crab-eating raccoon	8	0	3	3	2	2	3	2	4	3	8	38

Experiment 2

Microwave radiometers were used to discover annual flooding patterns in the Pantanal over a 9-year period. Maximum inundation always occurred near the end of, or after, the rainy season, which typically lasts from November to February. The period of maximum inundation never occurred before February or after June for the 9-year period.

Experiment 3

Another group of scientists noted each mammal observed, and the month in which it was observed. The frequency of individual animals observed and the number of mammal species observed is located in Figure 1.

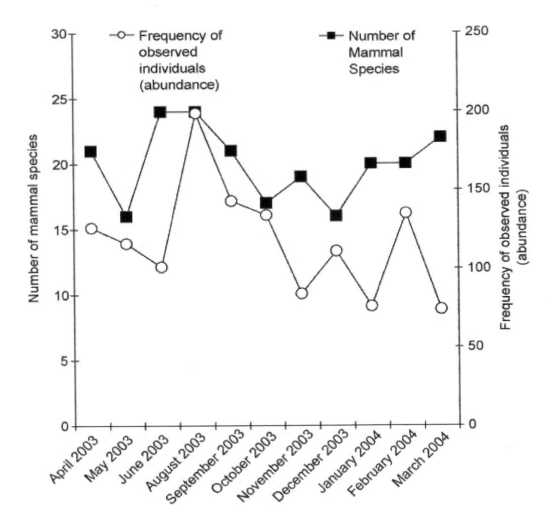

Figure 1

1. During which 2-month period was the number of capybara sightings lowest?
   A) May-June 2003
   B) Sept-Oct 2003
   C) Dec 2003-Jan 2004
   D) Jan-Feb 2004

2. Based on the information provided in Figure 1, the lower number of different animal species occurred in:
   A) May 2003.
   B) June 2003.
   C) January 2004.
   D) March 2004.

3. For which animal was the number of sightings in February and March 2004 to the number of total sightings the highest?
   A) Capybara
   B) Crab-eating raccoon
   C) Crab-eating fox
   D) Pampas deer

4. Does the information provided in Figure 1 back up the claim that "The frequency of observed individuals is lower during the dry season, when the land dries out and an expansion of terrestrial habitats occur."
   A) Yes, the lowest frequency of observed individuals occurs in March 2004, the transition from the dry season to the wet season.
   B) Yes, the highest frequency of observed individuals occurs in March 2004, several months into the dry season.
   C) No, the highest frequency of observed individuals occurs in August 2003, the transition from the dry season to the wet season.
   D) No, the highest frequency of observed individuals occurs in August 2003, several months into the dry season.

5. Which of the following is the most reasonable estimate of the number of gray brockets expected to be seen by the scientists in April 2004 if they had extended their study?
   A) 1
   B) 3
   C) 6
   D) 9

6. Had the experiment been carried on in July 2003, which of the following is the most reasonable estimate for the number of mammal species spotted that month?
   A) 12
   B) 15
   C) 17
   D) 22

Passage 2

The behavior of real gases generally agrees with the predictions of the *ideal gas law* at normal temperatures and pressures. However, at low temperatures or high pressures, real gases begin to deviate from the predicted behaviors. A series of experiments was designed to discover the reasons behind this deviation.

Experiment 1

A constant amount of a real gas is inserted into a container at pressure 1 atm. A force of attraction exists between real gas molecules that does not exist between ideal gas molecules; as such, these gas molecules bunch together to a certain extent. The volume these molecules occupy can be considered an "excluded volume" and is a negligible fraction of the volume of the container. The volume of the container is decreased, consequently increasing the pressure of the container. As the gas is compressed, the excluded volume slowly becomes a much greater fraction of the volume of the container. As a result, the volume of the real gas is larger than expected from the ideal gas law. This process is shown in Figure 1 below.

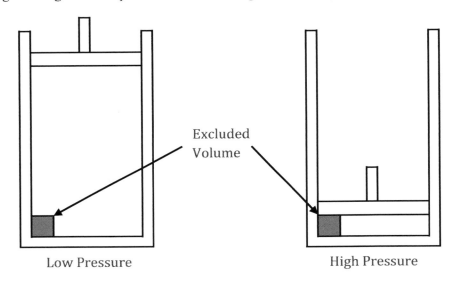

Figure 1

Experiment 2

Another experiment is designed to compare the pressure and volume for samples of 3 different gases – hydrogen (H_2), nitrogen (N_2), and carbon dioxide (CO_2). A constant amount of each gas, at constant temperature, is added to the container below. The pressure, in atmospheres (atm), was measured at several different volumes, in liters (L), and a plot of the pressure versus the product of the pressure and volume is shown in Figure 2.

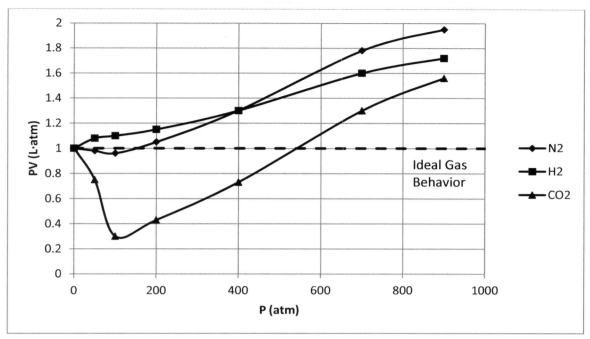

Figure 2

1. According to Figure 2, which gas deviates most from ideal gas behavior at 200 atm?
   A) N_2
   B) H_2
   C) CO_2
   D) None of the gases deviate from ideal gas behavior.

2. According to Figure 2, what is the expected volume of H_2 at 1000 atm?
   A) 0.0016 L
   B) 0.0018 L
   C) 0.0020 L
   D) 550 L

3. According to the information presented in Experiment 1, what would have occurred if an ideal gas were used instead of a real gas?
   A) The gas molecules would have exhibited greater attraction and the resulting volume would have been smaller.
   B) The gas molecules would have exhibited greater attraction and the resulting volume would have been larger.
   C) The gas molecules would have exhibited less attraction and the resulting volume would have been smaller.
   D) The gas molecules would have exhibited less attraction and the resulting volume would have been larger.

4. The data provided in Figure 2 backs up the information provided in the passage because:
    A) all 3 gases exhibit ideal gas behavior at low pressures.
    B) all 3 gases exhibit ideal gas behavior at high pressures.
    C) all 3 gases exhibit ideal gas behavior at low volumes.
    D) all 3 gases exhibit ideal gas behavior at high volumes.

5. At which of the following pressures are the volumes of H_2 and N_2 the same?
    A) 0 atm only
    B) At 200 atm and 400 atm only
    C) At 0 atm and 400 atm only
    D) The volumes of H_2 and N_2 are never identical.

6. The Van der Waals constant, a, for the 3 gases is shown below:

Gas	a
N_2	1.39
H_2	0.24
CO_2	3.59

Based on the information, which of the following must be true?
    A) For all pressures, the relationship between the volume of a real gas and the gas's Van der Waals constant a is direct.
    B) For pressures under 400 atm, the relationship between the volume of a real gas and the gas's Van der Waals constant a is direct.
    C) For all pressures, the relationship between the volume of a real gas and the gas's Van der Waals constant a is inverse.
    D) For pressures under 400 atm, the relationship between the volume of a real gas and the gas's Van der Waals constant a is inverse.

Passage 3

Vapor pressure is the pressure exerted by a vapor in thermodynamic equilibrium with its solid or liquid phase at a given temperature in a closed system. When a solute is added to a solvent, the vapor pressure of the solvent is less than the vapor pressure of the pure solvent. Thus, the boiling point of a solution will be greater than the boiling point of the pure solvent because the solution will be heated to a higher temperature in order for the vapor pressure to become equal to the external pressure.

The boiling point of the solvent above a solution changes as the concentration of the solute in the solution changes. Several experiments are carried out to determine how different solutes change the boiling point of several different solvents.

The boiling points of several different solvents are determined experimentally. The results are listed in Table 1 below. Additionally, several different solutes, and the number of ions they dissolve into in water, are listed in Table 2.

Table 1	
Solvent	Boiling Point (°C)
Benzene	80.1
Water	100.0
Acetic Acid	118.1

Table 2	
Solute	Number of particles
Sucrose	1
NaCl	2
CaCl$_2$	3

Experiment 1

Different amounts of each of the solutes were added to 100 g of water and the boiling points of each solution were observed. The results are listed in Figure 1 below.

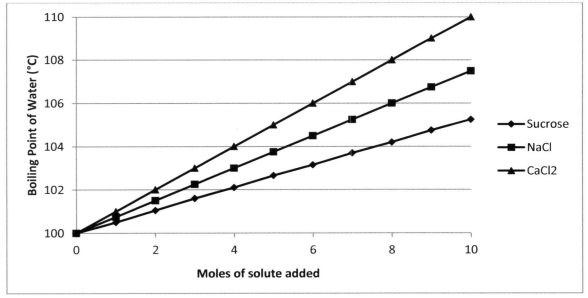

Figure 1

Experiment 2

Experiment 1 was repeated with acetic acid as the solvent. The following boiling points were obtained. $CaCl_2$ broke up into 3 particles when it was dissolved in acetic acid.

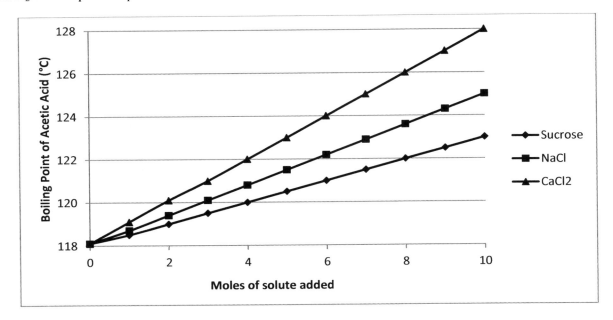

Figure 2

Experiment 3

Experiment 1 was repeated with benzene as the solvent. All 3 solutes produced approximately the same change in boiling point, as shown in Figure 3.

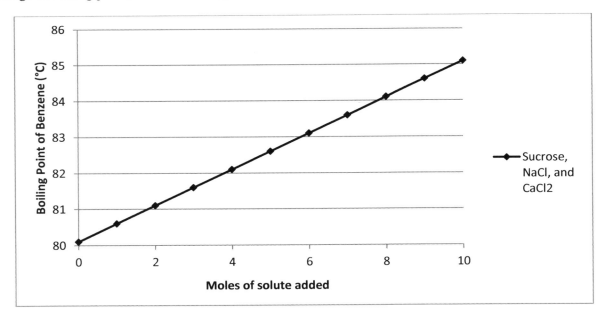

Figure 3

1. Based on the information provided in Figure 1, one can determine that as the number of particles formed by a solute increases, the boiling point of a solvent containing that solute:
   A) increases.
   B) decreases.
   C) increases, then decreases.
   D) decreases, then increases.

2. Based on the information provide in Figures 1 and 2, how many particles does a molecule of NaCl break up into when dissolved in acetic acid? (Assume that molecules can only break up into a whole number of particles.)
   A) 1
   B) 2
   C) 3
   D) It cannot be determined from the given information.

3. Based on the information provided in Experiment 3, one can determine that:
   A) 2 moles of sucrose produces more particles than 3 moles of NaCl.
   B) 2 moles of sucrose produces more particles than 3 moles of $CaCl_2$.
   C) 2 moles of sucrose produces the same number of particles as 2 moles of $CaCl_2$.
   D) 2 moles of sucrose produces more particles than moles g of sucrose.

4. Two moles of compound X is dissolved into 100 g of benzene and a boiling point of the solution is 82.5. You can tell that compound X:
   A) dissolves into more particles than NaCl does in benzene.
   B) dissolves into more particles than $CaCl_2$ does in benzene.
   C) dissolves into more particles than sucrose does in benzene.
   D) all of the above.

5. The control of Experiment 1 is:
   A) the number of moles of solute.
   B) the number of grams of water.
   C) the boiling point of the solution.
   D) the solute used.

6. Fourteen moles of NaCl are added to 100 g of acetic acid and the boiling point is observed. What is the most likely boiling point of the mixture?
   A) 132°C
   B) 128°C
   C) 124°C
   D) 120°C

Passage 4

A study was set up to determine how two different copper-nickel alloys, A and B, resisted corrosion from seawater. The composition of the two alloys is listed in Table 1.

	Table 1								
	Percent mass of total alloy								
Alloy	Copper	Nickel	Iron	Manganese	Zinc	Carbon	Lead	Sulfur	Impurities
A	All of the Remainder	9.0 – 11.0	1.0 – 2.0	0.5 – 1.0	0.0 – 0.5	0.00 – 0.05	0.00 – 0.02	0.00 – 0.02	0.00 – 0.10
B	All of the Remainder	29.0 – 33.0	0.4 – 1.0	0.5 – 1.5	0.0 – 0.5	0.00 – 0.05	0.00 – 0.02	0.00 – 0.02	0.00 – 0.10

Experiment 1

When Alloy B is exposed to clean seawater at 16°C, a thin, protective surface film forms naturally. The film forms over the first few days but takes 2-3 months to fully mature. Figure 1 shows the amount of copper discharged, in parts per million (ppm) at several different times during the process. As the amount of copper discharged decreases, the strength of the film increases.

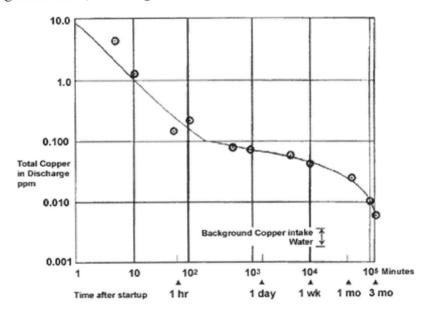

Figure 1

Experiment 2

Experiment 1 is performed again, but at several different seawater temperatures, and the amount of time until a film capable of protection forms is measured. The results are shown in Table 2.

Page 416

Table 2		
Location	Temperature	Time
Arabian Sea	27°C	2 – 3 hours
Pacific Ocean	18°C	1 day
Arctic Ocean	2°C	1 – 2 months

Experiment 3

Next, both Alloy A and B were tested for corrosion rates in 3 different types of seawater: quiet, flowing, and tidal. Once a surface film forms, the corrosion rate tends to decrease over a period of years, while the growth rate of the protective film increases, then decreases. The corrosion rate, in micrometers per year (μm/yr) was measured for each of the 2 alloys over a period of 14 years. This information is shown in Figure 2.

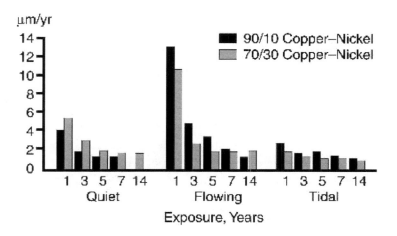

Figure 2

1. Under which of the following conditions will a copper-nickel alloy experience the least corrosion?
   A) Alloy A in flowing seawater after being exposed for 14 years
   B) Alloy B in flowing seawater after being exposed for 14 years
   C) Alloy A in quiet seawater after being exposed for 1 year
   D) Alloy B in tidal seawater after being exposed for 14 years

2. According to the information provided in Experiment 1, after which of the following amounts of time would the strength of the protective film of Alloy B be highest?
   A) 10^2 minutes
   B) 10^3 minutes
   C) 10^5 minutes
   D) 10^6 minutes

3. Which of the following could be the amount of iron in 50 g of Alloy B?
   A) 0.1 g
   B) 0.3 g
   C) 0.6 g
   D) 1.0 g

4. What is the expected copper discharge, in ppm, for Alloy B after 10 minutes?
   A) 10.0
   B) 1.0
   C) 0.1
   D) 0.01

5. A new nuclear power plant is planning on using copper-nickel pipes to dispel seawater, used for cooling, into the ocean. If the outtake pipes for the power plant are located in an area that regularly experiences ocean tides, which alloy should be used and why?
   A) Alloy A, it experiences less corrosion than does Alloy B under tidal conditions.
   B) Alloy B, it experiences less corrosion than does Alloy A under tidal conditions.
   C) Alloy A, it experiences more corrosion than does Alloy B under tidal conditions.
   D) Alloy B, it experiences more corrosion than does Alloy A under tidal conditions.

6. The Caribbean Sea's tropical waters feature average temperatures of 25°C and fluctuate by no more than 3°C. Which of the following is the best estimate for the amount of time it would take for Alloy A to form film capable of protection under these conditions?
   A) 1 – 2 hours
   B) 2 – 3 hours
   C) 3 – 4 hours
   D) It is unable to be determined from the information given.

ACT Science: Conflicting Viewpoints Passages

Conflicting Viewpoints Passages

- **Conflicting Viewpoints Passages** always contain exactly 7 questions.
- Conflicting Viewpoints Passages typically take the most amount of time out of the 3 passage types. Each one involves approximately a page worth of reading, featuring at least 2 opinions on a subject and some introductory material.
- Unless reading is your strongest subject, you should typically save the Conflicting Viewpoints Passage for last because of the great amount of time it takes to complete.
- Remember the active reading strategies we've discussed over the last few strategies and apply those tactics as you work your way through each passage.
- Let's look at an example Conflicting Viewpoints Passage and some typical questions:

In the 1940s, scientists thought all genetic material was contained in structures called *chromosomes* and that chromosomes had been found only in the nucleus of a cell (not in the cytoplasm).

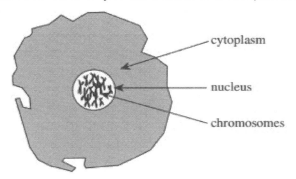

Chromosomes are composed of 2 types of molecules, proteins and deoxyribonucleic acid (DNA). Proteins are composed of subunits called *amino acids*. DNA consists of chains of subunits called *nucleotides*. The parts of chromosomes that are responsible for the transmission of genetic information are called *genes*.

Two scientists in the 1940s debate whether genes are made of proteins or DNA.

Protein Hypothesis

Genes are made only of proteins. Proteins make up 50% or more of a cell's dry weight. Cells contain 20 different amino acids that can be arranged in a virtually infinite number of ways to make different proteins. The number and arrangement of different amino acids within a protein form the codes that contain hereditary information.

In contrast, only 4 different nucleotides make up the DNA found in cells, and they are believed to form chains only in certain ratios. As a result, the number of different combinations that DNA can carry is much smaller than the number that proteins can carry.

DNA Hypothesis

Genes are made only of DNA. DNA is found exclusively in the cell's nucleus, whereas proteins are found throughout the nucleus and cytoplasm. Additionally, the amount of protein in a cell varies from cell type to cell type, even within the same animal. Though DNA is less abundant than proteins, the amount is consistent from cell type to cell type within the same animal, except for the *gametes* (the reproductive cells). Gametes have half the amount of DNA as other cells in the body. Gametes also have half the typical number of chromosomes. Thus, the amount of DNA in a cell is correlated with the number of chromosomes in the cell. No such correlation is found for proteins.

Example 1

The scientist who describes the DNA Hypothesis implies that the Protein Hypothesis is weakened by which of the following observations?

A) For a given organism, the amount of protein in the gametes is half that found in other types of cells.
B) For a given organism, the amount of protein in different types of cells is not the same.
C) Protein molecules are composed of many subunits.
D) Proteins are found only in the nucleus.

For questions like this, focus on what points the scientists disagree. In the DNA Hypothesis, the scientists proclaims: "Thus, the amount of DNA in a cell is correlated with the number of chromosomes in the cell. No such correlation is found for proteins." According to this scientist's logic, the lack of correlation between the amounts of protein in different cells weakens the protein hypothesis. So, our answer must be **B**.

While reading these passages, always be sure to note times in which the 2 (or more) opinions disagree and agree. There will always be at least 1 question relating to these differing or agreeing opinions.

Example 2

By referring to the observation that DNA is found exclusively in the nucleus while proteins are found throughout the cell, the scientist supporting the DNA Hypothesis implies that genes are made only of DNA because which of the following are also found only in the nucleus?

A) Amino acids
B) Proteins
C) Gametes
D) Chromosomes

Other questions only require finding information from the passage. Since we're referring to the DNA Hypothesis, let's focus there. "Genes are made only of DNA. DNA is found exclusively in the cell's nucleus, whereas proteins are found throughout the nucleus and cytoplasm." Since we know from the introductory material that "Chromosomes are composed of 2 types of molecules, proteins and deoxyribonucleic acid (DNA)," it makes sense that the scientist believes that chromosomes cannot be found anywhere else but the nucleus, as that is the only place DNA exists. The answer is **D**.

PRACTICE EXERCISE

Passage 1

Viruses can be found in every living organism, but today, their evolutionary origins, and their relationship to the evolution of living species, is still being debated. Many in the scientific community argue that viruses are alive, while others consider them to be something else entirely.

Scientist 1

Today, the debate is not about whether or not viruses are alive, it about what it means to be "alive". Viruses are incapable of replicating themselves. They require help, a host organism, to do so. Viruses both have and are capable of passing on genetic material, such as RNA and DNA, and also have a protective shell around their genome. However, they are not capable of making the proteins needed to copy their genome. Consequently, every other organism on earth *is* capable of these things. The fact that other organisms have an ability that viruses do not draws a clear line of separation between the two. I argue that that line is between "living" and "non-living".

The most important factor for being alive is the ability to take something from one's environment and use it to create energy. Plants, animals, fungi, and bacteria are all able to turn resources into energy. Viruses, on the other hand, do not: all of their energy is stolen from other organisms.

Cell theory states that all living things are made of cells. Since viruses are not made of cells, they are not alive. Even though viruses have genetic material, this genetic material does not actually *do* anything. It is simply an instruction manual, and without another organism to carry out the instructions, the virus is capable of nothing.

Scientist 2

Life is diverse, and organisms always find a means of getting what they need to survive from their environment. Organisms rely on a certain amount of material, both biological and non-biological, to be available. Organisms adapt to rely on the resource which is the least restricted by the environment in which they reside. Any organism that fails to adapt to its environment ceases to exist.

Viruses are no different from other forms of life. Their niche is minimalist; they have no need for glucose, so have no need to consume other organisms or use photosynthesis to create their own glucose. They have no use for water to diffuse the molecules that make up themselves. Viruses are successful because they are simple.

Only two traits are necessary to qualify as living – the ability to pass DNA on to future generations and the ability to adapt to changes in the environment. Viruses are capable, excellent in fact, at both of these criteria.

Remember, cell theory was created before the existence of viruses was known. If viruses were known back then, would the theory have been changed to accommodate them? Perhaps the list of criteria for life would be very different.

1. Which of the following ideas is most consistent with cell theory?
   A) If an organism is alive, then it is made up of cells.
   B) Viruses are not made up of cells.
   C) Any organism that contains DNA must be made up of cells.
   D) The combination of cells and DNA is essential for life.

2. With which of the following ideas would both scientists agree?
   A) Viruses are too simple to be considered successful organisms.
   B) Viruses are capable of passing on their DNA.
   C) An organism must be capable of surviving on its own to be considered alive.
   D) Cell theory should be revised to include viruses.

3. The lamprey is a species of jawless fish that is a parasite, which only obtains its energy from another organism known as the host. This information furthers the argument of:
   A) Scientist 1.
   B) Scientist 2.
   C) both scientists.
   D) neither scientist.

4. The idea that an organism needs to be capable of creating the proteins needed to replicate itself to be considered alive is encompassed by:
   A) Scientist 1.
   B) Scientist 2.
   C) both scientists.
   D) neither scientist.

5. How would Scientist 2 most likely react to the discovery of a type of virus that makes use of glucose?
   A) Since the organism needs glucose, it cannot be considered a virus.
   B) This virus must be part of an environment in which glucose is the easiest means of survival.
   C) This type of virus must be grouped in with other non-living organisms.
   D) Because this virus uses glucose, it must be capable of creating its own proteins necessary to replicate itself.

6. A new type of virus is found that is capable of surviving in both humans and reptiles. This information invalidates the ideas of:
   A) Scientist 1.
   B) Scientist 2.
   C) both scientists.
   D) neither scientist.

7. A new type of virus has evolved that is considered a one-celled organism. How would Scientist 1 react to this information?
   A) The presence of a cell does not make an organism necessarily alive.
   B) This type of virus is alive because of cell theory.
   C) The presence of a cell does not keep the organism from being alive.
   D) The organism is still a virus and, as such, is not alive.

Passage 2

Recently, some diet plans have encouraged the consumption of high amounts of fat and small amounts of carbohydrates in order to lose weight. Two nutritionists debate methods of losing weight below.

Nutritionist 1

Generally, butter, bacon, and fried chicken are foods on the naughty list for most diet plans. New research has shown that the high-fat, low-carbohydrate diet not only allows, but even encourages, dieters to eat as much butter, bacon and fried foods as possible. These nutritionists argue that it is not fat but excess carbohydrates, like those found in potatoes, bread, and desserts, which cause many of the ailments that plague Americans.

Diets high in fat and low in carbs lead to *ketosis*, a process that changes the way your body uses energy. When the body doesn't get enough energy through carbohydrates, it starts to use other sources of energy. Stopping carbohydrate consumption prevents the intake of glucose. The kidneys start to convert glycogen back into glucose to normalize the level in the body. While this happens, lipolysis breaks down the fat in fat cells, which allows fatty acids to enter the blood stream. Once the stores of glycogen are depleted, the kidneys start to produce ketones from fatty acids. Ketones supply energy to the brain and muscles. At this point, the body switches its energy source from carbohydrates to fats.

If the diet is properly followed, weight loss is guaranteed. Additionally, there are few stringent restrictions for the diet: most foods with few carbohydrates are fine to eat. While the diet can be known to cause headaches initially and some amount of irritability, being able to turn your body into a fat-burning machine more than makes up for a few minor problems.

Nutritionist 2

It seems like every year a new fad diet comes along promising to revolutionize your body. Most of these, however, prove to be just that – fads. The most effective way to lose weight and keep your body healthy is through a balanced diet and exercise.

The most effective way to lose weight is to burn more calories than you consume. If you burn 500 more calories than you eat every day for a week, you should lose about 1 or 2 pounds that week. Most Americans don't get nearly enough weekly exercise; 30 minutes a day should be a starting point, not an endpoint.

In order to help limit the number of calories you consume, start out small. Drink plenty of water and eat vegetables to help you feel full. Avoid buying tempting foods, and always use a plate – standing in front of the fridge or pantry to snack is one of the biggest temptations in everyday life. Finally, stay busy – many people get into the habit of eating because they are bored, not because they are actually hungry.

The low-carb, high-fat diet is not the best way to encourage healthy eating habits, and the amount of weight lost by the diet is too much to be healthy. Remember: if a diet plan sounds too good to be true, it probably is!

1. The Inuit of the Arctic eat a diet heavy in animal proteins and fats and low in plant-based material because of their environment. This diet helps back up the ideas of which nutritionist?
    A) Nutritionist 1
    B) Nutritionist 2
    C) Both nutritionists
    D) Neither nutritionist

2. How would Nutritionist 2 react to the statement "Diets high in fat and low in carbs lead to *ketosis*, a process that changes the way your body uses energy"?
    A) The ketogenic diet doesn't involve exercise, so it won't help you keep weight off.
    B) Avoiding carbohydrates encourages unhealthy eating habits and an unbalanced diet.
    C) Ketosis can cause you to lose weight, and continuation of the diet will help keep the weight off.
    D) Changing the processes of your body is even unhealthier than not exercising.

3. Both nutritionists agree that:
    A) The low-carb, high-fat diet will not keep weight off long-term.
    B) The low-carb, high-fat diet does cause weight loss.
    C) Your body does not get enough energy to keep up brain function during ketosis.
    D) Eating vegetables is the best way to convince your body that you are full.

4. Which nutritionist would most likely subscribe to the "food pyramid", which suggests that people eat 2-3 servings of dairy, 2-3 servings of meat, 3-5 servings of vegetables, 2-4 servings of fruit, and 6-11 servings of bread or pasta daily?
    A) Nutritionist 1
    B) Nutritionist 2
    C) Both nutritionists
    D) Neither nutritionist

5. The primary difference between the argument of Nutritionist 1 and 2 is that:
    A) Nutritionist 1 uses more scientific reasoning in his or her argument.
    B) Nutritionist 2 uses more scientific reasoning in his or her argument.
    C) Nutritionist 1 does not address disease as much as Nutritionist 2 does.
    D) Nutritionist 2 does not address exercise as much as Nutritionist 1 does.

6. The purpose of lipolysis is to:
    A) add fatty acid to the blood.
    B) break down fat cells.
    C) deplete glycogen stores.
    D) minimize the intake of glucose.

7. Nutritionist 2 would most likely recommend all of the following to lose weight except:
    A) eating fruits and vegetables.
    B) exercising daily.
    C) using weight-loss pills from a pharmacy.
    D) avoiding eating too much of one food group.

Passage 3

According to the Big Bang Theory, the entire universe emerged in a single explosive moment approximately 13.7 billion years ago. Recently, however, new theories have been developed to compete with and/or modify the Big Bang Theory. Three of these theories are shown below.

Theory 1

The standard interpretation of the Big Bang Theory insists that the explosion that formed the universe didn't just occur at some point in space and time – it *was* an explosion of space and time. Time did not exist before the Big Bang.

According to string theory, seven additional, hidden dimensions exist in space in addition to the three we experience normally. In these extra dimensions, strange things can happen. A *brane*, or 3-dimensional world embedded in higher-dimensional space, exerts powerful forces on other nearby branes. Vast quantities of energy lie bound up in the forces of these branes, and a collision between branes could unleash those energies. From the inside, the result would look like a tremendous explosion. Theoretical characteristics of this explosion match the observed properties of the Big Bang, including the microwave background. The energy in these explosions eventually turns to matter, and gives rise to the universe as we know it. Space within the branes expands, and as the distance between the branes grows, attractive forces between the branes grow as well. Eventually, a new collision occurs, and a new cycle of creation begins.

Theory 2

A cyclic universe creates more problems than it solves. Cycles imply that time flows in a definite direction. But, unfortunately, there is no way to address what came before the Big Bang until we understand why the "before" precedes the "after". The addition of more universes shows that, in the big picture, time does not flow so much as it advances both backwards and forwards symmetrically.

Equations governing individual objects do not care about time's direction. If you have a movie of two billiard balls colliding, you have no way of telling if the movie is going forward or backwards. However, if you add more objects, say a billion atoms inside a container, then past and future look very, very different.

Our universe has been evolving for 13 billion years, so it clearly did not start in equilibrium. Instead, matter, energy, space, and time must have begun in a state of very low entropy, or chaos. Understanding how this happened is key to understanding the process that brings our universe into being.

Theory 3

There is no need to find a solution to time's beginning because time does not exist. If you ever try to get your hands on time, it slips through your fingers. Maybe people can't get ahold of time because it isn't there at all.

Change creates the illusion of time. Each individual moment exists in its own right, complete and whole. As we live, we seem to move through a succession of these moments. But what are they? Each of these moments coexists at once. As such, if each moment of the universe, each of its configurations, each possible location of every atom, exists simultaneously, there is no past that flows into the future.

Thus, the Big Bang never arises because there is no time. Think of your memories: the only evidence you have of last week is your memories. The only evidence we have of Earth's past are fossils and rocks, but these rocks and fossils exist in the now as well; we can examine them in the present. Each of these moments may be linked together, even though they all exist simultaneously. They create the appearance of a sequence from past to future, but there is no evidence of an actual flow of time.

1. Which of the theories claims that the Big Bang never occurred?
   A) Theory 1
   B) Theory 2
   C) Theory 3
   D) All of the theories claim that the Big Bang did occur.

2. Theories 1 and 2 most disagree on the point of:
   A) how the Big Bang occurred.
   B) the cyclic nature of the universe.
   C) the existence of time.
   D) the direction in which time flows.

3. All of the theories use real-world examples to help explain their ideas except:
   A) Theory 1.
   B) Theory 2.
   C) Theory 3.
   D) All of the theories use real-world examples.

4. Which of the above theories deviates least from the Big Bang Theory?
   A) Theory 1
   B) Theory 2
   C) Theory 3
   D) All 3 theories deviate greatly from the Big Bang Theory

5. According to Theory 1, large amounts of energy are created by the:
   A) intersections of dimensions.
   B) collision of dimensions.
   C) collisions of "branes".
   D) intersections of "branes".

6. According to the information provided by Theory 1, which of the following helps backup the Big Bang Theory?
   A) A microwave background
   B) The flow of time
   C) The collisions between atoms
   D) The high entropy of particles on Earth

7. On which of the following ideas do the authors of Theory 1 and Theory 3 agree?
   A) Change makes people think that time exists.
   B) Time began after the Big Bang Theory happened.
   C) Time moves in many directions at once.
   D) At certain points in the universe, time has not existed.

Passage 4

Since its discovery by Westerners in the late 19th century, the Giant Panda has befuddled scientists. For many years, it was believed to be a type of raccoon, similar to the red panda. Other scientists make the case that the giant panda is a bear after all. Two scientists make their cases for the giant panda below:

Scientist 1

The giant panda has too many characteristics in common with the raccoon family to be put into the bear family *ursidae*. Two major features confirm that the panda has more in common with the raccoon than the bear: its bones and its teeth.

Giant pandas are descended from the same ancestral carnivores as bears, raccoons, dogs, and cats and are placed in the order Carnivora. However, giant pandas have almost entirely lost their ability to eat meat! As a rule, bears are omnivorous – they eat a variety of things, including meat and plants. Bears are typically opportunistic eaters; they eat whatever is available to them. Not so for the giant panda, whose diet is made up almost entirely of bamboo.

Additionally, the giant panda's skeletal structure and behavior are closer to other members of the raccoon family, like the red panda, than to bears. One of the biggest pieces of evidence here is the presence of the giant panda's special sixth digit, which acts like an opposable thumb. This digit is an extension of a bone in the giant panda's wrist and helps it grip bamboo shoots and strip them of their leaves.

Lastly, giant pandas have well-developed molars and do not hibernate in winter, none of which are exhibited by bears. Giant pandas should be placed in the raccoon family for good.

Scientist 2

In the 21st century, biologists no longer have to resort to subjective means of classifying animals. Today, we can use genetic testing to figure out how to classify living organisms, and the giant panda is no exception.

Molecular studies of the giant panda's DNA suggest that it is a true bear and part of the family *ursidae*. Although it differentiated early in history from the main bear stock, the giant panda's closest living relative is the spectacled bear of South America. These two bears have more than a little in common – both eat very little meat, and both are the only living members of their own subfamilies, giving them both many peculiarities in the bear family. In fact, even the spectacled bear eats a fair portion of bamboo, though it generally sticks to the bamboo heart instead of the plant's leaves.

Despite the shared name, habitat, diet, and the presence of the pseudo thumb used to grip bamboo, the giant panda is only distantly related to the red panda. In fact, molecular studies have placed the red panda in its own family, *ailuridae,* instead of the *procyonidae* family that raccoons belong to currently. Nothing more than convergent evolution gave these two animals similarities.

1. How would Scientist 2 respond to Scientist 1's comment that "Two major features confirm that the panda has more in common with the raccoon than the bear: its bones and its teeth"?
   A) While a definitive means of classifying animals, other methods are now available.
   B) Placing an animal into a family based on its structure is not as effective as basing an animal's family off of molecular characteristics.
   C) Classifying animals based on bones and teeth is a more modern technique than anything we currently have.
   D) Giant pandas are too large to be part of the raccoon family.

2. Both scientists agree on which of the following?
   A) The giant panda and spectacled bear are closely related.
   B) The giant panda and red panda are closely related.
   C) The giant panda and spectacled bear both eat highly herbivorous diets.
   D) The giant panda and red panda both have a sixth digit.

3. It is discovered that the giant panda occasionally eats meat. This discovery most affects the argument of:
   A) Scientist 1.
   B) Scientist 2.
   C) both scientists.
   D) neither scientist.

4. Which scientist believes that the red panda should be placed in its own family, away from both raccoons and the giant panda?
   A) Scientist 1
   B) Scientist 2
   C) Both scientists
   D) Neither scientist

5. A new mammal is discovered in the highlands of China that eats only bamboo. How would Scientist 1 go about classifying the species?
   A) Analyze the molecular structure of the new mammal.
   B) Analyze the physical structure of the new mammal only.
   C) Analyze the both the molecular structure and physical structure of the new mammal.
   D) None of these things.

6. A new mammal is discovered in the highlands of China that eats only bamboo. How would Scientist 1 go about classifying the species?
   A) Analyze the molecular structure of the new mammal only.
   B) Analyze the physical structure of the new mammal.
   C) Analyze the both the molecular structure and physical structure of the new mammal.
   D) None of these things.

7. Scientist 1 most likely believes which of the following?
   A) All bears have well-developed molars.
   B) Bears typically do not hibernate in the winter.
   C) Bears are adapted to be able to eat a variety of foods.
   D) Because the spectacled bear eats little meat, it is not a true bear.

Science Practice Exercises Answer Key

Introduction

Passage 1
1. B
2. C
3. A
4. B
5. D

Passage 2
1. D
2. B
3. B
4. C
5. D
6. C

Passage 3
1. C
2. A
3. B
4. D
5. A
6. A
7. D

Understanding Charts and Graphs

Passage 1
1. D
2. A
3. A
4. C
5. A

Passage 2
1. A
2. A
3. C
4. B
5. B

Passage 3
1. C
2. B
3. C
4. C
5. B
6. B

Passage 4
1. C
2. D
3. D
4. C
5. C
6. A

Understanding Questions

Passage 1
1. C
2. A
3. C
4. C
5. B

Passage 2
1. C
2. B
3. C
4. A
5. A

Passage 3
1. B
2. B
3. B
4. C
5. A
6. A

Passage 4
1. C
2. B
3. B
4. B
5. A
6. C
7. B

Analysis Questions

Passage 1
1. B
2. D
3. D
4. A
5. D

Passage 2
1. B
2. B
3. A
4. C
5. B
6. C

Passage 3
1. B
2. C
3. A
4. D
5. D
6. C

Passage 4
1. A
2. C
3. D
4. C
5. A
6. A
7. D

Generalization Questions

Passage 1
1. C
2. D
3. A
4. B
5. B

Passage 2
1. C
2. B
3. B
4. D
5. C

Passage 3
1. B
2. B
3. A
4. C
5. D
6. C

Passage 4
1. D
2. D
3. B
4. D
5. C
6. A
7. C

Data Representation Passages

Passage 1
1. C
2. C
3. B
4. C
5. B

Passage 2
1. C
2. B
3. C
4. C
5. C

Passage 3
1. D
2. A
3. A
4. A
5. C

Passage 4
1. B
2. B
3. B
4. D
5. B

Research Summaries
Passages
Passage 1
1. A
2. A
3. C
4. D
5. C
6. D

Passage 2
1. C
2. B
3. C
4. A
5. C
6. D

Passage 3
1. A
2. B
3. C
4. D
5. B
6. B

Passage 4
1. A
2. D
3. B
4. B
5. B
6. D

Conflicting Viewpoints
Passages
Passage 1
1. A
2. B
3. D
4. A
5. B
6. D
7. B

Passage 2
1. A
2. B
3. B
4. B
5. A
6. B
7. C

Passage 3
1. C
2. B
3. A
4. A
5. C
6. A
7. D

Passage 4
1. B
2. D
3. D
4. A
5. B
6. A
7. C

ACT Essay: Introduction to the ACT Writing Test

Even though the ACT Writing Test is elective, it is to your benefit to opt into taking this portion of the test. The ACT Writing Test is not exceedingly difficult, but does require knowledge of the expectations of the task in order to score well. As with other timed writing tasks, you have a limited amount of time, 40 minutes to be exact, to produce an approximately two- to three-page essay. To successfully complete this task, you need to have a game plan to tackle this essay efficiently and effectively.

What Should You Expect from the Essay Prompt?

While the ACT Writing Test used to be a simple persuasive writing task, the 2015 revamp to the ACT Writing Test now requires that you write an argumentative essay that includes the evaluation and analysis of three perspectives that are provided in the prompt, the development of your perspective, and the explanation of the relationship between your perspective and those given. Your perspective can be one of the given perspectives or one that you develop on your own. However, be cautioned that by coming up with your own perspective, you will have to analyze four perspectives as opposed to three, creating more work for yourself than is necessary.

How Should You Format Your Essay?

For this essay, you will be utilizing a standard format, including an introduction, multiple body paragraphs, and a conclusion. However, the content of these paragraphs, especially the body paragraphs, will be important to fully addressing the prompt. Below you will find the organizational structure we recommend:

The Best Format for the ACT Essay

Introduction: Brief discussion of the general topic provided in the prompt leading to a clear thesis statement that presents your perspective. Be sure that you use your own wording.

First Body Paragraph: Analyze one of the perspectives you did not choose. You will need to provide at least one specific example related to this perspective.

Second Body Paragraph: Analyze the other perspective you did not choose. You will need to provide at least one specific example related to this perspective.

Third Body Paragraph/Additional Paragraphs: Analyze the perspective you chose and explain why you have chosen this perspective. You will want to utilize two specific examples to support your analysis. Based on your preference, you may choose to use one paragraph for this portion or split it into multiple paragraphs.

Conclusion: Recap your reasons for supporting your chosen perspective. Be sure to utilize different wording than you did in your introduction.

How Will the Essay Be Scored?

Your ACT essay will be scored by two professional graders. They will each grade your essay on a scale of 1 to 6 in four categories: **Ideas and Analysis, Development and Support, Organization**, and **Language Use and Conventions**. The sum of all of those scores will provide a raw score between 8 and 48. From this raw score, a scaled score will be given with the maximum score being 36.

ACT Scoring Domains Overview

Ideas and Analysis: Essay exhibits the writer's ability to provide effective ideas and acute evaluations of the multiple perspectives on given issue. Skilled writers appreciate the issue they are asked to address, the purpose for writing, and the audience. The writer's ideas are appropriate for the task.

Development and Support: Essay exhibits the writer's ability to examine ideas, provides justification, and strengthen an argument. Skilled writers explain and scrutinize their ideas, discuss implications, and demonstrate through examples. This aids the reader's understanding of the rationale about the issue.

Organization: Essay exhibits the writer's ability to organize ideas with precision and intent. Organizational decisions are essential to successful writing. Skilled writers organize their essay in a way that clearly demonstrates the connection between ideas and guides the reader through their analysis.

Language Use and Conventions: Essay exhibits the writer's ability to utilize written language to express arguments clearly. Skilled writers effectively use the conventions of grammar, syntax, word usage, and mechanics. They modify the style and tone of their writing to communicate successfully to their audience.

PRACTICE EXERCISE

<u>Directions</u>: Write a practice essay using the prompt provided below.

Does Technology Make Humans More Connected?

One of the many intended uses of technology is the ability to increase our connections with each other. We can be in constant contact with our family and friends via social media websites, texting, or various apps. However, it is not uncommon to see people glued to their smartphones, even when they are around other people. Some believe that this inability to interact with those around us due to our addiction to technology makes us more lonely than connected. Others argue that technology allows us to stay connect with all of our family and friends, present or not, simultaneously, ensuring that we are never lonely. The role technology plays in our lives continues to increase, but does this technology truly make us more connected? Given the time that most people spend using technology even when others are present, it is worth examining the implications and meaning of the quality of the connectivity that technology offers us.

Read and carefully consider these perspectives. Each suggests a particular way of thinking about the quality of the connectivity that technology offers us.

Perspective One	Perspective Two	Perspective Three
Technology keeps us connected in a way that face-to-face communication cannot. If anything, we are too connected because we know too much about each other. Using the technology we have, we can never be lonely even if we are not as actively engaged in real life interactions.	Technology is increasingly making us more and more isolated. As technology begins to play a greater role in our lives, our ability to interact with each other in person will continue to dwindle. With our lost ability to interact will go our ability to empathize with others and our connections to reality.	Each person makes a conscientious decision either to be actively engaged in real life interactions or to focus on social media and other online interactions. It is not the fault of the technology that certain individuals lack the self-control to stop themselves from focusing on online interactions while they are with other people.

Essay Task

Write a unified, coherent essay in which you evaluate multiple perspectives on the quality of the connectivity that technology provides us. In your essay, be sure to:

- Analyze and evaluate the perspectives given
- State and develop your own perspective on the issue
- Explain the relationship between your perspective and those given

Your perspective may be in full agreement with any of the others, in partial agreement, or wholly different. Whatever the case, support your ideas with logical reasoning and details, persuasive examples.

ACT Essay: Prewriting

Due to the time constraints of the ACT Writing Test, you might be tempted to start writing without planning your essay. However, this is a mistake. Prewriting is essential not only to allow you to effectively organize your thoughts, but also to save you time when you are writing your essay. You should spend approximately 5-7 minutes on the two steps of prewriting: brainstorming and planning.

Brainstorming

Brainstorming can be done in various ways; there is no right or wrong way to brainstorm. Use the method that works for you because brainstorming should be quick and effective. A list of methods for brainstorming that you can use is outlined below:

Brainstorming Methods

Listing: This method is just like it sounds. You can start by making a bulleted list of ideas for examples and your thoughts that will later be organized while you are planning.

- Perspective
- Example
- Your opinion

Mind Mapping: This method involves drawing a map consisting of topics, terms, and ideas that you circle and connect with lines.

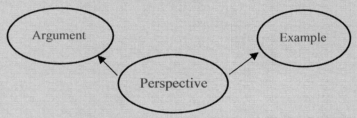

Outline from General to Specific: This method involves making an outline with the perspectives as the most general bullet, your opinion as the next step, and the example as the most specific bullet.

- Perspective
  - Argument
    - Example

Brainstorming from Specific to General: This method involves coming up with your examples first. Then, you can decide which perspective the examples will support.

- Example- Perspective 2
- Example- Perspective 1
- Example- Perspective 3
- Example- Perspective 2

Planning

In order to plan your essay, you will make a brief outline of your "game plan" for the essay. This will not be written in complete sentences, but simply terms or ideas you want to include in each paragraph. You will find an example below:

Planning Outline

- Introduction
  - Thesis: discuss my perspective
- First Body Paragraph: Perspective 2
  - Argument
    - Example
- Second Body Paragraph: Perspective 3
  - Argument
    - Example
- Third Body Paragraph: Perspective 1
  - Argument
    - Example 1
  - Argument
    - Example 2
- Conclusion

PRACTICE EXERCISE

Directions: Write a practice essay using the prompt provided below.

Is Live Television Becoming Antiquated?

Television used to require that you tune in to watch your favorite shows when they aired. Starting with the advent of the VCR, technology slowly began to develop to allow us to watch our favorite programs on our own schedule. On-demand television viewing has been made a reality by products such as DVR and online streaming services. This change in the way most people view television begs the question: is watching live television outdated? Given the many ways in which people can view television programs in an on-demand format, it is important to consider whether the broadcast of live television programming is still a necessity.

Read and carefully consider these perspectives. Each suggests a particular way of thinking about the necessity of live television broadcasts.

Perspective One	Perspective Two	Perspective Three
Despite the advent of on-demand programming, there are certain live broadcasts that are better when viewed right as they air, such as sporting events and news programs. By removing live broadcasts, you are forcing those who do not want or cannot financially participate in on-demand viewing to do so against their will.	On-demand television viewing allows you to watch your favorite shows when they are released, just as you would watch the show as it is being broadcasted live. The change in format has the potential to save broadcasting companies money without significantly affecting those who want to watch live television.	Given the fact that there are people who still prefer to watch their favorite shows live and the fact that continuing live broadcasts does not harm those who prefer to watch shows on-demand, it is preferential to continue to offer live broadcasting of television shows.

Page 443

Essay Task

Write a unified, coherent essay in which you evaluate multiple perspectives on the necessity of live television broadcasts. In your essay, be sure to:

- Analyze and evaluate the perspectives given
- State and develop your own perspective on the issue
- Explain the relationship between your perspective and those given

Your perspective may be in full agreement with any of the others, in partial agreement, or wholly different. Whatever the case, support your ideas with logical reasoning and details, persuasive examples.

ACT Essay: Introduction and Thesis

The following fact is vitally important to how you do on the ACT Writing Test: **most of the professional readers of the ACT Writing Test have read thousands of essays**. Why is this important? This means that you have to write a strong essay using all of your writing knowledge to stand out in order to get a higher score. The core of the essay begins with your introduction and thesis; your introduction and thesis are where you make your first impression, so make them count.

Introduction

Your essay's introduction should grab the reader's attention. Some students make the same general mistakes that make their introductions incomplete, dull, or wordy. Here are the most common mistakes to avoid:

Common Mistakes Students Make in the Introduction

- No clear thesis or a vaguely worded thesis
- Relying heavily on clichés and generalities
- Repeating the prompt word for word
- Extensively describing your examples in the thesis

Thesis

Your thesis provides the focus of your essay by establishing your argument and its main ideas clearly and succinctly, sometimes briefly stating or referencing the examples you will use to support your thesis. You will find the qualities that make for a good thesis below:

Qualities of a Good Thesis

- **Novelty**: Make your thesis more impactful by making it unique. Use your own distinct wording.
- **Clarity**: Although you may understand what you are thinking, the reader may not. Make sure your thoughts are conveyed very clearly in your thesis.
- **Brevity**: Strategically pick your wording so that you make your argument without being too long-winded.
- **Confidence**: Make it clear that you believe what you are writing.

PRACTICE EXERCISE

<u>Directions</u>: Write a practice essay using the prompt provided below.

Can Graffiti Be Deemed an Art Form?

Graffiti has become more than just public defacement. Some individuals are attempting to establish themselves as legitimate artists. Art dealers and buyers are even beginning to take this art form seriously. Certain pieces have been moved to museums and galleries or have been sold to the highest bidder for significant sums of money. However, this form of art still requires the breaking of the law. Not to mention that the art itself is subject to being scrubbed away, painted over, or stolen by other enterprising artists. There is no way in which these artists can copyright their work or even take full credit for it. Due to the questionable legal standing of graffiti, can it ever truly be deemed a legitimate art form? Given the legal implications of encouraging the production of graffiti, it is important to consider whether graffiti can ever be regarded as a genuine form of art.

Read and carefully consider these perspectives. Each suggests a particular way of thinking about the classification of graffiti as a legitimate art form.

Perspective One	Perspective Two	Perspective Three
Graffiti should be viewed as legitimate art. The only difference between graffiti and other forms of art is the medium being utilized. What makes a painting using spray paint on an exterior wall any different from a painting using oil paints on a canvas? There is no real difference in the art world.	It is irresponsible to promote the production of art that is created illegally. Graffiti is a public nuisance, not a form of art. These artists are disrespectful of the building owners and the taxpayers who have to pay for the graffiti to be removed. Recognizing these artists is only asking them to continue their disruptive activities.	Graffiti should not only be considered a legitimate art form, but also should not be illegal, assuming that the artist gets the permission of the building owner prior to the production of the art. This would allow the artist to take credit for the work and be recognized for his or her creative talents.

Essay Task

Write a unified, coherent essay in which you evaluate multiple perspectives on the classification of graffiti as a legitimate art form. In your essay, be sure to:

- Analyze and evaluate the perspectives given
- State and develop your own perspective on the issue
- Explain the relationship between your perspective and those given

Your perspective may be in full agreement with any of the others, in partial agreement, or wholly different. Whatever the case, support your ideas with logical reasoning and details, persuasive examples.

ACT Essay: Body Paragraphs – Analysis and Examples

Analyzing the Perspectives

As part of your essay, you must analyze all the perspectives provided in the prompt, even if you do not agree with all of them. Obviously, you want to spend the most time and effort analyzing the perspective that you are taking. We recommend that you come up with one specific example for each of the perspectives that you are not supporting and two specific examples for the perspective that you are supporting. The more specific the example, the better. Here is a refresher on setting up your body paragraphs:

What to Include in Your Body Paragraphs

- **First Body Paragraph:** Analyze one of the perspectives you did not choose. You will need to provide at least one specific example related to this perspective.
- **Second Body Paragraph:** Analyze the other perspective you did not choose. You will need to provide at least one specific example related to this perspective.
- **Third Body Paragraph/Additional Paragraphs:** Analyze the perspective you chose and explain why you have chosen this perspective. You should utilize two specific examples to support your analysis. Based on your preference, you may choose to use one paragraph for this portion or split it into multiple paragraphs.
- **Conclusion:** Recap your reasons for supporting your chosen perspective. Be sure to utilize different wording than you did in your introduction.

Address the Complexity of the Issue

As with any highly debated topic, the issues chosen for the ACT Writing Test are going to be complex, opinion-based topics. This means that there will not be an obvious right or wrong perspective. While the ACT wants you to support your perspective, they also want to see that you can show recognition for the validity of the other perspectives.

For example, consider a sample opinion on preferred ice cream flavors: vanilla, chocolate, or strawberry. You may love strawberry ice cream due to your love of fruit, but you can also understand that some people may not like the flavor or the strawberry seeds. In your essay, you might include something like this:

"Although some may not like strawberry ice cream for various reasons, such as a dislike of the flavor or a hatred of the strawberry seeds, strawberry ice cream is the superior ice cream flavor."

This shows that you understand that others may not agree with you, and you are expressing your understanding of the complexity of the issue.

PRACTICE EXERCISE

<u>Directions</u>: Write a practice essay using the prompt provided below.

Should Females Be Encouraged to Pursue Careers in Math and Science?

Gender equality is an ongoing battle. While it may seem that women are slowly gaining equality with men, it appears that women are not pursuing math and science careers. In fact, the rate of women getting computer science degrees dropped by 19 percent in a span of 25 years, and only one-fifth of physics Ph.D. recipients each year are female. Some argue that we should not force women into careers that they are not interested in pursuing. Others believe that women are not being encouraged from a young age to pursue math and science careers. Women have the potential to offer valuable perspectives to these career fields, but should females be encouraged to pursue careers in math and science? Given the low number of women pursuing math and science careers, it is important to consider the implications of encouraging women to gain degrees in these fields.

Read and carefully consider these perspectives. Each suggests a particular way of thinking about encouraging women to pursue careers in math and science.

Perspective One	Perspective Two	Perspective Three
Women should receive encouragement from a young age to pursue math and science careers. Parents should be encouraged to give their daughters building sets, science kits, and doctor's kits in addition to, or even in replacement of, kitchens, dolls, and dress-up outfits. Girls should be told they can pursue careers in any field they like.	The root of women not pursuing math and science careers is not encouragement. Females have the same opportunities to pursue these careers, but choose not to do so due to a lack of interest. Therefore, we should not waste time and energy pressuring women into careers in which they are not interested.	Encouraging females to pursue science and math careers is up to the parents. If the parents want to offer their daughters toys that promote math and science careers, that is their prerogative. Teachers should be offering equal encouragement to all students in all fields of interest, so in this way, females should have an equal opportunity to become interested in math and science careers.

Essay Task

Write a unified, coherent essay in which you evaluate multiple perspectives on the encouraging women to pursue careers in math and science. In your essay, be sure to:

- Analyze and evaluate the perspectives given
- State and develop your own perspective on the issue
- Explain the relationship between your perspective and those given

Your perspective may be in full agreement with any of the others, in partial agreement, or wholly different. Whatever the case, support your ideas with logical reasoning and details, persuasive examples.

ACT Essay: Conclusions

Conclusions

In comparison to the other parts of the essay, the conclusion should be the easiest part to write. You simply need to reiterate your thesis and provide a brief recap of your arguments. While you should try to write a few sentences, a one-sentence conclusion is better than nothing when you are short on time. If you have the time to spare, you can improve your conclusion by briefly mentioning the other perspectives and the complexity of the issue. However, you should avoid the mistakes listed below:

Mistakes to Avoid in Your Conclusion

- Beginning with an overused transitional phrase, such as "In conclusion" or "In summary"
- Stating the thesis for the first time in your conclusion
- Introduce a new idea or topic not already discussed in the essay
- Include evidence that should be in the body paragraphs
- Ending with a rephrased thesis statement without any substantive changes

---

PRACTICE EXERCISE

<u>Directions</u>: Write a practice essay using the prompt provided below.

Is It a Requirement That Great Leaders Be Outgoing?

Typically, politicians are viewed as outgoing people. You might imagine them joyfully shaking hands with voters, laughing as they enjoy coffee in a diner full of constituents, or holding events attending by throngs of people. However, the reality is that some politicians are introverted. They do not dislike people or public speaking, but they do tend to be reserved and prefer to socialize with smaller, more intimate groups of people. It may seem like an extroverted person would be best suited for a leadership position, but are great leaders always outgoing? Given the importance of strong leadership, it is important to consider whether being outgoing is a necessity to being a great leader.

Read and carefully consider these perspectives. Each suggests a particular way of thinking about whether being outgoing is a necessity to being a great leader.

Perspective One	Perspective Two	Perspective Three
Being extroverted is a necessary quality of great leadership. To be a great leader, you must have an outgoing personality in order to effectively connect with other people to sway them to agree with your ideas. Outgoing personalities also allow the leader to project greater confidence, which is a quality that makes people more trusting of a leader.	Outgoingness is not a requirement of being a great leader. Being outgoing has its benefits, but so does being reserved and introverted. It depends entirely on the circumstances. Great leaders of the past have had vastly different personalities, yet managed to gain public respect for their varying leadership styles.	Of the various character traits that humans can possess, being outgoing is an advantageous trait for a leader. However, it is only one of many traits. Other less favorable character traits can outweigh the benefits of being extroverted. Thus, it is a combination of advantageous character traits, as opposed to one, that makes a leader great.

Essay Task

Write a unified, coherent essay in which you evaluate multiple perspectives on whether being outgoing is a necessity to being a great leader. In your essay, be sure to:

- Analyze and evaluate the perspectives given
- State and develop your own perspective on the issue
- Explain the relationship between your perspective and those given

Your perspective may be in full agreement with any of the others, in partial agreement, or wholly different. Whatever the case, support your ideas with logical reasoning and details, persuasive examples.

ACT Essay: Organization

Organization is critical to writing an effective persuasive essay. By properly organizing your essay, you allow the reader to better understand the arguments you are making. Fortunately, the steps to improving your essay's organization are straightforward.

General Organizational Structure

> ### The Best Format for the ACT Essay
>
> - **Introduction:** Brief discussion of the general topic provided in the prompt leading to a clear thesis statement that presents your perspective. Be sure that you use your own wording.
> - **First Body Paragraph:** Analyze one of the perspectives you did not choose. You will need to provide at least one specific example related to this perspective.
> - **Second Body Paragraph:** Analyze the other perspective you did not choose. You will need to provide at least one specific example related to this perspective.
> - **Third Body Paragraph/Additional Paragraphs:** Analyze the perspective you chose and explain why you have chosen this perspective. You should utilize two specific examples to support your analysis. Based on your preference, you may choose to use one paragraph for this portion or split it into multiple paragraphs.
> - **Conclusion:** Recap your reasons for supporting your chosen perspective. Be sure to utilize different wording than you did in your introduction.

How to Organize a Paragraph?

Paragraphs are the building blocks of your essay. Creating separate paragraphs within your essay allows you to more effectively separate your ideas. We have already covered how to organize your introduction and conclusion in prior lessons. Here are the components of organization that you should use in each of your body paragraphs:

> ### Components of a Body Paragraph
>
> - **Topic sentence:** The topic sentence gives your paragraph direction by laying out the main idea. Each paragraph will include a topic sentence as the first sentence.
> - **Support:** Support will be provided over multiple sentences. This is where you provide your examples and explain how those examples support your main idea.
> - **Ending:** This is the final sentence of the paragraph. It is your chance to wrap up the paragraph and transition into the next paragraph.

How to Create Internal Organization?

While properly ordering the paragraphs within your essay and organizing your ideas within your paragraphs are important elements of organization as a whole, there are other organizational techniques that can be used to make your ideas more effectively connected and understandable. Here are those techniques:

Organizational Techniques for Your Essay

- **Cohesion:** There are various elements that will give your essay coherence, which will unify the ideas within your essay using word choice and sentence structure techniques. Here are various means of creating cohesion in your essay:
  - **Synonymy:** This means that you utilize a synonym of a word used in the prior sentence in the next sentence.
    - **Example**: Cardio, or aerobic *exercise*, includes activities such as running, swimming, cycling, and walking. Aerobic *workouts* are often intended to burn calories as opposed to building muscles.
  - **Pro-forms:** This involves using pronouns to refer back to a noun in a prior sentence.
    - **Example**: *Exercising* can be more fun than you might imagine. *It* can be made more exciting by doing different activities, listening to music, or inviting a friend or group of friends.
  - **Repetition:** This technique entails using one word from the prior sentence in the next sentence.
    - **Example**: *Exercising* is vital to maintaining your weight. An exemplary method of *exercising* is *walking*. *Walking* is inexpensive and low impact.
  - **Transitions:** Transitioning should be used not only between sentences, but also between paragraphs. Try to focus on using transitional phrases more than transitional words. Here are some common transitions:
    - **Indicate similarity:** that is, that is to say, in other words
    - **Indicate opposition:** but, yet, however, nevertheless, still, though, although, whereas, in contrast
    - **Indicate addition:** and, too, also, furthermore, moreover, in addition, besides, in the same way, again
    - **Indicate cause and effect:** therefore, so, consequently, as a consequence, thus, as a result, hence
    - **Indicate examples:** for example, for instance, after all, an illustration of, even, indeed, in fact, of course
- **Focus:** Be sure to keep similar ideas together within each paragraph. You do not want to begin a paragraph discussing one topic and then provide an example related to another topic.

PRACTICE EXERCISE

<u>Directions</u>: Write a practice essay using the prompt provided below.

Are Parents Violating The Privacy of Their Children on Social Media?

Social media has opened up a vast array of concerns. One of these concerns is whether parents are violating the privacy of their children by posting photographs and videos of the children online. While the photographs and videos may be adorable, the children have no say in the publishing of these pictures and videos that may ultimately stay on the Internet into their adulthood, but is it really a violation of privacy since parents have been embarrassing their children with photographs and videos long before the advent of the Internet? Given the growing number of parents posting photograph and videos of their children to social media, it is important to consider the implications of these social media posts on the privacy of children.

Read and carefully consider these perspectives. Each suggests a particular way of thinking about whether parents posting photographs and videos of their children online is a violation of the children's privacy.

Perspective One	Perspective Two	Perspective Three
The epidemic of parents posting photographs and videos of their children online is so rampant that there is a term for it, "oversharenting." This epidemic may not negatively impact all children, but even the small chance that it will negatively impact some children should be enough to necessitate laws to protect the privacy of children from this oversharing by their parents.	Parents give their children the gift of life, so they have the right to make a variety of important decisions for their children. If the parents were irreparably harming their children, it would be wrong. But a few embarrassing photographs and videos will not negatively impact their children in the future. Thus, they should be allowed to post whatever they want about their children online.	There should be a modification to social media that would allow parents to post photographs and videos of their children and give children the ability to remove those photographs and videos in adulthood. This would allow the parents to share the proud and amusing moments with their children while still allowing the children to maintain their privacy in the future.

Essay Task

Write a unified, coherent essay in which you evaluate multiple perspectives on whether parents posting photographs and videos of their children online is a violation of the children's privacy. In your essay, be sure to:

- Analyze and evaluate the perspectives given
- State and develop your own perspective on the issue
- Explain the relationship between your perspective and those given

Your perspective may be in full agreement with any of the others, in partial agreement, or wholly different. Whatever the case, support your ideas with logical reasoning and details, persuasive examples.

ACT Essay: Style

Not only will the professional readers be scoring your essay based on your arguments, support, and organization, but also writing style. What is style? Here is how the ACT rubric defines style:

- **The use of language enhances the argument. Word choice is skillful and precise. Sentence structures are consistently varied and clear. Stylistic choices are strategic and effective.**

The three elements discussed in this lesson will help you score higher in this category.

Language Usage

The readers want to see that you are using a great variety of higher-level vocabulary words. In addition to showing that you know complex words, varied word usage shows you know a greater range of words. Here are some synonyms to replace the most commonly overused words:

> ### Improving Your Vocabulary Usage
>
> - **Replacements for 'good':** marvelous, superb, valuable, exceptional, positive
> - **Replacements for 'bad':** atrocious, dreadful, rough, unacceptable, dissatisfactory
> - **Replacements for 'better':** improved, superior, more appropriate, more suitable
> - **Replacements for 'important':** critical, imperative, influential, significant, vital
> - **Replacements for 'very':** absolutely, decidedly, eminently, profoundly, surprisingly, unusually
> - **Replacements for 'explain':** analyze, demonstrate, explicate, expound on
> - **Replacements for 'keep':** retain, accumulate, amass, conserve, possess
> - **Replacements for 'know':** appreciate, perceive, recognize, comprehend, differentiate
> - **Replacements for 'like':** admire, appreciate, adore, cherish, fancy, relish, savor
> - **Replacements for 'more':** extra, additional, spare, augmented, expanded, increased
> - **Replacements for 'nice':** cordial, friendly, amiable, charming, delightful
> - **Replacements for 'think':** consider, conclude, deem, surmise, speculate
> - **Replacements for 'use':** apply, employ, manage, operate, utilize, wield
> - **Replacements for 'take':** capture, receive, seize, acquire, obtain
> - **Replacements for 'want':** desire, require, aspire, covet, yearn
> - **Replacements for 'give':** deliver, present, permit, furnish, indicate, produce